EUGENIO MONTALE, THE FASCIST STORM, AND THE JEWISH SUNFLOWER

This book uncovers one of the great hidden sagas of modern literature. During the Fascist period in Italy, Eugenio Montale, the most significant Italian poet of the twentieth century and a future Nobel laureate, fell in love with Irma Brandeis, a brilliant young Jewish American Dante scholar. Their romance came to an end after five years, but its literary echoes were profound. Throughout his career, and in some of his greatest poetry, Montale's works abound with secret codes that speak to a lost lover and muse.

There were good reasons for such secrecy. Montale's publisher, Piero Gobetti, was beaten to death by the Fascists. In 1938, following the enactment of anti-Semitic laws in Italy and just before the outbreak of the Second World War, Brandeis risked returning to Florence to try – unsuccessfully – to persuade Montale to leave his homeland. She returned to America, never to see him again.

Montale's poems, written in an evocative hermetic style, are explored here within their rich biographical and historical context, made possible through recently published archival materials. Offering fresh translations and readings, this book brings to life the intersecting mythology of some of Montale's most important poems and reveals a major thematic link in his life and work.

(Toronto Italian Studies)

DAVID MICHAEL HERTZ is a professor in the Department of Comparative Literature at Indiana University, Bloomington, and the author of *Angels of Reality: Wallace Stevens, Charles Ives, and Frank Lloyd Wright*, as well as other books and essays on modern poets, artists, and musicians. He is a member of the National Council on the Humanities, and has twice served as chair of Comparative Literature at Indiana University.

DAVID MICHAEL HERTZ

Eugenio Montale, the Fascist Storm, and the Jewish Sunflower

UNIVERSITY OF TORONTO PRESS
Toronto Buffalo London

Toronto Buffalo London
www.utppublishing.com

Reprinted in paperback 2015

ISBN 978-1-4426-4538-7 (cloth) ISBN 978-1-4875-1999-5 (paper)

Toronto Italian Studies

Library and Archives Canada Cataloguing in Publication

Hertz, David Michael, 1954–, author
Eugenio Montale, the fascist storm, and the Jewish sunflower / David Michael Hertz.

(Toronto Italian studies)
Includes bibliographical references and index.
ISBN 978-1-4426-4538-7 (bound).

1. Montale, Eugenio, 1896– – Criticism and interpretation. 2. Montale, Eugenio, 1896– – Relations with women. 3. Brandeis, Irma. 4. Poets, Italian – 20th century – Biography. I. Title. II. Series: Toronto Italian studies

PQ4829.O565Z65 2013 851′.912 C2013-903942-2

University of Toronto Press acknowledges the financial assistance to its publishing program of the Canada Council for the Arts and the Ontario Arts Council, an agency of the Government of Ontario.

Canada Council for the Arts Conseil des Arts du Canada

Funded by the Government of Canada Financé par le gouvernement du Canada

If he [Montale] speaks several times of his God ("Toward Siena," "The Garden"), or the God of his woman ("Incantation," "The Garden"), it seems to me that there is an evident religious tension that he expresses with myth. There is God or Christ, in the personal sense of a non-sacred Christianity that yields concrete images of the Divine; in an occidental ambience and therefore Christian, with a Greek influence, not possibly proven otherwise. A presence *extremely mediterranean,* the accent is biblical, more than principally evangelical (perhaps because of the influence of his *Jewish* lover?). Above all if she was Jewish, she was not Christian. The Christian images [are] only a transposition of the Divine for the poet.

—Rina Sara Virgillito

The work of art was the sole means of rediscovering Lost Time.

—Marcel Proust

With what meditations did Bloom accompany his demonstration to his companion of various constellations?

—James Joyce

When time leans on his dykes, then thine be his allconsciousness and memory flower forth in a flame.

—Eugenio Montale, as translated by Samuel Beckett

The love that moves the sun and the other stars . . .

—Dante

Contents

Acknowledgments

As H.V. Morton noted long ago, Bergamo has one of the best-preserved piazzas in Italy. It is located high above the city, in the medieval *città alta* (high city), surrounded by ancient streets, a rich assortment of architectural treasures, and precious artworks. The città alta is perched above the larger modern city of Bergamo, which stretches out on the Lombard plain below. Gaetano Donizetti, who later achieved great fame and wealth as an opera composer, was born just outside the gates of the città alta, in a poor man's apartment on a road that slopes downward towards the lower city.

Some years ago, thanks to a grant from Indiana University's West European Studies Department, I spent my late afternoons on the hill of San Vigilio, located even higher up, overlooking the città alta. I often worked from my scenic perch on the patio belonging to the wonderful Bar-Trattoria "al Castello," which was run by a warm Italian family. The food was excellent and earthy; the view was spectacular (a picture hangs in my office at Indiana University). On a clear day, it was possible to make out the great cathedral of Milan in the distance. There were several unforgettable afternoons with remarkably clear light that summer.

One day the proprietor of the trattoria, Giacinto Marchetto, introduced me to Rina Sara Virgillito, a local professor of Italian and classics who had known the poet Eugenio Montale. I soon realized that she was an accomplished poet in her own right, with a significant body of published works. We sat and talked for hours on the hill above Bergamo. She spoke of the great Italian poets – Montale, D'Annunzio, Ungaretti, and others – the story of Montale's murdered publisher, Piero Gobetti, and much more about the vibrant, neglected history of Italian literature.

A translator and critic herself, she gave me a number of her books, one of them a critical study on the works of her friend Montale. I carried them back to Indiana University to deposit in the Lilly Library, where they remain today. What stayed in my mind more than anything were her stories about Montale and *l'ebrea americana* – the Jewish-American woman Irma Brandeis, who had inspired his greatest poetry. Virgillito spoke eloquently about the brilliant syncretic vision of Mediterranean culture that Montale had invented because of Brandeis's presence in his life. My new friend died a few years after that meeting, but she had planted the seeds of curiosity with her intriguing commentary on Montale and Modernist poetry in Italy.

Among the many others who helped me penetrate into my subject in Italy were two of the most respected Montale experts in Italian academia, Rosanna Bettarini and Franco Contorbia. At the Gabinetto Vieusseux, a library once headed by Montale himself, Gloria Manghetti and Albarosa Albertini were especially helpful. The assistance of all the research librarians in the library's special archive for contemporary studies was generous and substantial. Ernestina Pellegrini, a close friend of Rina Sara Virgillito, served as a mysterious link between my initial meeting with Rina and the city of Florence. In 2005, Ernestina met me outside the Gabinetto Vieusseux and presented me with Virgillito's personal copies of Montale's great poems, and I was able to read his warm dedications to Virgillito in the volumes. Virgillito's marginalia proved especially fascinating, affecting some of my final remarks on the readings of the poems. High on another Italian hillside, this one near Fiesole, Ernestina helped me decode a cryptic passage written lightly in pencil at the back of Montale's *La bufera e altro.* I was excited to discover these thoughts from Virgillito; they linked my initial conversations with her to the final stages of my project. Ernestina, a professor of literature at the University of Florence, has catalogued the papers of Virgillito and deposited them in the state archives. They merit further study.

I also wish to record here my extremely memorable meeting with Alessandro Parronchi (1914–2007). At the time of our meeting, Professor Parronchi was one of the last surviving members of the intellectual and artistic group that gathered with Montale in the Caffè Giubbe Rosse in Florence in the 1930s and 1940s. I will always remember the warm hospitality he and his lovely family extended to me on a warm June day in 2005. I am very grateful for his gift of his own book of writings on the poet, *Quaderno per Montale.* A prolific author on many subjects, Professor Parronchi was one of the great figures in the humanities in Italy, one of the giants of his era. It was due to the intellectual generosity of Francesco Smeraldi, whom I met by chance while reading at I Tatti, that I was able to find him.

In Monterosso al Mare, the crucial site of Montale's youthful summer home, Sandro Dinari, Giovanna Stretti, Vittorio Vargiù, and Dr Luca Tortorolo (a descendant of the Montale family) were among the memorable personalities I encountered. Vittorio's remarks on the evolution of the Monterosso area and the meaning of the glass shards that run along the stone walls of Italian country estates were unforgettable.

At Indiana University, Peter Bondanella and Giancarlo Maiorino are to be thanked for many years of encouragement relating to all things Italian. If I had not met them, I would not have written this book. Jane Lyle, Dan Pyle, and Dr Ermanno Conti offered expertise of many sorts along the way. It was more than kind of Dr Conti to read my manuscript, not once but twice. My research was at first encouraged by the university with a series of smaller grants from the Department of Comparative Literature and from the Office of the Vice-President for Research. Early on, I especially appreciated the larger New Frontiers Travel Grant, one that I had not even expected, which was awarded by the Office of the Vice-President for Research. Later, when my project was in critical need of further support, funding from the Office of the Vice-President for Research, the College of Arts and Sciences, and the Department of Comparative Literature made this publication possible. I am extremely grateful.

New Yorkers Jonathan Galassi and Luciano Rebay were both intellectually open and generous. Galassi – poet, translator, publisher – was always happy to share information about Montale, and he encouraged my research with enthusiasm over a period of years. Luciano Rebay, Ungaretti Professor of Italian at Columbia University, freely discussed valuable scholarly information about his personal encounters with both Irma Brandeis and Eugenio Montale. I speak of Galassi and Rebay frequently in my work and cite them.

At Bard College and in Annandale-on-Hudson, Irma Brandeis's home and academic base for many years, a number of people extended themselves to me – Jean Cook, Bernard Tiegert, the late Anyss Wilson, Frank and Ruth Oja, and Helene Tiegert, current librarian and archivist. Jean Cook, Irma Brandeis's friend and caretaker and the executrix of her estate, gave me invaluable insights. She shared her manuscripts, photographs, and memories with me, in many ways settling important issues in Montale studies with her evidence.

At Princeton, Ted and Renée Weiss were open and warm, receiving me in their home when I travelled to the university to read in the archives of the *Quarterly Review of Literature*. Between chamber music sessions with Renée (who plays the violin very well), the Weisses and I spoke about Irma Brandeis and her mysterious Italian poet for many hours. Ted Weiss, now deceased, made many penetrating observations about Montale, Brandeis, and modern poetry in general. Our conversations enabled me to fill in crucial pieces of the Montale-Brandeis puzzle from the American point of view.

At the Sarah Lawrence College Archive, Abby Lester was especially helpful. Columbia University and Barnard archivists, particularly Donald Glassman, were also very kind.

I thank Helen Vendler and Willis Barnstone for inspiration in my study and appreciation of great poetry. Their fine work has contributed to a ripening of my sensibilities over many years.

The late Ron Schoeffel guided this book through several drafts. His editorial wisdom and enthusiasm for this book were a great joy for this particular scholar, so immersed in pursuit of his subject. I will always remember his kind and insightful help with this project. I thank his marvellous colleagues at the University of Toronto Press for all their good work. Special mention must also go to managing editor Anne Laughlin, copy editor Angela Wingfield (who read my book with such empathy for the topic and attention to detail), Eric Carlson for his excellent help with the technical aspects of the pictures, and Val Cooke, who designed the perfect cover for the book.

Permission to quote the work of Eugenio Montale is granted by Arnoldo Mondadori Editore s.p.a. The poems reprinted and translated are "Portami il girasole ch'io lo trapianti"; "Lontano, ero con te quando tuo padre"; "La speranza di pure rivederti"; "Nuove stanze"; "Palio"; "Notizie dall'Amiata"; "La bufera"; "Gli orecchini"; "La frangia dei capelli"; "Giorno e notte"; "Il tuo volo"; "Iride"; "L'orto"; "La primavera hitleriana"; "L'ombra della magnolia"; "L'eroismo"; "Clizia dice"; "Interno/Esterno"; "Credo"; and "Quartetto," all by Eugenio Montale, taken from *Tutte le poesie* (copyright Arnoldo Mondadori Editore s.p.a., Milan). Permission to reproduce the writing and translations of Irma Brandeis has been granted by Jean Cook on behalf of the Irma Brandeis estate. Material from volume 11, number 4, of *The Quarterly Review of*

Literature is reprinted with the permission of the Quarterly Review of Literature Archives, Manuscripts Division, Department of Rare Books and Special Collections, Princeton University Library. Materials from the Glauco Cambon correspondence have been quoted with the permission (and with non-exclusive rights) of the Archives and Special Collections at the Thomas J. Dodd Research Center, University of Connecticut Libraries, Storrs, Connecticut. Excerpts from selected Irma Brandeis papers and correspondence are published with the permission of the Sarah Lawrence College Archives. Permission to reprint a letter previously published by Luciano Rebay in the *Forum Italicum*, volume 16, number 3 (winter 1982), has been granted by the *Forum Italicum*, Center for Italian Studies, State University of New York. The brief excerpts from pages 6, 13–14, 19, 20, 22, 25, 27, 296, 298, 303–4, 305, 312, and 319 of *The Second Life of Art: Selected Essays by Eugenio Montale*, edited and translated by Jonathan Galassi (copyright 1977, 1978, 1979, 1980, 1981, and 1992 by Jonathan Galassi), are reprinted by permission of HarperCollins Publishers. All quotations are indicated in the endnotes. Every effort has been extended to reach copyright holders of all quoted material. If some rights holders of quoted content have been overlooked, those persons should contact the author, care of the University of Toronto Press, 10 St. Mary Street, Suite 700, Toronto, Ontario M4Y 2W8, Canada. Any remaining permissions issues will be resolved before subsequent editions of this work are printed.

Finally, I gratefully acknowledge Rachel, my wife, and Rafi, my son, for everything that the warmest love and companionship can mean. Special thanks to them for their excellent company as they followed me around Tuscany and Liguria in search of the footsteps of Irma and Eugenio. Rafi was one year old at the time of my sabbatical research trip. The Italians, who love *bambini,* warmed up to him, and because of that, we were treated like celebrities as we wandered about the Tuscan countryside and the Ligurian shore in search of Montalean traces. The sight of my wife and son framed by the background of the Italian countryside remains permanently imprinted in my mind, a continual source of remembered pleasure.

EUGENIO MONTALE, THE FASCIST STORM, AND THE JEWISH SUNFLOWER

1 The Clizia Myth and the Secret Cycle

He found himself ... already aided ... by Clizia's star, by the umbrella of her sunflower.

– Eugenio Montale

Montale's Secret Reader

In the fall of 1938 Eugenio Montale's life was disintegrating. He was deeply unhappy, even suicidal. Some of the problems had been festering for years. His Fascist bosses were about to fire him from his post as director of a prestigious Florentine library because he was not a member of their party. In his letters his disgust is apparent in the way he refers to the famous library, the Gabinetto Vieusseux, with its initials "GV" slyly rewritten as "WC" (for water closet, toilet). He was correctly worried that Benito Mussolini, to whom he refers with obvious sarcasm, was about to drag Italy into a huge war. His personal life was even worse. For many years he had been entangled in an absurdly complicated relationship involving two different women. Both were extremely jealous. His American lover, Irma Brandeis, had just travelled to Florence, giving him an ultimatum: *Leave with me now or forget about me.* He had been involved with her since the early 1930s, writing a steady stream of brilliant love letters to her, but they had never managed to get together permanently, even though both clearly wanted to do so. In the meantime he had been supported for years by an older Italian woman, Drusilla Tanzi Marangoni, who was already married to someone else. Each woman now clearly knew about the existence of the other. When Drusilla heard about Irma, she threatened to hang herself or jump out of various buildings. Montale was torn between these women, wondering in his most foolish moments why the two of them simply could not be friends, perhaps existing in some sort of bicontinental ménage à trois.

Historical events were about to sweep away this personal turmoil. In March of 1938, Hitler, acting in open defiance of the treaty that Germany had signed in Versailles at the end of the First World War, sent his armies into Austria. He described his forced annexation of Austria as an *Anschluss*, or "connection." Frightened by the ease with which the Nazis had absorbed his northern neighbour, Mussolini decided to make a strategic alliance with them. Hitler came to Italy in May. The Fascists, receiving him warmly, staged one of the largest propaganda events in history. It included a tour of Florence, Montale's home city. Anti-Semitic laws were enacted that summer. A chasm opened up. The Second World War was about to begin. Montale would never see Irma Brandeis again.

While Montale never managed to escape to New York to reunite with Irma, she became the main character in his poetry, a central figure in a body of work that would come to be considered some of the greatest lyric writing of the twentieth century. He would write about her for the rest of his life, and the resulting poetry eventually earned him a Nobel Prize. But Montale's voice had also been shaped by historical circumstance, and some of that formation took place years before he met Irma Brandeis. His greatest era as a poet was prompted by the Italian Fascist period (1922–43), which had begun some seventeen years before the outbreak of the Second World War. During this period Montale invented an intimate and secretive poetic voice for modern love poetry that was also distinctly anti-Fascist. This gentle but highly compacted poetry was conceived in a time of murdering for political agenda, mass movements of men and war machines, angry swarming crowds, mass hysteria, and global propaganda. Capturing these frightening images in his work, the Italian writer created a poetry of refined sentiment in a vulgar era. He spoke neither to a nation nor to posterity but to a single person, a disguised lover.

While writing much of his greatest poetry in the 1930s and 1940s, Montale consciously resurrected an old form of poetry, the *trobar clus*. *Trobar clus* refers to the "closed song" format of Provençal poetry of the late twelfth and early thirteenth centuries. Its style was marked by allusion, yet was elusive and hermetic, with esoteric words and rhyme schemes. In contrast, the opposing style, *trobar leu*, was light and easy to understand.[1] In his love poetry, and in much of his greatest verse, Montale speaks intimately to a secret listener via the trobar clus device known as the *senhal* – a protective cover name, or false identity, that the Provençal troubadour invented for his lady. It would have been too dangerous to name her directly in the lyrical love poetry of the era. Familiar to the poets of Dante's circle, the senhal was used first in medieval and then in Renaissance poetry, imported into Italy from Provence.[2] Montale's trobar clus of the Second World War era is an ingenious reworking of a poetic practice that dates back eight hundred years.

The identity of this mysterious *tu* (you), who usually seems to be a lover in Montale's poems, changes over time. She is at first Arletta (Anna degli Uberti, his youthful flame) and possibly several other women. Only later does she become Clizia (Irma Brandeis), Mosca (Drusilla Marangoni, his long-time companion and eventual wife), the Vixen (the poet Maria Luisa Spaziani), and several other female listeners of lesser importance. At the end of his life his secret listener becomes Clizia once again. The reader becomes part of this exchange as well. When we read Montale, we too become intimate with him. Montale's voice talks to a fictional character, and we overhear their interaction. We peer pruriently into their dialogue. When we delve into Montale, we are witnessing an intense inner drama, written out in the form of a meditation spoken to an absent lover.

In his book of 501 sonnets, the poet Willis Barnstone based the structure of his poems on the idea of a "Secret Reader." Montale's listeners – or Secret Readers, to use Barnstone's phrase – change over the course of time. But the speech acts that organize the patterns of his poetry always make a rhetorical structure that conveys an understanding of intimacy. The lonely voice of the poet needs to speak to a lover or an intimate friend. Montale's imagination requires a caring ear. As a result, we partake of his carefully constructed intimacy as we read. And we are placed in the rhetorical position of his Other, his absent friend, as we read him. After a while, we too are engaged in the conversation.

While he is a poet of history and ideas, Montale is above all a love poet. In the vast majority of his poetry it is the force of love that enables him to speak and to formulate his rhetorical stance. In order for Montale to write his best poems, he must speak to his *tu*. He even wrote a short poem about this problem, which he entitled "Il tu" ("The You") and which begins with a knowing wink: "Thrown off the track by me, / the critics go on and on about / how my 'you' is an institution"

(*I critici ripetono, / da me depistati, / che il mio tu è un istituto*).[3] The focal point of Montale's voice is most often the single listener who hears the poet's richly complex utterances. One of the most intriguing challenges of many of the best Montale poems is to gauge the nature of the relationship between the poet-speaker and the *tu* or you, the lover-hearer. Solving this puzzle unlocks the secrets of Montale. He was moved to address different secret female readers at different points in his life, but they are always solitary listeners. It is easy to retrace their names in the rich notes and commentaries on his poetry, but only one of those Secret Readers, Irma Brandeis, became an elaborate symbolic construction in his poetry. Transformed into a half-human goddess in the greatest Montale poems, she became Clizia, a symbolic presence of transcendental significance.

The Clizia Myth and the Secret Cycle

The first half of Montale's career as a poet was chiefly dedicated to creating three great books, which fit together in a larger pattern. His first book of poetry, *Ossi di seppia* (*Cuttlefish Bones*), published in 1925, is generally considered to be one of the most compelling books of Italian poetry in the twentieth century. It is perhaps one of the greatest books in all of modern poetry. While *Cuttlefish Bones* is on the surface a hermetic and at times gloomy contemplation of the alienated modern self, projected against the back-drop of a particularly rugged strip of the Italian Riviera, the social and historical underpinnings of the work explain Montale's later stance. Irma Brandeis does not appear in her literary incarnation in this great first book, but it contains the magical words that summoned her, the poetry that attracted her to the poet. Here Montale fashions his secretive style, writing to his unnamed listener, while at the same time developing his personal rebellion against the political and cultural ideas that dominated his era.

These underpinnings surface with increasing clarity in subsequent works, foremost among them Montale's next two collections: his second book, *Le occasioni* (*The Occasions*, 1939), based on his Florentine years, and the more abstract *La bufera e altro* (*The Storm and Other Things*, 1943, revised until 1956).[4] It is in these books that Clizia first makes her appearance as a character. *The Occasions*, ominous and tragic, is a deep meditation about love in a time of increasing menace – Fascist Florence in the late 1930s, just before the outbreak of war. Clizia evolves in the course of Montale's poetry. When we first meet her, she is a dashing young woman, with a red scarf that resembles the *bandiera stellata* (Star-Spangled Banner). At this point, she is modelled on a real person, a young woman whom we can see in old pictures: Irma Brandeis, whose initials (I.B.) are used to assign the secret dedication of the book. As the poems evolve to cover the disturbing circumstances of the late 1930s, she transforms, leaving her real-life model behind. Eventually Clizia becomes something more than a mere senhal for the poet's beloved Irma.

The Second World War explodes in the next book, fittingly entitled *The Storm and Other Things*. The architecture of this collection is held together by the recurring theme of the apotheosis of love in the hour of loss. Now Clizia is a goddess with X-ray eyes and supernatural wings who, in her effort to represent the hope of humanity, flies across the ocean to confront her enemies. The senhal takes on a life of its own in this book, assuming a transcendent meaning within the history of culture. Clizia becomes a symbolic entity that pushes upward on the scale of meaning, evolving from the merely human to the divine in Montale's complex poetic expression of her. As he continues to write to Clizia, she changes. At first she is still a lovely woman at times, with blonde bangs, flashing eyelashes, and a bright red scarf. The objects around her – her clothing, her cigarette smoke and ashes, her bracelet – are continually used to evoke her. Then she grows wings, even resembling a type of sphinx. Adorned with jewellery, and even made partly of gems herself, Clizia becomes a god-woman. Forged out of the magic of metaphorical construction, she is now a combination of human, bird, rainbow, flower, and sun. Eventually transformed into a goddess, she suffers torn wings and a bloodied throat in a quasi-Zoroastrian struggle between good and evil. Finally, she flies into the sun, bedazzled with light, consuming herself in a sacrificial act of divine luminosity.

The Storm subsides in an unsettling post-war conclusion. Montale viewed his first three books as "three canticles, three phases of a human life."[5] They are written in a dense, hermetic style, filled with complex imagery that is hard to decipher.

There is a final canticle, however, written many years later. After the war Montale gave up writing poetry for some time, working as a cultural journalist and eventually writing thousands of pages of criticism. The fragmentation of his career as a poet into two parts obscures the thematic obsessions that connect them. Eventually he began to write a new type of poetry – simpler, clearer, and more ironic. Clizia now reappears. In a final group of twelve poems (thirteen counting the somewhat earlier poem "Heroism") she is once again a beautiful young woman reading poetry in a pensione on the outskirts of Florence, while stretched out languorously on a chaise longue.

Montale was fascinated by the sunlight, the blue of the Mediterranean Sea, and the rugged coastal hills of his birthplace and childhood summer home. He prefigures his beloved in his contemplation of light, particularly in the famous poem in *Cuttlefish Bones* about the sunflower that follows the course of the sun across the sky, taking on the colours of the sun in its yellow flowers. Then he meets his human sunflower in the 1930s. After he loses her, she becomes transfigured in his writing as an intricately constructed symbolic presence. As a sun goddess in the poems, she becomes the symbol of the symbol that attracted her in the first place. This is a Borgesian complexity that existed not in fiction but in life itself.

Many hidden secrets of Montale's writing are uncovered by a reading of the poems that in some way are touched by Irma Brandeis, are concerned with symbolic concepts associated with her, or are directly about her. The senhal, the fictional name for this beloved, is Clizia. Montale's Clizia is named after Ovid's Clytie, a nymph who, because she suffered for the love of the sun god Apollo, was eventually turned into a sunflower. Of such great consequence is Clizia in Montale's poetry that the collected poems about her might well be read as a complete entity in themselves and published under a separate title, *The Clizia Poems*. Taken together, these poems are a cycle of works that can almost be traced through Montale's entire creative life as a writer. This book offers the first in-depth reading of them in English as the Clizia Cycle, an entity apart from Montale's other poetry and set in a cultural context.[6] This is also the first full-length study of Clizia that shows her from the American point of view, taking into account Brandeis's significance in the production and dissemination of the Clizia myth and looking back, in fact, at Montale's work from Brandeis's perspective as a translator and publisher of his poetry in the United States. Read as a whole, the Clizia poems are a complete entity in themselves, and they stretch through the three "canticles" of his greatest period to the poignant, playful poems of remembered passion that he wrote at the end of his life.

There is a double story, however, that needs to be told about Eugenio Montale and Irma Brandeis. One story is the unfolding mystery of the literary expression in the poems, including the developing mythic pattern that emerges in the imaginary world of the poems inspired by Brandeis. This can only be uncovered by closely reading the interrelated Clizia poems, tracing the patterns of the emerging Clizia saga, one poem at a time. There are great rewards to be had by going slowly, poem by poem, to uncover the full literary expression of the Clizia story, especially in light of new evidence. The other story is the micro-biographical and historical saga of Brandeis and Montale as their lives unfold. While a full biographical treatment of their lives is beyond the scope of this study, I do explore Brandeis's direct role in inspiring the strongest of Montale's poems and her role in publishing them in English (this has been too often overlooked, even neglected), and Montale's anti-Fascist stance as directly expressed to Brandeis. The historic context, as a whole, remains important. As the double story is uncovered, poetry and biography, art and life, intertwine in revealing patterns.

Clizia is also one of the most profound mythic creations in all of modern literature. Montale was well aware of the achievements of James Joyce and Marcel Proust, writing about them many times in his voluminous literary criticism. Montale's Clizia is at least as significant as Joyce's famous Jewish everyman, Leopold Bloom, a remodelling of the Ulysses myth in modern terms. Owing to its sustained attempt to recapture the lost lover in words, a search that lasts more than forty years, the Clizia Cycle rivals the meditations on time and memory – set against the historical background of the Dreyfus trial and the First World War – that hold together Proust's gigantic *À la recherche du temps perdu* (*In Search of Lost Time*). Clizia, who has origins in the classical world of Ovid, also has Jewish overtones, but her mythic structure is much more intricate, stretching back into early Christianity as well.

Montale created an interconnected body of poems by developing a secret symbology that stretched across the span of his entire writing life. What we have is a set of interconnected poems, not a *romanzo* (novel) or a linear narrative. The imaginative processes most characteristic of poetry enabled Montale to take bigger risks, assuming more imaginative liberties than any novelist could have undertaken. At the same time, the poetic voice allows for more secrecy and requires fewer words. A novelist would have to explain, to contextualize at length *within* the form of the work. The hidden story is suggested through the unexplained juxtaposition of the poems. While there is no extant romanzo, there is an implied narrative to uncover. My commentaries show how the poems might connect *outside* the form of the work. There is enough suggested in the interlocking symbols to let the reader discover much of the connecting drama that links the poetry. The revealed Clizia Cycle emerges as one of the great achievements of modern literature, until now neglected as an entity. For the first time we can see the Clizia myth in its entirety.

The Jewish Beatrice, the Sweet New Style, and Fascism

Montale, who translated Shakespeare, was keenly aware of the culture of love poetry in European literature. One key source was the *Dolce Stil Novo* (sweet new style) generated by Dante and his colleagues in the late thirteenth century. The phrase *sweet new style* appears in Dante's *Purgatory* (XXIV) when Bonagiunta Orbicciani da Lucca describes the sound of Dante's love poetry. While Dante is never far from Montale's grasp, Montale was also aware of the writing of one of Dante's colleagues and immediate predecessors, Guido Guinizzelli (1240?–76?), as he was working up to his uniquely contemporary style of love poetry. There are only about twenty extant Guinizzelli poems. One in particular, "Al cor gentil rempaira sempre amore" ("Love Repairs Always to the Gentle Heart"), describes a new type of idealized love in which the beloved takes on the nature and appearance of an angel and a kind of divine status. Guinizzelli's beloved is bathed in a divine solar light; she is his saviour and goddess. It is only this level of love that can bring the human heart to perfection for this champion of the sweet new style of Dante's era.

With the cadences of his Italian poetic heritage in mind, Montale created another Dolce Stil Novo in the maelstrom of the mid-twentieth century. His Clizia eventually becomes a divine angel who faces off against the demonic forces of his era. In his great essay on Dante, presented at the International Congress of Dante Studies in 1965, Montale mentions Guinizzelli's creation of the "*donna salutifera,* the lady who heals and redeems, which is the most evident theme of the entire school [of the Dolce Stil Novo]."[7] In the same essay he quotes Irma Brandeis's study of Dante. She was clearly his twentieth-century donna salutifera, enabling him to heal and redeem in his own time.

The listening lover Clizia rarely responds in the fictional construction of Montale's poetry, but Irma Brandeis, an intelligent Jewish-American writer and Dante scholar, did reciprocate in a variety of ways, eventually becoming a collaborator in projecting Montale's work into world literature. Even as a very young woman, she was one of the first American critics to realize his importance. After she met the poet in 1933, she reviewed his first book of poems in the *Saturday Review of Literature* just three years later. They corresponded thereafter, reading and translating poetry together. In the process she fell in love with him, and he with her. During this period Montale wrote some of his greatest poems, directly inspired by her. He included them in his love letters to her, mailed from Florence to New York City. Later in life Irma Brandeis even helped him become better known in the English-speaking world by editing a special edition of the *Quarterly Review of Literature* that was devoted completely to his work. Published in 1962, it contains a number of her own translations of his poetry and even begins with a critical essay analysing the mythic character that Montale had based on her. Her interest in Montale surely transcended the merely personal aspects of her relationship with him, for she was quite happy to publish the poetry that he wrote to other women. Without doubt, she was aware of the importance of her own literary task in disseminating Montale's writing. A gifted scholar and writer herself, she published an accomplished book about Dante, one of their many common intellectual interests. One of the reasons that Dante was important to Montale is that Dante was important to Irma Brandeis. Her writing on Dante informs our knowledge of the fictional persona that she inspired.

Montale created the senhal of Clizia to protect both his Jewish-American donna and himself, as he wrote poetry addressed to her during the height of the war years. She is the beloved reader who remains unidentified in the poetry – a beloved reader who might never read her poet or who seemed at one point to have no chance of ever reading him, especially during the long period of separation in which the poems were written. While Irma Brandeis would indeed read him years later, the poet could not have known this as he wrote his early work.[8]

Montale found a new voice, using both old and new materials, thus preserving a fluent and seamless connection with his Italianate tradition. He managed to revitalize the significance of the Greek philosophers, the Bible, the troubadours, Dante, Shakespeare, the French Symbolists and their Italian descendants, and much more while writing in a Modernist voice, full of doubt and anxiety. Like Eliot, he forced a dialogue between a cultural inheritance and the contemporary dilemma of humanity. But the results were very different, having been sparked by the donna salutifera from New York City.

Clizia is modelled on a Jewish-American woman, yet she evolves into a Christian symbol, described at one point by Montale as a "Christ-bearer." He clarified this quite explicitly in a letter to Glauco Cambon, his close friend and always one of his most astute critics (see chapter 6).[9] In the letter Montale outlines the heart of his Clizia myth. It is one of the most revealing pieces of auto-criticism ever written by a great poet.

The precedents from the European past – Dante, Guinizzelli, Mariology, various heretical traditions – are all the more effective and important because of the fresh context of the twentieth century. Clizia is Montale's best defence against what he calls – in key poems in the cycle – the era of the *tregenda,* the "hellish pandemonium" of shouting men and stomping boots, which had thwarted or inverted the values of a civilization. Montale constructs a system of meaning around the complex symbol of his absent or present beloved. Irma Brandeis is apotheosized into an all-suffering sun goddess who carries her own sun burning deep within her. In appreciation of her Jewish origin, he portrays her sun, which glows in many places in the poems, as Middle Eastern at times, shining over the Levant, the palm trees, and the wadis of the south.[10]

Montale's ingenious Dolce Stil Novo revival allows him to fashion a Clizia to trump Dante's Beatrice or, rather, to co-opt her. In his rewriting of Beatrice into Clizia, Montale invents a new character who is even more universal because she dissolves the barrier between great cultural divides, joining Greco-Roman, Christian, and Jewish traditions during one of the most disastrous periods of the twentieth century. And the real-life model for Clizia, a gifted professor and author herself, writes back and even reviews her poet's books. She eventually translates his works and publishes them, along with a critical essay that discusses the character modelled on her. She is perhaps the most unusually active muse in literary history. An excerpt from her own translation of Sergio Solmi's essay on Montale, published in her Montale issue of the *Quarterly Review,* shows how engaged she was in furthering the reputation of the poems. Solmi, rendered in her English words, speaks directly of the mythic character that Irma Brandeis inspired:

> As early as the "Mottetti" the feminine "other one" is glimpsed in the secret corridors of a personal history, presented to the reader's eye in a vague melange of indefiniteness, pure possibility and lightening-like evocation ... Later still this figure is so steeped in the poet's inner life that she becomes the angelic monster of a personal mythology: witness the mysterious figure of the "Nuove stanze" ["New Stanzas"] (1939), muse or witch, bent over the chessboard of which she alone can "compose the sense" – reflex of the world which, as its tragedy approaches, moves in an apocalyptic light along the clear lines of "metaphysical paintings." Still later, in *La bufera* [The Storm], this feminine principal will expand in further images and undergo more complex metamorphoses.[11]

Beatrice Portinari, Dante's model, is passive by comparison. If Dante could have known, he would have had reason to be jealous. James Joyce has similar cause for jealousy. If his friend Italo Svevo (the pen name for the businessman and writer Aron Ettore Schmitz, 1861–1928), the principal model for Leopold Bloom, had campaigned fiercely for *Ulysses*, translating it into another language with a group of influential friends, Joyce would have had similar help.[12]

Searching the history of Western civilization for heretics who can somehow account for his new Judeo-Christian goddess in opposition to the blasphemy and absurdity of modern culture, Montale eventually recreates the Dolce Stil Novo trope of Guinizzelli, inventing a literary lady to worship in his poems who has a divine power, an exalted status that both threatens and redeems the cultural order that gives meaning to his world. Montale turns to other forgotten figures, among them David Lazzaretti and Nestorius. Lazzaretti, a self-appointed nineteenth-century messiah, is remembered for his heretical rebellion near Mount Amiata in southern Tuscany. Nestorius, who lived in fifth-century Byzantium, doubted the divinity of Mary, arguing that Jesus was the son of a human mother and had essentially two entities or incarnations, one human and one divine. Montale's vast knowledge of his tradition enables him to articulate Clizia's eventual incarnation as a twentieth-century Dolce Stil Novo heroine, a daring combinatory refashioning of Beatrice, Ovidian myth, and Christian themes and motifs, with Jewish undertones. Montale, who refers to himself as a Nestorian heretic in one of his most dramatic poems, attempts to save his cultural tradition by searching its margins at a moment of great peril, stretching back into the forgotten corners of the European culture in order to save it.

History, Biography, and the Carefully Kept Secrets of the Work of Art

It is easy to make moralistic judgments about what one should or should not have done in the Fascist era. Montale courageously joined the philosopher Benedetto Croce to sign the "Protest Against the Manifesto of the Fascist Intellectuals" in 1925. Later, after his appointment as director of the Gabinetto Vieusseux, he was more accommodating. On the one hand, he would, out of necessity, readily solicit support for the library from Mussolini's son-in-law, the powerful Galeazzo Ciano. On the other, he would privately mock Mussolini in his letters to Irma Brandeis, sarcastically calling Mussolini "the Cardinal" because of the dictator's well-known novel about a promiscuous cleric, or make fun of lesser Fascists, such as the "cardinalist" lady who said at dinner, "We have to be pretty. We are the wives of the winners."[13]

Quietly defiant and lacking proper Fascist credentials, Montale eventually lost his job as director of the Gabinetto Vieusseux. He also had too many Jewish friends, an increasingly problematic position for the leader of a cultural organization in Italy in the late 1930s. As he pointed out to Giacomo Debenedetti, the Jewish-Italian critic and Proust translator, Montale himself was even labelled as "Jewish" at various points in his life. In addition to the various Jewish women who became heroines of his poetry, he was friends with Italo Svevo, Roberto "Bobi" Bazlen, Umberto Saba, and others, and he helped many of these acquaintances when it was highly dangerous and unpopular to do so.

During the worst of the war years Montale suffered quietly, withdrawing into the rich mental life of his poetry. There he found the meditation and peace that perhaps enabled him to survive. Montale was not a hero in a conventional sense. He did not confront the Fascists with the directness of, say, the poet and novelist Cesare Pavese, the writer Leone Ginzburg, or Montale's own sadly doomed publisher, Piero Gobetti. For this reason, perhaps, he was always fascinated with the Chaplinesque anti-hero.[14]

Some American poets of the mid-twentieth century, Ezra Pound and T.S. Eliot most conspicuously among them, were stained with anti-Semitic ideologies and views. In sharp contrast, Montale, writing as an anti-Fascist in a Fascist country, was philo-Semitic. Ezra Pound, who lived in Italy during the Second World War, was imprisoned in an open cage and then sent to jail after the war for his anti-American and anti-Semitic radio broadcasts. Montale knew Pound personally and, in his second career as a journalist, wrote about him, praising the American poet's talent and criticizing his political foolishness. Montale the anti-Fascist gives us a significantly different view of literary Modernism in poetry in this era. In "Iride" ("Iris"), one of the high points of the Clizia Cycle, the poet cries out to his Jewish-American donna salutifera, directly comparing the *naufragio* (shipwreck) of his people (the Italians, brought to ruin by the Fascists and their Nazi alliance) to the "shipwreck" of her people (the Jews, destroyed by the Holocaust).

With Montale, the connection between art and life matters a great deal, for it helps us to understand the full significance of his achievement. This connection is vital despite the fact that he wrote in an era in which the modern poem was conceived as a self-contained artefact, existing as a solid entity on a page and always inferior to any necessary commentary that would explain it. This was the era of Eliot, I.A. Richards, and High Modernist New Criticism. We need no more proof of the importance of these figures to Brandeis than the fact that she referred to Eliot and Richards when she first reviewed Montale's *Cuttlefish Bones* in 1936.

I.A. Richards's critical works, originally published in the twenties and disseminated in the thirties and forties, were known to both Irma and Montale. Richards (1893–1979) was one of the pioneers of modern "close reading," bringing new analytical techniques to bear on the intricacies of the literary work of art. Eliot's position, which was so well known at the time, argued for the autonomy of the work of art, with every great literary "masterpiece" locked in a self-referential network of classics. These classics were to talk more of each other than of the biographical and historical subject matter that generated them. The poem was a construction made out of words that held a latent power, a fool-proof objective correlative that could be provoked in the reader. Cultural conditioning was unnecessary for this to happen; the text could do it by itself. For Brandeis and Montale, poetry could stand almost as an objet d'art, as solidly constructed out of words as a rare Chinese vase is made out of hard materials, a solid object that could exist without context or commentary. Historical and biographical explanation would be extraneous, unnecessary, and intrusive, not only to their private dignity but to the notion of art.

For those of us looking back from a new century that will develop its own critical methods, it is important to see Brandeis and Montale in their proper historical and cultural context. They believed that Montale's poetry should project the full intended meaning of the text, regardless of the carefully guarded private life and historical circumstances that generated the poems. The objective correlative of the poems was far more crucial than the history and biography behind them. Irma was always torn about how much of her relationship with Montale should be known and how much should be hidden from view. She felt that it should have nothing to do with the reading of the poems, that they must stand alone. I am sure that much of her reasoning had to do with her desire and need for privacy. We must remember, too, that Montale and Brandeis were living in the era of New Criticism, which stressed a reading of literature without context.

Owing to this literary sensibility, the medieval senhal was the perfect device for the poetry of High Modernism that was later generated and championed by New Criticism, and for New Criticism itself, which shunned all biographical and historical commentary. Even the dominant critical sensibility of the mid-twentieth century dictated that Clizia's identity could be kept a secret and regarded as an irrelevancy. The biographical silence demanded by New Criticism helped to justify the great trepidation that Brandeis felt as the gifted Glauco Cambon grew closer and closer to revealing her true identity in his criticism. Responding to some of his insightful criticism on the poet, she both compliments Cambon and warns him off:

> I liked greatly your notes on the literary tack with Montale, but not the questioning on Clizia, with its suggestions that your book will approach the poems through the life. Don't do it. Save all that for some future work of biography. True criticism and true reading does not require such identification and they are, in any case, partial and misleading. You know too little of the story in any case, as you will no doubt someday see ... Don't make a dark face. I think am speaking to Montale's best critic. I know the value of your work, and hold it to be precious. I think of you fondly.[15]

Cambon pressed ahead, and Brandeis could not resist helping him, although she did so with reluctance. On 25 December 1980 her ambivalence was still evident. She called herself a "poor reader" for Cambon because she was at the heart of his subject to a much greater extent than even he could have known: "Of the Montale ms. I cannot speak at all, except to thank you for letting me have it. There is something so painful for me in this close encounter that even my awareness of how much you have to teach doesn't overcome my reluctance to go on. Have you yet submitted it to a publisher? If not, I have a note or two I could share with you when you return. I think there may be too much textual analysis. But I am a poor reader for this book."[16]

Yet some of Brandeis's actions indicated that she wanted her connection to Montale's poetry to eventually be known. At the very least, she wanted to make the original inspiration behind some of the poems available for study by serious scholars. For this reason she did not destroy the 155 letters that Montale wrote to her in the 1930s. Instead, she deposited them in 1983 in the archives of the Gabinetto Vieusseux in Florence, the library in which her romantic adventure with Montale had begun so many years before, with the understanding that they would be sealed for twenty years and then made available for scholars to study. They were finally published in an excellent scholarly edition in

May 2006, an event that generated considerable excitement in the Italian press.[17] Most of the published letters are in Italian, but approximately thirty-seven are in flawed but sometimes brilliant English; another twelve are half English and half Italian. Considering their historical significance (written just before the war) and the evident depth of feeling in them, these letters amount to something of a classic. The poet himself repeatedly compares his letters to the very famous thirty-seven love letters that Keats wrote to Fanny Brawne in 1819–20, letters written in the far more tranquil post-Napoleonic era.

As time passes, the context that provoked Montale's writing becomes more and more significant. The defining point in the lives of the poet and his beloved was the destructive mid-century vortex that whirled together the forces of civilization and its discontents. George Steiner, writing with wit and brilliance in his *In Bluebeard's Castle,* reminds us that "we now realize that the extremes of collective hysteria and savagery can coexist with a parallel conservation and, indeed, further development of the institutions, bureaucracies, and professional codes of high culture."[18] Among the administrators of the "final solution" were men who admired Goethe, Rilke, Mozart, and Bach. Some of them were competent musicians who could perform great music, capable even of arranging an evening of chamber music within yards of a gas chamber. Culture has never been a guarantee against barbarism. Steiner points out that Martin Heidegger, one of the most important philosophers of the twentieth century, wrote one of his greatest works on Hölderlin while in close proximity to a concentration camp. Hitler visited art museums and attended the opera during his state visit to Italy in 1938. He enjoyed culture more than did Mussolini, who was a mediocre novelist. Hitler would have liked to have been a painter or an architect. Had he not been rejected by the Vienna Academy of Fine Arts, history might have been different. Had it been possible, Hitler might have been happy as a painter or even a glamorous opera composer like Wagner, whose operas he loved.

Montale was probably the most significant poet of the twentieth century who dealt with this great paradox in his finest works. In his poetry he returns again and again to the irreconcilable extremes of human nature as he ponders a world that creates both the forces of the storm and the forces of love. On the one hand, he sees Hitler, Mussolini, and the destructiveness that overwhelmed European civilization in the mid-century. On the other, he sees his beloved Jewish-American Dante scholar. How can both be real? How can both be part of what human beings are? What purpose can there be to a humanity that has given a new meaning to *bestial*, a meaning that would even make the beasts ashamed? Montale is the poet who realizes the ramifications of this paradox, who is contemplating the great teachings of Western culture and staring down the brutality of Fascism at the same time. As a grand Orphic meditation on the significance of the contrast between brutality and civilization, his poetry surpasses the work of great figures such as Rilke, Stevens, Eliot, Lorca, and certainly Pound and Eliot.

We must read Montale against Eliot. The two were acquainted, having met several times. Eliot arranged for one of the first Montale translations into English, and Montale translated Eliot into Italian. Each dominated the era in his own way, Eliot in English and Montale in Italian. I am disturbed by certain aspects of Eliot's impressive little book *Notes towards the Definition of Culture,* written in 1948; Steiner, writing in the 1970s, was equally troubled. There is a chilling lack of compassion in the book for what happened in Europe just a few years before it was written. The ovens were barely cold at that point, the gas barely turned off. Still, Eliot came up with this appallingly ignorant little footnote: "Since the diaspora, and the scattering of Jews amongst peoples holding the Christian Faith, it may have been unfortunate both for these peoples and for the Jews themselves, that the culture-contact between them has had to be within those neutral zones of culture in which religion could be ignored: and the effect may have been to strengthen the illusion that there can be culture without religion."[19]

Eliot seems to have been willing to ignore the fact that religions grow out of one another, as do cultures, and that followers of one religion can be the spiritual and cultural ancestors of another. Resembling his model of literary classics, his model of culture is inert, sealed off, even medieval in its stated intention. For him, high culture, the arts, and education are for the few, not the many. For him, the dull majority of people are better off if they maintain their residence and cultural roots within the little village in which they were born. Education and knowledge can bring unhappiness. Going outside the protective framework of a village culture to venture into a world of conflicting views and practices is not necessarily a desirable activity. It is ironic that the same Eliot who expressed these strange, reactionary views also wrote some of the most adventurous poetry of the twentieth century.

Montale preferred to bring together, through the force of love, what the far colder and crueller Eliot understood as forever separate, even in 1948. Nevertheless, they are united by a similar drive to find a grand dialogue in their literary activities, a dialogue linking the certain classics of the past with the uncertainties of the present. Eliot, of course, was a literary giant, and Montale was one of his important European translators and probably deeply influenced by him. However, we need a wider picture of the interrelations of world poetry, culture, and Modernism for the twenty-first century, and to know Montale better in relation to Eliot and other Anglo-American figures is a step in the right direction.

A Surprise in the History of Style

The poetic language that Montale used to accomplish his purpose is a surprising innovation, finding its origins in an obscure pre-Modernist poetic style and originally developed in the fin de siècle. Montale's reconfiguration of this style is a perfect nod to the European past, tying in elegantly with the decision to resurrect the Dolce Stil Novo practice of the secret code. He was a virtuoso of metaphor, along with other poetic figures, and at the same time he was one of the keenest observers in the history of poetry. He often claimed that he never invented anything, that he only described what he saw. It is a strange fact of literary history that one of his precursors was Stéphane Mallarmé (1842–98), the French theoretical poet who envied the expressive intensity of music and the visual arts and who became famous for his difficult and abstract language. Mallarmé set the tone for the century that followed, and Montale was one of his last great descendants. Montale obviously read him with dangerous intensity. Montale's critical statements often strangely echo Mallarmé's, while at the same time saying very different things about the notion of poetry. When writing to his American lover, the Italian even quotes an obscure sonnet by the French poet, admitting his connection to the increasingly remote past of *belles-lettres* when he says that he has "to write in a language no one understands and can no longer be adapted to life today."[20] In his small body of poetry Mallarmé, who was somewhat of a snob, avoided the everyday, the political, and the social reality of his existence, shunning these aspects of life as if they were unclean contaminants of his pure poetry. Montale did just the opposite, rooting his poetry carefully in the world around him, directly absorbing the social and historical forces of his era with dramatic and even explosive power.

Another sign of Montale's post-Symbolist sensitivities was his obvious fascination with the arts, something that he also shared with

Proust. Aside from the sensitive study by Gian-Paolo Biasin, critical commentaries on Montale often overlook the fact that he was a gifted amateur painter with a close affinity to the work of Giorgio Morandi. Even more important, Montale was a serious student of music who almost considered it as a career. He studied voice with the famous baritone Ernesto Sivori, and, as Biasin has noted, he was fascinated with the music of the great French composer Claude Debussy.[21] The vocabulary, concepts, and forms of music influenced his poetry throughout his life. His early poems had titles of musical instruments and compositions, especially those taken from Debussy's piano scores ("Minstrels," with the epigraph "After Debussy," and "movimenti," taken from Debussy's "mouvement" in *Images*, book 1), and at least a few of which he heard in concert in Genoa in 1917.[22] Montale's Debussy poems have the quality of melding the psychological experience of sounds and visual phenomena that is unique in Debussy's music and typical of the poetry of his era. Both Montale and Debussy were masters at recreating the experience of perception, each in his respective art form.

His deep interests in music and art gave Montale more than a second profession as a cultural journalist, although he worked for many years at one of the best Italian newspapers, the *Corriere della Sera,* as a music critic and general cultural commentator. His artistic interests also contributed to his poetic technique, and his remarkable verbal gifts make him as great as his unique historical position makes him important. Montale was a painter and composer, but he was a master of these arts through his own art of poetry, emulating the qualities of each of these art forms as they informed his own senses, and, in doing this, he vastly enriched the visual and aural vocabulary of his poetry. His gifts were obviously stimulated by his childhood summer home at Monterosso al Mare, located in the Cinque Terre. There the steep slopes rise almost directly up to the sky from the sea, creating a long, rugged coastline where the water echoes resoundingly as it pounds the rocks and the pebbles, and the light is continuously changing. Dawn and sunset take place at different points in time up and down the greatly varied heights of the seaside hills and along the coast.

Montale, who learned his music from Maestro Sivori, was therefore a poet who knew how to think like a musician. Montale described his symbolic language in terms of *chiavi* (keys), *armonici* (harmonies), and *pedale* (pedal or pedal point), concepts he borrowed from the vocabulary of music. Each chiave is a symbolic area, a cluster of key images that intone the primary meanings of his poetry. A pedale of images is a repeated reference, like the continuous drone of a pedal point. Monterosso and its environs constitute the first tonality, and it is never far from his attention. The second chiave is based in the images of storm and marauding hordes that conjure up the brutality of the Second World War. This often appears as the ominous drone of the pedal point of war and destruction. The third key clusters around the symbolic imagery of Clizia, the goddess of the sunflower. Together these function as the principal tonalities of the Clizia Cycle, interlocking tonal areas that resound at the foundations of Montale's symbology, with one key area at times dominating the others. Each symbolic chiave is rich in memory and meaning, overlapping with resonant armonici of meaning. For Montale, the associative powers of words function like a musician's harmonies.

Montale's ingenious attention to detail makes him a great master, a master of – to borrow from some titles of his late poems – *suoni, luci,* and *colori* (sounds, lights, and colours). A poet with his own inner zoom lens, his sharply observant eye sweeps in to catch detail, and he meticulously records what he sees, blowing it up to huge proportions on the page, creating a whole new context out of the highlighting of observed phenomena. He did just as well, or perhaps even better, with the sounds around him, recording them with his ear and amplifying them with his words. If he is given the time and the attention he deserves, he will bring his reader deeply into the felt experience of life. His masterful powers of poetic suggestion can be viewed with particular clarity in a number of places in this study. Montale was writing during one of the most extensively covered periods in history. We have access to newspapers, photographs, newsreels, archives, memoirs, and correspondence; all of these are useful for uncovering Montale's story, but none of these is the equivalent of his expressive poetry. Here history and biography give us a rare opportunity to see how poetry works and how actual events kindle the poetic imagination. For example, the intensely evoked setting of the short poem "Nuove stanze" ("New Stanzas") can be read in these pages along with Irma Brandeis's description (and several extant photographs) of exactly the same interior – her residence at 54 Costa San Giorgio – that is to be found in the poem. Montale's great poem "Palio" may be compared here to Bernard Berenson's prose description of this famous Siennese horse-race. Both of these poems and texts can be found in chapter 4. Finally, the scenes and events in "La primavera hitleriana"

("Hitler Spring") may be contemplated in the context of the 1938 prose description by *New York Times* reporter Frederick Birchall and the reconstruction of exactly the same event by art historian D. Medina Lasansky – Hitler's visit to Florence (see chapters 5 and 6). These comparisons show where poetry begins and prose ends. The intensity of Montale's unique powers of observation fuels his poetic imagination and generates the myth of Clizia, but the same Montalean intensity, sparked by the meticulous observations of sights and sounds, also makes the poet a vital witness. In Montale's poems, the details of observed phenomena record the emotional memory of calamitous moments in the twentieth century. In Montale's voice, the great power of the most evocative poetic language preserves a brave, eloquent protest in the time of the tregenda.

2 Murder, Manifestos, and the Poems of the Cinque Terre

If it is a crime to incite people to violence, I boast now of committing that crime.
– Gabriele D'Annunzio

Don't ask us for the phrase that can open worlds, just a few gnarled syllables, dry like a branch.
– Eugenio Montale

Montale and D'Annunzio

Piero Gobetti, the publisher of Montale's first book of poems, was beaten so extensively by Fascist followers of Mussolini that he died a short time afterwards. This fact alone makes Benito Mussolini and *il ventennio,* the twenty-year era of Fascism, more than mere historical background to the writing career of Eugenio Montale.[1] Some knowledge of Mussolini and his era is necessary in order to see how and why Montale later created Clizia. The prehistory of Clizia – the period in which Montale discovered his own powers as a great poet – is characterized by his discontent with the 1920s' Fascist culture in which he was forced to live.

Eugenio Montale was thirteen years younger than the Italian dictator who dominated the culture of his early life. Born in the port city of Genoa on 12 October 1896, Montale was raised there and in Monterosso al Mare, a small seaside town in the Cinque Terre, the rugged coastal region to the south. His father, Domenico, a successful lawyer, businessman, and importer, built a villa overlooking the sea in Monterosso in 1905. A cousin, Lorenzo, built another fine house nearby. A large, lush Mediterranean garden linked the two homes. Montale spent his summer vacations at the villa for the next twenty years. That home and the personalities Montale encountered in Monterosso provided a source of poetic material for the rest of his life. The sounds, smells, sights, and tastes of the coastal region of Liguria – particularly of Monterosso and the Cinque Terre area – permeate his poetry, forming a basic vocabulary of psychological perception that articulates his thought.

Montale's rather stern father wanted his sensitive son to follow in the traditional masculine role of lawyer and businessman, but young Eugenio was artistically minded.[2] He was initially attracted to opera music, which he first heard with his family in the famous Teatro Carlo Felice in Genoa, and he spent a great deal of time in the opera house as a boy. Giulio Nascimbeni, Montale's Italian biographer, refers to the poet as a "singer manqué."[3] Vocal training became very important for Montale during his teenage years. Before long, he had advanced sufficiently in his studies to sing the challenging "Il lacerato spirito" ("The Weeping Spirit"), Fiesco's famous aria from Giuseppe Verdi's *Simon Boccanegra,* an opera steeped in the history and legend of the poet's native Genoa. Soon afterwards he began studying with the eminent Italian baritone Ernesto Sivori, a great master of that particular Verdi role. The maestro encouraged Montale in his music studies, detecting the potential for a rich, wide-ranging baritone voice in his student. Montale did consider the possibility of becoming an opera singer, but he lacked the extroverted personality necessary for the professional life of a performer. He was, as he recalls, a "fish out of water."[4] He abandoned his plans for a singing career, but his sensitivity to the arresting immediacy of musical sound stayed with him. At around this time he wrote the first draft of "Meriggiare pallido e assorto" ("To Rest at Noon Pale and Engrossed"), a poem he later published in *Cuttlefish Bones.*

Montale came from a large family. He was the youngest of four brothers, and he also had a sister, Marianna (1894–1938), with whom he read widely in French literature and European philosophy, including Saint Augustine, Pascal, Schopenhauer, and Nietzsche. Marianna, in turn, received guidance from a Barnabite priest, Father Giuseppe Trinchero, who stimulated her intellectual curiosity. When Marianna brought her younger brother to meet Father Trinchero in September of 1915, the priest was greatly impressed with Montale's sensitive and lively mind. Aside from Marianna's influence and, indirectly, Father

Trinchero's encouragement, Montale was essentially self-taught, with little formal schooling and no university education. Nascimbeni credits Marianna for Montale's initiation into the world of words and ideas. It was she who first saw how very different he was from his brothers, with his passion for books, his predilection for meditation and fantasy, and his obvious unsuitability for a standard desk job in a business such as the one founded by his father, which traded in dye and other chemicals.[5]

Like Hitler and Mussolini, Montale was a soldier in the First World War. In the autumn of 1917 he was sent to an officers' training camp in Parma. While there he met the writer and critic Sergio Solmi, the Futurist Cesare Cerati, and Marcello Manni, who wrote the lyrics to the Fascist song "Giovinezza." Later he was sent to the northern front, where the fighting with the Austrians was fierce. Unlike Giuseppe Ungaretti, another veteran of the First World War, Montale did not choose to write vividly about his war-time experience, instead finding his voice in Post-Symbolist abstraction. *Cuttlefish Bones,* the first book he wrote after the war, includes a short poem that refers to Valmorbia, a little village in the Trentino region near where he had been stationed. This poem is strangely detached, as if the poet needed to transcend rather than observe the morbid environment of war. It is one of the few recollections of war-time experience in his writing, although there are minor echoes of the First World War in his later poetry. Another of these echoes is in a little "motet," a short poem that contains a reference to a "ballerina bomb," an explosive device used in that war.

Although they could not have been more different, Mussolini and Montale shared the same great antecedent – the hugely gifted but politically flawed Gabriele D'Annunzio. D'Annunzio (1863–1938) was one of the most popular writers in the world during the early years of the twentieth century, though he is relatively forgotten outside of Italy today. An author of novels, plays, journalistic essays, tracts, and much more, he was above all an extraordinarily gifted poet. With a private life as controversial as Byron's, D'Annunzio possessed a nationalistic vision and energy reminiscent of Whitman, and he was fascinated with Nietzsche's conception of the amoral *Übermensch* or "Superman." D'Annunzio was also a great Wagnerite, listening to *Tristan und Isolde* for hours on end. The luxuriant Romanticism of the music drama celebrating the tragic release of adulterous passion was a perfect stimulant for the Italian poet, who in his prime was one of the most notorious lovers in Europe.

A dashing and colourful personality, D'Annunzio was well known for his flamboyant shift from the political right to the left in the Italian parliament in March 1900.[6] He was a true war hero, serving with distinction in the army, navy, and air force during the First World War. Despite being blinded in one eye when his airplane crashed in 1916, he fought on through 1918, with his military career culminating in a daring assault on the harbour city of Buccari and a dashing flight over Vienna. Gifted, charismatic, and celebrated, D'Annunzio was also one of the most formidable figures in Italy. He was Mussolini's chief rival during the gestation period of Fascism. The poet even invented much of the symbology of Fascism, which Mussolini later co-opted. D'Annunzio was the first to wear a black shirt and fez, and the first to punish his opponents by forcing castor oil down their throats. This procedure, if administered with too excessive a dose, can actually cause death by diarrhoea. He kept thirty-five watch-dogs at his lakeside villa perched above the Lago di Garda. When he completed a poem, he required that the church bells be rung in the nearby village of Salò.[7] He doused himself with pungent perfumes, so overwhelming for some that they had to leave his company. He believed the artist to be a Wagnerian superman, not bound by conventional morals or the common inconvenience of repaying debt. At the entrance to his villa, he had two signs – "Beware of Dog" and "Beware of Master." The artist, for D'Annunzio, was a romantic man of action and a dangerous man.[8]

Unfortunately D'Annunzio's raid on the small Adriatic port city of Fiume became the prototype for the new Italian nationalism. Now known as Rijeka, Fiume bordered on Yugoslavia and Italy, and both nations claimed it after the war. In September 1919, D'Annunzio and a group of followers attacked and captured the city. They occupied Fiume in violation of international law, holding out for more than a year until they were finally driven out by the Italian military.

It was at Fiume that much of the symbolism of Fascism was devised.[9] D'Annunzio dared Mussolini to come and fight with him, but Mussolini chose to remain warily on the sidelines, even censoring D'Annunzio's remarks in his newspaper. Undaunted, D'Annunzio released a string of nationalistic pronouncements on how Fiume and the Dalmatian coast were part of the manifest destiny of the Italian race. God was behind the territorial expansion of the Italians and their rightful "destiny," he insisted.[10] In many ways, his attack on Fiume set the tone for the coming Fascism. Before the Italian military ended the occupation in December 1920, he made a speech each day from a balcony, with emphatic rhetorical gestures. He also reintroduced the ancient Roman salute, devised colourful religious symbolism to praise his heroes and "martyrs," and invented the Fascist war cry of "Eja, Eja, alalà," which was to be satirized many years later by Montale in "Hitler Spring," his most powerful anti-Fascist poem.[11] Mussolini eventually used D'Annunzio's theatrical innovations far more effectively for his propaganda campaigns.

Hero and Anti-hero

Montale returned to Genoa after the war, rejoining his many literary and artistic friends in the vital port city. There were two important literary cafés in Genoa in the early 1920s. The Caffè Roma was the preferred base of the "dannunziani," led by Mario Maria Martini. Among these D'Annunzio admirers were a significant number of proto-Fascists, who were especially numerous after the Fiume incident. Had Montale frequented the Caffè Roma, Italian poetry would have developed very differently. But he preferred the company at the Caffè Diana, where he attended the other important literary klatsch. The Caffè Diana was the gathering place of the pacifists, who were anti-D'Annunzio in both politics and style. There Montale met Angelo Barile, Adriano Grande, Pierangelo Baratono, and Camillo Sbarbaro. Among the best-known of the poets associated with *crepuscolarismo* (crepuscularism) and a connoisseur of coastal lichens and mosses, Sbarbaro had fin-de-siècle roots in Huysmans and the French Symbolist movement. But Symbolism was extremely theoretical, and actually an apolitical style, divorced from the everyday world of social life and more concerned with the internal workings of the mind and detailed contemplation. Montale wrote much of *Cuttlefish Bones* during the period that he was going to the Caffè Diana. He also read voraciously, often spending six to seven hours a day in the library.[12]

Montale's relationship with D'Annunzio is extremely important and extremely complex.[13] D'Annunzio was one of the most famous Europeans of the early twentieth century and one of the most important Italian writers to appear on the international scene in hundreds of years. Already fifty-five years old by the end of the First World War, he was from a previous generation, with his aesthetic beginnings stretching back to the Romanticism of the previous century. He was popular and notorious, a creature of the developing modern frenzy of celebrity.[14] In some ways, D'Annunzio seemed to be a poet with a special understanding of the developing modern world. His poems in praise of weapons, speed, and power fed directly into the ideology of the Italian Futurists. Montale, in contrast, had his literary roots in the dandyish café dreamers of Genoa, particularly the "crepuscular" writers, with their fondness for the fin de siècle and the contemplation of intricate detail and intimate observation. Nevertheless, Montale's writing, not D'Annunzio's, evolved into a vividly modern voice.

Pantheistic abandon attracted D'Annunzio. For him, nature was the energy of Eros, the fount of ego, the life force. His description of his encounters with it can even seem strangely sexual. While he was enormously gifted, his egotism and literary bombast permeated his writing and made his work seem prematurely dated as the sentimentality of the nineteenth century gradually gave way to the scepticism of twentieth-century Modernism. Nature in Montale's poems, while impeccably evoked with all of the possibilities of language, is aloof and disconnected from the aspirations and fears of human beings. Montale often defined himself in terms of what he was not, and he made it abundantly clear that he was not another D'Annunzio. Eventually the new literary sensibility moved in the direction of the understated Montale.

For Montale, D'Annunzio was the Italian Victor Hugo. In his reflections on the relationship between his famous precursor and Fascism, Montale describes D'Annunzio's dated "bumpkins and trumpet," his patriotic *Canzoni della gesta d'oltremare* (*Songs from across the Sea*), often read aloud around the bourgeois dining table, and the amorality of his dramatic and fictional characters.[15] It is important to contrast the zealous speakers in D'Annunzio's lyric poems and his overblown heroes with the introspective speaker of Montale's poems. Montale created an unseen anti-hero, who serves as a watcher, a keeper of the vigil of faith.

In the nineteenth century the French poet Stéphane Mallarmé began as a devoted Wagnerite, touting the greatness of the quintessential Romanticist along with many other French writers of his generation, but he eventually became suspicious of the overt symbolism of Wagnerian operas, arguing that he preferred the subtler anti-hero, the "hero who is no one," to Wagner's great heroes. Montale, similarly, was a quiet, introverted personality who preferred the persona of the modest anti-hero in his writing to the heroic voice of D'Annunzio. Never a self-styled dramatic dandy and never a partisan in open defiance of Fascism, Montale was a self-proclaimed nobody, another "hero who is no one," often describing himself as a mere "witness." It is a stance that he maintained from his early writing to his sceptical late poem on heroism, written in 1975.

Poetry and Murder

In Italy in the mid-1920s a writer or publisher who was too outspoken against the government could be in great danger and even murdered. It took only a few short years to get to that point as Italy's post-war democracy steadily deteriorated. By 1922 the government of Luigi Facta had proved impotent against the rising tide of Fascism. While the Italian army could easily have put down a Fascist rebellion, Facta and King Vittorio Emanuele III could not agree on a plan to counter a scheduled Fascist march on Rome. In spite of recommendations from his cabinet, Facta never ordered the army to take action. As the date of the march grew closer, the king decided that he preferred to take a chance with Mussolini. The Fascists finally staged a badly organized rag-tag march to Rome on 28 October 1922. Without the firm opposition of the Italian king, this was all the Fascists needed to seize control of the government. Mussolini remained in power from 1922 until 1943. He was the longest-governing political leader in modern Italy. But he dismantled the parliamentary order of Italy's young democracy to establish authoritarian rule.

It took some time for Mussolini to consolidate his authority as dictator. Until 1924 there was still a strong political and cultural opposition and, therefore, some hope that Italy's fragile democracy would survive. The defining moment of Fascism was the murder of Giacomo Matteotti (1885–1924), the secretary general of the Socialist Party. It is easy to understand why Matteotti seemed dangerous to the Fascists. Only thirty-nine years old in 1924, he was articulate, outspoken, and energetic. As Mack Smith points out, "Matteotti published in foreign newspapers the shocking details about how Fascism relied for its success on violent intimidation and unprecedented financial corruption," and he wrote a book attacking the new regime.[16] He dared to stand up to Mussolini in Parliament. An account of one of their last confrontations, in June 1924, gives a sense of the enmity between them. In spite of boos and catcalls from Mussolini's allies, Matteotti made an anti-Fascist speech that greatly moved his audience. As a result an enraged Mussolini exclaimed, "You should receive a charge of lead in the back."[17]

A week after this incident, Matteotti disappeared.

Mussolini was forced to order an investigation, which eventually led back to people close to him. While the investigation was under way, the non-Fascist sector of the Parliament walked out in protest. This turned out to be a terrible mistake, leaving the Fascists in the government with an open field. After some time three men were finally implicated in the murder. One of them was an American, Amerigo Dumini. Born in St Louis to Italian immigrants, he had returned to Italy to become an investigator for the government press department. The other two were Cesare Rossi, head of the press department, and Giovanni Marinelli, the treasurer of the Fascist Party. It was Dumini who had hired four toughs to kidnap and beat Matteotti, but things quickly got out of hand. Dumini and his men had grabbed Matteotti outside his home on 10 June, forcing him into a waiting car, where they stabbed him to death. Dumini's pack of enforcers had already beaten three members of Parliament, but this time they had actually murdered one of Mussolini's opponents. It became impossible to hide what had happened when two witnesses, a street sweeper and a lawyer, came forward to identify the licence plate of the automobile fleeing with Matteotti and his kidnappers. In spite of the evidence, Mussolini denied his connection to the crime and asked for a vote of confidence. Since the opposition had walked out in protest, there was little to oppose him in Parliament. He was victorious, with a vote of 252 to 21.[18]

By July, Mussolini had ordered that newspapers and other media were not to report on anything that might disrupt the state. From this moment the dictatorship was truly in place. It had been clear for many years that an essential component of Fascism was the use of brute force without regard to any higher authority. Now it was undeniable, and yet many Italians at the time passively accepted it.

Historians generally agree that Mussolini was for a time greatly weakened by the Matteotti affair. While Mussolini was hovering at the edge of a precipice, Giovanni Gentile, his leading cultural adviser, entered the arena in April 1925 with his "Manifesto of the Fascist Intellectuals." Intended to show public support among the intelligentsia for Mussolini and his policies, it contained an impressive list of 250 signatories, among them such luminaries as Filippo Marinetti, Luigi Pirandello, Giuseppe Ungaretti, Ardengo Soffici, and Alfredo Panzini.[19]

Montale joined the opposition, choosing to side with Benedetto Croce (1866–1952), the renowned philosopher and critic, and leader of the remaining group of intellectuals who still openly defied Mussolini.[20]

Croce's anti-Fascist statement, titled "Protest Against the Manifesto of Fascist Intellectuals," appeared on 1 May. Luigi Albertini, Gaetano Salvemini, and Giovanni Amendola lobbied intensely in the major cities to gather signatures.[21] The signatories eventually numbered in the hundreds and included even more distinguished figures than did Gentile's manifesto. Along with Carlo Cassola, Luigi Einaudi, and Luigi Salvatorelli, the young Montale signed the statement.[22] It was an act of bravery in itself.

While Croce was suspicious of Mussolini, he had wavered on Fascism until this point. But in 1925 his stance was unequivocal. In his 1 May statement of defiance Croce bluntly described Fascism as "an incoherent and bizarre mixture of appeals to authority and demagogy, of professions of reverence for the laws, ultra modern concepts and moth-eaten bric-a-brac, absolutism and Bolshevism, unbelief and toadying to the Catholic Church, flight from culture and sterile reachings towards a culture without a basis, mystical languours and cynicism."[23] He had permanently broken with Gentile, his former protégé and colleague. From this point on Croce and all who signed his "Protest" were marked as potentially dangerous opponents of Fascism. There was no going back for him – or for Montale.

Montale's anti-Fascist stance had been kindled steadily within the circle of Italian intellectuals who admired Croce's thought. Although he was not a close associate of the philosopher, Montale knew Croce, having met him twice in Florence before the Second World War.[24] The link between them is preserved in the essays that Montale wrote about the older critic and philosopher. In "Aesthetics and Criticism" he describes Croce as "the last of the great critics who had faith in life and who considered man as the sole true and concrete expression of universal life."[25] Montale, a great critic himself, was attracted by Croce's warm humanism, which stretched directly and deeply back into the nineteenth-century liberal idealism so crucial to the Risorgimento and the rise of Italian democracy, and then all the way back to Dante and beyond.

Croce's ideas were particularly noteworthy for Montale because he dared to criticize the fin-de-siècle tendency to divorce spirituality and thought. Montale, who specifically cites a substantial portion of Croce's vast writings on aesthetics, admired the way that Croce vigorously disagreed with the reductive positivism and scientism popularized by Hippolyte Taine and others.[26] In order to refute the positivists, Croce created a theory of poetic language that equated intuition and expression. His chief objection to positivism, and the related concepts of realism and naturalism, stemmed from his belief that they led inevitably to obvious distortions of pedantry and reductive thinking, hiding what he saw as the true condition of human nature. Montale mentions the essay in which Croce wrote his boldest confrontation of positivism, "On the Character of the Most Recent Italian Literature," but Croce's theory of creative intuition permeated his enormous body of writings and spanned well beyond literature into history, politics, law, and aesthetics.

Croce was after a more flexible account of creativity, and he was opposed to the use of artistic expression to promote nationalism.[27] Montale explains Croce's views on the unity of the arts, claiming that it was Croce who taught him to see the interdependence between Romantic poetry and music, European architecture and the development of polyphony, fin-de-siècle painting and musical impressionism, expressionism in poetry and Schoenberg's innovative new sounds.[28] This Crocean attitude became part of Montale's own fascination with the arts, particularly (in addition to poetry) painting and music. For Croce, "an artist is such only insofar as he creates an object in which he recognizes himself and which was not exactly in his expectations." The poem, the picture, and the musical composition are not copies of an image "preexistent in the soul of the artist." The artist perceives himself in his creation, but there is something in his work that goes beyond his understanding. Thus art is more than technique, and criticism must be more than the mere analysis of technique. A poet must dream "in the presence of reason."[29]

Montale saw the later Croce as approaching something like a Freudian theory of sublimation, but for Croce it was sublimation with an inherent sense of religious value. The human being, struggling for freedom, must defeat the "dark forces" of the vitality within human nature itself, with art as an important component in the struggle. The elemental energy in humanity contains a barbarism that must be controlled and even purged.[30] In a 1950 essay Croce writes that "everyone feels in himself the wild beast (to call it 'animal nature' might be to malign the animals)."[31]

While he was never a mere disciple of Croce, Montale does display a Crocean sensitivity and a refined individuality, qualities in startling contrast to the brutality of European life in the 1930s. This sensibility is antithetical to the irresponsible and poorly reasoned theories of race, sociology, and power that came into fashion in the 1920s and 1930s. Montale's Crocean affinity remained with him throughout his life, descending from his early readings of Croce and remaining part of his bulwark of inner conviction as he defiantly contemplated the full implications of Fascism and Nazism in the 1930s and 1940s. Montale, however, did not share Croce's lack of understanding for the new experimental poetry, with its roots in the French fin de siècle, or his general hostility to Modernism.[32] It is Croce's inability to leave behind the nineteenth century for the twentieth that ultimately distinguishes their points of view.

Another important figure in the Crocean circle was Piero Gobetti (1901–26), the publisher of Montale's *Cuttlefish Bones,* who, like Matteotti, was one of the dwindling number of people who dared to stand up to the Fascists. Gobetti, whose base of activities was the northern city of Turin, ironically was similar to Mussolini at the beginning of his career in that both men started out as journalists with socialistic views. Gobetti, however, remained a socialist, and his activities were especially alarming to Mussolini because of his determination to disseminate democratic and anti-Fascist views in the press. In his short life Gobetti published two important journals, *Il Baretti* (1924–8) and *La Rivoluzione liberale* (1922–5). *Il Baretti* was named for Giuseppe Baretti, who published *La frusta letteraria* (*The Literary Whip*) in Venice in the 1760s. Gobetti wanted to brandish a literary whip in the 1920s, which was a dangerous era for such defiant ambitions.

The delicately framed, bespectacled Gobetti began to make frequent trips to Genoa in the early 1920s. He met with the lively circle gathered in the Caffè Diana, where he found poets, writers, and intellectuals who were willing to articulate a liberal vision of aesthetics apart from the dominating trends of Dannunzianism and Futurism.[33] By 1924 Montale had joined Sergio Solmi, Frederic Chabod, Natalino Sapegno, Raffaello Franchi, and others to contribute to the first issues of Gobetti's *Il Baretti.* Surprisingly, the politically outspoken Gobetti insisted that poetry and politics should not mix. Montale disagreed and submitted a piece of political criticism to the *Rivoluzione liberale*.[34] While Gobetti did not print that piece,[35] he did publish Montale's Crocean essay "Stile e tradizione" ("Style and Tradition") in *Il Baretti* in January 1925. Montale was at that time still relatively young, only in his late twenties. It was courageous of him to circulate his views in a review edited by Gobetti, who was already a marked man.

Italy in the 1920s was a dangerous place in which to fire off a broadside against the coarse nature of Italian popular culture, and that is precisely what Montale did in the essay he wrote for Gobetti. Critiquing the vulgarity of Italian mass culture, he argued that the connection between the everyday experience of life and the act of writing was never strong in Italy. Economic, social, and historical forces had not appeared in any significant way in Italian literature for many centuries, whereas this topic had been treated with great power in French literature, starting with Rousseau and Stendhal. Montale was aware that Dante, who had infused *The Divine Comedy* with the political and social dramas of his era, was a great exception. He wrote, "In Italy there is practically no literature that is civilized, refined, and popular at the same time, and there never may be; it is lacking precisely because a median society, a familiarity with non-vulgar attitudes, a habit of them, is lacking: i.e., a widespread intellectual well-being and easiness without great heights or vast depths."[36] Croce, repeatedly lauded as a champion of clarity, is here described as working for an isolated elite in a larger culture of vulgarity.[37] Montale saw Croce as the master who understood the connection between style and tradition. In an Eliotic remark Montale adds, "Tradition is continued not by those who want to do so, but by those who can."[38]

Style is the focus of the poet's attention. He dismisses the grandiose pronouncements and sentimental humanism of D'Annunzio, Giosuè Carducci, and others, criticizing them chiefly on the basis of their style. Following Croce's critique of D'Annunzio, Montale argues that these are poets who offer little but "Jacobin rages, Supermanism, and Messianism," poets who could not formulate a real style that would resonate with the best in Italian writing. A successful new style "perhaps will come to us from the sensible and shrewd disenchanted, who are conscious of the limits of their art and prefer loving it in humility to reforming humanity."[39] Little is said on the message of poetry, which is probably what saved Montale from getting into trouble when he published his essay. Style, that is to say, the new literary excellence, will come "from good usage." In his call for a newly understated rhetoric Montale expressed quiet defiance in his critique of the overblown writing of the day. He was already putting his theoretical ideas into practice, developing a soft but subversive poetic voice, based in a densely complex poetic style that would be perfect for his purposes. It would take several decades to see the full ramifications.

Montale saw early on that Fascism, in spite of its hostility to the freedom of creative artists, needed to justify itself with cultural achievements, and this, for better and worse, became one of Mussolini's obsessions. Montale was aware that Hitler was a failed painter, and Mussolini a failed novelist. As unsuccessful artists, Hitler and Mussolini were eager makers of their own myths and extremely sensitive to the power of persuasion in all manner of symbolic expression. Both were aware of the power of symbols in the manipulation of masses of people. The cultural apparatus that Mussolini steadily built up around Gentile and others was massive in scale. The control of the media and of the flow of information was always more important to him than was the implementation of effective policy or the actual production of armaments. He unleashed an intricate process of valorization that was meant to justify the pseudoscience of Fascist ideology. Napoleon had done this some 130 years before, distributing eagles to his troops and resurrecting an intricate system of imperial Roman symbolism. Mussolini, following D'Annunzio's charismatic example, set the later pattern for Hitler. The symbols of imperial Rome were even more attractive to Mussolini, who exploited them whenever possible.

The valuation of art is related to the symbolic procedures of politics and propaganda, but the social process of art always takes a more complex and elusive route to the amassing of cultural assets.[40] The great achievements of a civilization are seldom brought about by docile artists who follow orders. Nevertheless, the Fascist dictator wanted to control the symbolic processes of culture from the top down. The unpredictable mind of the free artist was too risky to be left unchecked. In spite of their foolhardy support of Mussolini, both D'Annunzio, an undisciplined late Romantic, and Marinetti (1876–1944), the author of the Futurist Manifestos, were eventually viewed as suspect by the very authoritarian regime that they supported. Mussolini, as Montale observed, was often suspicious of the artists. They were too dangerous to be left unsupervised.

More dangerous to Mussolini were his fellow journalists, and for this reason Montale's friend and publisher Gobetti was singled out for elimination in a manner resembling the fate of the far more powerful Matteotti. When an artist or a poet was judged untrustworthy, he could to some extent be isolated and subdued, but the polemical writer, the professional shaper of opinion, had to be permanently silenced. Accordingly, Mussolini sent a telegram to the prefect of Turin, commanding him to "make life difficult for this silly opponent of the government and of Fascism [Gobetti]."[41] Around the time that Matteotti was murdered in Rome, Gobetti was harassed and beaten in front of his home (which Montale had visited several times) by a Fascist squad. Gobetti was allowed to leave the country, and he fled by train to Paris in 1926, where he hoped to start a new publishing house. Montale, who met Gobetti when his train stopped in Genoa, was one of the last of his friends to see him alive. Gobetti had noble ambitions: "I do not wish to promote libels or trivial polemics like the displaced Russian grand dukes; I wish to promote a cultural program in the sense of European liberalism and of modern democracy." But this was not to be. In February 1926 Gobetti died in Paris of pneumonia at the tragically young age of twenty-six, his health broken by his ordeals.[42]

In 1925 Luigi Albertini, the Milan-based editor of the powerful *Corriere della Sera,* and Giovanni Amendola, the liberal-conservative politician and monarchist, made some last-ditch attempts to confront Mussolini. Since the dictator still enjoyed the support of the king and the army, all such manoeuvres failed. By January Mussolini had either silenced his opponents or minimized their influence. He openly assumed responsibility for state-supported murder and extortion, and no authority remained powerful enough to punish him.

In Montale's reflections on the Fascist era he recalls that Benedetto Croce and Gaetano Salvemini were the most important among the remaining opposition, mentioning also Giovanni Amendola, Antonio Gramsci, Carlo Rosselli, and, of course, Gobetti.[43] Amendola, who had earlier fought off with his umbrella an assault by goons, was eventually killed in an attack by hundreds of Fascist militia in 1926. Carlo Scorza, a member of Parliament, led the attack in the street. Rewarded for this and similar efforts, Scorza later became secretary of the Fascist Party.[44]

But the mysterious development of a great poet cannot be instigated or controlled by dictatorial force. While the Italian dictator was consolidating his power, the poet emerged. He was very different from the commanding national poet that the Fascists would have preferred. In 1925 Eugenio Montale, at the age of twenty-nine, signed the anti-Fascist manifesto and wrote and published his first important literary essay (the Crocean "Style and Tradition") and his first in a series of articles championing the Italian-Jewish writer Italo Svevo.[45] Most important, Montale saw his first book of poetry into print. The brutality of the era was undeniable. In an atmosphere of murder, manifestos, and marches *Cuttlefish Bones,* one of the truly significant books of poetry written in the twentieth century, made a quiet appearance.

Poems of the Cinque Terre

The 1920s was a great decade for Modernist literature. Something new was in the air. A number of the most significant literary works of the twentieth century appeared within the period of time stretching from the 1919 Fiume episode to Croce's anti-Fascist manifesto of 1925. Four volumes of Proust's *In Search of Lost Time* appeared between 1920 and 1925; the last volume came out in 1927. Two major works appeared in 1922: T.S. Eliot's "The Waste Land" and James Joyce's *Ulysses.* In 1923 Wallace Stevens published his great first book of poems, *Harmonium,* and Jorge Luis Borges his *Fervor of Buenos Aires*. Also in that year Rainer Maria Rilke published his *Sonnets to Orpheus.* Montale's *Cuttlefish Bones* appeared shortly afterwards, in 1925. Two other canonical works of twentieth-century literature, Franz Kafka's *The Trial* and Virginia Woolf's *Mrs. Dalloway,* also were published in 1925. Montale's *Cuttlefish Bones* is clearly in a class with all of these, and there are considerable similarities of style and thematic concern.

Cuttlefish Bones is divided into six sections. In Italian they are "In limine," "Movimenti," "Ossi di seppia," "Mediterraneo," "Meriggi e ombre," and "Riviere"; in English they are "At the Threshold," "Movements," "Cuttlefish Bones," "Mediterranean," "Noons and Shadows," and "Seacoasts." There is something both specific and abstract about these terms. They concern important but indeterminate aspects of psychological perception and experience. They suggest concepts of arrival, movement, the play of light and shadow, the time of day, and most of all the general evocation of the Mediterranean topos. Only one of the section titles names a specific object, the bones of the cuttlefish, which is also the overall title of the book. The cuttlefish, *Sepia officinalis,* indigenous to the Ligurian waters off Montale's childhood home, is related to the octopus. An invertebrate, it does not have a particularly firm skeleton, but it does have a bony, calcified under layer. The cuttlefish changes colour and texture with great rapidity, taking on the appearance of its surroundings. It is known for its flexibility and for the ink it releases in order to change its pigment. When that ink is released externally, it can darken the waters around it. These abilities allow the cuttlefish to hide and confuse its enemies, a quality that must have appealed to the poet. Montale did not title his great book after the living fish itself, which, if nothing else, is certainly fascinating to watch as it effortlessly changes colour, blending in with the variations in the sea bottom. Instead he chose its remains, its flimsy skeleton. The reference is to the skeletal remains or bones of a fish that knows how to adapt to its surroundings in order to hide. The implications of the strangely anti-sentimental title are enormous.

One poem, "Meriggiare pallido e assorto" ("To Rest at Noon Pale and Engrossed," 1916, revised in 1922), particularly captures the unique seascape of the Cinque Terre and the poet's reaction to it in a few intense lines. One of Montale's earliest poems, it is taught to students all over Italy today and frequently included in anthologies. *Meriggiare,* the first word of the poem, is an almost untranslatable verb, which in English means something like "to rest in the hottest point of the afternoon, avoiding the heat." *Meriggiare* is the first of five infinitives that power the poem: *meriggiare* (to rest at noon), *ascoltare* (to hear), *osservare* (to observe), *sentire* (to feel), and finally, *seguitare* (to follow). All of this sets up a search for an answer to the question in the rhetoric of the poem: what does it mean to do these things? The speaker of the poem hears blackbirds calling out and snakes crawling in the dry soil, and observes ants piling up in little mounds, all the while aware of the distant sea palpitating far below. Above, in the peaks of the hills, cicadas screech in the hot sun, but the sought-for answer seems to be that all of life is summed up in nothing more than following a "wall topped with glass shards from a broken bottle" (*una muraglia che ha in cima cocci aguzzi di bottiglia*).[46]

In his 1946 prose piece "Intenzioni (Intervista immaginaria)" ("Intentions [Imaginary Interview]"), one of the short writings in which he gives us a glimpse of his method, Montale quotes a famous phrase from Jean Baptiste Racine (1639–99) to describe how deeply attached to his landscape he quickly became early in his writing career. If the date of this early pessimistic poem is correct, it is perhaps the earliest in *Cuttlefish Bones:* "But by 1916 I had already written my first fragment '*tout entier à sa proie attaché*': 'Meriggiare pallido e assorto,' of which I later revised the last stanza. The prey was, it's understood, my landscape."[47]

In the words of the great French tragedian, Montale saw himself as "entirely affixed to" his "prey." This connection was to be deep, visceral, permanent. However, Montale had found more than his landscape of choice. He had found his fundamental stance towards the interrelationship of the human being and the natural world and his technical means of communicating that stance. The dry heat of the Mediterranean sun, with the shining sea below and in the distance, the languid mood, the indifference of human beings to one another, the solitary nature of the intensely observing mind – it all comes through in this short poem.

Here the poetic "I" is absorbed in detailed observation. The small and seemingly unimportant becomes profound. Sensations are inverted. Expected relationships connecting spatial and temporal experience of visual and aural stimuli are pulled apart and reconstituted. The poet uses language to bring us up close to his perceptions and emotions. Words serve as microscope, telescope, and microphone in odd combinations and juxtapositions. Small details are blown up and become huge. A delicate sound is greatly amplified. Faraway things become close. These are some of the great Montalean moves.

Gian-Paolo Biasin compares the treatment of objects in horizontal and vertical axes in the poem to the objects in a Modernist seascape by Giorgio Morandi, thus bringing out the power of Montale's painterly eye.[48] The central image, with which the poem begins and ends, is of the observant poet-speaker beside a garden wall baking in the hot Mediterranean sun. The poet is hearing sounds high above in the echoing peaks or of the sea far below. Or he is simply watching a line of red ants. The natural world is vibrant and alive. But it has no meaning. Everything, even the vast sea, is to be traced from following the jagged line of a broken bottle that runs along the top of a stone wall, gleaming in the sunlight. (Glass shards were originally set in stone along the tops of walls to keep petty thieves from jumping over them to steal chickens or fruit. Even today the stone walls that run along the boundaries of choice properties in Liguria and Tuscany are commonly topped with broken glass.)

Nature and the setting, while they are hypnotically compelling, seem cruel and indifferent. There is no anthropomorphic meaning to be read into the now-pointless presence of the natural world. Its impact on the mind, however, remains overwhelming even without that purpose. Not only has Montale affixed himself to his subject by 1916 but some of the most distinctive qualities of his style have already appeared – the meticulous observation of detail, the mixing of small settings and large vistas, a type of camera zoom effect that allows him to move in close and then pull back for a wide-angle view. For Montale, there is a universe within the minutiae of the seafront setting outside his childhood home. Using his astute powers of observation, he projects a macrocosm from his small focus of intense observation.

To Shun Nature or Begin with the Real?

Even if Montale had written nothing more, with the appearance of *Cuttlefish Bones* he had earned an eventual place for himself in world poetry. From Mallarmé onward, there is an anti-linear element to the play of words in modern poetry. At the core of this trend is a group of great figures whom the noted Symbolism scholar Anna Balakian identified as the poets of the Post-Symbolist mode.[49] Among them are Eliot, Rilke, Valéry, and Jorge Guillén. These are poets who wrote slender volumes, but whose words counted. Montale is one of the last in this great line. In these writers, poetry begins with the charge that is produced when two words placed side by side are rubbed together in the mind. This charge is given off by sound, sense, and placement; in linguistic terms, there is an interplay of phonological, semantic, and syntactic factors. These poets explore how words signify meanings in a variety of directions so that this ambiguity of meaning becomes a source of expressive potential, a technique used to expand the range of poetry. It was intended to make the poetic work more of a concrete entity, not an illusory, verbal fabrication. The new poetry purposefully attempts to undermine *logos* as a conscious point of intent. The best of this poetry never displays a naive indulgence in obscurity for its own sake. It instead reflects a conscious attempt to expand the possibilities of language. While the function of language for a great poet such as Montale is related to the concepts of the deconstructionists of late-twentieth-century academia, it is essentially very different. The general idea of the modern poets, who wrote for the most part in the first half of the twentieth century, was to make language more palpable, more of a self-contained expressive system, with a new poetry referring to new types of meaning by turning towards the elemental power of words, and not a critical project to show the failure of language to signify logocentric meanings. Montale made this explicit while explaining poetry to a lay audience on Italian television when he said that poetry was "vertical" and "short," whereas prose was "horizontal" and "long." He was after the suggestive power of words.[50]

Mallarmé made famous the general practice of hyperbaton (placing words in unusual order), and he also developed a new theory of semantic play, which he called the *tierce aspect* (third aspect) of poetic language.[51] This third aspect comes from the semantic blending of words that do not seem to go together until they are placed in combination by the poet. "The poet," he wrote, "must establish a careful relationship between two images, from which a third element, clear and fusible, will be distilled and caught by our imagination."[52]

These features, unusual word order and semantic experimentation, come into Montale's stylistics. Certainly he used both, although his purpose and results were very different from Mallarmé's. The distinctions are of paramount importance. Mallarmé first and foremost turned inward and towards abstraction, away from an exact observation of nature: "The Decadent or Mystic Schools (as they call themselves ...) find their common meeting-ground in an Idealism which (as in the case of fugues and sonatas) shuns the materials in nature, avoids any thought that might tend to arrange them too directly or precisely, and retains only the suggestiveness of things."[53] Montale used some of the same intensity of technique to do exactly the opposite. For him, nature was always a point of departure. Observation of life was the initial inspiration of each poem. "The important thing," asserts the Italian poet, "is that in me the translation from the real into the symbolic and vice versa is always unconscious. I always start with the real. I don't know how to invent anything."[54] Montale's propensity for hyperbaton, his frequent placement of things in unexpected parts of a poetic sentence, is an expression of his unusual powers of observation. He tends to play with a detail that other poets would miss, giving it a prominent semantic position. Thus an observed colour or texture can illuminate a poem with a great wash of light, or light can be hidden by a great cloud of dust, or a soft but distinct sound can seem strong and almost overwhelming. These perceptions are combined in unusual ways to create fresh effects that defy the normal expectations of syntax and semantics. Then there is the thickened texture of the language, which we find not just in Mallarmé and Montale but in various poets from around the world, among them Gerard Manley Hopkins, John Donne, Wallace Stevens, Francisco de Quevedo, Giorgos Seferis, Federico Garcia Lorca, T.S. Eliot, and Ezra Pound. In the Italian tradition, difficult or seemingly inaccessible modern poets such as Giuseppe Ungaretti, Salvatore Quasimodo, and Montale were described by some critics as practitioners of *ermetismo* (hermeticism), particularly after the publication in 1936 of Francesco Flora's *La poesia ermetica*.[55] Nevertheless, in the larger phenomenon of world literature, the foregrounding of the texture of words in a manner that challenges the reader is a stylistic tendency that has occurred at different times and for different reasons.

Great poets may not be made by great critics, but they are at least made *known* by great critics. The valorization process in great poetry, as in all art, is a long chain of social activity, generated from within the mind of the creative artist, who must first absorb old work by precursors and rivals to create something new and fresh to say. After this comes the social and political struggle for publication, publicity, and dissemination. In addition to his Italian and French precursors and his great Italian critics and contemporaries (Contini, Parronchi, Calvino, and the long list of writers of commentaries), Montale must be linked to Eliot and Richards, the twin gods of modern poetics, both of whom published important works in the 1920s.[56]

Italianists will always point out Montale's Italian roots, and they are right to do so.[57] They start with Dante and the Dolce Stil Novo. Foscolo and Leopardi and above all D'Annunzio are obvious Italian precursors who anticipated the Modernism of Montale. Finally, Sbarbaro, Gozzano, and Giovanni Boine were sophisticated and European, aware of world literature at large and far closer to the understated style of Post-Symbolist poetry than to the bombastic writing of D'Annunzio and the Futurists. However, Montale soon surpassed them as he reached out to a wide range of sources for inspiration.

Mallarmé invented something new and something that was known and absorbed by writers all over the world. Was Montale most profoundly influenced by non-Italian precursors or was he uniquely Italian in origin? The truth is somewhere in between. Montale's artistic parentage was both Italian and non-Italian. His awareness of early modern French culture is well documented in his youthful diary, *Quaderno genovese.* Like his friends among the Crepuscularists, a group of Italian Post-Symbolists, he was well read and sophisticated. Even though he had little formal schooling, Montale was a poet who knew and absorbed world literature and culture.

Eugenio Montale's early work is a poetry of twentieth century Post-Symbolism that proposes a pact between a remote master, who creates poetic works that are challenging, and a group of expert interpreters. The poetic work is difficult to enter, almost an object in itself, existing in a kind of multidimensional form on the page. We find it difficult to know the master, who wants us to focus on the intricacies of the language, and he poses a speaker, who becomes a personality, shielding us from the master, and him from us. Most important, the work was intended to be this way when it was brought into existence by its creator. The obscurity of the difficult Modernist work eventually served Montale well when he had to write a relatively impermeable form of poetry during the Fascist era, under the shadow of a regime that he detested.

Language is a continually spinning web that always generates new structures, ever-changing strings or sentences that give off meanings. Each language is an evolving web that structures itself in a different way. Meanings overlap and emanate; words give off semantic possibilities, potential meanings that are stimulated by each web. Existing within the web of language, poetry is a construction set apart from the common world of linguistic texture out of which it springs. Poetry is made of language, but culture marks its language apart from all others, bestowing upon it a special status. For the great poets and critics of the mid-twentieth century, it seemed to exist in a new concrete mass of its own – a real object. The purposeful construction of many meanings, polyvalence, is not a fault of the inaccuracy of language, but it is a feature to be explored, to be savoured by connoisseurs of words. It is a feature that will achieve the solidity of poetry as an entity apart from the rest of the world. It is an expressive device, to be exploited by minds capable of exquisitely exact meaning, like harmonic ambiguity or tonal ambiguity in music, or certain types of abstraction in visual art.

Poets who work towards this solid kind of poetry work in different languages, so each has to build the web differently. They are speaking a kind of language of their own, however, which cuts across the cultures. Writing in different languages, Montale, Rilke, Stevens, Guillén, and Yeats are among those who speak the same poetic language. But this is a question of family resemblance rather than mimicry and repetition. Each poet has a unique song to sing and a different story to tell.

In some poems of *Cuttlefish Bones* Montale speaks to himself, to the sea, his father, or even to us. The speaker is both intimate and distant. We know him well by the end through the intensity of his precise observations about the Cinque Terre, but we do not know his name or anything else that would make him easily accessible to us as a fictive character. However, as he progressed in his writing, Montale developed another personality. This is his listener, his secret and absent lover. The listener first appears in the late poems of *Cuttlefish Bones*, some of them published in the 1928 edition. These poems prefigure the pattern of the senhal in the great poetry to come. Montale begins to address his poems to an unnamed female figure who offers symbolic hope of escape and redemption.

One of these late poems, "Casa sul mare" ("House by the Sea," 1925), is particularly significant because it was translated and published by Irma Brandeis herself; thus it was obviously part of their ongoing dialogue of secret reader to poet to secret reader to publishing translator and back again – a process that stretched from Brandeis's first readings of *Cuttlefish Bones* to the end of their lives. In "House by the Sea" the poetic "I" speaks to an unnamed *donna,* an enigmatic woman who offers the speaker some sort of salvation that is beyond him and most others. Beyond helping himself, the poet wants to help the donna find a *varco,* a route of escape through a net of entrapment, which may not be available to him.

One factor that may have prompted Irma Brandeis to translate this poem is that she was well aware that it prefigured many of the poems that later featured her own symbolic incarnation. The fleeing donna, tracing a path to spiritual salvation, would be the essential symbol of the great poetry to come in Montale's next books. Directly addressing his unnamed lady, the poet writes, "*Ti dono anche l'avara mia speranza*" (In Irma's words, "I offer you my miserly hope").[58] At this early juncture the unidentified woman may have been Anna degli Uberti, the model for the Arletta senhal in Montale's poetry. A youthful infatuation for the poet, Anna was a lovely young woman whose parents rented a house from the Montale family in Monterosso, very near the Montales' own summer home. The daughter of an Italian admiral, Anna was obviously fundamental in sparking the early impulses that made Montale a poet. She turns up in other poems in *Cuttlefish Bones* and elsewhere in the poet's writings. The donna may also be Paola Nicoli, a Peruvian woman of Genovese origin whom Montale met in Florence in the late 1920s.[59] While scholars differ on which of these two women inspired which specific poems in Montale's early works, there is no question that in the subsequent poetry Brandeis eclipsed them both. She became the inspiration for the poet's intricately constructed female symbol of hope, even appearing, in her incarnation as Clizia, in the seaside Ligurian setting of Montale's early writings. In *Cuttlefish Bones* the poet discovered how to speak to his *tu,* his informal "you," his disguised but devoted listener who would be there to hear his meditations. Her identity would change over the years.

These last poems of *Cuttlefish Bones,* addressed to the unnamed donna, are also significant because they are filled with an intensifying pessimism that uses Dantesque language to reflect Montale's anxiety about the deteriorating political situation of the late 1920s.[60] Via Dante's model, political and social critique began to permeate Montale's writing from this point. At times, his poetry now seems to almost choke with a kind of suicidal desperation. In writing this first book, he also found his secretive political voice, a development that was probably stimulated by a pessimistic response to the tumultuous early years of Fascism.

Montale began his poetic career with a masterpiece that did not derive from his encounter with Irma Brandeis. In writing this first work, Montale also discovered a substantial part of the repertoire of his symbolic expression. He never abandoned the images generated by the Cinque Terre world that he had captured in *Cuttlefish Bones.* While the best poems of *Cuttlefish Bones* are great in themselves, they also have another significance in Montale's oeuvre. They are symbols that attracted the symbolized until the two met and joined. The poems that Irma Brandeis read before she met Montale are the poems that caused her to become infatuated with him. These poems, created during the early Fascist era of the 1920s, contained images that would later express her presence in the works of the poet. Brandeis was lured by the images of the master symbolist who would later define her meaning in his poems.

3 Love in Fascist Florence

Une rose dans les ténèbres …

– Mallarmé, as quoted by Eugenio Montale to Irma Brandeis

Stormy weather, since my Irma and I ain't together …

– Ted Koehler, paraphrased by Eugenio Montale for Irma

Fascism and Culture

In "Il fascismo e la letteratura" ("Fascism and Literature," 1945), written just two years after Mussolini's fall from power, Montale recalls that a woman was admitted to the Reale Accademia d'Italia (Royal Academy of Italy), the newly formed Fascist academy for intellectual and cultural excellence, because she had written extensively about Il Duce's beautiful hands in the *Corriere della Sera*.[1] The formation of the Reale Accademia was announced on 7 January 1926, and the academy was officially launched by Mussolini in October 1929. Initially it had sixty members. Mussolini bestowed an odd and heady mixture of benefits and privileges on the academicians. All members were to be referred to as "Your Excellency" in formal conversation. Each member received a monthly stipend of 3,000 lire, free first-class travel on all Italian trains, and an elaborate dress uniform. Many of the initial members were far more distinguished than the woman who wrote about Mussolini's hands. The famous Italian playwright Luigi Pirandello was one of the more accomplished early members. Although Montale thought of Pirandello as essentially un-Fascistic, he felt that Pirandello compromised himself with his publicly pronounced pro-Fascist sentiments in the furor after the murder of Matteotti. Among the other founding members were

Giovanni Gentile, the Futurist poet Filippo Marinetti, the great scientists Enrico Fermi and Guglielmo Marconi, literary and cultural figures such as D'Annunzio, Ada Negri, Gioacchino Volpe, and Giovanni Papini, and the composers Pietro Mascagni and Ottorino Respighi.[2]

Mussolini, with Gentile as his chief cultural adviser, attempted to revitalize a culture by initiating change from a centralized supreme authority. Both the obvious and the complex aspects of culture were of importance. At the coarsest level, the ancient Roman salute was resurrected as the modern Fascist salute (later co-opted by Hitler for the Nazi salute). Achille Starace later devised the *passo romano,* the Italian version of the goose-step.[3] Fascist attempts to manipulate the symbology of culture ranged from these coarse gestures to much more intricate issues, including critical speculation on how to revive the modern Italian novel. Montale describes Mussolini as a mediocre writer – "a yellow journalist and failed serial novelist" – who nonetheless had read widely and understood that Fascism needed an enduring literary manifestation to record some sort of genuine expression of the Italian people. Mussolini needed a fresh impetus from literature and the arts, sprung naturally from the people to shore up his new political and social hierarchy. In Montale's view, however, the dictator could not make it happen. Instead, Fascism was "a time of intimist prose writers, exquisite essayists, ascetic, fakiresque poets."[4]

From a literary point of view, Montale saw the futility of the Fascist efforts, viewing the Fascist era as "unfavourable" for artistic creativity. An oppressive and heavy-handed political climate does not automatically cause a poet to push back in defiance. In the Fascist era it tended to stifle and sterilize. Montale recalled the many who joined the National Fascist Party (PNF), not out of political conviction but mostly to retain jobs and gain opportunities.[5] Expanding on the criticism of Italian culture that he presents in his 1925 Crocean essay on style, Montale again brought together Italy's cultural history and the character of its national literary expression. He viewed Italian literature as the slowest to evolve in Europe: "Our literature has been, and probably will remain even after Fascism, the most static, the most indifferent to the contingencies of life, the least faithful interpreter of the times in which it is written."[6] He pointed out the not-so-subtle pressures on poets and novelists in the Fascist era. While relatively less oppressed and restrained than were their German counterparts under Nazism, the Italian writers were nonetheless intellectually enslaved: "In essence, one could put the plaint of adolescence or one's grandfather's slippers into prose or verse, or confabulate some long drawn-out nineteenth-century story;

one could converse with one's own transcendent ego in the convoluted style of the new *trobar clus;* but in no way was it permitted to react directly to one's own time, to criticize it, denounce its ways, deride its defects."[7]

It is ironic that Montale mentions the use of the trobar clus to somewhat sarcastically describe writers who hid their real concerns with obfuscating self-absorption and trivial preoccupations, for the technique of the trobar clus was also crucial for *his* developing style. To create a closed style in this era was of the utmost importance to Montale. It was a rebellion, rooted, as he wrote in his essay on Croce, in the exploration of poetic language, and it was developed in opposition to the large-scale vulgarity that he felt surrounded him. He did not become a self-absorbed bore, like the unnamed Italian writers he describes, and for Montale there was always to be a key to his "closed style," based in the meticulous observation of his lived experience. Most of all, he confronted his historical and social circumstances critically and powerfully in his poetry.

In the 1920s the full implications of Mussolini's rise to power were not yet clear. The early years of Fascism were not characterized by the vitriolic racism and anti-Semitism of the late 1930s. Gradually Mussolini was able to win over some of his earlier critics by awarding them memberships in such attractive new entities as the Reale Accademia. Some of the early cultural achievements, especially in the plastic arts, seemed impressive and promising. The new school of Italian rationalist architecture established by Gino Pollini, Giuseppe Terragni, Carlo Enrico Rava, and others was as freshly original as any of the Modernist styles in Europe. Jewish architects such as Gino Levi-Montalcini and Giuseppe Pagano were among the leading innovators and at first were by and large accepted as such. Pagano was an early Fascist and a member of D'Annunzio's band of irredentists at Fiume. (Sadly, he later joined the Italian resistance movement and perished in a concentration camp.)[8]

The art critic Margherita Sarfatti, Mussolini's Jewish paramour and publicist, was his mistress from around 1918, following him through his rise to prominence in Italian journalism and the Socialist Party. She helped him formulate many of his early pronouncements about art and culture, and she stuck with him through the early years of his rule. In 1926 she published *Dux,* her hagiographic biography of Mussolini; it eventually appeared in eighteen languages. She finally fell out of favour with the dictator around 1929 when he began to prefer younger women. While Mussolini increasingly distanced himself from her in the early 1930s, she was allowed to make a propaganda tour of the United States on his behalf in 1934, meeting with President Franklin Delano Roosevelt, the publisher William Randolph Hearst, and many other important Americans at around the same time that Irma Brandeis was getting to know Eugenio Montale in Florence.[9]

When Enrico Bemporad offered Montale a new job at his publishing house in Florence, the poet decided to leave Genoa. He arrived in Florence in early February 1927 to begin work for Bemporad. From his first days in the city Montale began frequenting the Caffè Giubbe Rosse in the Piazza della Repubblica, often stopping there on the way home from Bemporad or after meals, meeting other gifted young Italian writers such as Piero Bigongiari, Tommaso Landolfi, Mario Luzi, Alessandro Parronchi, Arturo Loria, and Leone Traverso.[10] The circle of literary and artistic friends that he found at the Giubbe Rosse soon replaced those at the Caffè Diana in Genoa. Many of these figures collaborated on the avant-garde magazine *Solaria* (1926–34), a lively, but doomed, liberal publication of Italian belles-lettres in the late 1920s and early 1930s. However, there are lasting implications in the cultural importance of the literary figures who wrote for it. Its editors sought to place Italian literature within the larger context of the developing European Modernism. The writer Elio Vittorini claimed that *Solaria* and the *solarini* who wrote for it were "anti-fascist, European internationalist, anti-traditionalist."[11] Montale wrote on Charlie Chaplin and cinema, translated Eliot, and published his own poetry in *Solaria.* In his piece on Chaplin he describes a bittersweet quality and finds a surprising complexity in the great filmmaker: "Chaplin seems to me to be a difficult artist; the Jewish basis of his art and his undeniable sadness, the two- or three-sided nature of his humor, seem hardly accessible to the 'public.'"[12] Montale produced a lively string of articles and book reviews during the *Solaria* years, only a small percentage of which appeared in the journal. In the meantime his own poetry was treated in important review articles in *Solaria,* and his growing reputation is evident in its pages, as is the emerging significance of Giuseppe Ungaretti, Salvatore Quasimodo, and Umberto Saba. It was the critics of *Solaria* who first made the case for these writers as the four great Modernist poets in Italian literature.

By the early 1930s there was a growing rift in the cultural life of Florence between the internationalists, who gathered in such places as the Giubbe Rosse and published in *Solaria,* and the nationalists, who were increasingly provincial. Fascist critics denounced *Solaria* as too cosmopolitan and worldly, qualities that smacked of Jewishness. The journal's writers did indeed favour Jewish internationalism and even studied the Jewish qualities of Italo Svevo's writing as a desirable feature of his work. According to Vittorini, "they called us dirty Jews because we used to publish Jewish writers and because of all the good things we said about Kafka or Joyce. And they called us jackals. They called us hyenas. They called us ditch diggers."[13]

There are indications that the writers at the Caffè Giubbe Rosse felt they were under siege, even though in most respects they were left alone by the authorities. Alberto Moravia noticed something more behind the insular habits of those who gathered at the café in that era. The atmosphere there was not open and freely creative. Instead it was ominously silent, marked by a distinct intent to avoid overt communication. "There were as many as twenty or thirty literary people who didn't speak or confined themselves to joking remarks. I remember that Montale constantly hummed scales, because he had studied voice … Italian literature was characterized by the presence of men of genius, among them Montale, Landolfi, Delfini, Penna, Saba, and so on. But all of them were encased in a hermetic impenetrability, and at the same time, perhaps as a reaction to Fascist grandiloquence, they tended to underline the mediocre or even squalid characteristics of daily life."[14] Like Montale, Moravia had had an important literary success in the 1920s with the publication of his first novel, *Gli indifferenti* (*The Indifferent Ones*, 1928). The work displays a cultural pessimism similar to that of *Cuttlefish Bones*, but as a writer of prose, which almost always has greater clarity than the densely worded Post-Symbolist favoured by the poets at the Giubbe Rosse café, and with a Jewish father in his background, Moravia was eventually even more suspect than Montale.

Montale met Drusilla Tanzi soon after moving to Florence. At least a decade older than Montale, she was to be his lifelong friend and companion and eventually his wife. At the time of their meeting Drusilla was married to Matteo Marangoni (1876–1958), a highly respected art critic who taught at the University of Pisa, corresponded with Bernard Berenson, and wrote many books on Renaissance art. Drusilla Tanzi came from a Jewish-Italian family and the Trieste-based intelligentsia that Montale knew well through such close literary friends as Italo Svevo and Roberto "Bobi" Bazlen. One branch of the Tanzis had intermarried with the Levis of Palermo. One of the Levi children, Drusilla's niece, became the prominent Italian writer Natalia Ginzburg, whose husband, Leone, was killed by the Fascists.[15] Ginzburg was another of the young Italian writers whose stories first appeared in *Solaria.* In a letter to Italo Svevo written in June 1927 Montale wondered whether Drusilla was also related to Dr E. Tanzi, one of Svevo's friends. Montale was a great champion of Svevo's writing, and he was extremely pleased to find that Drusilla shared his ardent admiration.[16] An interest in Svevo certainly brought the two of them closer together.

Montale's prospects improved in 1929 when there was a vacancy at the famous Florentine library, Gabinetto Scientifico Letterario Vieusseux, after Bonaventura Tecchi, the previous director, left for a new post in Brno, Czechoslovakia. Count Giuseppe della Gherardesca, an old-fashioned liberal, found Montale's independence and literary distinction appealing, preferring him over Fascist applicants. He gave Montale the job in March 1929.[17] Montale went to work in the medieval Palagio di Parte Guelfa, headquarters of the Gabinetto Vieusseux. It was just a short walk from the Caffè Giubbe Rosse. In June he rented a basement room in the apartment of Matteo and Drusilla Marangoni at 6 Via Benedetto Varchi.

Giovan Pietro Vieusseux, a young Swiss, and Gino Capponi, a Florentine aristocrat, had founded the Gabinetto Scientifico Letterario G.P. Vieusseux in the early nineteenth century.[18] Vieusseux was a businessman who appreciated the cosmopolitan atmosphere of Florence. He initially set up the Gabinetto as a reading room where foreigners visiting Florence could meet and browse through publications from all around the world. Vieusseux soon added a circulating library next to the reading room, featuring books written in the major European languages. The most important Italian writers frequented the Gabinetto in the nineteenth century, including Giacomo Leopardi and Alessandro Manzoni. European visitors included Stendhal, Arthur Schopenhauer, William Makepeace Thackeray, Émile Zola, André Gide, Rudyard Kipling, Aldous Huxley, and D.H. Lawrence. The list of notable American readers is impressive, too. Among the distinguished visitors were Henry Wadsworth Longfellow, James Fenimore Cooper, William Dean Howells, William and Henry James, Charles Eliot Norton, Mark Twain, and Edith Wharton.[19]

The head position at the Gabinetto Vieusseux was certainly a plum for an Italian writer, and Montale was suddenly well installed in Florence. While his anti-Fascism may have helped him in the beginning, it left him vulnerable, and he eventually lost his job in 1938. For almost ten years, however, the library gave him a valuable platform from which to exercise his broad and international literary interests. In spite of the rise of Fascism the Gabinetto had a long-standing liberal tradition and a commitment to the international dimension of literature stretching directly back to its founders. It was also an ideal setting for the initial personal and literary interactions of Montale and Irma Brandeis.

A small amount of dissent was tolerated in the early Fascist years, especially when such tolerance had its political and public-relations advantages. Croce, who was too well known abroad for the type of treatment given to Gobetti, was to some extent harassed, marginalized, and partially censored, but he was ultimately left alone. Similarly, the Gabinetto Vieusseux in Florence, a research library with a large international membership, was also left largely intact until the late 1930s, perhaps because it was useful in the propaganda campaign to win foreign support for the Fascist regime. Montale, who was not a Fascist, increasingly found himself obliged to court the ruling party in his efforts to keep the library running in the Depression era. Political pressures became much greater over time.

Irma Brandeis and the Sunflower

Irma Brandeis was born in New York City on 3 February 1905. Her family was related to Louis Dembitz Brandeis (1856–1941), one of the most important Jewish Americans of the early twentieth century. Known as the "people's attorney," Louis Brandeis often represented liberal causes. He was appointed to the Supreme Court by President Woodrow Wilson, who often sought his advice.[20] The first Jewish justice in U.S. history, Brandeis assumed his seat on the Court in June 1916. Triumphing over opposition from anti-Semites and big business interests, he served until 1939. During his long career he fought for minimum wages, shortened working hours, and life insurance for labour, and he challenged the very powerful American railroad monopolies of the early twentieth century. Judge Brandeis was also an important early proponent of Zionism and other Jewish causes.

Irma was the daughter of Dr Julian and Pauline "Polly" Aaron Brandeis. She was raised in the brownstone house at 8 West 83rd Street in Manhattan, near Central Park and the Museum of Natural History. She received her early education in the New York City public schools and later attended Hunter [College] High School.[21] Years later, in a letter to Luciano Rebay, she acknowledged the importance in Montale's poetry of her Jewish-American background: "My father and Louis

D. Brandeis were second cousins. Both branches of the family were Austrian (for I do not know how many generations) before coming to the United States in mid-century. My grandfather married an English Jewess and my father married the daughter of a German Jewish family. I tell you this so that you will avoid reading Montale's references to Palestine or Canaan or the East as colorful background rather than as awareness of a two thousand year old blood heritage – and therewith a confraternity which deserves more thought than I think it has had."[22]

Nevertheless, Irma's family was secular, very Americanized, and not religiously observant.[23] The home provided a highly cultured environment for Irma and her brother, Frederick. Dr Julian Brandeis had strong literary interests and even published a comic novel, *The Extraordinary Exploits and Experiences of Munchausen, M.D.*, in 1924. Irma's mother, Pauline, sang beautifully. Her father, an accomplished amateur musician, accompanied Pauline on a fine pre-war Steinway grand piano; Irma recorded her memory of his sensitive pianistic touch in her journal.[24] Dr Brandeis's father, Frederick Brandeis (1832–99), was a composer and pianist who studied piano in Austria with Carl Czerny, a pupil and early interpreter of Beethoven. After emigrating to the United States in 1848, Frederick Brandeis appeared as a soloist with the William Wallace Company and toured the country. He also served as an organist at various Catholic churches and a synagogue in New York City.[25]

In the early 1920s Irma was a student at Barnard College. Bright and creative, she was a member of Phi Beta Kappa and wrote poetry. Her major fields were English literature and Romance languages. She later attended graduate school in philosophy at Columbia University. While the records show that she had a strong interest in French, her passion through the 1930s was Italian language and literature. Arthur Livingston, Helen Huss Parkhurst, and Dino Bigongiari were among the most prominent of the Italian professors who taught her during her studies at Barnard and Columbia.[26] She remained closest to Livingston, soon finding fault with the Fascist sympathies of Bigongiari. However, she became quite close to Bigongiari's cousin Gino. Gino, who was staunchly anti-Fascist, had been her Italian instructor at Barnard, and after graduation Irma became romantically involved with him, eventually travelling with him in Europe. While they never married, they remained lifelong friends.

Irma Brandeis was a member of the class of 1926. Although she graduated in October 1926, she attended the June commencement ceremonies in the spring of 1927.[27] After graduation her first job of importance was as literary secretary to Julia Dunn, whose husband, Gano Dunn, was one of the most important electrical engineers of his era and a trustee of Barnard College. Julia Dunn, who wanted to write a study on comparative religion and culture, needed a bright assistant, well versed in languages, and the brilliant young Irma was well suited for the job. The Dunns took her to Europe with them in the fall of 1929, and it was in their company that she first saw Italy, becoming completely captivated with the beauty of Rome. Writing from Florence in November 1929, she described her first impressions of Florence to Gino Bigongiari: "Must I say it? *I love it here.* I do not want to go home. Italians could be as much my brothers as anyone could, and some Italians, more, maybe. And I want to live for at least a little while at Naples, Capri, San Gimignano, Rimini, Padua, Mantua, Portofino, Sestri Levante, Venice."[28]

Irma worked for Julia Dunn until 1930, but she had not had her fill of Europe.[29] She travelled overseas again in March of 1931 and managed to stay abroad for ten months. During this period she met up with Gino Bigongiari, and the two toured together. She started her European sojourn in France, where her brother, Frederick, who had recently married the very wealthy Lyndal Heller, kept an apartment. But Italy attracted her more. In the fall of 1931 Irma met the gifted young writer Leo Ferrero (1903–33) in Florence. Ferrero wrote both poetry and prose, including an important anti-Fascist memoir, *Diario di un privilegiato sotto il fascismo* (*Diary of a Privileged Person under Fascism*). Ferrero knew Montale personally and moved in the best Florentine literary circles of the era. It was he who gave Irma Brandeis a copy of Montale's *Cuttlefish Bones.*

One poem in *Cuttlefish Bones,* "Portami il girasole" (Bring Me the Sunflower), written in June 1923, has a particularly intense incantatory power, and it is one of the loveliest of all modern Italian poems. It prefigures Clizia, since it was written and published well before Irma met Eugenio. Irma would have read it shortly after Leo Ferrero gave her a copy of *Cuttlefish Bones* in the 1930s, and she could easily have commented favourably on the poem to Montale himself, directly and in person, when she met him several years later. On one level, at least, the poem is about the mutability of all things, a mutability powered by the energy of the sun and to which the sunflower, flush with its light, beckons.

> Bring me the sunflower so I can plant it
> in this, my salt-burned place,

and show all day to the sky's mirroring blue
the anxious desire of its yellow face.

Straining towards clarity are darker things,
they consume themselves in a flowing
of colours, these colours in musics. To disappear
is then the adventure of ventures.

Bring me the plant that leads
where blond transparencies in flight
and life vaporizes as essence:
bring me the sunflower made crazy with light.[30]

Afterwards the sunflower will become Irma's senhal, and Montale will refer to her as Clizia, the sunflower goddess, in many of his most important poems. In "Hitler Spring" and its Dolce Stil Novo epigraph Irma is signified quite specifically by the sunflower, which in Italian is the *girasole,* the "turn-towards-the-sun," or the flower that turns towards the sun. In this much earlier poem the key images appear in the first stanza: the sunflower, the patch of ground, the salt spray, the reflective mirroring blue of the Ligurian sky. They have the same intentionally tangible and humble solidity as those of "The Lemons," another early poem in *Cuttlefish Bones* (and, also, translated by Brandeis). In both poems the fantastic, vivid colours – blue and yellow – are obviously fully saturated with Mediterranean light. Here the sunflower is in motion by the last line, lifting its golden face towards the light. Craving the sun, it is filled with *ansietà* (anxiety).

In the second stanza the symbols generate larger abstractions. Darkness moves towards light. The sunflower, planted in the salty earth, turns towards the sun, as in all things there is a turning towards brightness, and finally towards nothingness, towards an unknowable void. Everything moves towards an evaporation into essence. Even colours sublimate into music, and the greatest of all adventures is simply to vanish. In the last stanza, the *ansietà* of desire now becomes *impazzito* (crazed or maddened). The sunflower has been driven mad by its desire for light.

The poem should be contrasted with Baudelaire's "Correspondances," which Montale had probably memorized. They are alike and different in important ways. Many years earlier Baudelaire wrote: "vast as the night and as the clarity of day, perfumes, colors and sound respond to one another." We might also compare this poem to the images of fruit in Rilke's *Sonnets to Orpheus*, where the German poet calls out to "Dance the orange. Fling the warmer landscape / out of your soul so she glows ripely in / her native winds!"[31] Rilke creates a similar meditation on the combinatory melding of sensory perception in the psychology of the mind at around the same time, but without Montale's bittersweet reserve.

Classified by botanists in the genus *Helianthus* of the family Asteraceae, the sunflower has a number of important physical attributes that make it ideal for its coming symbolic role in Montale's poetry. First of all, it originated in America. It is tall and graceful in appearance, with short, blonde-yellow flower petals and a round central disc that is sometimes yellowish, but most often brown or purple. The sunflower also has practical uses, producing oil, dye, and edible seeds. It might serve admirably as a symbol for a beautiful and pragmatic woman with short blonde bangs and an oval face. As we will learn from later Montale poems, this fits well with the way Irma Brandeis wore her hair in the 1930s. While the hairstyle is a good match, the hair colour is not. Brandeis was a brunette. For her poetic incarnation, as Renée Weiss has quipped, "Montale put a wig on her."[32] In mid-summer the sunflower can grow to the height of a tall woman and even higher. Also, it is a hardy plant. Clizia, Irma's senhal, was a symbol of resilience, even steely toughness at times.

The American Beatrice Walks into an Italian Library

Already a devoted admirer of *Cuttlefish Bones*, Irma Brandeis went to call on Eugenio Montale at the Gabinetto Vieusseux in Florence in the early summer of 1933.[33] At the time of her visit she was twenty-eight years old, a graduate student at Columbia, and already teaching on the faculty of fashionable Sarah Lawrence College, located nearby along the Hudson River. But her true ambition was to become a writer. She had already published her own poetry and short stories in the *New Yorker* magazine, and she had begun work on a novel.[34] Like many American expatriates of the 1920s and 1930s, she had come to Europe to find inspiration for her version of the Great American Novel.

Montale was not available when Irma first walked into the Gabinetto Vieusseux and asked to meet him, but he appeared the next day and introduced himself while she was studying at one of the reading tables in the library. There were obvious sparks. In a long letter to Gino Bigongiari dated 20 July 1933 Irma described her first meeting with Montale, giving a detailed account of their animated discussion:

> When I first went to the library I took all the courage I could find and asked for Eugenio Montale. You remember, he wrote the book of poems, *Ossi di seppia,* which I love but could not make you read. He is the director of Vieusseux – but he was not there. Certainly I wouldn't have the nerve to ask again; but when I went back the next day, the clerk knew me and said, "*Se vuol vederlo, signorina, il direttore è qui, adesso*" (If you want to see him, miss, the director is now here).
>
> We became friends! We talked about Ezra Pound and T.S. Eliot and England and America and Italy. And the next day when I went back to the library he came out to find me, and promptly again the next. He lent me the best novel I have read so far, and made me a list of possible recent books. He told me all about his visits from Peter Riccio, his notions of Dino Bigongiari. And leaned back in his chair looking faintly malicious and rather lazy, face to face with a musty, rather lovely fresco on the flat, cold wall of his office – a huge, subterranean room with a painted, vaulted ceiling and a modern desk and modern books and a modern poet, polite and weary and neatly dressed.[35]

In addition to common acquaintances such as the critic Peter Riccio and the Columbia professor Dino Bigongiari, the two young writers clearly had much to talk about, and we can gauge something of the animated nature of the conversation from Irma's description. Writing again to Bigongiari on 2 August, she perhaps wanted to put her very handsome friend at ease by describing Montale as physically unappealing, but she was clearly infatuated with the Italian poet, whether or not she found him attractive in a conventional sense, and she did not deny how taken she was with his poetry: "He is very gentle, very simple, quite ugly, and often dull. Montale is no less his book [*Cuttlefish Bones*] than this prematurely old/young man. But his poetry leaves me *esaltata* [exalted, infatuated]."[36]

In the summer of 1933 Brandeis and Montale began an intense and tormented relationship, the initial phase of which lasted until 1939. It was also the beginning of an intellectual and artistic interaction that would last until the end of their lives.

Irma Brandeis was attractive. This we can see easily in photographs of her taken in the 1930s. In an image from 1933 Irma's face is delicate and sensitive, with a clear complexion, large, expressive, widely spaced eyes, a substantial but attractive nose, and a lovely mouth. It is a face of intelligence and beauty. At that time she had short, stylish hair with bangs. She seems sophisticated, contemporary, and possessed of a distinctly feminine elegance and mystique. Her hairstyle and oval face could have called to mind the bright yellow petals and round disc of the sunflower. In his writing, the poet adds many specific details about Irma: her hair, her jewellery, her scarf, her sunglasses, her cigarette smoke wafting into the air. Even her little travelling bookcase turns up in a late poem. These details come in a variety of settings – in a Florentine pensione, on the Bellosguardo hill overlooking the old city of Florence, at the Siena Palio, in the countryside, by the ruins of an ancient Etruscan port city, and depicted, with sad finality, in a dockside setting as she boards a boat to sail for the United States in 1938, presumably for the last time before the war. These fragmented elements of memory bring her old snapshots to life, recreating the emotion of lived experience on the printed page. While many of Montale's poems about her seem to have begun with his own contemplation of a photograph, the poems carry a telling charge of emotional energy that articulates felt experience in a manner beyond the range of any photograph. We must remember, however, that we are discovering her through the mind of her lover, and everything is filtered through the scrim of her senhal as Clizia, a completely separate entity within the imaginary space of Montale's poetry.

Obviously an intelligent and gifted woman, Brandeis had already had some considerable experience with Italian culture by the time she met Montale. She had translated short articles and essays from Italian, including some by Columbia professor Giuseppe Prezzolini.[37] Working with a collaborator named Hannah D. Kahn, Irma had translated Tobia Nicotra's book on Toscanini, which was published by Knopf in 1929. This was an early biography of the Italian maestro, covering his formative years through his rise to an international career. The rise of Fascism is in the remote background of the biography. Nicotra, for example, only briefly mentions the proto-Fascist D'Annunzio, who praises Toscanini from his temporary outpost in Fiume. It ends with Toscanini's musical triumphs in Italy and the United States in the late 1920s. While it has interesting remarks on music and Toscanini's ideas of interpretation, it says little or nothing about his political problems under Mussolini, which occurred later in the 1930s.[38]

After working as a literary secretary for someone else, Irma Brandeis began to develop her own literary projects. In the 1930s she wrote criticism and reviews for the *Saturday Review of Literature* and fiction for the *New Yorker.* Some of her fiction is set in Italy, and Montale avidly read her work in the *New Yorker*, commenting on several of her short stories in his letters to her. She also published her original poetry both in the *New Yorker* and in the "Books" section of the *New York Herald Tribune.* But she wanted a steadier income, and she decided to try for a job in academia. Upon receiving strong recommendations from her Italian professors (Bigongiari and Livingston), she was hired by Constance Warren, the president of Sarah Lawrence College, to teach Italian in September 1932. Brandeis soon gave language instruction in both French and Italian at the college, occasionally venturing into the teaching of literature. She taught at Sarah Lawrence for ten years, continually rehired by President Warren in a series of temporary contracts that ended in 1942.[39] For a short time she worked for the Office of War Information, helping to prepare foreign-language broadcasts for Italy. She briefly considered going to work in the magazine business, applying for an editorial position at the *New Yorker.* Eventually her first post in academia led to a second position at Bard College, which began in 1944. While she taught at Sarah Lawrence, Brandeis also continued her graduate studies, enrolling in the department of philosophy. She took classes in French and Italian as well.[40]

We do not need to go much beyond Montale's poetry to know that during her visits to Florence Brandeis often stayed at the well-known (and still extant) Pensione Annalena at 34 Via Romana, near the Pitti Palace and the Boboli Gardens. In the 1930s the pensione had a veranda overlooking its own walled-in gardens. In March 1931 Brandeis recorded some impressions of the Annalena in her journal: "The far side of the wall is broken by a French window – a broad balcony that runs along one face of the house. There are chairs and tables – the sun pours in – straight on into the room. And below is a garden – a big garden, Italian style, with towering trees beyond which one sees no houses – there is a wall with vines – a gate – shrubs in leaf, a few flowers (but it's early for flowers) – a pond – birds! – and over everything deep warm sweet pouring light. Now one can not only bear it, but love it here – in a special way."[41] This scene later turns up, described in great detail, in poems that Montale wrote very near the end of his life (see chapter 8).

Today the veranda overlooks a nursery. It is also directly across the street from a little-used entrance to the Boboli.

The Annalena is located in a neighbourhood of Florence known as the *Oltrarno* (the other [side] of the Arno). A number of significant Montale poems specifically name areas in or near the Oltrarno. For example, the very densely worded poem "Costa San Giorgio" is named for a small street that climbs up a steep hill overlooking the Arno on the Oltrarno side, at a sharp angle, winding eastward from the Via Romana near the southern bank of the river. Starting in 1931, Irma rented a small apartment at 54 Costa San Giorgio.[42] This site, too, is charged with significance in the Clizia Cycle and may well be the setting for some of the greatest poems in the cycle, among them the very dramatic "New Stanzas." Montale and Brandeis mention the Costa San Giorgio several times in their letters, and it appears in Brandeis's journal. The narrow and winding street was obviously a favourite site for a *passeggiata,* an evening walk for the lovers. Another poem that concerns a specific topos in the area is "Bellosguardo Times." This poem is about the view from the Bellosguardo hill, another short walk from the pensione and the Costa San Giorgio.

The Pensione Annalena is named after a famous fifteenth-century widow, Annalena Malatesta, who resided in the building. She had been given the house by Cosimo Medici the Elder. In 1441 Annalena's husband, Baldaccio d'Anghiari, so enraged his enemy, Bartolomeo Orlandini, that Orlandini arranged to have him eliminated. Baldaccio was killed and beheaded in the Palazzo Vecchio across the river. The body was tossed out of a window of the palazzo into the piazza. Annalena learned of her husband's death while waiting for him with their newborn son in the house on the Via Romana. She was only twenty-two at the time. Annalena's child died a few years later. After this second tragedy she turned her house into a home for single women. It eventually came to be called the Casa Annalena. Annalena Malatesta joined a nunnery and died in a convent in 1490.[43]

The Pensione Annalena was a popular residence in the 1930s among artistic Americans who were passing through Florence. Irma Brandeis was one of the many notable guests. The pensione and the Via Romana area are important loci in much of the great Clizia poetry that Montale wrote in the 1930s. A number of important late poems, written in the 1970s, depict Irma and Eugenio at the Annalena in surprisingly vivid detail.

The art historian James Thomas Flexner gives an excellent sense of what the Pensione Annalena was like in the 1930s for an American abroad. In the spring of 1933 he met Edith Ives, daughter of the great American composer Charles Ives, at the Annalena. This was close to the time that Irma first appeared there: "The pensione was on the far side of the Arno, facing the Boboli Gardens. It was up several flights of stairs in an old palazzo, and it was run primarily for young students and artists … The pensione was a simple place where everyone ate at one table, and you ate what was put before you."[44] Although it is across the Arno, the ancient Oltrarno neighbourhood of Florence, in which the Pensione Annalena and the Costa San Giorgio can still be found, is at most a fifteen-minute walk from the city centre and the Palagio di Parte Guelfa, home of the Gabinetto Vieusseux in the 1920s. The Palagio di Parte Guelfa is just a few hundred yards from the Caffè Giubbe Rosse, centre of the literary and artistic ferment of the 1920s and early 1930s. All of the key locales in Florence were in close proximity. Today it still possible to retrace the steps of Irma Brandeis and Eugenio Montale on a morning walk in Florence.

Montale and Brandeis were soon completely smitten with each other. Later he would write that the "thunderbolt" of love came while they were dancing and singing "Parlez-moi d'amour" (a French tune that was popular at the time) and chattering about his poetry. Around two weeks after he had met Irma, Montale left Florence for a brief vacation, travelling first to Paris and London and then to the Queens Hotel in Eastbourne, England. While there, he wrote the poem "Eastbourne," one of the first in which Irma appears as a character. Almost immediately in his letters – which he began to write practically as soon as he had left – he introduced the possibility of his moving with Irma to the United States. Writing in a somewhat melodramatic tone, he imagined four outcomes: she could move to Europe, he could move to the United States, they could endure long winters and reunite each summer, or he could simply kill himself. They arranged a rendezvous in Genoa, which would be Irma's last stop before she boarded a ship back to America. If they had not already physically consummated their love in Florence, they did so at the Hotel Bristol in Genoa. Both remember the erotic bliss of 5 September 1933 in their written recollections.[45] Many months later the poet wrote to his American lover in a blur of Italian and English, comparing the visceral experience of passion on that 5 September to the mere idea of love in the abstract or philosophical sense: "… *in realtà odio il platonismo e credo che nella vita non esistono altro che i 5 Settembre con varianti e aggiunte* [I hate Platonism and believe that in life nothing exists besides the fifth of September with variants and additions] … And if I dream you I don't dream your Soul, I dream your lips, your eyes, your breast, and the rest which is not silence. I daresay that the rest is the best and Shakespeare knew it."[46]

The Lover as Poetry Critic

As many scholars have noted, Irma Brandeis functions in Montale's work as a modern-day parallel to Dante's Beatrice and Petrarch's Laura. Scholars still debate the identity of Laura, who was probably a young aristocratic woman from Avignon. Beatrice Portinari, mentioned everywhere in Dante's works, was originally his childhood neighbour. She married Simone de' Bardi in 1287, then died prematurely in 1290. We know little else about her. Dante married Gemma Donati around 1285, but she and their various children are never mentioned in his writing. We know even less about Gemma than we do about Beatrice. Laura, Beatrice, and the ladies of the Dolce Stil Novo were silent, brought to life and preserved in the works of the poets who admired them. The American Beatrice, in contrast, made the first contact with her poet, initially reading him and then visiting him at his place of employment. Unlike her medieval predecessors, she spoke and wrote back to her lover, and she was an important sponsor of his work.

Irma and Eugenio exchanged many letters across the Atlantic in the winter of 1933–4. While Brandeis's letters are no longer extant, many of the important themes and images in Montale's poetry emerge in his correspondence. In September 1933 he remembers the Costa San Giorgio, which will soon turn up as the title of a great poem. He mentions the poem and the little street frequently in his letters. He tells Irma – in a mixture of French and Italian – that "*mi sento come una bouteille à la mer*" (I feel like a bottle in the ocean), using an image that he will use much later in "Su una lettera non scritta" ("On an Unwritten Letter"). He writes that the Pensione Annalena, the site of his last poems to Irma, "is in mourning" now that she has gone back to New York. He refers to Siena, with its famous horse-race and medieval neighbourhoods, later to be conjured in his great poem about the Palio.

More important, the poet, with great seductive power, describes Irma's eyes (they are first "Austrian eyes," then "almond shaped"; eventually he concentrates on the iris), earrings, and bangs ("I'm sure that the little *frangia* on your forehead will follow me in[to] the grave"), and even her cigarette butts (he actually saved them), and he associates her with the "rainbow." These are all important features of the beloved that will later be distilled into art. He is obsessed with her face, frequently begging for photos of her, with earrings and without or with hat and without. At other times, phrases are used in the letters that will appear again in poems written many years later. He repeatedly uses the word *fede* (faith) to describe his feelings for her, eventually writing *"ho fede in te"* (I have faith in you), a line from 1933 that he will rework near the end of his life (probably in 1979) in one of his very last poems about her. The line *"Se Dio esiste"* (If God exists) anticipates the playful tone of another late poem with the line *"dio con barba"* (God with a beard) written in 1978.[47] He anticipates Irma's deification in his poetry, addressing her at one point as a "beautiful and gentle-fingered Goddess." Even greater in importance than this early look at the source of Montale's imagery are the evident underpinnings of the thematic story of the myth of Clizia. These surface over time.

Mixed in with the language of love are the kinds of affairs of literary business that would certainly have fascinated two young, active writers with much in common. Montale is very conscious of Irma's Columbia connections, among them Professor Arthur Livingston, who founded the foreign press service. He is jealous of his friend, the gifted Jewish-Italian writer Arturo Loria, who left in October 1933 for a speaking engagement and some limited teaching at Columbia. Loria was going to be in alarmingly close proximity to Irma, while Montale was far away in Florence. Aware of his own literary importance, Montale clearly wants Irma to see whether she can find him similar work in the United States for a year or two. He promises that he can have Croce, Pirandello, and Berenson – certainly three of the greatest names associated with Italian culture at the time – as his sponsors. Knowing that Irma was greatly impressed by *Cuttlefish Bones,* he slyly lists the articles about him that have appeared in the Italian press. He wants her to know that Croce is very impressed with him: "the Cardinal's enemy the famous man of Naples who has written *l'Estetica* … he [Croce] likes my poems more than other modern poetry: so he said to Mr. Berenson."[48] It is clear from the context that Mussolini is "the Cardinal" and Croce is his "enemy."

There is much talk of literary interest. Writing from the Giubbe Rosse, he sends a list of recommended authors and their books: Flaubert's *L'Education sentimentale,* Gogol, Fromentin's *Dominique,* Svevo's three books, Fournier's *Grand Meaulnes, Don Quixote,* Dante, Marivaux's plays, Molière's *Don Juan,* St Simon, Chateaubriand, and the poetry of Tristan Corbière, Rimbaud, and Mallarmé. While it is a strongly French list, he is particularly fond of the southern European characters of Don Juan and Don Quixote and, at least here, not enthusiastic about Leopardi and Valéry.[49] In the letters Montale comments on Irma's writing, particularly the series of stories she was publishing in the *New Yorker* (he mentions "Baggage," "Sato," and "Lady Alone"). He eagerly sends his poems. Wanting to know if she has received his "La Punta del Mesco," he describes the *punta* itself, so crucial to his formation and jutting so impressively into the Mediterranean Sea, as merely "*una piccola penisola della Liguria orientale*" (a little peninsula of eastern Liguria).[50]

He also sends important insight about his poetics, much in keeping with the more developed critical statements that he will later make elsewhere: "For me poetry is a question of memory and pain. Put together the most possible number of memories and spasms, and to use in the form most interior and direct ... I don't have fantasy, it takes years for me to accumulate a few poems. The material execution then is rapid, often it is a question of minutes."[51] He connects his ideas to specific poems that he has already published in *Cuttlefish Bones* and to his new work, the first poems that will later be included in *The Occasions:* "Surely, it's not possible to pick up a philosophy in my poems. But there is a sort of philosophy: perhaps idealism in the first poems, mechanicism in the more recent (for ex. *Stanze*). Life is an addition of painful movements (?): necessity is the Rule; but the miracle, the *contingenza* exists also (*In limine, Casa sul mare*) for the 'happy few.' I don't think I belong; but the happy few do exist. I hope you, Irma, will belong. You have a splendid temper; the blind Gods and Goddes will help you."[52] Here the incorrect spelling of *goddess* is exactly the same as in his last letter to Irma, written at the end of his life, when he writes her one last time to tell her that she is his "Goddes."

At the end of a long letter in early October he writes down a line from Stéphane Mallarmé – "*une rose dans les ténèbres*" (a rose in the shadows), quoting from "Surgi de la croup et du bond," a famous poem dating from 1887.[53] It is one of the most ambiguous and most dense of the Mallarmé sonnets, evoking an image of a pair of lovers painted on an urn who are about to kiss but never quite do. It turned out to be strangely prophetic for Irma and Eugenio, who never quite managed to get together in a serious way, although both were desperate to do so.

Aware that Irma is modern, American, and young, Montale does not try to overwhelm her with his European learning. Part of the seductive power of the letters comes from his clever use of American popular culture in his tender expressions. In another October letter he writes, in quotation marks, "guilty of loving you." This phrase is taken from "Guilty," a song by Gus Kahn, Harry Akst, and Richard A. Whiting that was popular in the early 1930s:[54] "If it's a crime then I'm guilty, / Guilty of loving you." As he knew well, he was already "guilty" of loving two women at the same time or loving one and staying with another, but Irma did not know that yet.

Later Montale makes clever references to the vaudeville singer Sophie Tucker, the songwriters Harold Arlen and Cole Porter, and the African-American singer Paul Robeson, who became famous for his rich bass and leftist politics in the 1930s. Montale also includes some ingenious cartoons he had drawn for Irma, filled with caricatures of their mutual friends and acquaintances, perhaps inspired by the *New Yorker,* in which she was publishing her stories.

After learning that Irma's father had died on 23 October 1933, Montale writes back immediately on 6 November, expressing great compassion. He says how much he would have liked to talk with Dr Brandeis in his "bad" English or in French. "I remember how many times and the manner in which you spoke of him and I understand how you must have loved him and how much he must have loved you."[55] The death of Irma's father had a significant impact on Montale, and the event turns up later in an important short poem and a short story that provide two of the most important clues for unlocking the secrets of the myth of Clizia. The rich literary discourse is frequently interrupted with outbursts of passion. On 19 November 1933 Montale tells Irma, "There are days when I would die happy after having spent a month with you (thirty days and thirty nights)," and soon afterward, "I want you very much ... I can truly put my life in your hands, when and where you want."[56] He also sees a great literary value to their relationship, comparing it with another famous poet's love affair. "I tell you once and for always that I (but I am not consumptive and am not Keats) believe I love you with the same passion, and alas!, with the same sensuality as Keats loved Fanny Brawne."[57] Not content with that dramatic statement, he again takes up the model of Keats and Fanny Brawne in another letter later that month.

Writing on 7 December, Montale explicitly says that he will call Mussolini "the Cardinal" in his letters to Irma, although in later letters the dictator is also assigned another ingeniously derogatory nickname, the "Brass Scoundrel." The poet already senses a great divide between what the Cardinal stands for and what his "goddess" represents: "I will name HIM the Cardinal, if you'll agree. The everlasting Cardinal doesn't like our love. Tant pis pour lui. I see your almond-shaped eyes, Irma; they are here, brighting in my cellar. I love them, and your words also. Think of me, if you can."[58] Her eyes will be of great importance in the symbology of the poetry to come. Here they are already in juxtaposition to the image of the Cardinal, an opposition that will assume greater and greater significance as time passes.

At times he wonders in his letters if maybe the "Cardinal" is not so bad after all, if maybe the United States "needs" a similar "cure" (he points out the frequent lynching of African-Americans in the 1930s), but his instinctive dislike of Mussolini soon comes through with greater consistency. Included in the letter of 7 April 1934, after the customary account of various concerts and other cultural matters, is an astounding poem, with the Cardinal and his followers singing in some of the stanzas, unleashing the Fascist war cry. Irma is in the other stanzas. Here the tendency to divide the world up into a polarity of good and evil, to be developed in later and greater poems in Italian, first turns up in a charming poem that Montale, indulging exuberantly in the (to him) foreign sounds of English, had written expressly for Irma.

In the poem the Cardinal asserts, "I am the golden bull," with the "key" to the "cash," and his followers cry out in approval ("Blood blood! / Birth copulation and death!"). A "Miss Brandeis," who is described as "half drunk," responds in nonsense syllables, but by the end the poet writes that she is standing in a "rainbow" while the Cardinal "squeezes" what seems like a globe of the world (Montale does not specify exactly), and "the world falls."[59]

Here we first see Irma in the context of the rainbow, an association that will be developed in the great poem "Iride" ("Iris"). The egoism of Mussolini, the falsehood behind it, the Fascist war cry in his support – all turn up later in "La primavera hitleriana." Montale's image of the Cardinal squeezing the world anticipates the comic scene in Chaplin's film *The Great Dictator,* which will not appear until 1940 and in which Mussolini is lampooned as Benzini Napaloni and Hitler is Adenoid Hynkel. Peter Riccio, as Rosanna Bettarini informs us, made a mistake in his book on Fascism when he called the poet Charles Péguy a painter, and Montale is making fun of him. "Lady Bat" stands for Irma, who is absorbed in her "Thomistic" reading. Other figures satirized in the poem and in the comments directly below it are Dino Bigongiari and his wife (Lady DB) and Arturo Loria (Arthur). The WC is the Gabinetto

Vieusseux. *WC* is a derogatory term for the library that Montale uses throughout the letters to Brandeis.

Montale's disturbing descriptions of Fascism continue. Writing on 23 April 1934, he mentions the Florence Club, where there was a rather orgiastic indoctrination for thirty poets who stripped to put on black shirts. Ungaretti, his great rival and contemporary and much in favour with the Fascists, was there. After describing the scene, Montale quotes a little quatrain by Corrado Govoni (1884–1965). Govoni ends by saying that he hates spring: "*odio la primavera*." It is another forerunner of Montale's later "La primavera hitleriana." Montale ends this section of the letter with "Really spring is not here, spring is dead." Eliot's famous phrase from "The Wasteland," "April is the cruelest month," already has a new sense here. Later it will be May that will be the cruelest month when Montale describes Hitler's May visit to Florence in "La primavera hitleriana."

In a letter dated 1 May 1934 he describes in great detail another mass Fascist spectacle, this one a militaristic celebration at the Cascine, the riverside Florentine park. The letter of 9 May begins with the greeting "Oh my baby / My curly headed baby." This line comes from a lullaby, sung in a grand spiritual style by Paul Robeson.[60] The touching lyrics are the words of a black man or woman, in this case performed by the son of a former slave, singing to a beloved "curly-headed" child.[61] Robeson's performance sends a strong anti-racist message, his magnificent voice booming about the humanity of the African-American to the world at large, as powerful in its own way as the knock-out punch that Joe Louis delivered to Max Schmeling in 1938. Montale was writing to his Jewish lover, using the same address, and his words sing off the page even today. This tender intimacy makes a strong contrast with the Fascist orgies described in the April letters.

Behind the telling and ominous descriptions of Fascism, the voluminous cultural chatter, and the unceasing signs of tenderness, though, something was wrong. By early May Montale was back-pedalling in his letters. Discussing the upcoming summer in the 9 May letter, he says that he will probably go to France in August, possibly for around fifteen days or maybe more. "We could have a retreat, but for a thousand reasons I haven't changed my lodging, which is not well-suited for such a purpose." He had been living with another woman all along, but he does not say so yet. Then he adds, somewhat reassuringly, "I haven't remained long with the women I've loved … You are the last and the strongest and the definitive one of a series that is made up of two or three names in all." While he is proposing a mere "fifteen days" of "happiness," not a whole summer with her, he ends by saying, "I live for you."[62] He sounds very much like a man trying to see a woman he wants as a mistress, seeking convenient access and no obligation.

By June the hedging in his letters has become even more obvious. While his letter of 1 June 1934, again mentions the erotic magic of 5 September at the Bristol Hotel, he is clearly starting to feel anxiety about Irma's return to Florence. He writes, in English, with some evident shame, "If you think of me with contempt you are right because men should be strong and energetic; I am perhaps a little woman, a little whore ... And life has hurt me too much ... it's possible that my way will be this one: to want to see you and to love you once more before dying." Then he adds, "I don't love you in my way; I love you in all ways."[63] There is a lot of evasive commentary in the letter of 5 June. He complains that Irma has forced him into an "either/or" situation. Finally, not wanting to push himself into a major confrontation, he says, "If you undertake the trip I will wait for you with open arms. If you believe I'm in a rabbit hole-joke [*sic*] intentionally don't come, I will not condemn you, because I can't obligate anyone into heroism and I understand the need to be heroic to love me ... in this condition. You will see how I suffer but don't be afraid ... Remember that I adore you."[64] He signs off with "Yours, Arsenio," using one of his favourite pen names, which is also the title of the famous autobiographical poem in *Cuttlefish Bones*.

Irma did not pick up on the troubling signals in Montale's letters. In the summer of 1934 she returned to Europe, clearly expecting that the romance would continue to blossom. Everything seemed fine at first. Montale himself wrote a detailed description of "the inexpressible agitation" with which he greeted her arrival at the train station on 3 July, trying to reach her even before she disembarked from the train. She was "even more beautiful" than he had remembered: "I kissed you; I had my heart in the throat. We took a porter, a cab. I gave you (I suppose) a gardenia. The cab ran thru Ponte Vecchio and reached Annalena."[65] But at some point after she had arrived in Florence (probably on 5 July) Irma discovered the existence of the other woman in Montale's life, Drusilla Tanzi Marangoni. Montale writes about her "surprise" and his "desperation" after he told her the truth. They sat down to dinner at the Piazzale Michelangelo to contemplate their situation. When Irma found out about her rival, she laughed at first, thinking it a pretext of some sort, designed to stave off further involvement. Then she became furious, threatening to break off the relationship, and later, after becoming more reflective, remarked that she would rather not have known. They both hoped that time would take care of the situation.[66]

Drusilla turned out to be a formidable rival. In spite of the fact that she was already married to Matteo Marangoni, Montale had grown increasingly close to her in the late 1920s. He had rented the basement apartment underneath her house at 6 Via Benedetto Varchi. Before long he found himself inextricably involved in a long-term ménage à trois. A forceful woman with sophisticated literary taste, Drusilla soon became a fierce ally and supporter of Montale's literary interests, and Montale, while he was drawn to Irma, could never deny the indebtedness he felt towards Drusilla or ever bring himself to sever his ties with her.

Without letting on that something was wrong, Irma described her activities to Gino Bigongiari again on 8 July 1934: "For the present I see E.M. at noon for an aperitivo, and again in the evening for dinner. After which we walk on the Costa San Giorgio, or take a carrozza to Le Cascine or climb down from the Piazzale. It is possible we go to Venice next week for a species of theater festival during which Max Reinhardt will produce the Merchant of Venice outdoors in the Campo San Trovaso."[67]

They arrived in Venice on 14 July. In spite of the intermittent arguments about Drusilla, Montale and Brandeis had, according to the poet, at least "four splendid evenings." He even recorded the name of the gondolier who rowed them around the canals, and he carefully describes his ecstatic reaction to a few precious kisses in the gondola. Friends came to join them, defusing some of the tension. At times conversation devolved into fights about politics. When Irma effectively called Montale a Fascist by telling him that he "belonged to Dino B[igongiari]'s party," he felt guilty, writing in a letter that he sent to her much later, "Never man was more humiliated, but you were right."[68] For him, this was even worse than the threatening "shadow" of Drusilla. Nevertheless, Irma also managed to enjoy herself. Writing home on 15 July, she observes that "everybody is in Venice and we meet everybody."[69] They saw a number of the Italian writers and artists of the day there, among them the respected writer Diego Valeri and the composer Mario Castelnuovo-Tedesco, who later taught Nelson Riddle.

On the way back to Florence they stopped in Padua, taking refreshments at the famous Caffè Pedrocchi. In early August they were still quarreling, with Montale fighting for some sort of dignified position in response to Irma's understandable indignation: "I deny that what I said to you yesterday was in contrast with the last of my letters from Italy or what you said at the Piazzale Michelangelo. I deny to have … let you come knowing that these two months would for us be the first and the last. I deny that I should or could massacre someone before being certain of your affections. I deny to having had a program regarding you."[70] Sounding a theme that would get stronger over time, Montale was already worried about what would happen to Drusilla if he broke things off to leave with Irma. From 15 to 17 August they were in Siena, where they attended the Palio. Montale had to share a room with Francis Criss, an American painter, who painted a remarkable portrait of Irma Brandeis at around that time and who, the poet complained, snored heavily.[71]

Although Irma returned to America greatly disappointed, the two continued to correspond. If anything, Montale, now threatened with the possibility of losing contact with Irma forever, became even more seductive and intriguing in his letters. He filled them with lively commentaries on literature, amusing cartoons, classical and popular music, the Fascist political scene in Florence, and culture in general, always including touching expressions of passion for Irma. He wisely encouraged her to write. At the end of October he told her not to worry about Scholastic philosophy and Saint Thomas Aquinas but instead to write more stories like her "Sato," which had been published in the *New Yorker.* He sent an account of a taxi accident, illustrated with a little drawing, that they both used in later short stories. By late November he was able to dismiss Drusilla and the crisis in July as "our little scuffles of the summer." He told Irma again that she was the only woman in his life who mattered, the "unique example of generosity, harmony, and style that I have found in my life." By December he put it in musical terms: "*sei una specie di basso continuo, di pedale della mia vita*" (you are a species of basso continuo, of pedal point in my life).[72] She was increasingly the subject of and even a character in the poems that he sent to her in his letters.

On 7 February 1935, amid commentary on his freshly created "motets," concentrated new poems mostly inspired by Irma, Montale was back to discussing the idea of joining her in America if she could find work for him. He included some basic background for Irma, telling her that he was born in October 1896 and remarking on his lack of formal education, saying that he only finished the Technical Institute of Genoa. Clearly evident in this letter is the fact that not only does Irma know about Drusilla, but Drusilla now knows about Irma as well;

Drusilla is very dramatic, threatening suicide, when she discovers that she may lose Montale. "After 20 months of hell, always increasing, because I live struggling between the desire to finish everything with a bullet to the head and the horror of preventing her from doing that, because her brother did it and I think she is capable of doing it."[73] On the one hand, he says that he is worried about Drusilla's broken foot and bad eyesight, while on the other he says that he has made it understood that he wants to marry Irma and that Drusilla is insanely jealous. Amid all this, he insists that he is an honest man and that Irma is the one thing in his life that makes it worthwhile. He openly describes his strange situation, referring to the two men living in his house – the husband, Matteo, and his son, Andrea, who feign not to know what is going on, and remarking that "he does not know what they might do to him tomorrow."[74]

Irma responded to Montale's letter of 7 February on 21 February, completely exasperated with him and with Drusilla's threats of suicide. It is probably the only letter still extant out of the dozens, perhaps hundreds, that she wrote to Montale, since most of the others were purportedly destroyed by Drusilla:

> If I think any more about your Feb. 7th letter I won't answer it at all, so I must write now, quickly, as briefly as I can. It made me sick at heart … That you would have let me go on, forever no doubt, planning, begging at Livingston's door, asking everybody for help …
>
> I think you believed you were making everything plain to me, while making nothing plain. You said: give me 6 months to make this difficulty straight. Even a year. That was quite easy to do. You were never going to tell that you knew it was impossible? Here's the situation: a hysterical woman threatens to commit suicide and so holds two other people's lives in suspense as long as she may live …
>
> I love you, worse luck. Anything you do to hurt yourself, you do equally to me. I cannot bear this unheroic, almost ludicrous sorrowful life we lead … You gave me a dreadful (entirely unprepared) blow this summer, and another today. It is not true that you warned me before last summer; you wrote me that it would be "heroic" to come, but did not give me even the faintest clue to why. It was not something a person unskilled in female intrigue could guess … Last June I could still manage to be bitter and angry and alter my feeling towards you. It's too late now. I'm in love with you; and perhaps I despise what you've done, but it makes no difference. The common solutions I suppose are to cry about [it], write about it, or make love to someone else.

> Forgive this if it sounds unlike me and awful. My heart has hit upon an unpleasant way of beating, very fast and on the surface of my skin.[75]

It was possibly never sent to the poet, since Irma included it in the trove of letters she deposited in the Gabinetto Vieusseux in the early 1980s. Whether or not she sent it, Montale had already written to Irma again, encouraging her to write a projected article about his poetry, telling her charmingly, "I am not terrorized (*terrorizzato*) by the idea of your study 'about EM,' and I believe you are extremely prepared (*competentissima*) to write it."[76] Trying to help her, he explains his poetry, explicating words and concepts such as his puzzling use of *turbina* (whirling) and the "voice of the lover" in *l'oscura* (the dark). He had already used these images in poems she knew from *Cuttlefish Bones,* and he would use them again in later poems inspired by her.[77] Not for the first time, he again mentions her bangs and earrings, which will turn up later in a set of "pseudo-sonnets" he will write in the early 1940s.

In the middle of a long letter in Italian, written on 6 April, at first concerning his meetings with now forgotten figures such as Gertrude Stein's brother Leo and Barco Tartari, an American admirer of Pound, Montale suddenly bursts out in English: "*Io sono* [I am] Arsenio Gatu Ratu, the boy in blue jacket, the brother of the man who wore the *stiffelius,* the boy who cried on leaving you in Genoa, the boy (of 38 years) who was half dead waiting you at the station of Florence the 3rd July 1934. I know my faults, my mistakes, my weakness; but I *know* that I am worth of you (*si dice così?* [is that right?]), I know that I was born for you and that you are the only hope and the only thing of my life."[78] At the bottom of the letter he includes a memorable line in English: "Dont [*sic*] think love is a pair of silk stockings you may change easily."

Clearly Irma could not forget about her Italian poet, and he was not about to let her do so. Even in June 1935, almost a year after she had learned of the existence of her rival, Brandeis was considering the possibility of resigning her post at Sarah Lawrence College in order to move to Italy and join Montale. From her apartment at 53 West 12th Street in New York, she wrote to Constance Warren on 11 June in some detail about her predicament, hinting at the reason for her possible departure: "I am holding my Sarah Lawrence contract, unsigned while waiting for a most important communication from Italy, which should be here within three or four weeks. I have had news recently which may (although this is barely possible) result in my having to go abroad to live for the next few years. This has, of course, absolutely no connection with a job of any sort, nor would I ask you to accept such cryptic information were the factors of this situation not both personal and painfully complicated. May I, then, delay the signing of my contract – or may I sign it with the understanding that I could be released (between sessions of the college), if my grounds for leaving had no connection with other employment?"[79] Later that month, on 25 June, Montale wrote her another note that hit a higher level of desperation. Perhaps he was realizing that she was not likely to turn up that summer without some sort of significant signal from him: "And when I told you in Venice and in Genoa "vorrei avere un bambino da te" [I would like to have a baby with you] I was full of happiness and I felt the first time in my life like a young God. I love you. I want desperately your life and mine not to be destroyed by a stupid chance. Why have I not introduced you to X [Drusilla] in 1933? Perhaps you would be friends now, and she could have understood that two friends are better than one enemy."[80]

Possibly because of his dim-witted hope that his Italian mistress could get along with his American lover, the dramatic resignation at which Brandeis hinted in her letter to Warren never came to pass. Perhaps she knew even then that Montale was inextricably involved with Drusilla. Irma remained in the United States to teach at Sarah Lawrence for the 1935–6 academic year. She also published an important early article on Montale's poetry for the *Saturday Review of Literature* in July 1936, three years after her meeting with the poet at the Gabinetto Vieusseux and one year after she had seriously contemplated the idea of moving to Italy.

Irma's article for the *Saturday Review,* which she called "An Italian Letter," reveals a sharp and discerning critical mind. In her review she is full of praise for Montale's poetry, in which she has found something new and sincerely authentic. However, she sees artificiality in the Italian post-war cultural posturings, in Futurism, in the official proclamations about the new energy in Italian art. Her views on the limited cultural achievements of Fascism were similar to Montale's. Both were anti-Fascist from the start, and Irma's views anticipated Montale's essay on Fascism by almost ten years:

> The situation of the Italians in the field of literature (and, indeed, in all the arts) has been a curious one during the past twenty years when,

> on the one hand, the curve of decline from the Renaissance has appeared to be hurrying toward bottom level and, on the other, a new country has been officially proclaiming and seeking to stimulate a fresh pulse of life in this very sphere. Since the close of the [first] world war modern sculpture, painting, music, architecture, literature have been appearing abundantly in Italy. But there was a false link somewhere; contemporary Italian art has left its proper audience cool and distant – or manifesting at best a certain patriotic enthusiasm entirely without issue.[81]

Brandeis's opposition to Fascism extended to its cultural as well as political dimensions, and she detected, very much as did Montale, an artificiality in contemporary Italian culture. She was aware that the Fascist determination to create a newly revitalized Italy had made it necessary to celebrate the Italian artistic mythos in a new Romantic nationalism, but she deemed the effort unsuccessful, even in 1936. One exception was Eugenio Montale's poetry. In Montale she found something authentic and truly new. She perceived his work as hard edged, focusing on perception as a point of departure: "Montale's writing is hard, intense, empty of all superfluities. In diction it has an entirely natural lack of simplicity, appropriate to its intention. Its images are clipped sharp and hard from the immediate sensuous world."

Brandeis accurately sensed the reduced importance of the human condition in Montale, where human emotion or whim is no more or less important than the phenomenon of the sea pounding the rocks on the Ligurian coast. "Montale's anti-sentimental modern style has realigned poetic expression in a completely fresh way: For here is a physical world whose function is no longer that of background, but which has virtually changed places with man in that it is the mover and man the moved. The unaware, the unfeeling, the unintentional world performs in a single level with the conscious, the feeling, and the willing. The physical scene takes over mood or emotion. This activity in man of the irrational concrete is the personal seal on Montale's poetry."

While Brandeis does not offer many specific examples to justify this sweeping statement, this is a fine and perspicacious analysis of the startling originality so pervasive in *Cuttlefish Bones*. Montale is no longer a D'Annunzian god-hero riding a horse along the shore; he is a poet with a freshly sceptical eye, who "perceives" or "bears witness to the insignificance of man." Brandeis caught this transition and describes it brilliantly. She also offers an insightful comment about Montale's sense of entrapment in a random existence. This is especially apt considering that he would preoccupy himself with the paradoxes of time for the rest of his life: "the poet can find no way out of patterned time." Montale, as Irma understood him, knew that he was trapped in his now.

Brandeis mentions and quotes poems from *Cuttlefish Bones*, including "The Lemons," and several that would be included in Montale's second book, *The Occasions*. She includes a long passage in prose form from "La casa dei doganieri" ("The Toll-Keeper's House," 1930), and two moody evening poems, "Cave d'autunno" ("Autumn Cellars," 1931) and "Bassa marea" ("Ebb-Tide," 1932).[82] These three poems are steeped in the Monterosso coastal setting that is so crucial to Montale. Each of the two short poems, "Autumn Cellars" and "Ebb-Tide," is appended to the *Saturday Review* essay in a full translation by Brandeis, thus marking her debut as a Montale translator. Although the poems do not yet concern her as a subject, they have a place in the story of the Clizia Cycle because they attracted the attention of Irma as Montale's American reader and critic and she translated them. Clearly, the knowledge of Montale's recent work that Brandeis reveals in her article indicates an involvement with him that is deeper than that of a merely distant reviewer. With the publication of Montale's letters, we now know that he had been sending her his new poems, including several in which she has begun to assume her role as Clizia, in the mail along with his letters.

I.A. Richards, in an important 1926 review of T.S. Eliot's poetry, remarked that "when a writer has found a theme or image which fixes a point of relative stability in the drift of experience, it is not to be expected that he will avoid it. Such themes are a means of orientation." Brandeis quotes this passage to argue that Montale's Ligurian seacoast imagery offers exactly that orientation in his expressive vocabulary, noting that the sounds and sights of the Cinque Terre generate key conceptions (which Montale would call one of his symbolic *chiavi* or keys) that work together to form a complete poetic expression, and she places the worth of his poetry on a level with T.S. Eliot's. Eliot was famous by that time, but Brandeis makes it clear that Montale is in the same class, and the passage of time has shown her judgment to be correct. Eliot and Montale do have a similarity of importance in the history of modern poetry. Brandeis takes pains to show that Montale's poems are distinctly different, containing an Italian music that is unique and clearly unlike Eliot's Anglo-American English in a significant level of artistic style that goes far beyond the mere linguistic differences. Brandeis conveys the unequivocal conviction that Montale is a major new voice on the international scene, equal to any of the major Modernist poets writing at that time.

One of the most delightful curiosities in the history of poetry is that Montale's Beatrice read her poet and then went to Florence to meet him. After a period of romantic involvement with Montale that ended badly for her, she remained nevertheless convinced about the importance of his poetry. A few years later she reviewed and translated his work in a prominent American publication. Over time, meanwhile, she came to inhabit his imagination, developing into the most important character in his poetry.

The Podestà and the Poet

The Great Depression of 1929 had thrown much of the world into economic chaos by the early 1930s. In Italy, the Fascist control of centralized internal economic policies combined with complete dominance of the press and an efficient propaganda machine to give at least an appearance of stability and order. Economic conditions were worse in France and Germany. Still, many social problems were well hidden. Much of the country remained poor. This was particularly true of the south, where, it must be said, the democratic Italian governments that preceded Mussolini in the early years of the twentieth century had also done little to effect social progress. The poet and painter Carlo Levi, exiled to the remote southern region of Lucania for his anti-Fascist activities, described in considerable detail the impoverished and isolated existence of the southern peasants, in his memoir, *Christ Stopped at Eboli.*[83] Fascism, even in its most bellicose expression, did not touch large sections of the populace, who were too poor to view it as different from any number of invasive ideologies from the north. Mussolini, a master publicist, hid the true state of Italy from the people.

With the rise of Achille Starace to secretary of the Fascist Party in 1931, dissent became more and more difficult within Italy. When Toscanini refused to conduct "Giovinezza," the Fascist anthem, at a benefit concert in Bologna in May 1931, he was repeatedly slapped and insulted in public. He and his fearful family had to leave the city in the middle of the night in order to avoid a lynching.[84] A huge exhibit on the history of Fascism opened in Rome in 1932. On display were the castor oil and cudgels that had enabled the policies of intimidation and the forceful seizing of power in the early 1920s.[85] Further centralization of cultural policing followed the establishment of the Ministry of Popular Culture in 1935.[86] It became less possible for a person who was not a member of the Fascist Party to hold any sort of job in Italian cultural life, let alone a prominent post.

By the mid-1930s Mussolini's expansionist policies were leading irrevocably towards war and a binding alliance with Hitler. In spite of official pronouncements Italy was unprepared for great wars of conquest and empire, and when Mussolini attacked Ethiopia in 1935, he needed to use poison gas to guarantee a sure victory over the poorly equipped army of Haile Selassie. Nevertheless, victory over the Ethiopians was relatively easy, accomplished in about six months, and Mussolini announced the founding of a new Italian (Italo-Roman) Empire on 9 May 1936. Italy's alliance with Franco in the Spanish Civil War pushed the country further away from the Western democracies and closer to a binding alliance with Hitler. By 1937 Mussolini had begun an expensive three-year commitment of soldiers and arms to the Fascist cause in Spain. The invasion of Albania was to follow in 1939.

In Florence the local Fascist Party had slowly extended control during the previous ten years, gradually removing important opposition. The extinction of *Solaria* in 1934 marked the swing towards a monovocal nationalism in the city. Florence had been the site of a large and important English expatriate population since the mid-nineteenth century. With the invasion of Ethiopia, anti-British sentiment grew. Old businesses with English names – particularly hotels and restaurants – had to be given new Italian names.[87] Nevertheless, Mussolini had his supporters, even among the foreigners living in Florence. Figures such as Harold Goad, head of the British Institute of Florence, saw Fascism as an excellent defence against communism. Goad, not foreseeing that Mussolini's anti-British sentiment could lead to war, even wrote *The Making of the Fascist State: A Study of Fascist Development* (1934), a book that praised many of Mussolini's policies. The great art historian Bernard Berenson (whom Montale knew and admired) found himself increasingly isolated at I Tatti, his hillside villa overlooking Florence, although a small group of anti-Fascist Italians and foreigners were for a time still able to gather there. Harold Acton, whose parents owned the splendid La Pietra, a villa along the Via Bolognese, gives vivid accounts of the dwindling British population, many of them retirees, in his important series of memoirs. As conditions worsened for the English in Florence, Acton increasingly turned to Berenson's retreat for free and open conversation that dared to critique Fascism. There he found young Italians such as Guglielmo Alberti, Arturo Loria, and Umberto Morra, who openly criticized Il Duce.[88] Loria, who had travelled abroad several times to lecture in the United States, was also an editor at *Solaria* and a member of Montale's set at the Caffè Giubbe Rosse, where public criticism had to be much more subdued.[89] In sharp contrast, Giovanni Papini (1881–1956), a former Futurist who reconverted to ardent Catholicism around 1918, was an example of the new breed of conservative Florentine intellectual who supported Mussolini and his Fascist policies. Papini's *History of Italian Literature,* published in 1937, was dedicated to "the Duce, friend of poetry and poets."

Montale had for some time felt the pressure of heading a prominent post while working under the supervision of an increasingly hostile local government. In a letter to Irma in September 1935 he senses the possibility of another war, saying somewhat cryptically, "It is not certain that a European scourge will not break out now."[90] He is more demoralized and pessimistic in his letters to her in the late summer and fall of that year, writing with desperation from a variety of locales in northern Italy while travelling with Drusilla. The only truly bright spot in his letters is his developing friendship with the obviously brilliant Gianfranco Contini, whom he had described as his *miglior critico* (best critic) in a 1934 letter.[91] Contini, the son of a stationmaster from Domodossola, and who apparently spoke just about every European language and dialect, begins to emerge as a personality in the poet's correspondence.[92] In October 1935 Montale remarks in a letter to another old friend, Sergio Solmi, "If I hardly ever write to you it is always due to my state of mind, which could not be more depressed and bankrupt. It is not wise to pin everything on a little bit of literature, and renounce life itself, which after all is the unique thing that we have."[93] That November he asked Irma to send him a list of new American books, showing publishers and prices. He was worried that English and French books would no longer be allowed in Italy, owing to an angry Fascist reaction against the international pressures that had followed the invasion of Ethiopia.[94] While he was pleased about the new train station that the Fascists had erected, which he describes as "modern, rationalist, cubist,"[95] his sarcasm about Mussolini soon resurfaces in his letters, putting him at increasing risk of exposure by the censors. He sends Irma a lively description of dinner with the French consul in Florence, who is suspiciously empathetic to Fascist notions of world dominance: "The gentlemen and the ladies love the cardinal, onions, garlic, guitar songs and the crostini di beccaccia. They think Ausonia [Italy] is a lovely urine smelling country and '*Enfin il faudra bien lui donner des colonies a ces gosses*' [in the end it will be good to give the colonies to the kids], don't you think, Nanna? *Aufwiedersehen*, I'll ring up, *Salud y pesetas*."[96] After this description

Montale writes, "Don't drop me, I.B. You are the only Thing [*sic*] left to me."

By 1937 Montale and his literary friends at the Giubbe Rosse were under complete surveillance, their innermost circles probably penetrated by a variety of informants.[97] The racial laws were implemented in 1938. After that, open disagreement between the international Modernists and the regionally minded local Fascists was no longer possible.

For a time Irma Brandeis grew more distant from Montale, whom she had not seen since 1934. In the mid-1930s, stung by her discovery of Montale's entanglement with Drusilla Marangoni, she had become involved with Joseph Campbell, later a famous myth critic, and then Nicholas Stavrou Kaltchas, a political scientist then teaching at Sarah Lawrence College. Kaltchas, who wrote a promising book about the constitutional history of modern Greece, was taken ill suddenly and died young in October 1937. Brandeis was devastated, and her contact with Montale was at a low ebb throughout 1937. By 1938, however, her thoughts had already turned back to the Italian poet, and she was deeply concerned about him. From mutual friends she had heard about Montale's despair, a deep unhappiness attributed to both the relentless slide towards another war and his personal life with Drusilla. Irma wanted to confront him one more time and hopefully provoke a final break with Drusilla.

Fully aware that with every passing day Europe was becoming an increasingly dangerous place, she began to contemplate the idea of returning to Florence to see Montale. She described the worsening political situation in Europe in her journal in March 1938:

> Hitler is in Austria … [and] is expected in Vienna on his round of congratulations to his beloved and rewarded new subjects. He has a bodyguard of troops. There are armed forces round all the public buildings in Vienna (we hear by radio), no doubt to keep the riots of celebration from becoming too noisy for the sleep of the officials; over 150 important arrests were made today, no doubt to sober the reflections of the merry populace. The *anschluss* is perfectly safe and complete. German troops are in Austria and on the Italian border. They have promised Mussolini not to go beyond the Brenner Pass and M. has gritted his teeth and said he was perfectly glad about it all. Riots in London protesting Chamberlain's policy of non-interference. England has said she would back France up (immorally?) in her promise to help Czechoslovakia if Germany tries to take her – as she intends. France is not very populous. Italy is Germany's friend. Spain is

> at civil war. Russia is wracked by her own plots and counterplots. War in China. In Europe terror and anxiety, waiting for the next stop Germany will make toward European domination; that and the next word from England being the crucial matters …
>
> The borders of Austria re[main] closed to fugitives from the inside. Thousands have escaped by foot to Switzerland where the government will not maintain them or give them leave to stay. Jews arrested and their jobs taken away. Anti-Semitism in Italy.[98]

Tensions were high between the socialist government of Léon Blum in France and the Fascist leadership in Italy. If anything, the Italians were on even worse terms with Great Britain. Things grew even more ominous later that spring when Hitler came down to Italy in the first week of May to cement his alliance with Mussolini in an explosive show of propaganda and pageantry. In mid-July Mussolini became officially anti-Semitic, enacting new racial laws to align himself further with Hitler. None of this stopped Irma. In the summer of 1938 she made one last visit to Fascist Florence. She sailed from the United States on 24 June and travelled first to France, arriving by the first of July. She spent several days resting in Tours, a provincial city near the Loire Valley in west-central France. She slipped down to Italy after a little more than a week, making it to Florence by 18 July.

In 1934 she had found Montale eagerly waiting for her when she arrived at the train station. She preferred discretion this time, travelling to Florence without informing him ahead of time. At first she did not see Montale. Eventually her friend Helen Woodman went to tell him that Irma was back and wanted to see him. They saw each other on 26 July. On the next day Montale wrote a note to Irma, describing his reactions to their meeting: "Perhaps you didn't realize yesterday, between Cencio and Ponte Vecchio, coming back to Annalena, to have told me so great and decisive words … You were a great thing half in shadow to me, you are now an enormous and lighting thing. I saw once the iris of your eyes swimming and loosening shape and colours. It was in Genoa: I was tight to you, stuck heart and body to you and spoke on a child of ours!"[99]

Montale's English is flawed here, but important. "Iride" ("Iris") will be one of the great Clizia poems, and its central image is the iris of Irma's eyes. Already by the end of 1938 the very real beauty of Irma's eyes was gaining in symbolic power. Again, he speaks of having a child with her, then closes the letter by telling her that he will call at the Pensione Annalena that evening. The pattern continues for several days. For a brief period the trysts at the Annalena resume. But he disappoints her once again. She writes in her journal shortly after their reunion, "In the end 'what has happened' is the wrong question, nothing has happened."[100]

Irma had already left Florence when Montale wrote to her on 31 July. He begins in Italian, describing the insufferable Florentine heat of late July – "Suffocating Sunday. I'm in the WC to write to you, half nude, from the secretary's desk" – but he soon says, as he has before, that English is better for expressing his thoughts to her. She has given him an ultimatum, and he is struggling to respond, and he now realizes that his inability to act comes from deep within himself. "I know to be too poor, too weak, too miserable for you but I am surely one of the rare men who know what is love ... If you allow me to think of you and over all to ACT for you as you did crossing the sea two times for a man like me! ... I have a terrible enemy to fight in myself ... I am a third rade [*sic*] poet no one can make a genius of me; but I have to breathe and to discover in you the breath of God, the work of a Divinity!"[101] He will not leave with Irma, but he will soon transform her into a goddess in his cycle of poems.

Clearly, Montale was tempted to go to America with Brandeis for reasons that stretched beyond his very real feelings for her. He had never conformed and formally joined the Fascist Party, and he now knew that he was headed for trouble. Montale once quipped that he got the job at the Gabinetto Vieusseux because he was not a Fascist and that he lost it ten years later for the same reason.[102] By 1938 the friendly Count Giuseppe della Gherardesca had been replaced by another aristocrat, Count Paolo Venerosi Pesciolini, who was a Fascist sympathizer. Writing to his old friend Bobi Bazlen on 4 August 1938, Montale expressed the likelihood of his coming dismissal:

> You may know (but keep the secret!) that it is 90% certain that I will be sent away by the beginning of September. This concrete act, connected to the recent racist provisions that you know about and others that will follow, has made me feel the necessity of rejoining [Irma Brandeis] at great trouble [*coûte que coûte*] as you suppose. Do you understand me? Until yesterday it was possible to exercise *pleasure* in one part of my life and *duty* in another (Florence, the solitary life, as you know). It was possible to be sad (and rather horrible for me), to follow necessity and leave the rest; sad but quasi noble. But now I feel exactly the contrary, that it is properly my honor, my duty, to go toward that which was awaited for over five years without lamenting, without breathing (and two years without writing!) ...

Only it is *duty* not because my (and I believe our) feeling has perhaps grown; and *Fly* [Drusilla] had even been able to predict this outcome when she imposed with her blackmail years (I say years!) of separation!

Besides: if I lose this job it is characteristic of this blackmail that I be exhausted and rendered incompetent to work and defend myself. At present, it would not change the situation, the work you want that could sustain you … A cohabitation elsewhere (without surroundings, friends that lighten the load for me), would be even more difficult, and I believe make moreover new obligations for me (as in refusing certain help that keeps us together?) – that would knock me out completely.

The conclusion is clear: that I have many faults, but from 1932 until today I have done the possible and the impossible to resign myself and work and *not succeed for them;* while from the other side there is never a true gesture of piety and of comprehension. All is on the contrary done to humiliate me because they instinctively indicate that if I were humiliated I would be more submissive and work more to please them … when I have already wanted to leave … ([since] 1935); all to increase my obligations, my *duties*!!!

Perhaps it is done unwittingly. I want the best for the Fly, who I judge for many things a woman of great courage and great goodness. I owe her a lot and in many ways will remain very indebted to her. But am I then that scoundrel to whom she says yes one day and no the next? Is it right, this continuous contempt, this saying that my work and my prospects do not have any weight in relation to *her* life? Is it right to say this when she has a son … 25 years of age and a life already lived? Is it right to demand my continuous, total, definitive *humiliation*? Is it right to consider as sacred promises phrases such as "I will die in the basement," words uttered to be certain that the night will pass without suicide? …

Don't be scared, I do not ask for a response to these questions. I would like from you a general opinion. What other way of escape have I, between the blast of the revolver and the … steamship?

You will assume *no* responsibility in responding to this question. Think and reflect … I am very guilty and perhaps I had need of suffering, but it is certain that henceforth from this suffering I will no longer have any possibility of extracting a life, not even a life *sui generis.*[103]

This gloomy and dramatic letter offers a glimpse into both the political situation and the complex and tumultuous relationship between Irma Brandeis, Eugenio Montale, and Drusilla Marangoni. Montale displays a peculiar ability to compartmentalize his life. He had very much been living for the intimations of possibility in Irma's letters from abroad, letters that he claims had stopped coming two years earlier, and at the same time maintaining a dreary daily existence (if we are to take him at his word) in Florence. Describing his Florentine life as lonely and sterile, he seems trapped in his unorthodox relationship with Drusilla, with which he is deeply unhappy and which he appears, at least in this letter, to find deeply humiliating. Drusilla, who has already raised a son (her child, Andrea Marangoni, as the letter indicates, was at that time twenty-five years old), has made him feel that his own life and career are subsidiary to her priorities. Irma may have been all the more attractive because she was beyond his reach and seemed ready to devote herself solely to championing his work. In addition, Mussolini's enactment of new racist policies and the coming blow from the Fascists (clearly, he expected to be fired) had made him reconsider everything from a more pragmatic perspective. Now Irma had come to Florence once again, offering a way out. He considered it his duty to leave Italy and join her in protest.

Montale was deeply conflicted about whether to go to Irma or stay with Drusilla, but now that he had seen Irma once again, he was terrified of losing her and the imagined chance to escape to America forever. He wrote to Irma on 3 August and again the next day, explaining that he had been completely miserable without her for the last two years and promising to be free for her by the summer of 1939.

In mid-August they saw each other for the last time, in Siena, when Irma returned to Tuscany to see friends and to attend the Palio. On 16, 17, and 18 August she stayed just outside Siena at the Villa Solaia in Malafrasca, the country home of the Vivantes, a Jewish-Italian family. Afterwards she spent some days on Lussinpiccolo, a small Istrian island in the north. Montale tried to reach her, sending letters to her hotels in Italy and France. Her last night in Italy was spent, once again, at the Hotel Bristol in Genoa. She then returned to Paris, arriving on 25 August.[104] He had not given her the hoped-for definitive resolution, but he could not stop reaching out to her. Starting on 25 August, he wrote to her every day until 30 August, sending five desperate love letters in a row. Some of the letters are from Genoa and the Ligurian coast, where a family tragedy was about to take place. His sister Marianna was dying of cancer, and he had rushed home to see her.

In his letters the poet praises Irma's "marvellous hands," "the magical flute" of her voice, "the light of her intelligence." Comparing the abrupt nature of their parting to those of 1933 and 1934, he claims, "I live in terror of losing you." From the family home of writer Carlo Bo in Sestri he begs Irma to "write ... that you love me and you have trust in my words: that you think our link is a great and unbreakable thing." Back at the Giubbe Rosse in Florence he says he feels a horrible emptiness in everything that is not her: "I am finally convinced to have direction in life." Still remembering the erotic encounter of 1933 in the Hotel Bristol, he closes the letter with "many bathroom-like kisses." On 30 August he sends yet another missive to her Paris hotel, asking her to "write me that you love me, if possible that you are IN Love, with me and you have trust in my words and in our love destiny. I kiss your marvellous lips and everything of you."[105]

After a brief interlude Montale resumed his letter writing. He sent a letter from Monterosso on 7 September 1938, perhaps the only one written from there to Irma, something that makes it important in itself. He is in the house in which he grew up and "*Cuttlefish Bones* was born." He tells her that it is "that which you saw more or less from the train. A pagoda with three floors with large palms in front, a *giardino* [decorative garden] in decay and an *orto* [kitchen garden]." The "Orto" will be the title of a great poem that he will write to Irma in 1946.

A week later he writes, "There are many great rumors of war all around. Here is something more serious than X [Drusilla] between us. When this letter will arrive, what will the situation be?" On his way back from Monterosso he had stopped at Levanto, a coastal town on the other side of the Punta del Mesco. He describes for Irma the "frightened Jews, banished teachers, half destroyed businessmen" that he saw there. He tells her that both his dying sister and his mother, who is now also ill, are being treated with Roentgen rays.[106]

In mid-September Drusilla is flying into rages about Irma and threatening to commit suicide again. Montale claims that "until now every attack ends with a blackmail" and that he has to lie to achieve a truce with her. He now knows for sure that he will lose his job at the "WC" (the Gabinetto Vieusseux) very soon. He wants Irma to know that because the Vivantes are Jewish, they will probably have to leave the Villa Solaia, where she had visited them a little more than a month before. Soon afterwards he informs her that Leone Vivante's ownership of his estate will be questioned under the new anti-Semitic laws. War is threatening, sometimes seeming closer or further away with each passing day, but Montale says he finds comfort when, "from time to time, I dive in your light-stream."[107]

By the end of September Irma was busily preparing for Montale's emigration to the United States, attempting to secure him a visa for a fixed period of time and contacting various American colleges in the hope of finding him an academic position. But he could never give her a fixed date for his departure from Italy. He began to delude Irma and even himself with yet another excuse. He repeatedly wrote that he could not leave the country until he had received his final severance pay from the "WC," which he had been promised and which would enable him to finance his trip. In early October Montale returned to the bedside of his dying sister in Genoa, where the siblings reminisced one last time about their Monterosso childhood. It was his sister who had encouraged his musical and poetic interests, something that linked her to Irma in his mind. Before she died, the two of them recalled how, as a young man, he had sung operatic arias to her, perched on a rock above the seawater at Monterosso. After asking Montale to always remember her, she died on 9 October 1938 at the age of forty-four, leaving behind an eleven-year-old daughter.[108]

Montale writes at the end of October to describe his severance payout, which he now estimates will be between six hundred and seven hundred American dollars, still rationalizing to Irma about Drusilla, still trying to justify Drusilla's role in his life to her rival. Mysteriously, he switches the many lines of lover's praise that he has written to Irma about her eyes, earrings, lips, hands, and so forth. Now, suddenly, she is more ethereal. He tells her that she now "has no lips, no limbs, no eyes, no knees"; instead, she is "a holy Thing."[109] This is another early premonition of Clizia's transformation into the supernatural in the cycle as she evolves in the 1940s and 1950s. During this period he also sends more of his "motets," poems that are specifically addressed to her.

Montale was unsure about what to do, trying to find a way to extricate himself from his Italian lover and waiting to be fired. His despair is evident in another letter that he wrote to his friend Bobi Bazlen, this one on 29 October: "Regarding America, for I am not yet *licensed* … Only with the passport (that I don't have) can I expect to see the U.S.A. I can only have it in one month. I will be able to leave then, at the latest in February. And everything will be terrible. I may be able to succeed in shooting myself before February."[110] He wrote to Irma yet again, on 14 November, confessing that he had been hiding his head under his wing like a *struzzo* (ostrich).[111] He had thought he would be dismissed in October, not December or January. Again he tells her that he cannot get the money without the dismissal.

Montale was waiting for his final meeting with the *podestà* (town leader). One of the new and effective institutions of Fascism was the appointed podestà, who replaced the mayor chosen by democratic election in every Italian town and village. Finally, in late 1938, Montale was called before Count Pesciolini, the Fascist podestà of Florence.[112] He was first informed that the Gabinetto Vieusseux was to move from the Palagio di Parte Guelfa to the far more impressive Palazzo Strozzi, prominently situated on the fashionable Via Tornabuoni. The library was to be located just below the Fascist cultural institute in the giant palazzo and, most important, would be placed within the larger political context of Fascism and denied its older independent site. Montale was told that since he was not a member of the Fascist Party, he would no longer fit in. Accordingly, he was summarily fired from his post at the Gabinetto Vieusseux in early December 1938. On the first of December a formal explanation for Montale's removal was read at an assembly of administrative advisers to the library. Present at that the final meeting were the *podestà* (Count Pesciolini), the influential aristocrat Marquis Niccolò Antinori, the lawyer Paolo Terussi, and a number of Fascist professors – Jacopo Mazzei, Mario Salmi, Carlo Pellegrini, and Piero Rebora.[113]

Decades later Montale would refashion the story of his firing for his short story "Il colpevole" ("The Culprit"). In the fictionalized version Federigo, a young man who directs an "Institute for Popular Culture," represents Montale. Federigo's institute is very much like the Gabinetto Vieusseux, with a tradition stretching back into the nineteenth century of lending books in foreign languages to a variety of subscribers. The fictionalized institute, just like the real Vieusseux, had been changing its political and organizational orientation over the past few years, slowly pushing an increasingly isolated Federigo out on a limb by himself. Montale deftly changes a few letters to create a fictionalized Count Penzolini to replace the podestà who had actually fired him. Penzolini calls young Federigo (a name purposefully close to Eugenio) into his office to fire him: "I'm sure you'll understand this – it's rather too much of a good thing that a man without elementary allegiances … hem, hem (the Count coughed, without specifying quite what he was going to say) should run a cultural centre that is in line with political directives … I must inform you that next Thursday you must hand over authority to a successor who will be named within the next two days."[114]

A close friend, Alessandro Bonsanti, soon took Montale's place as director of the Gabinetto Vieusseux. Bonsanti had originally been among the literary companions at the Caffè Giubbe Rosse, which made this a particularly bitter outcome for Montale. Without steady work Montale now had to earn a modest living as a translator until after the war. He had worked at the Vieusseux for almost ten years, while also publishing essays and reviews on many of the great French and Italian writers of the day and carrying on a lively personal correspondence with some of them. His prestigious perch at the library had provided at least a minimal amount of financial security and visibility on the European scene at large. Now he was out.

Surely a substantial part of his misery was the result of his professional and political difficulties in Fascist Florence. The other problem was trying to decide whether to stick it out in Italy and stay with Drusilla Tanzi Marangoni or to run off to America to Irma Brandeis. By November Irma must have understood that nothing had changed since their meeting that summer. Montale was hedging on his American venture yet again. He simply could not bring himself to break with Drusilla and Italy. His letter of 26 November 1938 devolves into "monosyllables," as he himself admits, and he even writes them on the page – "bi ba bo, bi ba bo."[115] Perhaps he can think of no more words (he had written so many seductive ones to Irma since 1933) to use in making excuses for his endless delaying. His last line, written in English, has a disturbing finality: "I love you with my whole heart. Good-bye, E."

He would endure Fascist Italy through the coming war and remain in the company of the other woman in his life. He moved into an apartment with Drusilla in April 1939 and began to eke out a humble existence translating Eliot, Joyce, Steinbeck, and others.[116] Drusilla was destined to become Montale's Italian mainstay in his daily life, appearing only much later in his poetry and correspondence as "La Mosca" (The Fly). In the 1964 "Xenia" Drusilla is finally referred to as the "*caro piccolo insetto / che chiamavano mosca non so perché*" (the dear little insect / known as the fly, I don't know why). She is only slightly less nondescript in Montale's literary output than is Dante's wife, Gemma. By 1938 Irma had become the light of Montale's literary imagination, as incandescent in his poetry as Beatrice in Dante's. He stayed in Italy with Drusilla, but by the end of 1938 he was sending Irma poem after poem that was addressed to her and had been inspired by her. Later that winter, after he lost her, Montale sent Irma a Christmas gift, a volume of Leopardi poetry, *Canti,* edited by Leone Ginzburg. He wrote in pencil in the book "To the only begetter of my life," paraphrasing Shakespeare, who hundreds of years earlier had dedicated his sonnets to the young man known only to us as W.H. and praised him as "the onlie begetter."[117]

Montale's Florentine career had arrived at what seemed to be a disastrous dead end. The collaborative stimulus of *Solaria* was no more. He had lost his job. Hitler had come to Florence to celebrate his new alliance with Mussolini in May 1938. Irma Brandeis, his American paramour, had left for the last time before the war, and he had effectively lost her as well. Montale had also lost his beloved sister Marianna, who had died that October, a catastrophe that took a tremendous emotional toll and was extensively documented in his many letters to Irma. But the enormous personal and political tensions had provoked some of Montale's greatest poems. On 23 June 1939 Montale wrote to Brandeis yet again to tell her that he had prevented more of Drusilla's suicide attempts, one a potential hanging, the other an attempted leap from a seventh-floor window. Aware that he has become somewhat ridiculous, he says once again that he "adores her [Irma] more every day and that he breathes only because there is in the world her breath."[118] Asking her to give him the name of a cheap hotel somewhere in Brooklyn, he promises to show up in the not too distant future. None of this, of course, was going to happen. Montale also wrote to say that he was about to publish a new book made up of approximately fifty poems; he thought that she knew some forty of them. Unlike his endless promises to her, this was a sure thing. *Le occasioni* (*The Occasions*), his second book of poetry, ultimately dedicated to Irma Brandeis, was published in October 1939.

4 The Woman of *The Occasions*

I've projected the Selvaggia, the Mandetta, or the Delia (call her what you will) of the "Motets" against the background of a war that is both cosmic and terrestrial, without an end and without a reason, and I've pledged myself to her, lady or shade, angel or petrel.

– Eugenio Montale

Montale, the Philo-Semite

The first thing of importance to observe about *The Occasions,* Montale's second book of poetry (comprising work from 1928 to 1939), is that it is dedicated to "I.B."[1] Those are obviously the initials of Irma Brandeis. Following the Arletta poems that appear towards the end of *Cuttlefish Bones,* the developing pattern of an idealized I/You love poem,[2] recreated in a Modernist context, continues to unfold and mature, with most of the key poetry addressed to I.B. Clizia begins to take shape here, but she will not be named or fully formed until Montale's next book of poems, *The Storm and Other Things.* While Irma Brandeis is the dominant female muse of the collection, clues provided by Montale himself and by the ensuing critical debate indicate that some of the poems were written to other women.[3]

The poems from *The Occasions* that Brandeis published in her 1962 *Quarterly Review of Literature* issue were taken from some of the most pivotal moments in the lifelong dialogue between the poet and his beloved. The poems she included, with the titles as she translated them, were "The Balcony," "Buffalo," "Lindau," "The Way to Vienna," "For Liuba, Leaving," "Dora Markus," "In the Park at Caserta," ten of the twenty short Motets (which she first saw, possibly before anyone else, in her mail in the 1930s), "The Toll-House," and "News from Amiata." Brandeis offered an excellent and varied selection, but she omitted important poems that were specifically inspired by her and written directly to her, among them "New Stanzas" and "Palio," two of the greatest poems in the Clizia Cycle. It is hard not to wonder why she left certain poems out of her collection. Were they, perhaps, for one reason or another, too close for comfort?

The Occasions draws upon the rich Tuscan culture of poetry, music, the plastic arts, and even popular festivals such as the Palio horse-race in Siena. The most important literary source is the technique of the trobar clus – the closed or secret song – of the Florentine *stilnovisti.* Through Montale's re-creation of the trobar clus, medieval hermeticism meets the brutality of the twentieth century in Modernist poems of love.

Florence is a city of pristine Renaissance pattern and geometric precision. The hard surfaces of its facades and courtyards provide a source of imagery for some of the key poems in *The Occasions,* just as the Ligurian shore did for *Cuttlefish Bones.* The great Piazza del Campo of Siena, with its medieval architectonic forms, provides another important stimulus. The sounds of Tuscan aural culture abound in the imagery of *The Occasions,* stretching from the ringing of tower bells to the medieval motet. Finally, Tuscany and Liguria at large offer a wider repertoire of images, with Monterosso apt to reappear in Montale's poetry at any given moment.

In his important exercise in autocriticism, "Intentions (Imaginary Interview)," Montale compares pure poetry, which he comes closest to writing in parts of *Cuttlefish Bones,* to the more contemplative historicism in *The Occasions*: "*Le occasioni* was an orange, or rather a lemon, that was missing a slice: not really that of pure poetry ... but of the pedal, of profound music and contemplation."[4] The *pedale* or pedal is an important concept in Montale's poetics and is used throughout his three great books of poetry. The pedal tone in music is a kind of anchoring undertone that resounds through both harmonically sympathetic and conflicting sonorities. Certain themes and images resound in a similar way in Montale's poetry. This is not an aural characteristic worked into the sound of the poetry (which has a great music of its own). Rather, it is a musical conception applied to the intellectual nature of the poetry, based in the associative powers of key images that recur in different ways, as if different combinations of images can create related but varied chordal effects. Images of Monterosso, Florence, Tuscany, and so forth recur in Montale's writing as if they were resounding bass lines, each with a different tonality and harmonic overtones and each joining to focus the thematic message of his poetry in a unifying whole. Irma Brandeis describes the pedal technique in 1936 when she uses I.A. Richards's analysis of T.S. Eliot's recurring symbols to discuss similar unifying aspects of imagery in Montale's work. When the poet himself, in a letter from December 1934, told her, "You are ... a *pedale* of my life," he was explaining something of her symbolic importance in his poetry in addition to his very real explanation of his feelings for her.

The Occasions, the title of the book, says something significant about the difference between Montale's first book and his second. In this collection the occasion of the writing becomes more important than it was in the more abstract *Cuttlefish Bones.* Here the backdrop of history, politics, and passion that instigates the creation of the poems is less difficult to recover than in the earlier book, which was characterized by the almost impenetrable poem "Arsenio" and where professional exegesis is extremely helpful. Such a poem rivals the abstraction and narrative disjunctions of T.S. Eliot's early work (as in "The Love Song of J. Alfred Prufrock" or "The Waste Land"). Now Montale becomes less concerned with hiding the traces of human experience that engendered his poetry. His dense language, however, still makes the poems challenging, difficult, and, for some, obscure.

"Il balcone" ("The Balcony") begins both *The Occasions* and Irma's selections from the book for the *Quarterly Review.* The unnamed female figure in "The Balcony" seems to possess a certain luminosity in the uncertainty of nothingness and to be leaning towards the light. Only she can see the shining or gleaming light of a special aspect of life. The images of light and access to a unique vision of some sort are often signs of Clizia.[5] A woman, an unnamed listening "you" who is addressed by the poet, is the only one who can catch sight of "the life that gleams" (*la vita che dà barlumi*) as she leans forward out of a darkened window.[6] Whether or not this woman is Irma, there has been a great change in Montale's poetry. While there was no female presence implied in the first poem of *Cuttlefish Bones,* that is not the case with the first poem of *The Occasions.* An unnamed donna of light opens the collection.

Montale knew full well that he was borrowing from a Baudelaire title and a Debussy song, but the strength of his originality is so obvious at this point that both the French and the Italian poem benefit from comparison. Baudelaire's great line from "Le Balcon," his balcony poem, "*je sais l'art d'évoquer les minutes heureuses*" (I know the art of evoking happy moments), generates fresh treatment in Montale's writing. To be happy for a day, an hour, an instant, and to remember this happiness in a time of despair becomes an important theme in his later poetry. There is no doubt that he would have thought about his recent but past joy as he writes in a gloomy and disturbing present. Here the hard, focused nature of his modern language makes a sharp contrast with the sensuous evocations of Baudelaire's 1857 poem.

"Buffalo," "Lindau," and "The Way to Vienna," three short poems that Brandeis included in her collection, are examples of the ways in which Montale can suggest an exotic locale with a few deftly chosen words. They are travel poems, evoking a busy velodrome in a suburb of Paris, a resort in Bavaria, and the road to Vienna. Vienna may have added significance because Irma's family came from Austria.[7] Technically important and accomplished poems, they have some thematic and topical significance in the larger picture of the literary interaction between Brandeis and Montale, but they do not take the reader into the heart of the Clizia Cycle proper.

More telling for the study of the Clizia Cycle is the surprising number of strong poems in the first section of *The Occasions* that resonate with remarkably consistent sympathy for the plight of Jewish people, especially Jewish women, in Italy of the late 1930s. The first of these, "A Liuba che parte" ("For Liuba, Leaving," 1938), is an important short poem, published in Brandeis's *Quarterly Review* in the translation by Ben Belitt. Giulio Nascimbeni, Montale's biographer, mentions that Montale met a woman named Liuba Blumenthal at the train station in Florence. Although she had lived in Italy for many years, Liuba was leaving for England because of the anti-Semitic racial laws of 1938.[8]

"For Liuba, Leaving" has a Jewish ark image that recurs in the later poem "L'Arca" ("The Ark"). It emerges here for the first time in Montale's poetry. In the poem, Liuba, a Jewish woman fleeing Italy after the enactment of Mussolini's anti-Semitic policies, carries her belongings on her head in a hatbox as if it were an "ark," a miniature version of Noah's Ark, but one that is just as "seaworthy." It is just enough (*e basta*) for her "salvation" (*riscatto*).[9]

While Montale's subsequent translators have got it right, it is of historical interest that Ben Belitt's version (for Irma Brandeis) mistranslated *arca,* the Italian word for "ark" (as in Noah's Ark or *l'Arca di Noè*), with the English "arc," translating the ark riding out the flood (the sense in the Italian) as an "arc on the torrent" and therefore hiding the link with biblical Jewish culture.[10] The phrase "your scattered clan" (*dispersa tua famiglia*) refers not to the dispersal of Liuba's immediate family but to the Jews in general, and the poet clearly hopes that they will survive, as cats do, adapting to the emergency. The ark image from the Hebrew Bible shows that Montale could use a Jewish image as freely and as elegantly as he could a Christian one. Later he uses the ark symbol to describe how he carried his images in his poet's mind from place to place in his peripatetic life, as if he were carrying an ark. (See discussion of "The Ark" below.)

As early as 1926 Montale remarked to the famous Italian critic Giacomo Debenedetti that "in Milan I'm thought to be Jewish, because of the Svevo 'case.' If it were possible to be Jewish without knowing it, this would be my 'case': such is my capacity for suffering, and my sense of the ark, more than 'home,' made of a few affections and memories that could follow me everywhere, unobscured."[11] Like many of the writers of *Solaria,* Montale had been branded by Fascist critics as "Jewish," and this was a label that he did not mind.[12]

The Gerti of "Carnevale di Gerti" ("Gerti's Carnival," 1920) was modelled on Gertruden Frankl (1902–89), another Jewish woman. A more substantial poem, "Dora Markus" (1926–39), is included in Brandeis's *Quarterly Review* in a translation by Ben Belitt. "Dora Markus" may have initially been prompted when Bobi Bazlen sent Montale a photo of the real Dora, a pretty Jewish woman, or more accurately a cropped photograph of her pretty legs, but Montale has indicated in his remarks to critics and wrote in a May 1939 letter to Bazlen that Gertruden Frankl was also an inspiration for the poem.[13] Either way, in "Dora Markus" the personal nature of the mode of address reads very much like preparation for the Clizia poems. Montale himself refers to the pre-Brandeis references and to the post-Anschluss atmosphere of the poem in the letter to Bazlen, which was written a few months after the Nazi annexation of Austria.[14] "Dora Markus" features an early example of the storm image that will be developed as a resounding "pedal" of images in Montale's later work: storm-tossed birds slam against the lighthouse in the dark of night. Dora's "sweet oriental yearning" (*dolce ansietà d'Oriente*) refers to her Jewish origins. These are similar to images in other poems written to Clizia. In this poem we learn that Dora's true fatherland (*la tua patria vera*), like Clizia's, is Palestine, the land that would later become Israel.

These three poems capture Montale's compassion for the Jews, and for Jewish women in particular. We also know that these three female figures blended together in his mind because he refers to them in a touching passage from his late poem "Botta e risposta I" ("Thrust and Parry I"), which was written in the early 1960s and published in 1971. In one sweeping line he recalls the curls of the long-lost Gerti, Liuba in flight (this time he does not mention her in the context of the hat-ark image), and a sleeping Clizia (Irma) who is holding an esoteric or "euphuistic sonnet" in her hands but who lets it slip as her fingers relax when she falls asleep.[15]

Liuba, Gerti, and Dora are all prefigurings of the Jewish-Christian Clizia. All were Jewish women, and all were ultimately threatened by the Fascist culture of Europe.[16] Glauco Cambon aptly described the importance of their Jewishness for Montale when he wrote, "They are persecuted or in danger of being persecuted and they embody an unflinching loyalty to an ancient minority faith which entails spiritual survival in an age of horror."[17] These three female figures are important symbols in the proto-Clizia poems.

"Nel parco di Caserta" is included in the *Quarterly Review* with the title "In the Park at Caserta," in a translation by Maurice English. Caserta is the site of the great eighteenth-century royal residence that Luigi Vanvitelli designed for Charles III, the Bourbon king of Naples. The poem evokes the spectacular classical gardens in the park next to the palace, with fountains, lagoons, swans, and statuary.[18] It may also concern Eugenio and Clizia because Caserta is located near Capua, a topos where there are clearer signs of Clizia. However, the poem is more descriptive of a setting than it is evocative of a dramatic interaction between a man and woman.

The first unquestionably obvious Clizia poem in the sequence of Montale's published works, as Luciano Rebay has noted, is "Verso Capua" ("Toward Capua," 1938).[19] For this reason it is the most important of the poems included in *The Occasions* before the Motets. Montale first met Irma Brandeis in 1933. Now, five years later, Irma is about to leave for America for the last time before the war. This moment of parting generates the first certain appearance of Clizia in the poetry. Within the sequence of works arranged in Montale's poetry, Clizia's debut begins with one of the last moments.

Capua, originally settled by the Etruscans, has religious significance. Like "Là fuoresce il Tritone" ("There the Triton Surges"), the poem about the ancient town of Portovenere that Brandeis translated from *Cuttlefish Bones,* "Verso Capua" concerns a site of both pagan and Christian significance. Saint Priscus is said to have first preached Christianity in the

Campanian town of Capua. Once again, the characters of the poem are standing at a culturally charged locus, where Christian thought began to supersede the pagan world, but this time Irma Brandeis is the inspiration of the I/You rhetoric of the poem.

In the poem Clizia and the poet are in a horse-drawn carriage. The characters are north of Naples, near Capua and Caserta, travelling along the Volturno River, which flows more than a hundred miles from the Apennines until it empties into the Gulf of Gaeta. Outside, a swarm of tiny butterflies is fluttering around the harness of the carriage, and then a startling ray of light illuminates the forest by the river. Montale describes his beloved inside the carriage: "*e tu in fondo che agitavi / lungamente una sciarpa, la bandiera / stellata!*" (and you inside who for a long while / waved a scarf, your star-spangled banner!).[20] Montale does not try to describe Clizia in detail but merely uses one of the items she is wearing to evoke her. This is a metonymic device. An object next to Clizia gives us Clizia. While Montale uses this trope to great effect in his Clizia poetry in general, here it is her scarf, which doubles as a star-spangled banner, *la bandiera stellata.* The reference to the American flag is clear.

This is a beautiful description from a particular moment during what was perhaps one of the last excursions in the countryside before Irma's departure and the onset of war. There are a number of other poems that similarly describe such excursions, among them one to the Festa del Palio in Siena in 1938, another to the Etruscan ruins at Luni and, possibly, a visit to Caserta, which is just down the road from Capua. This is only the first time we will see Clizia's scarf, which turns up again in "The Red Lily" (1942). All told, there is little of Irma here but a great deal of sensuous description. Subsequent poems offer much more to provide pieces of the puzzle.

The Sacred and Profane Motets: Seeds of the Cycle

The Italian word *barbaglio* is a key to the elusive symbology of the "Mottetti" ("The Motets," 1934–40), Montale's series of twenty short poems published in the heart of *The Occasions. Barbaglio* means "the dazzle that comes from intense light."[21] It is a useful word – a *pedale* symbol – for uncovering the meaning of Montale's poetry. Where there is light in Montale, Clizia is often nearby. All Italian words pertaining to light, from *barlumi* to *solarità,* existed in a string of related images and associations in Montale's mind. They are essential to a substantial portion of his symbology in the Clizia Cycle, and at the heart of this symbology is the transcendent donna of the trobar clus, whom we come to know in the poetry as Clizia. Clizia's eyes, her hair, and even her jewellery reflect prisms of coloured light as she is transformed in Montale's imagination from a woman into the sunflower goddess of redemption.

Light was an essential source of thematic and symbolic expression in Dante. Irma Brandeis herself, in her fine 1961 study *The Ladder of Vision,* records her fascination with the images of light in Dante's works. Montale cites this study in an important lecture on Dante that he gave in Florence in 1965. *Luce,* Italian for "light," is a crucial word for Dante, Montale, and Irma. Light opens up meaning in Montale's writing and in *The Divine Comedy,* a work that absorbed much of both Brandeis's and Montale's intellectual energy. In the *Paradiso* Dante expresses the highest level of heaven in elusive, synaesthetic metaphors of light.[22] In Dante, Beatrice gazes at the full sun of noon, just as Clizia, the sunflower goddess, follows the sun. Just as Dante gazes at the reflection of the sun in Beatrice's eyes, so does the lover in Montale gaze at Clizia, who follows God's light. In Dante, the sun is always a symbol of God and wisdom, even in the *Inferno*.[23] Writing as a Modernist, Montale used light metaphors to help express what could be left of the unified spiritual vision of Dante in the maelstrom of the twentieth century.

Dante resonates throughout Montale's poetry, but in the Motets the Dantesque flickerings of heaven and hell are especially important because Dante scholar Irma Brandeis finally takes up her dominant position as the chief muse and addressee of Montale's poetry. It is a role that will grow in significance over time. The Motets are partly medieval in inspiration, taking their precedent from the Dolce Stil Novo practice of writing a trobar clus to a disguised beloved under the protective cover of the senhal. They are also named after a type of medieval music important to the culture of old Florence. The musical motet, from the French *mot* (word), is an essentially combinatory composition, originating as a piece of religious music, with either Latin text or wordless chant, and later crucial to the development of European polyphony. At first only in Latin, texts (hence the word *mot*) were eventually added from vulgar spoken languages (as opposed to Latin or Greek), such as French, Italian, and English. Motets date from the thirteenth century and were used by the troubadours. In the broadest sense, the vernacular motet, which evolved from the earlier church motet, incorporates both sacred and profane elements.[24] This is important for Montale because Irma's symbol begins from an earthly love affair and becomes a sacred symbol in the poetry, the exact reverse of the history of the motet. Since sacred and secular texts, including even the topic of amorous love, are at times mixed together in the long history of the motet, it is an appropriate frame of reference for the first stages of Irma's transformation from real woman into Clizia and beyond, into a Christ-bearing Jewish-American female symbol of salvation. In the poet's Motets, symbols of Clizia overlap in cultural significance, taking on amorous and religious overtones, recalling the hybrid history of the musical form.

Italian Modernist poets often are attracted to musical titles. Some examples are Umberto Saba's *Preludes and Fugues,* Giuseppe Ungaretti's *Hymns,* or Salvatore Quasimodo's *Drowned Oboe.* Montale's interest in musical references is common to more than just Italian poets, however. His use of the motet, like all musical references and vocabulary in modern poetry, is in general a poetic trope of the Post-Symbolists in the twentieth century. T.S. Eliot wrote "preludes" and "quartets," while Rainer Maria Rilke composed sonnets to Orpheus, the greatest mortal musician of classical mythology. Wallace Stevens used the variation form for many of his extended poems, and musical titles and references abound throughout his works.[25]

Montale's Motets are short and enigmatic, even, as the poet himself describes them, epigrammatic. They occupy a place in his oeuvre that is similar in significance to the preludes of Chopin, Debussy, or Scriabin. These short musical works hold stylistic keys that can unlock the secrets of larger musical scores by these composers. In the same way, Montale's Motets are preludes to the larger works to come in *The Occasions* and *The Storm and Other Things.* In style and content they connect to more intricate arguments in the longer works and encapsulate many of the themes in the longer poems. Turning back to the motet and trobar clus was a good move for Montale in the Fascist 1930s because he was able to reconsider models that would enable privacy and secrecy. Moving backward into the past also helped him to create a new style that was distinct from what he had achieved in *Cuttlefish Bones,* and it helped to furnish escape from a similar style, Post-Symbolism, which had similar qualities but different intentions based in fin-de-siècle aestheticism. For one thing, the love poetry of the more historically remote Dolce Stil Novo had a clear-cut strategic purpose, unlike the aesthetic and philosophical meditations of the more recent Symbolist movement.

The poems are conspicuously modern in technique as well, and there is a highly contemporary meaning to the notion of *barbaglio.* The Motets are like the flashes of brilliant light that come with the use of a flash-bulb, as if the poet is exposing a poetic vision that is illuminated for only an instant. Then darkness closes around again, hiding context and identification. Montale used the English word *flashes* in his poetry (a title for a section of his later book *The Storm and Other Things*). The *flash* stands for a split-second insight into the realm beyond the knowable, but it is also related to the flash of the twentieth-century flashbulb, and Montale referred on various occasions to his poetics of the snap-shot. In his introduction to his 1956 book of short stories, *The Butterfly of Dinard* (*Farfalla di Dinard*), he refers to his stories as "instantaneous flashes."[26] These very short stories are an expression in prose that is similar to the brief lyric utterances of the Motets. Two aspects of flashing light, medieval and modern, intermingle in Montale's mind.[27]

Photography is a point of departure for the intensity of contemplation in this series of fragments. The series of poetic snap-shots is similar to the jump from poem to poem in the Motets, one following the other paratactically, without explanation. The ephemeral nature of experience is thus captured in these twenty short works. Merging notions of snap-shot, motet, and trobar clus are crucial to the unique modern and medieval mixture of essential ingredients in Montalean poetics. The Motets are fragmentary, elusive wisps of expression and vision caught in language – a mysterious moment among moments, felt, then gone; remembered, but saved only through these fragments, which are a key to their meaning in the life of the speaker. They are sparks and glimmerings of the greater emanations of light to come in the longer poems that will follow. In them we get an early view of Clizia as a kind of superwoman, with paranormal eyes and powerful wings that can fly her across the Atlantic Ocean. The poet speaks to Clizia in most of these poems, but she is not named here. We encounter her name only in subsequent fuller, longer works.

Clizia, however, is named in a companion piece to the Motets, a short story entitled "Due sciacalli al guinzaglio" ("Two Jackals on a Leash"), which Montale published in the *Corriere della Sera* in February 1950. This remarkable short work of fiction and self-criticism gives us one of our clearest glimpses of his poetic project of the Clizia Cycle. Much of the story refers quite obviously to the literary procedures involved with the composing of the actual Motets:

> Many years ago, Mirco, a noted poet who today has changed professions, wrote in his mind and then transcribed on certain crumpled-up pieces of paper that he had put in his vest pocket, and at last published, a series of short poems, and addressed by air mail (but only on the wings of fantasy),

> to a Clizia who lived around three thousand miles away from him. Clizia was not really named Clizia, and the original Clizia one can find in a sonnet of uncertain origin by Dante, or someone close to him, sent to Giovanni Querini; and neither was Mirco really named Mirco, but the necessary circumspection does not alter the meaning of this little business. It is enough to identify the typical situation of this poet, and almost every lyric poet who lives besieged by the absence-presence of a distant lady, in this case of a Clizia bearing the name of the one who, according to the myth, was changed into a sunflower.
>
> The little poems by Mirco then formed a series, a little autobiographical novel, anything but dark in tone, born day by day. Clizia did not know anything about it and probably did not read it until many years later; but sometimes the news of her that reached Mirco furnished the spark for some motet; and in this way new epigrams were born and shot like arrows across the seas without the concerned lady offering any pretext for them, even unintentionally.[28]

The names of the characters Mirco and Clizia are so obviously Montale and Brandeis today that they seem slightly overdone, but even when they were published, they must have seemed part of a roman à clef to some informed insiders. By 1950 Montale was a full-time journalist. Mirco, like Montale, has changed professions. Mirco/Montale writes verses to Clizia/Irma, who is three thousand miles away, about as far as the distance between Italy and the United States. Writing in 1950, Montale explains the epistolary nature of the Motets as well as much of the Clizia poetry, openly referring to this work as a series that taken together forms an autobiographical novella (*un romanzetto autobiografico*). The connection between the motets and the mail is something that we can see with greater clarity since the 2006 publication of his *Lettere a Clizia,* which makes it clear that many of the Motets were actually mailed to Irma in the 1930s. The poems in the story were meant to be sent by mail to the distant lady, but they were sent only in the imagination. Every bit of news of Clizia could be enough to inspire a motet. And the distant lady in the story had done nothing to provoke the one-way I/You dialogue of the poems, even "involuntarily." However, the actual Irma Brandeis was actively involved with one of the liveliest exchanges of love letters ever written and was receiving her "motets" in the mail in the 1930s.

While no translation can ever quite capture the effervescent imagery and euphony of the Italian, translators have often been attracted to the

Motets, possibly because they are shorter and less difficult than other Montale poems or because their enigmatic nature has fascinated many readers and translators.[29] They are among Montale's most famous poems but not necessarily the best of them. Or rather, they are like haiku that hold secrets that capture the meaning of the longer and more involved poems on similar topics. We can compare them to the short poems of Williams or Pound or Richard Wright, which they clearly rival in range and quality.

The Motets begin with an epigraph, a line from the Spanish poet Gustavo Adolfo Bécquer: "*Sobre el volcán la flor*" (Above the volcano the flower). It is easy to think of a meaning for this. The volcano is very close to the many images of the storm in Montale's poetry: *bufera, nembo, tempesta,* and so forth. The volcano is the Fascist era. The flower is Clizia. There are twenty poems in the set, of which Brandeis included ten in the *Quarterly Review*.[30] She translated eight of them. This is another important act in the rare case of a beloved object of love poetry who later became involved in the literary fate of the author of those poems written and mailed to her.

At the end of "Two Jackals on a Leash" Montale concludes with an important warning: "Between understanding nothing and understanding too much there is a middle road, a *juste milieu*, that poets, instinctively, respect more than their critics."[31] Nevertheless, the poet also indicated, in a 1964 letter to Silvio Guarnieri, that the first three Motets were inspired by Paola Nicoli, the married Peruvian woman whom he met in Florence in the early 1930s.[32] He presents a different pretext for the poem in his letters to Irma Brandeis, saying that Irma is the only stimulant of the first of the poems and that the next two Motets were "commissioned" by a poetry lover named Maria Rosa Solari.[33] Either way, it is important to read the twenty poems as a consistent whole, since the artist presented them as such, and it makes little sense to read them while imagining the unnamed narrator or lover writing to two different women.[34] The female listener is all these women, and none of them. Montale was working with the emotions that he lived in his life, and fashioning them into art.

The first poem sets the tone for the series in the opening line, with the desperate statement of the poet lover, who proclaims that he "must lose" (*debbo riperderti*) his listening lover yet again, and cannot bear it (*non posso*), and that she, his listener, knows this (*lo sai*).[35] The unnamed lovers are in Genoa, an important point of entry and departure in Montale's poetry. The last line of the poem, "hell is certain" (*l'inferno è certo*), introduces a notion crucial for the whole sequence of Motet poems by conveying a sense of a modern version of a Dantesque *inferno*.

Although the poem may not have been written with her in mind, Brandeis, who included it in her collection in her own translation, was familiar with this dock-side setting for departure and loss, having lived it herself. She even describes it in her journal. Both Montale and Irma also describe in their written reminiscences the nearby Hotel Bristol and Carlotta's Ristorante, where they had their *ultima cena* (last supper), but these are not in the poem.[36] Sottoripa, the neighbourhood of medieval streets near the waterfront in Genoa, and the dock-side setting in general seem gloomy and infernal. The huge ocean-going ships in the poem are like great mountains of steel, and the great masts are like huge trees. Their looming shapes obviously are a conspicuous part of a modern-day hell for the poet, documenting the emotional impact of the port background in the mind of the speaker. An often neglected detail in the commentaries is the element of sound imagery. A droning, gnawing sound (*un ronzìo lungo*), possibly a dock-side crane, evolves into a screeching noise, perhaps brakes or some other machinery, which the poet compares to a nail scraping on glass (*strazia com'unghia ai vetri*). These combine to create an infernal sound world. The Genovese setting is also elaborated in the second Motet, which sets up a medieval context of banners and symbols, both good and evil, in the setting of the modern port city.[37] This symbolic pattern is greatly expanded in the poem "Palio," which concerns the enactment of the famous medieval horse-race in 1938.

Brandeis also translated the third Motet, "Brina sui vetri" ("Brine on the Windows"). Whether Paola or Irma inspired the persona of the unidentified donna is less important than Montale's recollection of the bursting sounds of the ballerina bombs used in the First World War. They exploded in the cliffs all night long. The poet's misery then recalls the current unhappiness that he feels as he writes the poem. Both are states of "exile."

The next, "Lontano, ero con te quando tuo padre" ("Far away, I was still with you when your father"), was the first of the Motets clearly inspired by Irma Brandeis. The prime authority who guarantees the importance of the Brandeis connection is Montale himself. In "Two Jackals on a Leash" Mirco reflects on the occasion that instigated this poem:

> One day Mirco found out that Clizia's father had died; he sensed her agony and greatly detested the three thousand miles that kept him far,

> too far from this mourning. And it seemed that all the anxieties and risks of his past life had converged towards the as yet unknown Clizia, towards a meeting that would take place many years later. Perhaps, he said to himself, the war prepared me for this. Because without Clizia my life had no sense, no direction. Dredging up his past, again he saw himself in several contested villages of Vallarsa, at Cumerlotti, Anghébeni, below Monte Corvo; finding himself again in mortal danger, but already assisted, with his knowledge, by the star of Clizia, under the little umbrella of her sunflower.[38]

Montale describes himself as Mirco, seated in a café, which one might imagine to be the famous Giubbe Rosse (this he does not specify), and writing this Motet in the margins of a newspaper. The poet is obviously referring to Irma's father, Dr Julian Brandeis, who died in the autumn of 1933.[39] Montale actually wrote a poignant and sensitive note to Irma in November 1933 when he learned about the death of her father. Here in his autobiographical "story," when he hears of Dr Brandeis's death, he feels a shock of recognition. He understands the importance of Clizia in his life. In the Motet it is as if he had survived the First World War because he was already protected by Clizia's special power, protected under the shield of her senhal:

> Far away, I was still with you when your father
> entered the darkness and left you with his good-bye.
> To what end then? The earlier
> suffering only saved me for this:
>
> that I didn't know you and should have; from today's
> blows I know – if from down there inflects back to
> an earlier time and returns me to Cumerlotti
> or Anghébeni – between exploding mines,
> the cries and forward push of the squadrons.[40]

As I am sure he intended, Montale is not clear on whether "today's barrage" (*ai colpi d'oggi*) is simply the psychological effect of the news of the death, the larger political situation, or the suffering that has come from the separation – or all of these. But his suffering in the present moment has clearly brought him back to a horrible memory of the past, where he recalls the explosions, the screaming, and the desperate movements of a human-made inferno, which, as a veteran and a witness, he saw to be the true nature of the First World War. These war images are the most vivid in all of Montale's poetry. The tone of this poem is similar to the desperate tone that the poet achieved in the first Motet, regardless of who may have inspired which poem. The lyric "I" says that he did not die before, in the first war, because it was not yet time to meet the beloved. This is an extreme expression of passion, consistent with the purpose of the whole Motets series.

"Addii, fischi nel buio, cenni, tosse" ("Good-byes, whistles in the darkness, waving, coughing"), which directly follows in the series, superimposes the medieval and the modern. In this poem Clizia and the poet are immersed in the *buio,* a darkness image with a history that takes us back to the many places of darkness and shadow in Dante. But this is the modern world, and the lovers are in a train station. Clizia is a bit like a modern Eurydice, not descending into the underworld but ascending towards her exit from the scene, which is achieved by boarding a train and disappearing into the darkness. Shortly thereafter, perhaps, the train vanishes through some tunnels into the mountains. The caged or entrapped "automatons" that the poet mentions are the Fascists and pseudo-Fascists of the era. They are like the drowned or trapped dead of the last poems of *Cuttlefish Bones,* the ensnared automatons of contemporary Fascist life. Montale himself often felt miserable and trapped, even suicidal, in this era.[41] The departing trains make a kind of music that Montale compares to a Latin dance, a *cadenza di carioca,* a type of samba rhythm. This is one of the many dance images in his poetry, here evoking the train sounds that seem sad and hypnotic as they recede in the distance.

Following this, the next Motet (the sixth) is a pivotal work in the whole sequence. The procedure that led to its creation is described in some detail in "Two Jackals on a Leash." Mirco/Montale is now in Modena, taking a passeggiata in the shopping galleries of this wealthy northern city, which is famous for balsamic vinegar and Ferrari sports cars. Mirco is still thinking of Clizia. Everything else seems fake as if it were an image "painted or projected on a screen." As Mirco wanders, he is troubled by the beauty and merriment around him, since he is unhappy:

> And then an old man in a braided uniform appeared before Mirco, dragging two champagne-coloured puppies on a leash, two small dogs that at first glance did not seem to be wolf-hounds or dachshunds or

> Pomeranians. Mirco walked up to the old man and asked him, "What type of dogs are these?" The old man replied, dryly and proudly, "They are not dogs, they're jackals." (This was spoken in a rough Northern manner; then he slipped away with his pair.) Clizia loved exotic creatures. How delighted she would have been to see them, thought Mirco! And from that day he never read the name of Modena without connecting that city with the notion of Clizia and the two jackals. A strange, persistent notion. That the two beasts could have been sent by her, almost by an emanation? Were they an emblem, an occult saying, a *senhal*?[42]

Other strange occurrences in the random flow of his everyday life appear to Mirco/Montale to be instances of the senhal of Clizia. Every time he discerns a sign of the beloved, he feels comforted. Finally he sits down to write a poem about this. That poem is the sixth Motet, which Montale reprints in its totality in the heart of his short story. Brandeis translated and included this poem to herself in the *Quarterly Review*:

> The hope even of seeing you again
> forsook me;
>
> and I asked myself whether upon this that cuts me off
> from every sense of you, this screen of images,
> swarm the insignia of death or whether from the past
> there yet may be on it, distorted and unstable,
> some glimmering of yours.
>
> (At Modena among the porticoes
> a blazoned servant led along
> two jackals on a leash.)[43]

The poem begins with the lines "*La speranza di pure rivederti / m'abbandonava*" (The hope even of seeing you again / forsook me). It is a line spun with a purposeful echo from the third canto of Dante's *Inferno*: "*Lasciate ogne speranza voi ch'intrate*" (Leave behind every hope you who enter). This is inscribed on a sign that Dante sees on a door to hell. In both cases the abandonment of hope is associated with the entry into hell, but, for Montale, hell is the reduction of the pleasures of everyday life to the false screen of images. The screen, explicitly described in the "Two Jackals" story, was first used in the poem that was written years before.

While there are clear signs of hell and death, there are also signs of *paradiso* in this small poem. This is chiefly from Clizia's *barbaglio,* which, rather than Brandeis's "glimmering," I would prefer to translate as her "dazzle-flash" or "dazzlement."[44] The light image, a sure sign of Clizia and her powers of salvation, goes with the light imagery of "Il balcone." This connection alone is an excellent argument for including "Il balcone" in the poems of the Clizia Cycle. Starting with her emanations in the Motets, Clizia becomes more and more dazzling as her cycle progresses, and she becomes less human, more of an angel, eventually even a goddess. This pattern is anticipated in miniature in the sequence of Motets.

The last three lines of "The hope even of seeing you again," as we know from Montale's explanation, are about another sign of Clizia, the two jackals on a leash that were sighted in Modena. Montale's self-quoting in the story makes this easy to unravel. Without the story I am not sure how a reader would easily discern the significance of the jackals. Montale, writing in the newspaper in 1950, decided to make explicit a meaning that was well embedded in symbolic language in 1938. We should also note that Montale, ever the elusive Modernist, specifically introduces the idea of the medieval senhal in his story, clarifying one of his most arcane uses of it.

Bettarini suspects that Montale sent Brandeis the seventh Motet in his letter of 2 November 1938, which would place its inception at just a few months after the poet had seen his lover for the last time.[45] The Motet, which begins with the line "*Il saliscendi bianco e nero dei*" (The black and white swooping of) concerns the lover's distress on the pier. Brandeis may have remembered something of the "anguish on the pier" (*crucci su lo scalo*) that she renders in her translation. In both the Montale poem and the Brandeis translation, birds are sweeping through the sky towards the sea, the aromatic air is rich with the thick scent of elderberry, and a drizzling rain clears up, but none of this natural beauty overcomes the "anguish on the pier."[46]

The same theme is treated in the first poem, which, if the critics are correct (in spite of Montale's declaration otherwise to Irma), was not inspired by Irma Brandeis, but the seventh poem is clearly a Clizia poem. It goes with the Sottoripa setting and mood of the first Motet, but now the poet has moved back from the immediacy of dock-side drama to details of the surrounding natural phenomena. While nature is a witness to the cruelty of the separation, it is indifferent. And the beloved has gone, sailing off without her poet lover. The scene of parting and distress has a universality about it that transcends the answer to the question of which woman inspired it. The reader will automatically assume that the two poems go together unless he or she knows too much.

The late poem "Interno/Esterno" ("Inside/Outside"), written in 1976, gives a fuller picture of this moment in Montale's life, quite specifically placing Irma/Clizia and the poet in a scene of dock-side parting and probably in nearby Sottoripa. Here he remembers her face long after she has left. In "Inside/Outside" we learn that the memory of the parting at the pier is something that he carried with him throughout his life.

Another Motet that attracted Brandeis's interest is one of the more obviously erotic poems in the collection. She included it as rendered in her own words in the *Quarterly Review,* translating Montale's very visceral last line "it is / still your life, blood of yours in my veins" (*è ancora / tua vita, sangue tuo nelle mie vene.*).[47] The more elegant words that begin the poem, "Here is the sign" (*Ecco il segno*), quite clearly indicate another senhal signal of the beloved. The light and sun images of the golden wall and the dazzle of dawn (once again the word *barbaglio*) are important clues. Cambon read the palm as a Jewish symbol, at least indirectly.[48] The tree is certainly typical of those found in what was then Palestine. And it is obviously evocative of the Levant, as are other symbols in Montale's poems that suggest the Jewish history of the Middle East. Taken together, the palm leaves and the dawn's light are somewhat reminiscent of an enlarged sunflower, which will be the ultimate symbol of Clizia, as explained in "Two Jackals on a Leash" and as exemplified in the culminating poems of *The Storm and Other Things* (see chapter 6).

The most important sign of Clizia is the *barbagli dell'aurora,* "the glittering" or "bedazzling" early light of "dawn," which burns the palm leaf. This is surely an indication of the sun goddess who will emerge in Montale's subsequent writing, reminiscent of the aura of light around Dante's Beatrice, and even anticipates much of Irma's later writing about Beatrice and light in *The Ladder of Vision* (1961). In addition, reflected or refracted light glowing on a wall is an important detail in later Montale poems with a Florentine setting. Finally, the sexual nature of the lovers' commingled blood is unusually clear for Montale.

The next two Motets, the ninth and tenth in the series, contain an outburst of fantastic images that, judging from the procedure narrated in

"Two Jackals on a Leash," are signs of the beloved that Mirco/Montale discovers as he wanders in his world – a green lizard, a flapping sail, a noontime cannon shot, and a clock.[49] The most likely signs are the images of lightning in both poems.[50] Even the image of a lizard, a reference from Dante's *Inferno* (as has been noted by a number of the translators and commentators), leads indirectly back to the notion of light.[51] The Italian words for *lizard* and *lightning* (*ramarro* and *fólgore*) are linked in the same Dante simile:

> Come 'l ramarro sotto la gran fersa
> dei dì canicular, cangiando siepe,
> folgore par se la via attraversa (Canto XXV, lines 79–81)

> [Just as a lizard darting from hedge to hedge,
> under the sting lash of the dog-days' heat
> zips across the road, like a flash of lightning.][52]

Montale's Motet begins with exactly the same imagery of lizard (*ramarro*) and whip (*fersa*): "*Il ramarro, se scocca / sotto la grande fersa / dalle stoppie ...*" (The lizard, if it darts / under the great whip / from the stubble ...)[53] Montale included a complete version of this poem in a letter to Irma dated 20 November 1938. The only difference between that version and the version published in his complete works is that the former has a different second line: "*come un colpo di frusta*" (like a blow of the whip). Montale finally opts for the more Dantesque "*sotto la grande fersa*" (under the great whip), a change that adds to the mixed flavour of Modernist snap-shot and *stilnovistic* feints.[54]

Another Motet is about the connection between music, dance, and the human soul. This poem is an important example of the vocabularies of music and dance as significant symbolic areas in Montale. *Furlana* (the forlane) and *rigodone* (the rigadoon), two old European dances, seem to convey positive contexts here. Their role in symbolizing the energy of Clizia should be compared to the *trescone, sardana,* and fandango in other poems, which have demonic energy, communicating the powers that oppose her. In rendering the poem in English, Brandeis makes one of the dances a polka, which perhaps was a mistake because the polka is a Polish dance. The dances, of course, evoke not only the dances themselves but also the lively music that generates their patterns.

With the second stanza the poem becomes a hymn to the voice of the beloved: "*La tua voce è quest'anima diffusa*" (Your voice is this soul that diffuses) or, as Brandeis puts it, "Your voice is this pervasive soul." Clizia sings here, whether it is "on wires" (*su fili*), "on wings" (*su ali*), or in "the wind" (*al vento*).[55] Singing is something she also does to positive effect in "Clizia at Foggia," another short story that Montale wrote about her.[56] Obviously, a fondness for opera and for music in general would have been another common interest for Eugenio and Irma. It is just as easy to imagine them sharing the pleasures of music as translating Donne in the Pensione Annalena, which, judging from Montale's late poems about her, they obviously did (see chapter 8). Montale refers to this Motet in his 14 January 1939 letter to Irma when he says: "Your voice is not do re la sol: is much more and I can't put it in verse."[57] He had already tried in the eleventh Motet, however, which ends with the solfège symbols "do re la sol sol," exactly the same notes plus one.

"Ti libero la fronte dai ghiaccioli" ("I liberated your forehead of icicles") offers an early look at Clizia as a divine figure in the miniature form of the short motet. She assumes her superhuman form here, but she still seems to be in danger. She has *penne* (wings), but they have been lacerated or torn. We will note other instances of the divine Clizia with wings in longer poems, and these wings have sometimes been damaged because of the moral and spiritual battles she must fight. Montale was extremely fond of birds and was one of the greatest bird watchers in world literature. Given his fascination with them, it is not surprising that Clizia takes on avian qualities as she evolves into her mythic transformation. Noting that Clizia's wings have been lacerated by cyclones (*cicloni*), the poet-lover carefully removes the icicles that congealed on the beloved's forehead while she was crossing the "high clouds" (*alte nebulose*).[58] Here the poet tenderly addresses a wounded angel who has flown high in the sky. The poem gives an early sense of the fragile but powerful superheroine who will emerge later in the cycle. As he pulls the icicles from her forehead, she awakens. A chill remains in the air, though it is noontime, and a long shadow extends from a medlar tree in some unspecified Italian square. Even the sun is chilled (*freddoloso*). They are separate from the others, who are described as the *altre ombre* (other shades). Montale himself described them to Guarnieri: "the other men are those who *don't know,* who ignore the possibility" of Clizia's "visitation from heaven" (Montale uses the word *oltrecielo* for heaven).[59] Montale is once again using the language of the *Inferno* to convey a sense of the damned souls in the modern-day Fascist hell that opposes Clizia. It is a practice he will continue in later and longer poems.

Jonathan Galassi identifies the forehead, icicles, and lacerated wings as three of Clizia's most important stilnovistic features, noting that they recur elsewhere in the later poetry.[60] Here the wings were damaged by cyclones as she attempted to return to Italy and to the poet. This is an early indication of the storm that she will face in other poems. Her flight up to the highest clouds is something that would be possible only for a winged goddess. It is important to see this poem as a prelude in relation to Clizia's developing appearance and purpose in later poems. But Montale does not use the name Clizia in his poetry until the next book of poems, *The Storm and Other Things*.

The next Motet, the thirteenth, begins a series of poems with significant musical references. It has a Venetian setting, with gondolas and palaces. Doors are shut against the beloved. A man is fishing for eels, and the poet identifies with him. Also, the eel is later connected to notions of Clizia. (See "L'anguilla," Montale's great poem about the eel, in which he links the eel and the rainbow symbols to Clizia.) Montale remarks that "the deceitful song might be Dappertutto's song in the second act of Offenbach's *Tales of Hoffmann*."[61] This would corroborate the diabolical quality of the poem, as the forces of darkness oppose Clizia.

Montale creates a complete world of sound in the following Motet, filling it with an exotic variety of references to musical sound. It is a poem best entered through the ear. Brandeis used her own translation in the *Quarterly Review*, beginning her version with the question "Does it storm hail or brine?" (Brandeis reverses the word order of the original, which is "*Infuria sale o grandine?*").[62] Brandeis's English, even more specifically than the Italian original, links the poem with the sounds of the storm so crucial to Montale's overall symbolic expression. Lush vegetation is pushed down by the brunt of the storm, but then an "underwater tolling" (*un rintocco subacqueo*) intones from the depths. (Brandeis translates this phrase, mistakenly perhaps, as "underwater cymbal.") A "pianola" of submerged voices resounds from underwater, rising in the frosty air. Finally, the poet-speaker hears his lover singing, her voice trilling a famous operatic aria.

Montale specifies two musical works in this Motet. The most obvious one is the "Bell Song" from Léo Delibes's *Lakmé*. This is the aria that the beloved sings at the close of the poem. Delibes (1836–91) was a French opera composer of the late Romantic period; appointed professor of composition at the Paris Conservatoire in 1881, he was perhaps the most important French composer to teach there after Bizet. Montale had a weakness for Delibes's type of syrupy operatic music.

One wonders whether Irma Brandeis actually sang some of *Lakmé* for Montale one day in Florence, especially since the two of them shared a passion for vocal music that reached back to childhood, and musical topics frequently turn up in Montale's letters to Brandeis. Anticipating Puccini's 1904 triumph, *Madame Butterfly, Lakmé* (1883) is an example of late-nineteenth-century French orientalism. It concerns the love of the Hindu beauty Lakmé for a British officer, who is torn between running off with Lakmé and returning to his regiment. Less fickle than Butterfly's Pinkerton, the soldier, after hesitating, chooses Lakmé and death at the end of the opera.

The "Bell Song" – also known by its text "Où va la jeune Hindoue?" – is a charming old chestnut in the operatic repertoire that is often used to show off the virtuosity of young sopranos. It is also an aria of seduction, in which Lakmé, following the instructions of her father, sings her exotic bell music in which she narrates the "legend of the pariah's daughter" to entrap and expose her lover. The number is a strange combination of coloratura gymnastics, French sophistication, and European impressions of oriental sounds. The cultural contrast between the Indian woman and the Englishman echoes the clash between the Jewish-American woman and the Italian poet. Indeed, the minor key melody that begins "Où va la jeune Hindoue?" almost sounds Hebraic.

Montale, whose fascination with Debussy predates *Cuttlefish Bones*, said that "the underwater tolling" sounds are "probably [Debussy's] La Cathédrale engloutie."[63] The piano prelude *Cathédrale engloutie* (*Sunken Cathedral*) contains parallel harmonies rising without traditional constraints and capturing Debussy's unique sense of orientalism. Rhythm does not pulse in this revolutionary prelude. Instead, the music seems to float. Time and space are expanded to new, unearthly limits. The long pedal in the heart of the prelude allows Debussy to suspend a modern evocation of a medieval organum over a delicately throbbing accompaniment. Montale would have liked the medieval qualities of the piece, which fits in well with the sound of a motet, and its thirteenth-century origins. Debussy is known for having pointedly eschewed the driving metric rhythm of Beethoven and the Romantics, and this prelude, with its floating and dreamy rhythm, is an excellent example of this stylistic change.[64]

In his 1949 essay "Words and Music" Montale made it clear that he did not care for bombastic settings of language in a musical composition. He preferred composers who allowed the full richness of poetry to come out in their settings. Among these was Debussy, whose influence is obvious in this Motet.[65] The aural nature of the Motet is very apparent. Montale hears a Debussy-style underwater tolling, a hellish pianola, and the famous but weird trilling of Delibes's "Bell Song" echoing in his Motet. There are three kinds of music here: avant-garde music of the early Modernist period; a kind of *musique concrète*; and a well-known, well-worn operatic aria. The sounds of music and the music of sound, both of which seem to have inspired him everywhere in his poetry, are crucial here in the generation of his private symbology.

The Motet "Al primo chiaro, quando" ("At first light, when") again contrasts the supernatural world of Dante and the modern world. Montale is also once again immersed in his train images, as in his earlier poem "Accelerato" and in "Good-byes, whistles in the darkness, waving, coughing," the fifth Motet. There are a number of train scenes in Montale that create startling images but actually describe the flickering effects of light and dark, land and sky, water and shore. "Accelerato," commonly thought to be an Arletta poem, is a particularly good instance of this. It is about travelling the short train route through the mountains from Genoa to Monterosso. The poem evokes what is seen through the window as the train passes through and out of tunnels. In the fifth Motet the view is from the track looking up at the open train windows before it departs. The flickering effects of momentarily exposed sea and sky recur in the fifteenth Motet, which concerns a train ride along the same Ligurian strip, possibly starting at the railroad station in Florence or Genoa.[66] The shimmering effects created by trains or other technological aspects of modern life here and elsewhere in Montale help him capture the ephemera of experience. This combines with the snapshot norm to create the qualities of modernity in his poem that make it more plausible to draw on the poetic heritage of the Italian literary past and at the same time preserve the freshness of originality. Thus Dante is allowed into a world that he could not have known, Montale's mid-twentieth-century world of trains, tunnels, telephones, electricity, warplanes, and so forth. The last two lines of the poem have a symmetry of rhetoric linking the phrases "at first light" (*al primo chiaro*) and "at first dark" (*al primo buio*) and concern the beloved. Her inspiration (signified by her "weaving") binds the two. Perhaps the linking of the beloved to the sunrise and sunset indicates that the poem commemorates a day of love, a tryst somewhere, demarcated by a train ride.

Brandeis translated the Motet "Il fiore che ripete" ("The flower that repeats") as well. In her words, the poet notices the flower when he is at the "edge" of a "crevasse" (*dall'orlo del burrato*), anticipating the vast abyss that is about to separate them. Then, with the "clank of metal gears" (*un cigolìo si sferra*), a funicular starts up, and he is carried away from her.[67] The space between the lovers soon grows enormous, the azure of the mountain air evolving quickly into darkness (*già buia*). Much as in the railroad contexts of other Motets, in this one the cranking modern machinery of the cable-car gears combines with the Dolce Stil Novo devotional tone to create a modern context for the poem. The lyric offers just enough information to enable the reader to imagine Eugenio and Irma, or Mirco and Clizia, with one of the two lovers descending in the funicular after a hike to a mountain peak, perhaps to admire the alpine flowers of the Dolomites, the lovely Italian Alps (but also where the poet served in the First World War).

The notion of an abyss separating the lovers calls to mind "The Balcony," the first poem of *The Occasions,* but the empty space has now become vast. Also, as Galassi points out, the image of a flower in the mountain rocks is reminiscent of the Bécquer epigraph of the flower above the volcano.[68] The single flower in a bleak and rocky landscape is an important image in *Cuttlefish Bones,* but in "The Motets" the flower has evolved into a Dolce Stil Novo symbol of love.

One of the densest of the Motets, the seventeenth in the series, serves as an interlude. This is the first Motet that does not directly address Clizia (or someone else) in the I/You rhetorical formulation. Instead of dance-like train rhythms, screeching cranes, or cranking funicular gears, there is chamber music consisting of country sounds. Frogs make a kind of natural music emanating from the marsh. The poet creates a composition of haze, dimly lit under a weakening sun, melding together a vista of bulrushes and rustling carob trees. Montale uses the word *ronzìo* in the first Motet to describe annoying dock-side noise, and again in one of the later pseudo-sonnets in *The Storm and Other Things* to suggest droning warplanes. Here it is used to describe the Coleoptera, the largest beetle, sucking on flowers.

The rich sensual imagery of the countryside smells, sounds, and sights prepares us for the next poem, which moves to an interior scene. This Motet, "Non recidere, forbice, quel volto" ("Don't cut, scissors, that face"), begins with a snap-shot: the poet protagonist himself is holding a photograph and scissors (perhaps also connoting the "shears" of time), looking at Irma's/Clizia's face in the photograph. Remembering a face that once looked at him attentively, perhaps lovingly, he realizes that the photograph is helping him to hold on to his increasingly fragmented memory of her. Then there is a chill outside. Montale describes a slicing blow, remaining purposefully unclear whether this blow is the sound of an axe against the acacia tree echoing in the crisp fall air or the greatly amplified sound of the scissors cutting the face out of the photograph. Perhaps the poet does cut it out, but we do not know, for the camera eye of the narrator cuts to nature, to the acacia tree and the cicada's husk. It is late autumn, and the November *belletta* (a Dantesque word), the November mud, is upon the land.[69] This Motet should be compared to the nature descriptions of the seventeenth Motet and the late autumnal season of the great poem "News from Amiata." The transition of the seasons, especially from summer to fall, is of importance in a full contextual reading of the Clizia Cycle. Autumn is a time of memory and despair, of letters written and never sent, and of great loneliness. (Late spring and summer, however, are periods of drama and confrontation.) Whereas Clizia seems to be completely, if only momentarily, absent from the seventeenth Motet, the eighteenth is almost directly about the absent or present Clizia. Here the indoor agony exemplified in the scene of the poet with scissors and photograph resonates with the outdoor setting of impending winter. Here she haunts him. Unlike the fantastic images of Clizia's wings and frosted forehead in the twelfth Motet, the photograph that is so crucial to the eighteenth may actually have existed. In the late 1970s Montale wrote a series of poems about photographs of Irma, particularly at the Palio of 1938, and other extant photographs from the 1930s have been published.

In the last two Motets the poet is resigned to a memory of Clizia that is more remote, more distilled, from the initial passion of sorrow and loss. She is depicted from a great distance in "La Canna che dispiuma" ("The reed that molts"), which Montale mentions having sent to Irma in his letter of 20 November 1938. Once again displaying supernatural powers of light projection typical of Beatrice, Clizia's eyes shine beams of light that cross, connoting her quasi-Christian status in the poems to come. Montale explicitly stated to Silvio Guarnieri that the "cross is a symbol of suffering" in this poem and that this suffering is evoked elsewhere in his poetry by the symbol of Ezekiel's wheel (see chapter 6).[70]

This next-to-last Motet ends with the phrase "and time passes" (*e il tempo passa*), and the final one begins with "but so be it" (*ma così sia*). It should be made clear that *così sia* is also the Italian phrase for "amen." Outside, the sound of a cornet rings out, giving the poems one more musical touch, and the swarming birds answer from the oak trees.[71]

The poet is inside, by his desk, staring at various souvenirs among his papers. He notes a reflection in a shell and a gleaming coin in a chunk of lava. These are the last glimmerings of Clizia's shining light. In yet one more reversal of D'Annunzio's effusive style, small things capture vast spaces and energies. But the poet still feels sterilized by his loss, as Mirco (in Montale's later short story) does in Modena where all the gaiety of city life seems like flat images on a screen. Montale concludes with a note of dejection: *"la vita che sembrava / vasta è più breve del tuo fazzoletto"* (life, which once seemed / vast, is smaller than your handkerchief). This is the last of the ten Motets that Irma Brandeis published, but this time she used the translation by Maurice English.

The View from Bellosguardo Hill

Set apart from the rest of *The Occasions* in its own special section is a poem from 1939 with the title "Tempi di Bellosguardo" ("Bellosguardo Times").[72] *Bellosguardo* means, quite literally, "beautiful view." The Bellosguardo area is in the Oltrarno neighbourhood, across the river and southwest of Brunelleschi's Duomo and the heart of the city. The Bellosguardo hill is well named. A twenty-minute walk from Piazza Torquato Tasso, it offers a unique perspective of the city of Florence and a welcome respite from the city heat just a few minutes from the urban centre. It is also one of the residential districts near the city centre that has a great historical tradition. Ugo Foscolo (1778–1827) wrote "Le Grazie" in his perch on the hill. There are many villas on Bellosguardo, and a number of them were and are occupied by noted foreigners. The villas are known for their splendid terraced gardens. Nathaniel Hawthorne stayed in the Torre di Montauto, which was reconstructed in the nineteenth century. Florence Nightingale was born at the nearby Villa Colombaia. The Via di Bellosguardo, a narrow street, offers a steep but pleasant walk up the hill. Henry James completed *The Aspern Papers* at number twenty, the Villa Brichieri-Colombi. The Brownings were guests there when it was owned by Mrs Isa Blagden (1849–73). The via also gives a well-known view of the Villa dello Strozzino, a lovely Renaissance house.

The little cul-de-sac near the Villa Brichieri-Colombi, outside the Villa Limonaia, offers a panorama of sites that are key to Montale's poetic expression – the Arno River and its bridges, Brunelleschi's Duomo, the Palazzo Vecchio, and the other great monuments of the *centro*, and, in the opposite hills across the valley, Fiesole and Maiano. The view is

The Punta del Mesco, Monterosso al Mare, site of Eugenio Montale's childhood home. This setting appears in poems that Montale wrote throughout his life. Photograph by D.M. Hertz

The Caffè Giubbe Rosse was a gathering place for many of the great anti-Fascist writers in the 1930s, including Eugenio Montale. Photograph by D.M. Hertz

Irma Brandeis in the 1930s. Photograph courtesy of Jean Cook

View of Florence from the Belvedere fortress near Irma Brandeis's rented apartment at 54 Costa San Giorgio. Photograph by D.M. Hertz

Francis Criss's portrait of Irma Brandeis. Photograph courtesy of Jean Cook

Eugenio Montale in 1933. Photograph courtesy of Jean Cook

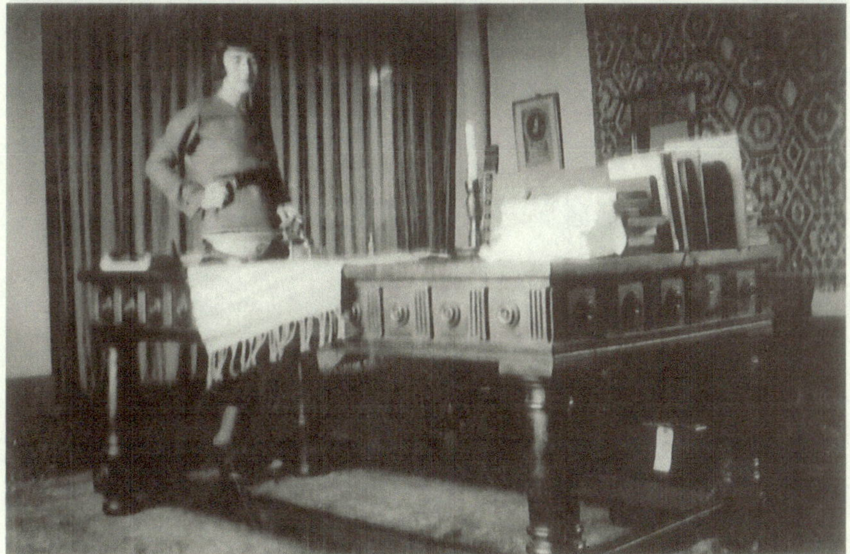

The studio apartment at 54 Costa San Giorgio, the setting of several key Montale poems, including "New Stanzas." The first photograph shows the apartment with the window open while the second has both Irma and the heavy curtain described in the poem. Photographs courtesy of Jean Cook

Images of Hitler and Mussolini in Florence should be read against Eugenio Montale's "Hitler Spring." © Banca Dati dell'Archivio Storico Foto Locchi Florence

Hitler and Mussolini near the Piazzale Michelangelo with Brunelleschi's great Dome in the background. © Banca Dati dell'Archivio Storico Foto Locchi Florence

Paolo Vivante, Elena de Bosis Vivante, Irma Brandeis, Leone Vivante, Camillo Sbarbaro, and Eugenio Montale after the Palio of August 1938. Photograph courtesy of Jean Cook

Irma Brandeis at Sarah Lawrence College in the 1940s. Photograph by Westchester Photo Service, courtesy of the Sarah Lawrence College Archives

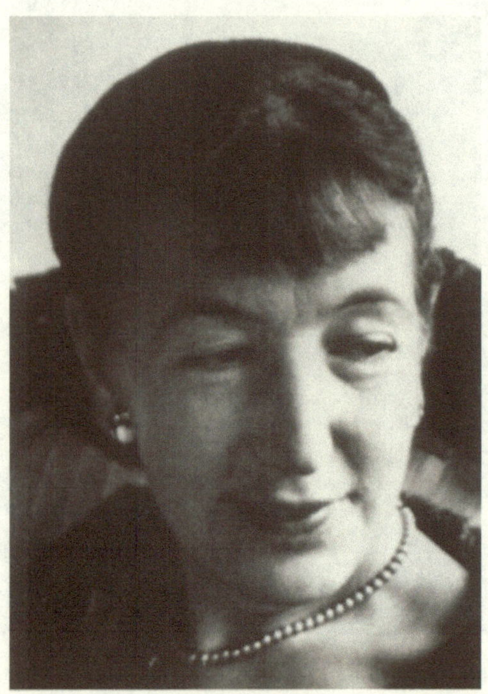

Irma Brandeis during her Bard College period. Photograph courtesy of Jean Cook

The aging poet Eugenio Montale. Photograph courtesy of the Newberry Library

View of the Pensione Annalena from the garden area below. Photograph by D.M. Hertz

The Pensione Annalena veranda and its adjacent garden are key settings in many late Montale poems about Clizia. Photograph by D.M. Hertz

Irma Brandeis at the Pensione Annalena in the 1930s. Photograph courtesy of Jean Cook

even more spectacular from the Torre di Bellosguardo, a former castle that is now a luxury hotel, which was once inhabited by Dante's friend Guido Cavalcanti. Near the hotel is the gated Villa Ombrellino, the former home of Mrs George Keppel, a close friend of the English king Edward VIII. In the 1920s and 1930s Mrs Keppel entertained many famous guests with her warm hospitality and fabulous views.[73] All of Florentine civilization, from the Etruscans to the modern age, stretches out before one's eyes from the Bellosguardo hill.

It is easy to imagine the many famous people who have strolled there over the centuries. Two of the most important were surely Irma Brandeis and Eugenio Montale.[74] This we can presume from Montale's great poem about Bellosguardo. The protagonist of the poem, the "I," speaks from the hill as he gazes over Florence. He has been wandering there, remembering an earlier visit with Clizia/Irma, perhaps the year before, meditating on the force of love and the threat of war as they affect his civilization. While he views the cultivated terraced gardens, he hears the soft sounds of civilized Florentine life echoing gently around him.

This is one of the most deeply sensual poems in all of Montale, and it is pivotal in his development of the senhal of Clizia. It is an unusual locus of sexual energy in the Clizia poems, for Clizia is almost always a figure of spiritual inspiration, half goddess, half human. In "Bellosguardo Times" the lovers embody the symbolization of eroticism and life. The amassing forces of death, the polar opposite, are the gathering Fascists and Nazis, who will erupt in the storm to come. Together the two opposites function very much like Eros, the life instinct, and Thanatos, the death instinct, in Freud's contemporaneous classic *Civilization and Its Discontents,* which was written in 1930.

There is a larger context as well and another theme as important as the first. The beautiful city of Florence here represents the threatened civilization that Montale contemplates so beautifully in "Boats along the Marne," a companion piece to this poem, also published in *The Occasions.* While "Boats along the Marne" has a pastoral French context, the lover-speaker in "Bellosguardo Times" takes in the beauty of Florence from the Bellosguardo hill, witnessing the calm before the storm. The time of its writing would have been only several months after Irma's departure and the announcement of the new racial laws. During this period Montale was describing the deteriorating situation in Europe in his letters to her. The Second World War was about to begin.

The poem is in sections that are so distinct in theme and tone that they are arranged very much like three movements in a musical composition. The first section uses the hendecasyllable, the classical Italian line. Accordingly, the twenty-three irregular hendecasyllabic lines are written in the most subdued classical tone of the three parts. It is fitting for the stanza that muses over the civilization at risk. It features an arresting juxtaposition of human life and landscape detail. The blending of seemingly unrelated but meticulously observed phenomena is something that Montale does very well. Here there is a fluid combination of the hum of evening lessons and rustling trees, a blending of orders of columns and cultivated willows, shouts emanating from hanging gardens, long laughter flowing over Florentine roofs. Trees and conversations meld, columns and plants blend, laughter and conversational hubbub buzzes over natural and man-made objects. The detailed signs of human life in combination with the foregrounded presence of cultivated nature in the city are evident throughout the poem. Observing the flickering lights below, the poet remarks that it is "*troppo triste*" (too sad) that such peacefulness is only ephemeral, as fleeting as the intermittent points of illumination that punctuate the larger darkness. A final "tail of light that crosses the heavens," perhaps serving as a marker of Clizia's presence there, closes the stanza.

In the second section the poet moves to shorter, choppier phrases, a line length of between seven and nine syllables. The change in rhythm and pattern is good for establishing his new subject. We see the magnolia, a primal symbol of the childhood garden in Monterosso, but there is a disturbance, a rising wind provoking "agitated chords." Next we encounter "fevered limbs" (*le membra di febbre*) that seem to be in furious motion, repeating in "a tight circle" (*al moto che si ripete in circolo breve*), as the abandoned cultivated beauty of Bellosguardo "gets lost / in the prism of a minute" (*si smarriscono / nel prisma del minuto*).[75]

Since 2006 scholars have had access to Montale's letters to Irma, which document the sexual aspects of their initial relationship. In them we read again and again of the poet's celebration of his beloved's knees, lips, hands, bangs, earrings, et cetera. In this poem we find piquant images of limbs, pulsation, sweat, and death. They describe a desperate act of lovemaking, which ends in orgasm, the death of the energy of the moment of love, "sweat that pulsates, death sweat" (*sudore che pulsa, sudore di morte*). Since Montale translated John Donne with Irma in the mid-1930s, he knew well the Baroque conceit of lovemaking: each consummated act ends in a little death. There is a desperate embrace.

Then it is over. The poet asserts that it is better to "die with knowledge" (*si muore sapendo*) than to choose life "that changes unaware" (*la vita che muta ed ignora*). Then the poet perceives the road descending down from the hill, passing loggias and herms, and he leaves with the lover.

But Montale is constructing a poetics of memory as the perhaps imaginary conjuring of the erotic shrinks away into the past. He speaks of an eternal passion. With each passing step down the hill as the moment of earthly passion recedes in time, Irma's love has already begun to transform into Clizia's unchanging love. It is this *"fedeltà che non muta"* (unchanging fidelity), as Montale writes here, that becomes the central symbol of divine light in the later "Hitler Spring," which is the apex of the great poems in the last of Montale's three books, *The Storm and Other Things*. By the close of the stanza there is a tension between the "passion of always" (*passione di sempre*), preserved in memory, and the passion in "blood and brain" (*un sangue e un cervello*). Eros on Bellosguardo, achieved under the shadow of looming Thanatos, will never be forgotten. In the first moment that the poet is alone, poetry, the act of reconstructing memory in art, begins.

The third and last section of the poem speaks of the *bufera* (storm). It is Montale's symbol for the coming war; the word will later become the famous title of his third book of poems. The storm follows the tranquility and beauty of the earlier scenes of Bellosguardo, and the erotic dream vision. Now the destructive power of the storm arrives: *"Il rumore degli émbrici distrutti / dalla bufera / nell'aria dilatata che non s'incrina"* (The racket of the roof tiles destroyed by / the storm / in the dilated air that doesn't fracture).[76] A shivering Canada poplar withstands the brunt of the storm. The poplar is probably a symbol of Clizia, since Montale elsewhere uses Canadian references to refer to her North American background (see, for example, "Iris"). The motion of descent is carried over from the last stanza, as we sense that the poet-speaker is still walking down from Bellosguardo. Human life and human works are still connected with unusual directness, as they were in the first section of the poem. Here there is a connection between human life and the marble of each step down the hill: *"il segno di una vita che assecondi il marmo a ogni scalino"* (the sign of a life that harmonizes with the marble of every little step). The I, now alone, is still high up and makes out the ivy that "shrinks from the solitary thrust of the bridges" over the Arno in the distance. Montale specialists often list ivy as a Clizia symbol, perhaps because it is often linked with notions of "everlasting life" and "fidelity" in Christian theology, and it turns up in two later poems that feature her ("Fiesole Window " and "Ezekial Saw the Wheel").[77]

The poet sees the mark of human cultivation – works, gardens, bridges over the waters – and the faces that go with them ("*opere misure e volti umani, piante umane*"). He wonders whether all of this will be obliterated. Once again, a sound comes over the gardens, here echoing over terracotta tiles. The morning glories are so fecund, they pull at their stakes. Will the hard work of civilization, the heavenly weavers of culture (*dura opera, tessitrici celesti*), come to nothing? Joseph Cary thinks the locusts that threaten these details of the garden, woven on the loom of men, are symbols for the black-shirted Fascists.[78] If so, they threaten the gentle gardens of the Bellosguardo hill. The poet judged the world situation correctly at the time of his writing. Florence was in great danger, and Montale's sense of the coming destruction proved to be accurate. The Germans, fearing the inevitable Allied advance on the city, would eventually use land mines in 1944 to decimate the very scene that the poet was contemplating at the end of the 1930s.[79]

In summation, the three sections of the poem each have a distinct purpose. Part 1 is the stanza of meditation on the threatened civilization. Part 2 is the stanza of passion, ending in the transfiguration of an erotic encounter into an unchanging memory of love. Part 3 talks of the bufera and the coming war. This is an important poem in the evolution of Irma into Clizia, for here Irma seems more flesh-and-blood woman, and the coming disaster of the war is related to a more immediate recollection of Irma in the recent past. If we move outside the realm of poetry and into speculation about Montale's actual life, we can guess that the gestation of the poem took place only a few months after Irma and Eugenio had seen each other, because Irma left for the United States for the last time before the war in the late summer of 1938. In December 1939, still some months before Italy entered the war, Montale sent his final letter to her. In later poems, as the poet sits his "vigil," Irma's symbolic incarnation takes on a sharper focus. Clizia will become a sunflower goddess with wings, bejewelled with dazzling raiment, a source of spiritual succour, a radiance of light against the night. In this poem, however, while she is unnamed and her identity remains hidden and protected, she is a woman.

The Distillation of Love

The last portion of *The Occasions* (Part IV) contains one of the strongest series of Montale poems and some of the greatest works in the

Clizia Cycle. It begins with an important epigraph taken from the fifth Shakespeare sonnet: "Sap check'd with frost, and lusty leaves quite gone, / Beauty o'ersnow'd and bareness every where ..." It is easy to guess why Montale would have chosen that epigraph. It prefigures the great despair captured in the poetry that it introduces. *The Occasions* ends with the melancholy desperation of the poet and the exile of the beloved, in "News from Amiata." Therefore, the epigraph of Shakespearean despair, signifying the barren winter, is certainly an apt choice for the culminating section of the book.

The last two lines (the couplet) of the famous sonnet tell us more: "But flowers distilled, though they with winter meet, / Leese but their show; their substance still lives sweet." Shakespeare's idea of distilling beauty and keeping it preserved safely in a time of winter is highly appropriate because Montale is remembering Irma just before the war. He is in a winter of the mind, or worse (he became suicidal for a brief period of time in 1938), and he has to keep his memory of her alive, if for no other reason than merely to preserve his sanity. We already have seen the beginning of this process as the erotic lovemaking in the second section of "Bellosguardo Times" transforms into "the unchanging fidelity" (*la fedeltà che non muta*), the unwavering love of Clizia. What has transpired in the flesh is distilled and preserved in the mind. As Helen Vendler has observed, the main point of the final Shakespearean couplet is that "show cannot be preserved but substance can." I also would note the "distilled / still lives" pun that she points out as "mimetic."[80] In the manner of this Shakespearean trope, Irma, whose physical presence has gone, will now be distilled into Clizia, preserved as a "liquid prisoner pent" in the forms of Montale's words. The idea becomes a new essence, a symbol that will enable the poet to say many things in the difficult years ahead and to articulate his thoughts with great power.

Part IV begins with a suggestive set of images, often described by Montale as a *pedale* or a *chiave,* connecting a group of poems that return to the Monterosso world that was so crucial to *Cuttlefish Bones* and which recurs throughout Montale. "La casa dei doganieri" ("The Toll-House," 1930), a well-known Montale poem, concerns a small house in the rocks near the family villa. It no longer exists. A number of commentators have seen the toll-house or customs house as a symbol of civilization at risk.[81] Since Irma Brandeis cites it in her 1936 article about Montale and includes her own translation of the poem in the *Quarterly Review,* it is part of the complete picture of her literary interactions with the poet. However, it is also part of the smaller and earlier Arletta cycle, which generates the rhetorical shape of many of the Montale poems. Brandeis translated "Bassa marea" ("Low Tide"), another Arlettian poem, in 1936. "Stanzas," which was written in the late 1920s, features a woman or goddess who prefigures many of the features of Clizia, but its early date of composition points once again to Anna degli Uberti.

"Punta del Mesco" ("Mesco Point," 1933), which Montale mailed to Brandeis in late 1933 or early 1934, clearly concerns the most prominent point in the Cinque Terre in general and in Monterosso in particular. Just northwest of Monterosso, and visible everywhere in the town, the Punta del Mesco juts out far into the sea, blocking off the Cinque Terre from Levanto and other points north. It can seem either ominous or lovely, depending on the weather. Its importance for Montale is exemplified by its prominence in his touching pencil drawing of the Cinque Terre, which can be found in the Gabinetto Vieusseux archives. The Montale house is situated just where the Punta del Mesco joins the mainland, couched at the base of the slopes, and with steep inclines on three sides. The sea is directly ahead. The poem captures the infernal smoke rising from the stone quarries that were extant there in Montale's youth. Arletta's trace is gently inscribed here. Just a footstep or a remembered gesture is enough to spark a meditation and a poetic act in Montale.

Brandeis chose to translate "La casa dei doganieri" as "The Toll-House." She included a full stanza in her 1936 *Saturday Review* article. The poem later intrigued her enough to cause her to revise her work and complete a full translation.[82] Like "House by the Sea," this poem concerns the very particular spot in Monterosso near the family home. The old toll-house was just above the family villa, high on the rocks in the direction of the Punta del Mesco: "You have forgotten the tollkeeper's house / on the height where the rock sheers, on the ledges."[83] And just like "House by the Sea," "The Toll-House" addresses an unnamed woman who prefigures Clizia. The poet describes a tanker with lights blinking beyond the Punta del Mesco and far off on the horizon. He again seeks a *varco,* his escape, and wonders whether it is to be found in the receding tanker. The unnamed female listener (here Arletta) is more qualified than is the poet for the desperately sought way out, as she was in the earlier *Cuttlefish Bones.*

The poems of *The Occasions* abruptly turn from the Monterosso seaside to the riverbanks of Florence. "Costa San Giorgio" (1933, revised in 1938) takes its title from a famous street that rises above the Arno at a steep incline. Irma Brandeis often rented an apartment at 54 Costa San Giorgio when she visited Florence.[84] The street is also near the Pensione Annalena on the Via Romana, where Irma stayed in the 1930s. There are a number of important later poems, written in the 1970s, that describe Irma and Eugenio at the pensione (see chapter 8). The proximity of the Annalena and the Costa San Giorgio makes this narrow, winding, and sometimes elegant street an important link between this poem and the late poems of the 1970s, some of which refer repeatedly to the Pensione Annalena.

Montale helped to place the poem "Costa San Giorgio" in its proper context when he described it in terms of "a pair walking on the well-known Florentine ramp, and a bit higher at one point ... it could in fact be called 'the Walk.'"[85] Brandeis writes about the importance of the street as a favoured setting for a walk as well, explaining to Gino Bigongiari that "the poem's name is the name of *my* street in Florence; it was written after an evening's long walk up the hill and thru the gates – E.M. and I."[86] In his letters to Irma, beginning in September 1933, Montale repeatedly refers to "Costa San Giorgio," often wondering whether she has read the poem or trying to explain its difficulties to her. In a letter to Gianfranco Contini dated 2 December 1935 Montale refers to the poem as a *carme* (Latin for "song" or "lyric"), explicitly describing it as a "despairing" love song.

The first five lines of the poem give us our best look at the Costa San Giorgio. It is unclear from these words whether the poet is walking with his lover or alone. In the poem, Montale describes a man lighting the streetlights along the Costa San Giorgio at dusk, while a will-o'-the-wisp (*un fuoco fatuo*) covers the street with dust (*impolvera la strada*).[87] The darkness recedes along the sharply sloping street as the man, riding a bicycle and carrying a ladder on his shoulder, moves from lamp post to lamp post, and after he has done his work at each stop, a light comes on, each one illuminating the night a bit more.

The poem has the Montalean feature of the minute detail enlarged meticulously against a background. This always creates an unusual or startling contrast, which at first seems difficult but eventually, after rereading and study, proves vividly descriptive. Here softly shining street lamps, lit one by one in the evening mist, reminiscent of the glow of the will-o'-the-wisp, cast drops of light on the slanted, twisting street.[88] There are other subtle contrasts between light and dark as the natural light of day ebbs and city street lights come on at dusk. Only an insect's glow and a veil over the moon are left for the lovers.

In the same December 1935 letter to Contini, Montale refers to the religious despair in the poem.[89] It is possible that the "Idol" he described in it is Christ: "Now the Idol is here, barred from us" (*Ora l'Idolo è qui, sbarrato*). The darkness obscures the fixed look of the Idol, which, the poet specifically says, "is on the Cross" (*l'Idolo è in croce*). It is worn down, almost lifeless, even without voice.[90] The religious references may have been prompted by the proximity of the Church of Santi Girolamo e Francesco alla Costa (1432), which is located across the street from 54 Costa San Giorgio. "Costa San Giorgio" is a first glimpse of the religious scepticism that is evident in "News from Amiata" at the close of *The Occasions* and in "Iris" in *The Storm and Other Things*, but its bitter pessimism also echoes the much earlier and very self-reflective poem, "Arsenio."[91]

Writing directly to Brandeis in September 1935, Montale made explicit his intent to suggest a Hispanic layering of meaning in the poem, saying that the *Idolo d'oro* (Golden Idol) in the poem is associated with the "conquistadores," referring to the "land of gold, fabulous," and the fable of El Dorado. It is one of the forms in his poetry that are "eternal mirages, softened, Christianized."[92] He also tells her clearly that there is a purposeful reference to Cervantes: "Maritornes is the servant who cures Don Quixote's bed-sores, and in this case a simple consoler of afflictions." The reference to Don Quixote, a character with whom Montale had a special fascination (equalled only by his fondness for Don Juan/Giovanni), appears at the end of the third stanza: "There is no respite, no value: Maritornes / no longer takes down her lamp / from the stable architrave." At the close of the poem Montale seems both horrified by the destructive nature of time and somewhat unsettled by the declivitous street winding downward towards the Via Romana, where the enemy Fascists and Nazis pass. The speaker of the poem refers to the narrow but storied street as having an "idiotic slope" (*stupida discesa*), and, much more ominously, he describes the pressure of a "silent foe / that crushes" (*il torchio del nemico muto / che preme*) lurking at the bottom of the street.[93]

Montale told Luciano Rebay that this poem was written for the Peruvian Italian Paola Nicoli,[94] but the references to Maritornes may be a symbol for Irma. The fragmentary nature of the poem and the fact that he had difficulty completing it make me think that he may have begun by writing for Paola and finished when he began thinking about Irma as Clizia, blending the initial inspiration with the more resounding implications of Clizia in his poetic meditations, in a manner similar to the evolution of the "Motets." However, I do not read this as one of the great Clizia poems. Instead, what is important is the site, the topos of the Costa San Giorgio, where he shared intense personal experience with Irma Brandeis and which is the point of departure for one of his pessimistic meditations.

Shortly after meeting Irma in July 1933 Montale took an August holiday in England at Eastbourne, Sussex, after stop-overs in Paris and London. One result of that trip was the poem "Eastbourne" (1933, revised in 1935). It is easy to spot Eastbourne's white cliffs in the poem. The revolving door of a hotel, with moving panes revolving on a pivot, reflects gleaming light in the moving glass surfaces, provoking thoughts of a gyre of turning circles. The tide rolling in is equated with the poet's passing life. Revolving glass doors, reflecting light, moving water – all evoke the inexorable flux of time for the poet. There are ominous images here also that go beyond the traditional poet's lament on the destructive forces of time. Here, while the poet is on holiday by the sea-shore, he sees a disturbing image of ex-soldiers, presumably from the First World War, mutilated (*i mutilati*), perhaps missing arms or legs, passing in wheel-chairs. All across Europe in the 1920s and 1930s it was common to see many thousands of maimed veterans. One war had passed, but others were coming.

As the Fascists were turning steadily towards colonial war and an increasing brutalization of Italian society in the mid-1930s, to Montale evil must have seemed to be winning, and evil had the upper hand in "Eastbourne": "*vince il male ... La ruota non s'arresta*" (evil is winning ... The wheel won't stop). We should compare this evil to the notions of evil in "Hitler Spring" and elsewhere, including later themes in Montale's pseudo-sonnets, and other poems that divide the universe into opposing forces of good and evil. The wheel is one of many images of the circle that turn up in Montale. Only a light in the darkness answers with a ray of hope: "*Anche tu lo sapevi, luce-in-tenebra*" (You knew it too, light-in-shadows). The "you" is an early instance of Clizia as a light goddess, and the "I" remembers Clizia while sitting by the shore, as if he were looking off into the horizon where she had disappeared as she sailed back to the United States. The poet is in England, a country that speaks her language, Irma's language. As he listens to the sounds around him, strains of "God Save the Queen" transform into "My Country 'Tis of Thee," but he sees nothing left of her on the burning shore where she has disappeared, and he finds bitterness in his English type of vacation, which he refers to repeatedly with the English phrase

Bank Holiday.[95] The recurrent use of *Bank Holiday* and the Eliotic tone ("The low, slow tide of my life is shambling in") recall "The Love Song of J. Alfred Prufrock" and its author, who worked in a bank.

"Corrispondenze" ("Correspondences," 1936) steals its title from one of Baudelaire's most important and famous poems, a poem in *Les Fleurs du mal* that Montale would have known by heart. Following "Il balcone," it is the second recycled Baudelaire title in *The Occasions*. The Montalean correspondence seems to lie between mythic and modern, with references to Orpheus, whom Rilke had recently made famous in his sonnets. Images of mid-century industrialism disrupt the Baudelairean context, creating a new and disturbing pattern of reference. Bursting lights and booming noises contrast with the interplay of the senses in the French poem. Vapours vacillate and disperse, leaving a glimpse of a train moving through the Ligurian coastal mountains. William Arrowsmith detects Clizia in the poem, perhaps as the "shepherdess without flocks," gazing at "flights diverging over the pass," while Contini has noted the French source material.[96]

Another poem with a French context is the far more complex "Barche sulla Marna" ("Boats along the Marne," 1933, revised in 1937). Here the reference is not to a French poet but to a lush French setting. It is one of the few Montale poems that create an abstract world of pure pleasure. Why the Marne? Why a French setting? Italian to his core, Montale here reverts to France, very much like Wallace Stevens does, to create an abstract sense of *plaisir*. In the first half of the twentieth century France was perhaps the foremost international symbol of cultivation and civilized pleasure. This poem is very important from the point of view of the world that had been destroyed by the war. Although France had been ravaged by the First World War, it was a site of pleasure and culture for Montale, who was very familiar with all facets of French civilization, including its music, poetry, and art. Most of all, the Marne, which meets the Seine just above Alfortville and runs generally eastward towards Germany, had been the scene of some of the most vicious fighting during the First World War. Since Montale was a veteran of that war, the Marne setting, now peaceful in the context of the poem, was obviously carefully chosen.

The beloved Florence of "Bellosguardo Times" and this halcyon European scene are part of the doomed Europe. For this reason Arrowsmith suggests we read "Boats along the Marne" with "Bellosguardo Times." "Boats along the Marne" offers exquisite moments of beauty and bliss in the world that will soon be destroyed.

In this poem unnamed lovers row gently down the river on a Sunday outing before they are ripped apart by their destinies. For Montale, the European vision of civilization branches out from Florence to France.[97] As the poet understands, the onset of passion and war will once more destroy this world of pastoral civility and meditative bliss.

In March 1939 Montale visited one of his close friends from the Caffè Giubbe Rosse, the novelist Tommaso Landolfi, at the Landolfi family estate in the tiny village of Pico Farnese. Pico Farnese is southwest of Rome, in Frosinone, the southern region of Lazio. The resulting poem, "Elegia di Pico Farnese" ("The Pico Farnese Elegy," 1939), is one of the most closed off of the great Montale poems. Dante Isella has found allusions interrelating the poem and Landolfi's novel *The Moonstone* (1939), which Montale was reading in page proof at the time.[98] This may account for some of the difficulty. However, there are important indications of the intense distillation process of Irma into Clizia in the "Elegia di Pico Farnese." Here we have an early glimpse of Clizia, the bird goddess who serves as a winged messenger. In the poem, "Love" (*Amore*) is flashing signals of anxiety from the wingtips (*frangia d'ali*) of the "frowning messenger" (*messaggera accigliata*). This avian messenger has a perfect plumage on her feathered brow, and the power to press persimmons until they are bled dry (giving the goddess rather human hands with great digital strength). Most important in terms of Montale's overall expression of her in his cycle, the messenger is already able to "keep vigil / over the few passing through the hordes of goat-men" (*e vegli / al trapasso dei pochi tra orde d'uomini-capre*).[99]

We have had another preview of the winged Clizia in the twelfth Motet, where she seems to have been wounded and partially frozen in the course of her efforts to aid the beloved. In the "Elegia di Pico Farnese" Clizia flies in sorrowful defiance against the Fascist hordes, who appear here for the first time in Montale's poetry. Montale may have borrowed the "horde" image from Eliot, who in "The Waste Land" (1922) writes, "Who are those hooded hordes swarming / Over endless plains ..." However, it is Montale, not Eliot, who specifically connects *his* hordes and swarms to the Fascists and Nazis of the 1930s. Also appearing for the first time is the notion of "standing vigil" as a witness against the activities of the hordes. Similar oppositions between the keeper of the vigil and the hordes are to be found in "New Stanzas," "News from Amiata," the three pseudo-sonnets, and "Hitler Spring."

"The Pico Farnese Elegy" also includes the first intimations of Clizia's derivation from the Ovidian Clytie, a derivation that will explain her later transformation into a goddess of sun and light. Clizia speaks "*parole / che il seme del girasole / se brilla disperde*" (words / that the seeds of the sunflower / would disperse should it shine). But the full implications of Clizia, the sunflower goddess who turns towards the sun, emerge only in *The Storm and Other Things.* The "Pico" elegy ends with an ominous image of a boy reloading guns. It is a symbol of the coming war.

Confrontation in Florence

"Nuove stanze" ("New Stanzas," 1939) is one of the key Clizia poems. Montale's statements in his criticism and letters clarify the importance that this poem held for him. Montale refers to "the sphinx of 'nuove stanze' who had left the east to illuminate the ice and mists of the north."[100] Her apotheosis, or transformation, is much more obvious in "Iris," as he himself points out, and there is an indication of it in "The Pico Farnese Elegy." But here Clizia is still very much a woman like Irma:

> After the last bits of tobacco
> have been snuffed out on the
> crystal plate with your gesture,
> the spiral of smoke slowly
> ascends to the ceiling,
> the bishops and knights on the chessboard
> watch in astonishment: and new rings
> follow the first, more alive than those
> on your finger.
>
> The fata Morgana that liberated towers
> and bridges in the sky has disappeared
> with the first breath of air; a window opens
> unseen, and the smoke starts up. There, below,
> another swarm stirs: a demonic horde
> of men who do not know your incense,
> on the chessboard of which only you
> can make any sense.
>
> My concern at one time was whether perhaps
> you also ignored the game that was developing

on the squares, and now a squall is at your door:
a madness of death not placated by a small
pay-off. If the lightning flash of your glance is worth little,
it demands other fires, beyond the thick
curtains that for you the god of
chance stirs up, when he helps.

Today I know you want this; the Martinella strikes
its sombre knell and frightens
the ivory profiles in a spectral
light of snow. But resisting and
winning first place in this solitary
vigil is he who can, with you, oppose the burning glass
that counters the pawns
with your eyes of steel.[101]

These "New Stanzas" are unusually significant because they are surprisingly direct and give us one of our clearest views of the original context that generated many of the Clizia poems, a view of Irma Brandeis and Eugenio Montale in Fascist Florence during the late 1930s. Once the context of Montale's concerns has been established, these lines are clear and easy to understand. In addition, some of Montale's particular qualities are evident, and so the poem enables us to know him more fully.

Montale wrote two important letters about this poem, one to Gianfranco Contini on 15 May 1939 (we know for a fact that he wrote only three more letters to Irma before the war) and the other to Silvio Guarnieri on 22 May 1964. First, in the 1939 letter to Contini, Montale compares "New Stanzas" to an earlier poem with a similar title: "I've followed up on my older 'Stanzas' ... These, which might be entitled 'Love, Chess, and Wartime Vigil,' ... are a little different. They're more Florentine, more inlaid, harder; ... The 'Martinella,' as you know, is the bell in the Palazzo Vecchio; sounding only, according to Palazzeschi, to indicate 'shame.'"[102] Here we can see that cultural background is important to Montale. Architectural detail evoked by symbol, both interiors and exteriors, a church bell – these are some of the isolates for his imagery. Montale makes an obvious analogy between the chessboard and the somewhat severe but intricate geometric patterns commonly used on facades and other surfaces in Renaissance Florentine architecture.

The 1964 letter to Guarnieri, written many years after the poem itself was written, is extremely helpful because it gives us a rare look at Montale as he comments specifically on one of his own poems: "'New Stanzas.' 'Another swam,' the war is about to erupt. The last days in Florence for Clizia. 'At your door.' Generic enough. But she was Jewish. 'The thick curtains' hang so that as chance would have it you do not see the worst. 'The burning glass,' the war, evil etc.[103]

The first thing to note is that in this letter, Montale very clearly refers to Irma as Clizia. The two have melded in his imagination at this point in the cycle. Next, Montale's understanding of Irma's Jewishness is part of his conception of the poem. The chance hanging of the curtain, stirred up by a breeze, is highly reminiscent of Mallarmé; the horror that the curtain hides is not. The Frenchman was one of the first great modern philosophical poets who used concepts of *hazard* (chance) to express abstract thoughts on the purposelessness of existence and to use that idea to create formal randomness and an aleatoric experiment in verbal-visual composition. For Montale, writing in 1964 about a poem created in 1939, there is a very different and very powerful purpose to the poetry. A powerful immediacy that comes from the context is as vivid for him as it was when he originally wrote it. The god of chance blows a breeze to stir the curtains to hide the swarming hordes from the beloved.

In the first stanza of the poem Irma's/Clizia's presence is more palpable than in any of the other Montale poems. We see Irma/Clizia making the small gestures that are remembered by a loving observer. The poet is talking to her. She puts out her cigarette with style in a crystal ash-tray. "*Lenta sale / la spirale del fumo*" (Smoke rises slowly to the ceiling). Next the poet's lens or camera eye zooms in on the chessboard to see the knights and bishops, turned towards the smoke by chance, perhaps, and so they seem to stare at the new rings of smoke that follow, compared to the rings on Irma's finger.

We feel *there.* It is summertime in Fascist Florence just before the war. Clizia, as imagined in the poem, has just come to Florence for the last time.[104] The Fascists have just adopted the racist policies of the Nazis. War now seems unavoidable, and the storm is gathering. Mallarmé wanted to purge the real events of everyday life from his poetry, leaving it pure. In contrast, Montale said that he always started with reality. The two poets used the same techniques, with different intentions and results. Here the cigarette smoke and the stubble in the ash-tray bring back the beloved, and yet they are elusive trifles from remembered experience, airy nothings upon which the whole logic of the poem rests. These are details that might occur to a great novelist, and judging from the close connection between the poem and an extant photograph of Irma Brandeis's apartment, the poem probably comes from an intensely lived moment in Montale's life, one he could never forget.

The poem begins with a meditation on spiralling smoke rings rising above a chessboard. Mallarmé might have begun a poem with similar images, but he would not have wanted to work it out with such clear thematic power and specific historical urgency. Both poets had an extraordinary ability to capture the meticulously observed detail, and a philosophical richness of thought for the possible implications that can come from such meticulous observation. The first stanza ends with an intriguing comparison between the rising smoke rings from the cigarette and the rings around the fingers of the beloved. Since the smoke rings are in movement, they are even more alive than is the inert jewellery.

As we try to unlock the secrets of the second stanza, we should remember that Montale was a gifted amateur painter. The fata Morgana (a type of mirage) in the smoke seems to set towers and bridges floating in the sky. It projects an image, a city that appears to float in a cloud. The image could be from Giorgio de Chirico, Marc Chagall, or one of Montale's favourite Italian painters, Filippo de Pisis or Giorgio Morandi. A cunning lover of words, Montale was probably aware of the Italian nuances of the fata Morgana. It is a mirage seen in the Strait of Messina, which separates Italy from Sicily, and in mythology it is created by the sorceress Morgan Le Fay. Her name gives the phrase its etymology. The fata Morgana and smoke dissipate, but the smoke starts up again when a window, unseen, opens. Only very recently two photographs of Irma Brandeis's apartment at 54 Costa San Giorgio have turned up.[105] Taken in the 1930s, one shows a window open to the exterior, with air and light flowing in. It is likely that the window in the poem was specifically modelled on this window, or on a similar one at the Pensione Annalena. The other shows Irma standing near her desk with thick curtains behind her.

Outside, below the open window, there is a gathering horde or swarm, visible as the cigarette smoke clears. Down there, outside the window and below, *in fondo,* this swarm is moving. (In the full cycle, *stormo, tregenda, orde,* connoting the diabolical hordes, also go with various words for storm, such as *nembo* and *bufera* to signify the Nazis or

Fascists.) In his remarks Montale clearly indicates that *stormo* is a war image. Here the warring pieces on the chessboard are compared to the hordes of Fascists on the outside in the *piazze* and *quadrati*. There is a hellish horde gathering with ever greater force. We first see mention of the horde in "The Pico Farnese Elegy." The Italian phrase for the horde used in "New Stanzas," "*tregenda d'uomini*" (a demonic horde of men), turns up again in "Hitler Spring," one of the climactic poems of the Clizia Cycle. It is one of the most important phrases in all of Montale. Its repetition indicates its importance. These Fascists, monsters for Montale, cannot understand the magical fragrance of the beloved, who is Jewish. If there is a meaning on the chessboard, it can be unravelled only by the beloved. The difficult language posing the notion that only the human perception of the beloved can organize the external meaning strikes me as a Mallarméan construction again, but with a difference.

In the third stanza the chess game motif transforms into another form of *il giuoco* (the game),[106] but this game is played outside in the public squares, which are compared to the squares of the chessboard. The rectilinear shapes of Florentine urban architecture blend with the squares of the chessboard. Now a storm (*nembo*) of Fascists, the "demonic horde of men" (*tregenda d'uomini*) introduced in the second stanza, are at the beloved's door. The storm is also connected to the "*follia di morte*" (a madness or frenzy of death), and the demonic horde (now caught up in its death frenzy) seems unimpressed by the brilliant lightning power in the defiant stare of the beloved, whom the poet is still addressing directly. Against the image of mad death the lightning of Clizia's fiery look is a powerful moral, erotic, human force that makes the human storm of evil outside evident to the speaker or poet.

The third stanza takes place in the past. The fourth takes place at a later date – the present, the "today" of the speaking of the poem. In the beginning Montale was there with Irma in a room in Florence. In the third stanza he remembers his thoughts about her in relation to the Fascists. In the last stanza he is thinking about it all again. Now he knows what she would want. Outside, the Martinella is ringing. It is the bell of the Palazzo Vecchio in the heart of Florence.[107] Montale says it rings only to signify "disgrace." Inside, the pawns turn up again, continuing the chess game. It is the time of the solitary vigil (*la solitaria veglia*). For Montale as the solitary watcher, sitting vigil in the presence of evil, this phrase turns up in many different guises in the Clizia poetry. Outside and inside are intentionally blurred, as are past and present. The poet takes us back to the chess game. They (the pawns, the lovers?)

are blinded by something burning. Clizia has eyes of great moral power and strength. Montale will oppose the death frenzy of Fascism with the beloved's eyes of steel (*occhi d'acciaio*). In the end, the beloved's beautiful eyes represent something more powerful, more truthful, and the poet must keep his faith and his vigil in this desperate time of destruction and death.[108]

There is a basic opposition here that is essential to understanding all of Montale's poetry. On the one hand, we find the images of teeming armies and pandemonium: swarm, squall, horde (*stormo, nembo, tregenda*). On the other, the images of the poet and the lover are set in clear defiance: the solitary vigil, the eyes of steel, the light (*la solitaria veglia, occhi d'acciaio, lampo*). Another pattern of opposition is created by the contrast of outside (*esterno*) and inside (*interno*). This opposition also turns up in other key places in the poetry (for example, "Café at Rapallo," and the late poem "Inside/Outside"). The crowd outside threatens the lovers' duet inside. The demonic swarm of men (*tregenda d'uomini*) is on the move. Montale describes the crowds in his very private poetry to Clizia. They are outside, increasingly threatening, increasingly massive in number. The lovers are inside, increasingly removed, recreated by intricate details. And the speaker is recalling both at a later point, the point of narration, or the point in time at which the narration takes place.[109]

Like Mallarmé, Montale moves by metonymy to great effect. Crucial to his method is the intense observation of a detail, from minute particulars, from things next to other things. This device is easier to see here than it is in most of his other poems. As the details are contemplated with greater and greater depth, they take on increasing meaning. An ingenious metonymist, Montale moves from frame to picture, from border to interior, often working from an intimate detail, which only one person could know about fully, that person being the co-observer and respondent to the speaker (here, Irma Brandeis). The rhetorical structure allows us to overhear what the poet tells her. He shifts his focus from a very particular detail to a whole scene, a larger historical situation of gigantic importance. And we can retrace the context as the poet addresses the absent lover.

One final bit of evidence gives us a greater understanding of the workings of a great poetic mind. Brandeis wrote a detailed and perceptive description of her rented apartment at 54 Costa San Giorgio. The text is undated, but judging by its place among the other entries in her journals, it is probably from early September of 1931. Since Irma rented the same apartment a number of times, the description is almost certainly of the same room that serves as the interior scene evoked in Montale's "New Stanzas":

> The studio is on the top floor and the house on a hill. It is a perfectly enormous room with a great window (yellow curtain) looking out on a double cypress tree and red-tiled rooves, the Palazzo Vecchio tower clear and close, the cathedral, a complete background of hills, and then Santa Croce and the river all the way out to the country and the tiny, flat trees near the Iron Bridge, and the hills on that side. There is no way to speak about this view. From the terrazza upstairs you can see all Florence except the Costa S. Giorgio and all the hills except the ones immediately behind.
>
> The floor is made of dark brown tiles, showing red where they are rubbed; and these the landlady keeps in a high state of polish. The walls are cream-yellow, with India prints and bits of fabric carefully hung, threadbare, mostly. The ceiling is dark red bricks faintly sloping up from either side to a centre beam, and the whole thing is supported by cross-beams and ribs of dark lovely brown wood.
>
> In the centre an enormous heavy brown table and a big throne chair to match. Two chests of drawers, one plain, old dark brown – the other very antique with a centre door that swings open and reveals a charming little painted scene in perspective – two divans covered in green cotton (one near the big window, the other in the middle of the opposite wall), a wooden chest for holding fuel, a low square coffee table covered with a variety of India print, and my hired piano (now meeker than a lamb). I have only failed to mention several chairs, several remarkably useless mirrors, and the stone. A list of objects doesn't reproduce the feeling of a room. This one is just right. For coming in, locking the door. Throwing off one's hat, and taking a deep, long breath.[110]

Curtains, mirrors, geometric designs on tiles on the floor – all important symbols in Montale's poetry – appear here. The view from the apartment looks out on the city below and across the river, and the sounds of the Martinella bell would have easily carried into this room from the Palazzo Vecchio on the other side of the Arno. The yellow curtains by the large window could well be the same curtains that form the mysterious barrier in the poem. Irma's journal makes clear the way in which the city beyond the window, and the events that would eventually transpire there, could seem tightly juxtaposed against the interior scene. Her detailed description gives us a sense of how the poet carefully selected details from the scene, arranging and intensifying their meanings to make them into telling, resonant symbols that convey a very dramatic story in very few words.

Traces of Clizia at Bocca di Magra and a Fascist Palio in Siena

In contrast to the Florentine setting of "New Stanzas" is the erotically charged "Il ritorno" ("The Return," 1940), steeped once more in the coastal environment that so extensively animated Montale's imagination. The epigraph of "The Return" indicates that the poem is set in Bocca di Magra, an area just south of the Cinque Terre where Liguria meets Tuscany. At Bocca di Magra the towering coastal mountains recede into the background, and there are some sandy beaches and wetlands. Here the River Magra spills into the sea. Luni, an ancient Etruscan port city, is just a kilometre or two away. Luni is the site of one of the late Clizia poems (see chapter 8). Clearly Irma and Eugenio visited Luni together, and so a longed-for visit to the nearby Bocca di Magra is also conceivable. Montale's own statements make it plausible that this poem concerns, as he says, a "hoped-for" return visit of the beloved to the Cinque Terre region: "We'll now see in a more extensive poem a whole landscape move and prepare itself, waiting for the hoped-for visit. It's the landscape of Bocca di Magra, at the border of Tuscany and Liguria, very resonant with the music of Debussy's sarabande and the musical exercises of the Queen of the Night in Mozart's *The Magic Flute:* the hellsnakes ... Clearly the stormy petrel angel owned a good gramophone."[111]

"The Return" is a highly erotic poem, with its distinct sexuality evoked in musical terms. Music, in addition to the music of noted natural sound, is once again important here. Montale indicates the Mozart reference himself: "musical aria, in which Mozart's Hellsnakes alone would not justify the final squall."[112] The sea squall could represent the coming storm often used to symbolize the Second World War in Montale, and the stormy petrel angel could stand for Clizia. "*Gli angui d'inferno / sentomi nel petto*" (The snakes of hell / I feel them in my breast), sings the Queen of the Night in the Italian version of *The Magic Flute.* Montale refers to the snakes of hell in his poem. He does not make it clear, however, either in his poem or in his comments, that this unnamed beloved is Clizia, or someone else. While some expert Montale readers think that this is an Arletta poem, there are so many poems about Clizia's departure and flight that it is hard to imagine there would not be at least one about a much-wished-for fantasy of return, especially in 1940.

In my reading of the poem, Montale imagines I.B. (to whom, after all, *The Occasions* is dedicated) turning up for a tryst near the shore. She puts *The Magic Flute* on the phonograph. The sea air is filled with strains from the Queen of the Night's aria, with its difficult arpeggios and scales running up and down the vocal range of the coloratura soprano. Montale also explicitly refers to Debussy's sarabande from the *Pour le piano suite* (1896–1901). This is a wistful, slow dance. The dignified parallel chords and modal style of Debussy's music give the dance a medieval air, and yet the complex harmonies make it distinctly modern. Debussy marks the score to be played "with a serious and slow elegance." It is ideal mood music for a Mediterranean setting, with a river opening into the sea, mountains rising in the background, blowing breezes, and flickering lights.

Irma Brandeis would have known that Dante refers to Lerici and the general coastal area of La Spezia in the *Commedia*.[113] The image of the ferryman Duilio crossing the Magra recalls Charon crossing the mythological Acheron or Lethe river, and its cultural resonance is both classical and Dantesque.[114] The tarantula bite at the end of the poem might indicate the tarantella, the famous musical "spider's dance" common to both Italian popular music and art music (Chopin, for example, composed a good one) and the consummation of sexual bliss.

While it is possible to construe but hard to substantiate a role for Clizia in "The Return," there can be no doubt about her importance in "Palio." One of Montale's most important and successful poems, "Palio" (1939) clearly picks up the story of the Clizia Cycle where it left off in the Florentine context of "New Stanzas" and carries it from Florence to Siena. While "New Stanzas" juxtaposes an intimate interior against a threatening exterior, "Palio" has Clizia and the poet in a huge swarm of people. Technically Montale worked up to his great achievement of "Palio" in several earlier shorter poems, among them "Buffalo," "Café at Rapallo," and "Vento e bandiere" ("Wind and Flags"). In each of these poems a great flurry of varied visual stimuli is effectively caught, codified, and combined in poetic language. Montale surpasses all of these in the more developed "Palio."

There could be no greater clash between a great medieval tradition in Italian popular culture – one that takes place in one of the most beautiful public spaces in all of Italy, the great fan-shaped Piazza del Campo of Siena – and the larger mass movements of crowds and machines that celebrated the alliance of Hitler and Mussolini in 1938. However, there was a strange resonance for Montale between the massed crowds that gathered for the medieval festival and the massed European crowds of Fascists and Nazis so characteristic of the 1930s. At first the Palio race was a genuinely serious competition. By 1938 it had become a festive ritual that took place in Siena, the Festa del Palio, more significant as a summer rite than as an actual horse-race. It was particularly the Palio of 1938 that concerned Montale, with its enigmatic clash of the Italian past and present.

Siena is one of the crown jewels of Italian civilization. Out of the way of the more discovered city of Florence, it has a uniquely preserved medieval centre, one of the oldest universities in Europe, and an important Gothic cathedral. It is rich in masterpieces by Duccio di Buoninsegna (1255–1319), Simone Martini (1280–1344), and Pietro and Ambrogio Lorenzetti (ca 1280–1348?), among others. Siena's greatest era of political power was in the late medieval period, when it was an economic dynamo that challenged neighbouring Florence.

The Palio grew out of the earliest forms of civic unity in the small Italian city-states. Dante mentions Palio racing, and there is evidence of medieval races in Florence, Verona, and Ferrara. Other ritual contests were also held in Siena, including the *elmora,* fought with wooden weapons (swords and lances); the *pugna,* which included fist-fighting; and the *battaglia dei sassi,* which, as the name implies, featured stone throwing. These events were more dangerous than the horse-race. Sometimes people were killed while participating in these contests.[115] Siena has held horse-races since around 1230, and the first Palio took place as a civic event in 1482, in the heart of the Renaissance period. It has been run every 2 July and 16 August since 1701. *Palio* literally means "banner," and the *Corsa del Palio* is the "Race (or Racecourse) of the Banner." The contestants represent the seventeen districts of the city, known as *contrade.* Each has a banner with an emblem, a medieval coat of arms dating back to the era when they represented competing military units. Preparations begin months before the day of the Palio and in actuality go on year-round in the life of Siena. Each district hosts huge ceremonial banquets in the streets of Siena on the night before the race.

Most of the Palio involves rituals of preparation, rivalry, celebration, and procession. The day of the race begins with a complex procedure of prayer, profanity, and singing. A high point is when each *contrada* brings its horse into the neighbourhood chapel for a blessing. Before the race a huge crowd swarms into the centre of the Campo, and there is great pageantry involved in the presentations of the contrade in a procession. Each contrada is represented by a *comparsa,* a company of marchers with a *duce* (leader), a *tamburino* (drummer), and a contingent of expert *alfieri* (flag wavers). The *tamburino* and *alfieri* make a spectacular team, providing an assortment of important visual and musical symbols.[116] Bells sound throughout, including the famous *sunto* bell on top of the fourteenth-century tower next to the Palazzo Pubblico. After many hours of festivities the Sienese are finally ready to run the actual race. A small cannon is fired to indicate that it is time to clear the track and line up the horses and jockeys. After the *mossiere,* the special umpire, drops the flag, the horses are off. They run around the perimeter of the Campo, circling the vast crowd in the centre. There is a great roar from the crowd. Some are in a trance-like state; others collapse from excitement or perhaps the summer heat. The race consists of three laps around the Campo, and it is over very quickly. Cannon fire signifies the conclusion. Visibility from the centre is very difficult. This information is crucial for understanding Montale's great poem.[117]

Irma first saw the Palio in the early 1930s with Gino Bigongiari. She attended the race in 1934 in Montale's company. Montale and Irma almost certainly attended the Palio together one last time on 16 August 1938, joining a group of Italian friends that included Elena Vivante and Camillo Sbarbaro.[118] Two late Montale poems, "Quartetto" ("Quartet") and "Nel '38" ("In '38"), also refer to the 1938 Palio. Taken together, these three poems provide a comprehensive picture of this moment in Montale's life and of the characters involved. There are also extant snap-shots taken near Siena in 1938, much discussed in Montale's letters to Irma.

The date of 16 August 1938 was, of course, dangerously late for a Jewish-American woman to be doing something so public and touristic in Italy, but a clearly courageous Irma Brandeis went to see the race with her friends. The August Palio race of 1938 was just a few months after Hitler's May visit to Florence, which is the subject of Montale's great poem "Hitler Spring." Only a month before this Palio, on 14 July, the "Manifesto of the Racist Scientists" had appeared in a Roman paper, the *Giornale d'Italia.*[119] It had obvious backing from Mussolini and the Fascist Party, and it was clearly an anti-Semitic document. Thereafter, it was plainly unsafe for Jews in Italy. Since Mussolini had bound Italy inextricably to Hitler and the Nazis in June, each passing day brought

Italy closer to war. By August, when Irma and her friends (some of whom had Jewish ancestry) went to the Palio, all Jewish people were marked targets, officially denounced for their racial background. Regardless of the anxiogenic nature of their personal relationship, the political context of this moment must have provoked still more anxiety for both Brandeis and Montale. Through the 1930s Irma's Italian friends had called her "Cassandra" because of her warnings about the Fascists.[120] Now Cassandra's warnings had come true.

It is quite clear that in "Palio" the poet is talking directly to the absent beloved. He is recreating the sensation of the Palio for her (and for himself) as he writes to her. The impending war and the sounds of crowd celebration blend the Fascist hordes with the medieval pageantry of the horse-race. The rhetorical structure has something of the love letter written but never sent, which is common in the poems in the Clizia Cycle:

Your flight then was not lost
in the gyration of a top
spinning out at the curb:
the racecourse that dissolves
its coiling finishes here
in the purple hollow
where a tumult of souls salute
the signs of Unicorn and Tortoise.

The flag throwing does not change
your face: too much heat has consumed
the signals that you detected, last forebodings,
this odour of turpentine and imminent
storm and this tepid drizzle
of clouds pulled upward,
a tardy salute in the glory of a fate
that even escapes destiny. From the tower
falls a sound of the bronze: the procession
continues with drums that pound out
the glory of the *contrade*.

It's strange: you
who watch the vast upheaval,
the hollowed-out bricks, the wavering

Montgolfier balloon of paper cut off
by the animated phantasms on the quadrant
of the immense clock, the arpeggiated
twisting of the swarms and the dazed wonder
that invades the snail shell
of the Campo, you retain
between your fingers the pre-emptory seal
that I had thought lost
and the light of before that disperses
on the heads and whitens them with its lilies.

An echo from before returns: "once upon a time ..."
(recalling the prayer that from the darkness
came to you one morning)

'not a realm but the thin
trace of filigree
without our leaving a sign
our fading footsteps

Under the ice-cold twists
weighs now a stony sleep,
the voice from the cellar

The bars with a cross shape don't scan
the light for the one who is lost
death does not have another voice
than that which spreads life.'

But another voice here flees
the prisoner's horror, and for it this *ritornello*
is no match for the flourish of furled lances
(Goose and Giraffe) that cross each other high up
and fall again in flames. A groan in the stands
at the passage of worn-out horses, saluted
with a single cry. It is a flight! And you forget!
Forget death
toto coelo achieved and therefore
the babble of the damned! It was *the* day
of the living. You see it, it appears immobilized
in the water of this ruby so populated

with images. The present dissolves
and the finishing line is there: over the mass
of banners, above the incessantly ringing bells
in unrestrained sky, beyond the view
of man – and you set it. You are high up
until the gyrating top checks its spiral,
but its cut furrow still stands. Then, nothing else.[121]

Montale begins the first stanza by referring to Clizia's "flight" (*la tua fuga*). There are many images of flight in Montale (see, for example, "Your Flight" and his use of numerous Italian words for flight, such as *fuga* and *volo,* in other poems). This is probably because Irma's various departures from Italy in the 1930s, in the face of Mussolini's growing commitment to Hitler and his increasingly dangerous racial views, played over and over again in Montale's mind. Her final departure before the war was a crucial event in his life and a central symbolic act in his poetry. Irma's last good-bye in 1938 meant at least two consequential things. First, the poet lost her, and that led to her literary re-creation as Clizia. Second, it signified Italy's devolution into war and defeat, which Montale had feared since the 1920s.

The spinning top, a recurring image in the poem, occurs in the first line: "Your flight then was not lost in the gyration of a top" (*La tua fuga non s'è dunque perduta / in un giro di trottola*). This refers to the fact that Irma/Clizia escaped, perhaps, returning one last time after a number of crossings in huge spirals over the Atlantic. Her movements blend in Montale's mind with the elliptical spiralling of the horses as they race around the Palio course, with the shouting and screaming spectators massed in the centre of the piazza. The Palio itself consists of three laps around the elliptical piazza. So the horses and riders also spin around the track like tops. Clizia's flight could have ended *al margine della strade* (on the side of the road or the race course), but it did not. She escaped, just like the fleeing Liuba (another Jewish woman) at the Florence train station.

The poet is writing to her as he recalls the past event of the race. In the now of the narration she is far away in America, but he remembers how they stood together in the *purpurea buca* (the purple hollow) of the piazza. There the great crowd of spectators saluted the flags and banners. The purple mouth or pit is an image for the famous seashell-shaped Campo of Siena. Irma and Eugenio and their friends may have been standing in the crowd or they may have had better seats in a private home or in the grandstand.

Each of the contrade, the competing neighbourhoods of Siena, has a special medieval insignia displayed on a banner, four of which turn up in the poem. The first two are the contrade of Unicorn (*Liocorno*) and Tortoise (*Tartuca*). Brandeis mentions that Montale knew the mayor's nephew, who personally showed them the list of all the races won by his contrada since 1613.[122]

Although well known to the Sienese who attend their beloved horse-race every year, the contrade are presented abruptly in the text of the poem, distorted by the lack of context for the uninitiated. They give the poem a special surreal quality because they are introduced without explanation, creating the effect of a close-up view, almost in the face of the reader. They are described in various ways throughout, without any specific context but giving the poem a particularly appropriate medieval character. This is one more indication of the way in which Montale indeed starts from reality, just as he says, but what he does with his observations makes them part of the imaginative superreality in his poetry. Any context or explanation is cut away so that only the immediacy of the moment is left. Montale does this type of thing very well, as well as any Modernist poet.

There is a strong presence of Irma/Clizia in the second stanza. Her defiant expression is celebrated in various ways throughout the Clizia poems as one of the most important of Montale's anti-Fascist symbols. Here she is unmoved by the dramatic "flag throwing." A variety of ominous sensory signals, including the scent of turpentine and of light raindrops, are an indication of the threatening "storm" (here the Italian word is *tempesta,* another image of the imminent *bufera*), the coming war. And so the poet tells her how he observed her unchanging expression, which is stalwart, which does not vacillate, like her unchanging love and her unswerving principles. These strong images indicate that disaster is coming, in spite of the revelry of the Festa del Palio. Even the floating hot-air balloon and the sounds of happy screaming suggest the *tempesta imminente.* The protagonists in the poem are in a crowd, but it is assembled for a celebratory purpose that could easily seem sinister. We should compare the tregenda, the diabolical swarm of men in "New Stanzas," to the crowds in "Palio."[123]

The disturbing symbols of sound and smell are interrupted when a blast of "bronze" falls down "from the tower." This is Montale's re-creation in his poetic language of the *sunto* bell high on top of the Mangia, the tall fourteenth-century tower adjacent to the Palazzo Pubblico. Sound imagery is as important as visual imagery in this poem, and this is a great example of Montale's ability to combine the two. The interjection of musical sound seems strange at first, until the reader realizes that it is the sound of the bells in the great campanile, announcing the victory. Soon drums pound as the "glory of the *contrade*" is acclaimed in the victory parade that follows. We might compare the sound of the bells, brass (there is also a trumpet), and drums to the Martinella bell in Florence, signifying disgrace in the shorter "New Stanzas." Once again, sound is an important source of imagery in Montale. All manner of sound is important, from nature to man-made noise, such as church bells, to every form of music.

There is a Mallarméan intensity of compacted language in "Palio," but it is used to recreate something very unlike Mallarmé's subjects. Mallarmé's lovely and delicate poems use a similar technique in a very different way. "Palio," in comparison, is a huge subject, something of enormous energy. Mallarmé never attempted anything like this great crowd scene. Whereas he stuck to abstract reflection and intricate detail, Montale creates in this poem a deep meditation on a very real and specific instance of a cultural event. This is an event of great social and historical significance because it was one of the last enactments of a medieval Tuscan ritual before the Second World War, which the poet attended in the company of his Jewish-American beloved, and it concerns the great cataclysm to come shortly after her departure.[124] Wallace Stevens is another virtuoso at composing dense thickets of language for expressive purposes. His writing can have a wild energy, particularly when he is stimulated by the exuberance and fecundity of nature.[125] But there is no poem in his oeuvre like Montale's "Palio."

In the third stanza the poet describes how Irma/Clizia observes (in the present tense: "*tu che guardi*") the complex visual scene of the Palio, the stones and tiles, the floating balloon, the shadow on the immense clock on the tower overlooking the Campo, until he comes to a particularly unusual combination of musical image and visual depiction of a huge crowd in the historic city centre: "the arpeggiated / twisting of the swarms and the dazed wonder / that invades the snail shell / of the Campo" (*l'arpeggiante / volteggio degli sciami e lo stupore / che invade la conchiglia / del Campo*). It all seems like a surrealistic vision until we realize that each item could easily be the result of the poet's meticulous powers of observation. Musical arpeggios are chords unfolding in sequential patterns in time, note by note, creating a cascade of tonal sound. The composer invents the pattern but not the chord. Certain patterns of arpeggios really do zigzag, and so do huge throngs of people pulling in one direction and then another. Here sound in the form of a musical image describes the visual waves of human movement in a crowd of human beings, a crowd that is in a stupor because of mass hypnosis, captivated by an ancient ritual and enthralled by the thrill of the race. These *sciami,* these swarms of humanity, should be compared to the *stormo* (a synonym) and the *tregenda,* the hordes of Fascists. The Sienese Palio is a remarkable instance of participation in an ancient ritual on a mass scale. The hordes of Fascists, far more threatening, make even the celebration of the Palio suspect.[126]

Clizia/Irma is the single heroine in this sea of benumbed humanity. The poet tells her directly, "You retain / between your fingers the preemptory seal / that I had thought lost." Light, never far from Clizia, is here again, shining between the fingers of the beloved. It is *"la luce di prima"* (the light of before). The various insignias of the contrade are compared to the *sigillo imperioso* that Montale had thought lost (*credevo smarrito*).What has been lost? The true honour of the Italian past, including this glorious medieval tradition in this gloriously preserved medieval Italian city. It is Irma/Clizia who holds the seal of honour that none of the Sienese can possess now.

Now comes an interlude, written in another past or time frame, signified by the phrase *"c'era una volta"* (once upon a time). It is a *preghiera,* a prayer once heard in the Dantesque darkness (*buio*). In most editions the time shift is further indicated by a different typeface or by italics. There are three four-line stanzas. The poet describes here a man who is lost, and the inference is that he is like the poet who is lost without Clizia. *Smarrito* (to be lost) is a favourite Montale word, recalling the lost pilgrim Dante. It returns with the lines "The bars with a cross shape don't scan / the light for the one who is lost" (*La sbarra in croce non scande / la luce per chi s'è smarrito*). The failure of "the bars with a cross shape" connotes the religious crisis, the failure of European Christianity, that is so strongly present in Montale at the time. Also, *sbarra,* which means "bar" or "rail," could suggest parallel bars, implying a gate but also the bars of a prison.[127] Montale may have wanted to suggest that the lost man in the interlude section of the poem is in a kind of Fascist prison, for that is what Italy had become for him. This narration within the narration is typical of Modernist poetry, where disjunctions in narrative voice become commonplace, but the device goes back once again to Mallarmé, who used italics to create a similar alternation between the present tense of narration and a dream state, in

"L'Après-midi d'un faune." Once again the purpose and content could not be more different.

The last section of the poem is nineteen lines long. In it we learn that the unnamed man in the earlier "prayer-dream interlude" is indeed a kind of prisoner, very much like the prisoner in Montale's later "Dream of the Prisoner." However, the great flourishes of the contrade at the Palio wash away the *ritornello* of prayer for the trapped prisoner, bringing him back to the great rush of life spreading out in the Campo. The colourful banners of the contrade clash overhead and seem to fall to the ground in flames. Montale refers specifically to Goose and Giraffe (*Oca e Giraffa*). In Italian, the crossed banners that fall in flames make a pun on *croce,* with *incrociano* echoing *sbarra in croce.* A sound image follows this striking visual image. A single collective groan emanates from the crowd in the grandstand as the horses parade by the onlookers. The phrase *un volo* (a flight) indicates that the horses are off and running once more, but *flight* here has a double significance because it also refers to Clizia's flight from Italy. The Italian word *volo* is close to *fuga,* with which the poem begins and which reappears at the beginning of this section.

If Clizia's escape and the explosive start of the horses go together, they both leave behind the spectators, who now seem like nothing more than a pack of babbling sinners. With the Dantesque phrase "therefore / the babble of the damned" (*l'ergotante / balbuzie de dannati*), the Palio crowds suddenly bear resemblance to those in the *Inferno,* where Dante hears the garbled voices of complaining sinners. Montale suggests but does not exactly say that all of the people at the Palio are damned and that he himself is also damned because he is trapped with them, a prisoner once again. These lines also recall the trapped dead at the close of *Cuttlefish Bones,* but here they seem more clearly damned to *inferno* rather than *purgatorio. Toto coelo* is Latin for "in all the heavens, everywhere." Death is *toto coelo,* everywhere, and it is in opposition to the vital nature of Clizia's flight, the *volo* or *fuga.* With the successful flight or escape the Palio crowd now resembles the *tregenda* and the *sciami* of Fascists in other poems and, to some extent, the trapped dead who populate the closing poems of *Cuttlefish Bones.*

The poet shifts back and forth in time as he speaks. At times he is writing to the beloved in a later present, without her. But then the present fades. This is the receding present of the writing of the poem, the point of narration of the speaker. The poet finds himself back with the beloved at the Palio. The finish line is in plain sight. They see the massed display of pennants of the contrade stretching out before them, and the race is playing out to its conclusion once again.

La trottola (the [spinning] top), another word that indicates movement or great whirling motion, turns up again in the penultimate line. Used twice, at the beginning and at the end of the poem, it is a key image evoking a twisting vortex of circular motion, crucial to the poem, perhaps relating to other circles in Montale and even those of Dante's *Inferno.* Circling beyond the crowds, the banners, the pealing bells, Clizia is airborne, gyrating like the top and the circling horses. Then comes the poem's strange and anti-sentimental end. Clizia's escape leaves an etched trace of flight, and "then, nothing else" (*poi, nient'altro*).

Clarity of description and obscure meaning intermingle in the poem in a delicate balance. Montale's lines clearly capture the flag-waving of the *alfieri,* and the sound falling from the tower is the sound of the *campanone* on top of the Mangia tower. There is a subtle shift of mood. At first Clizia seems justified in her indifference to the race, although the reader gets the feeling that the poet senses the excitement, and certainly the lively nature of the *festa* comes through in spite of Clizia's concerns. The prayer interlude seems to change something. Then after the interlude the poet tells Clizia to forget (her troubles) for a moment and to lose herself in the glorious race, which, as Dundes and Falassi say, is an expression of life itself.[128] The prayer section accomplishes a change of mood. At the beginning and the end of the poem Montale links Irma's/Clizia's flight, the flight of the horses in the race, and the motion of the gyrating top. All these are, in a positive way, a release of energy, a flight of the energy of life. In contradistinction, Irma and the racers leave behind the negative, the "babble of the damned," as they take off. In this way the poem gives us a sense of the double meaning of the Palio for the poet. The crowds are somewhat ominous, but the glory of the race is preserved for Montale, who still loves Italian culture deeply, no matter what, and in spite of the Fascists who are threatening his Clizia.

At first reading, "Palio" seems a baffling array of images. With study it reveals itself to be a miraculous example of how language can rival and even surpass the visual immediacy of painting or photography, while also using the vivid sound qualities of music, to create a sense of a scene from a particular series of psychological perspectives. Here Montale's intimate knowledge of the different arts (later to accumulate in a vast body of critical writing) seems to have borne fruit in his poetry. Qualities of painting and music, or images from them, are appropriated to make this poem so vivid. He is able not only to create the sensual immediacy of the experience but very specifically to use sounds and visual images to add to his desired moral undertone. Using all the senses, Montale constructs a combination of a recording and a picture made of language, a verbal canvas of Clizia and Eugenio at the Palio. Sights and sounds combine to give colour, motion, and speed to the Palio; language adds the specific emotional undertones that Montale wants. "Palio" is a great verbal construction that recreates a complex sensory experience. It is like a great Modernist canvas, in that the various parts of the whole at first seem disjunct, not logically connected, but when you step back from the painting and view it as a whole, it comes together in ingenious ways that you never suspected at first. The sights, sounds, and smells of the Palio in that fateful summer of 1938 are recreated. The poem calls to mind a Bonnard or Vuillard canvas that becomes clear as the viewer moves around and pieces the images together in the mind.[129]

A scene described in poetry has to be taken in sequence and then put together in the imagination. A painting made up of still images has to be scanned by the eye and then put together in the mind.[130] The diverse clusters of images fit together if one reads "Palio" enough times. The poem contains tremendous colour and vividness, including precise information about such details as the banners of the contrade and the shape of the famous piazza, and accurate evocations of the noise, sounds, and smells of the crowd at the horse-race.

Just as a first glance at a great Vuillard does not do justice to the painting, a shallow single reading of "Palio" will not suffice. The poem demands many readings, and with each rereading the vivid images create a time and place of felt experience with sharper and sharper clarity. One touches, tastes, hears, sees, and smells the experience with greater precision as the intricate assemblage of images comes into focus in the mind. Taken as a whole, the poem is one of the great compositions encompassing visual and aural experience in modern poetry. Along with the ominous mood of 1938, it captures the energy and colour and light and sound of that single moment at the Palio, recreated meticulously by the poet's careful craftsmanship. It is a flash of Montalean luminosity, a flash-bulb photograph of a moment in a life recorded in the technology of words and print.

Mallarmé's "third aspect" of poetic language, the distillation process that comes from the combinatory overflow of meaning in words, is of vital importance to Montale. The poet uses this technique to create with tremendous intensity a huge outdoor event with masses of people and great visual and aural stimuli. Also, there is a moral purpose and a clarity of tone that would not have been possible or even desirable for Mallarmé. This poem is one of the greatest of Montale's Clizia poems, which would be enough to give it an important place in the development of this study of the evolution of the senhal in his imagination, but there is also biographical evidence connecting the poem to the actual Palio of 1938. An example of this evidence is the important photograph of Montale, Irma, and their friends taken at the Palio in the summer of 1938.[131] Montale refers to this photograph, and others taken at the same time, in his 1978 poem "Nel '38." This is a crucial poem because it is about one of the last outings before the crisis point in Brandeis and Montale's complex relationship, a crisis that led to the final break and to the birth of the myth of Clizia.

The poem is also remarkable for its technical achievement. The economy of Montale's richly suggestive language in recreating the Palio might be compared to the large numbers needed onstage for a crowd scene in a grand opera. How many things can the eye and ear focus on at once? How can images make the mind remember, and how many diverse images can the mind hold in place in the temporal process of reading? Montale tests the limits of poetry and recreates with his richly evocative images the physical and emotional experience of being in a huge throng.

Bernard Berenson included observations on the Palio in his *Seeing and Knowing.* It is a passably good prose description, but no more than that.

> I had been sitting thru the first part of the Sienese Palio ... At last, at last the flag-waving ... was over, and the flashing by of the galloping horses would only take a moment more ... The sun had just set and the afterglow flushed from the red palaces that guard the theatre-shaped Piazza of Siena. I was watching the flicker of fading light when suddenly I became aware first of a creeping, then of a crowding, and finally as of a stream pouring into the paved arena until it was brim-full or (to change the simile) jammed tight. With what? If I had trusted my eyes I should have said with flowers from a herbaceous border, so multicoloured was what I actually saw ... In an instant I inferred that the mass, the crazy-quilt I was looking at, did not consist of flowers or patchwork. I knew, although in the growing dimness

> I could not distinguish heads or faces, and the jam was such that I saw no bodies, yet I knew that this floral canopy not only must be, but was actually, composed of human beings.[132]

Here the flow of colours and forms is described in a more prosaic way, and Berenson's description helps us to understand Montale's great poetic achievement better. Montale begins by closely observing the actual phenomenon of the Palio, and from there he creates something in language that expresses the complexity of the experience. A comparison of Berenson and Montale shows where prose ends and poetry begins.

Reminiscences from a Tuscan Mountain Top

The Occasions comes to a dramatic conclusion with the last poem in the collection, "Notizie dall'Amiata" ("News from Amiata," 1938). It is one of the important poems that begin in the epistolary manner, and it may well have begun its literary life as the text of an actual letter to Irma Brandeis. The great poem was written in the same year that Montale lost his job at the Gabinetto Vieusseux and thereafter considered leaving Italy for the United States. We know that Montale wrote at least sixteen letters to Brandeis from the beginning of September through to the end of November in 1938. Rosanna Bettarini and Gianfranco Contini, along with Giorgio Zampa, date the poem to late autumn 1938, indicating that it was written well after Irma had gone back to the United States.[133] Two other great poems in the Clizia Cycle, "Hitler Spring" and "Palio," are set in the full force of late spring and high summer. The autumnal setting in this poem contributes to its unmistakable sense of crisis.

Mount Amiata is an extinct volcano between Siena and Grosseto, stretching out over southern Tuscany. It is on the way from Florence to Rome, not too far south of Siena. In his remarks on the poem in Greco, Montale refers to the three or four nearby villages in the area with a Romanesque, as opposed to Florentine Renaissance, flavour.[134] Possible points of reference for him are Abbadia San Salvatore and Arcidosso, located on either side of the Amiata mountain peak. Montale's poems are often distinguished by the carefully recorded detail of topoi. The most significant images of place are Ligurian, Florentine, and Genovese, but here southern Tuscany becomes important. It is helpful to compare the quiet medieval villages and rugged rural setting of "News from Amiata" to the Florentine background that was crucial for other poems, such as "New Stanzas" or "Hitler Spring," or to the Sienese context of "Palio."

As things got worse in Europe, heretics and the site of their activities obviously took on increasing importance for Montale. The Amiata region was one such site because it was the home of the heretic David Lazzaretti, born in Arcidosso in 1834. Lazzaretti, who saw himself as a messiah, attracted a small community of followers to his mountain retreat on rocky Mount Labbro, a few kilometres from the peak of Mount Amiata. His charismatic sermons alarmed the religious and political authorities. On 18 August 1878, Lazzaretti led his followers, known as *gurisdavidici,* out of Arcidosso and up the nearby slopes. When the police tried to stop him, he resisted. He was shot through the head.[135] In a letter to Silvio Guarnieri in 1964 Montale specifically cites a study by Giacomo Barzellotti, *Monte Amiata e il suo profeta David Lazzaretti* (*Mount Amiata and Its Prophet David Lazzaretti*), in relation to his poem.[136] The book, which explores the Lazzaretti case in some detail, clearly had a deep influence on Montale. Lazzaretti's heretical notions made him in many ways comparable to Nestorius, another controversial figure who intrigued Montale and turns up elsewhere in the Clizia Cycle (for discussions of Nestorius see the commentary on "Iris" in chapter 6).

Amiata, then, is a region of daring heretical thinking, and heretical thinking was precisely what Montale needed at this point. The architecture and historical importance of its little villages signify an earlier, more anarchic, and less definitively formed Christian culture. Lazzaretti and Nestor are crucial symbols from what Willis Barnstone has so aptly described as the "other Bible."[137] These are the vast collections of texts and ideas that did not become part of the Judeo-Christian canon but which might somehow offer Montale a missing link that could revalidate the whole. It is this larger, more embracing context of what was left out of culture and religion that can save them for Montale. This is far different from the sealed-off divisions of culture and religion that Eliot described in his *Notes towards the Definition of Culture.* Eliot wrote in 1948 that Christians and Jews could never really know each other, because they were separated by Christian culture.[138] Montale came up with a different solution: if Judaism and Christianity were to be social and cultural barriers separating him from his beloved, then he would create a new religion based on his worship of her.[139]

The ominous north wind intoned in the poem is reminiscent of Shelley's "Ode to the West Wind," and it is plausible that Montale, who was beginning his new career as a translator of English and American writers, would have reread Shelley at this time. In the Shelley poem there is a sense of coming winter and storm, and a yearning for death and for a giving of oneself over to nature, but here it is because of the speaker's despair over more specific issues. The autumnal setting of "News from Amiata" is the time of San Martino, the Italian Indian summer, and it is related to the autumnal setting of "Iris," which is another poem of climactic importance in the Clizia sequence, but there the tone of the poem is very different.

Fortunately Montale's English-language readers can benefit from the fine translations by Jonathan Galassi and William Arrowsmith, as well as the insights in an interesting translation impression by Robert Lowell.[140] While those versions are invaluable, it is particularly intriguing for those who wish to study the Clizia mystery to consult the earlier translation by Irma Brandeis because this poem so particularly concerns her. Significantly she used her own translation of it in the *Quarterly Review* issue, not a translation made by one of her capable collaborators. One cannot help but wonder why she included this wrenching personal poem in her own translation and left out others that were also obviously written to her but which are more elusive and difficult to unravel (thereby giving her more of a cover). By 1962 the war-time "News from Amiata" was certainly old news, but Irma knew perfectly well that she was the addressee in the poem. While not named or described, she is present (once again) as an offstage character; she is the beloved persona spoken to in the poem. By 1962 she had become the devoted interlocutor, translating the poem for later generations. In Irma's translation we have her English version of a love poem written with the rhetorical structure of an unsent love letter that was originally intended for her and had been written more than twenty years earlier:

The fireworks of threatening weather
might be murmur of hives at duskfall.
The room has pockmarked beams
and an odor of melons
seeps from the store-room. Soft mists
that climb from a valley
of elves and mushrooms to the diaphanous cone
of the crest cloud over my windows,

and I write you from here, from this table,
remote, from the honey cell
of a sphere launched into space –
and the covered cages, the hearth
where chestnuts are bursting, the veins
of saltpetre and mould are the frame
where soon you will break through.
Life that enfables you is still too brief
if it contains you. The luminous ground
unfolds your icon. Outside it rains.

* * * *

Could you but see the fragile buildings
blackened by time and smoke,
the square courtyards with their deep wells
at center; and could you see
the laden flight of the night birds
and, beyond the ravine, the twinkling
of the Galaxy that soothes all wounds!
But the step that echoes long in the dark
is of one who goes alone and who sees only
this fall of shadows, of arches and of folds.
The stars sew with too fine a thread,
the eye of the tower stopped at two,
even the climbing vines are an ascent of shadows,
and their perfume bitter hurt.
Return tomorrow colder, winds from the north,
shatter the old hands of the sandstone,
overturn the books of hours in the sunrooms,
and let all be pendulum calm, dominion, prison of sense
which does not know despair! Return still stronger
wind from the north, wind that endears
our chains and seals the spores of the possible!
The paths are too narrow, the hooves of the black donkeys
clicking in file raise sparks,
from the hidden peak magnesium flares reply.
O the slow drip of rain from the dark shacks,
time turned to water,

the long colloquy with the poor dead, the ashes, the wind,
late-coming wind, and death, and death that lives!

* * * *

This christian fracas which has no speech
Other than shadows or laments,
what does it give you of me? Less
than was snatched from you by the tunnel
plunging gently into its casing of stone.
A mill-wheel, an old tree-trunk,
last boundaries of the world. A heap
of chaff blows off; and, venturing late,
to join my vigil to your deep sleep
that welcomes them, the porcupines
will sip at a thin stream of pity.[141]

The first stanza sets up the rhetorical structure of a letter, which gives us the premise for the whole poem. The speech act that powers the first Italian stanza is one of written address: "*ti scrivo di qui, da questo tavolo / remoto*" (I write to you from this place, from this far-off table). In Irma's translation the lines read "I write you from here, from this table, / remote, from the honey cell / of a sphere launched into space." The sensuous nature of experience is singularly remarkable here, although this is always one of Montale's great features. The vital sound image of *murmure d'arnie a tarda sera* (the murmur of beehives in late evening) is like the crackling sounds underfoot in the later "Hitler Spring" or the swarms of butterflies around the horse carriage in "Towards Capua." The smell of melons through floorboards, also a wonderful descriptive detail, is a sensory image worthy of a great novelist who wants to make a scene come alive for readers. It is even better in poetry. In his remarks on the poem Montale also refers to the wooden texture of the medieval architecture.[142]

The rhetoric of the poem has great seductive power. Life without the beloved in the little Italian mountain town in the countryside has a sensuous fullness, an observation that does not seem to make sense at first. How can things be so fecund, so redolent, without her? In the Italian the eighteen hendecasyllabic lines that begin the poem have the rhetorical strategy of a great Shakespearean sonnet. Montale uses all of his poetic gifts to describe the beauty of the land and the sensuousness of life in the little village near Amiata. Then come the lines "*La vita / che t'affàbula è ancora troppo breve / se ti contiene!*" which Irma translates as "life that enfables you is still too brief if it contains you." This notion is similar to the handkerchief metaphor in the last Motet ("life, which once seemed vast, is smaller than your handkerchief"), but here there is greater expressive power. This abundant fullness of life in the little village near the Amiata summit, a fullness evoked so effectively by the poet, is still too puny if it also contains the beloved. Life is not good enough for Irma and her "icon" (Clizia). Finally a last detail closes the opening stanza: the rain. "*Fuori piove*" (Outside it is raining), the poet writes from Mount Amiata to his absent lover in the United States. The poem begins with the image of the poet-speaker writing to the beloved in an interior, a rented room or a hotel in Arcidosso or Abbadia San Salvatore. The windows are fogging up from the moisture because of the downpour outside.

The second stanza moves from the sensitively rendered interior to an external view of the small town near Mount Amiata. The rain has slowed to the point that it allows a stroll outside in the narrow medieval streets. We should note the architectural detail of the medieval Italian town in this stanza, especially with the Italian words *cortili quadrati* (square courtyards). For thousands of years everyday Italian culture has revolved around the piazza. The town square has always been the centre of everyday life in Italy, the site of the market, the place of gossip, the social seat of religious life, with church façade and campanile always en face. The architectural significance of the piazza in Italy has been documented magnificently in Pepi Merisio's *Piazze d'Italia,* with text by Carlo Bo.[143] The town squares evoked in this poem do not have the fan shape of the much larger piazza in Siena. This is the Romanesque square of the little village. Here there is a greater mass of an earlier architectural style, with heavier ironwork and wood. Montale explicitly refers to the square courtyards with their drinking wells in the middle. The lonely poet or lover, walking alone in the dark in the old medieval *cortili,* discerns the many shadows cast by the old medieval arches and stone ledges in the narrow streets. The old village is black with time and soot.

Then comes a startling contrast. The poet looks up to see night birds and a twinkling galaxy. This is balm for every torment (*la fascia d'ogni tormento*) which, as Brandeis puts it, "soothes all wounds." Montale would have been keenly aware of the close punning connection between *fascio,* the bundle of sticks that symbolizes the Fascists, and *la fascia,* the bandage that heals the wounds inflicted by the sticks. The poet spots a campanile, a tower, something that can be found in every old Italian town. The clock is fixed at two o'clock (*alle due*). Images of vines and their fragrance round out the stanza. After this the Shelleyesque gesture in the poem occurs, recalling the wild destructive wind of the "Ode to the West Wind." Here the poet stops talking to his lover. Montale addresses the cold north wind, invoking it to whip into the narrow medieval streets of the little town near Amiata: "*Ritorna domani più freddo, vento del nord*" (Return tomorrow colder, winds from the north).[144] Arrowsmith observes that the north wind also evokes the Nazi north, and, of course, this makes sense geographically because Germany lies to the north. However, this does not explain Montale's invocation of the wind. Why would he want to usher in the evil winds of the north unless he knows that they are coming anyway, and he is saying, in effect, "Come and get us if you dare"? Whether or not the Nazis can be found in this portion, the whole last section of the stanza is a twentieth-century *Inferno,* as if the linear plan of Dante had been sucked out, leaving only the brilliant Montalean imagery. In the very narrow medieval *borgo,* rain drips from the old hovels, yet the hooves strike hellish sparks on the cobblestone street, and these are echoed from the peak of the old volcano on top of Amiata as if the devil were responding in order to signal preparation for hellish activity. In a striking image of the relativity of time Montale writes that time melts away: "*il tempo fatto acqua*" (time made water). The dead and the ashes are all blown together in a living death, just as they are in the *Inferno.*

In the last stanza the poet talks directly to the beloved again. The crux of the section is Montale's great outcry, exposing his struggle with Christianity at this time. This crisis has already been expressed with some subtlety in "Costa San Giorgio" and "Palio." Now it is out in the open:

Questa rissa cristiana che non ha
se non parole d'ombra e di lamento
Che ti porta di me? (192)

[This Christian fracas which has
no speech other than shadows or laments.
What does it give you of me?]

Questa rissa cristiana (This Christian fracas), at least as it was then culminating in what was to be a Nazi-Fascist Europe, does not give the poet very much.[145] Brandeis's version, more than any of the subsequent translations, obscures the desperation in the answer to the question. In Arrowsmith the "Christian wrangle" is "less than the marsh ... silting behind its dam of cement."[146] In Galassi, it is "less than what the mill-race softly silting / in its cement basin stole from you."[147] Both give the sense of mud gathering in the storm sewer. *La gora* is the key. It is Italian for a man-made drainage canal that empties into a larger body of water. The wrangle of religion as it has evolved into the reality of modern Fascist culture has left the poet with less than what is washed away through the *gora,* and that means he is left with nothing of his beloved Irma. This is a desperate and dramatic outburst. It is directly addressed to Irma/Clizia, and even in 1962 Brandeis chose to soften the tone of its critical outcry against the European Christianity of its era. Montale is now a heretic, possibly a wild rebel like David Lazzaretti of nearby Arcidosso. In a later poem he claims to be a Nestorian heretic. Montale is questioning the markers of belief and value in his civilization.

Montale began to refer to himself as a keeper of the vigil in "New Stanzas" and "The Pico Farnese Elegy." He refers once again to his vigil-keeping role in "News from Amiata." It is a key concept in the Clizia Cycle.[148] He refers to it quite openly here in the last poem of *The Occasions* as *la mia veglia* (my vigil). In the absence of Clizia the poet is alone, but his destiny is to keep watch as disaster occurs, to sit vigil as a witness, in the hope that he and his civilization can be redeemed, can survive the era of the tregenda. It is not a heroic role. The last two lines of the poem close with images of *porcospini* (porcupines). In the Brandeis translation they read, "porcupines ... will sip at a thin stream of pity." Brandeis knew full well that Montale had written to her in November 1935 to say, "I love you Irma with all my tenderness. Forgive my faults, my mistakes, my ugliness of mind and features. I am the porcupine holding the little dish, the little dish, the empty dish – and hope God will pour his milk in the *piattino* [little plate]."[149]

Finally, "News from Amiata" also has imagery of "threatening weather" and a gathering storm that is crucial in Montale's symbology. As in "New Stanzas" and "Palio," inclement weather is on the way. In Montale, storms and hordes are signals of the threat to the peaceful inner world of the poet and the beloved, a dissonant "sonority" of interlocking symbols. There is also a sense of progression in the last poems of *The Occasions.* The solitary environment of "News from Amiata" contrasts markedly with the huge crowds conjured up for "Palio" and with the intimate scene of the lovers in "New Stanzas," who are desperately hiding in the Florentine interior while the hordes gather outside. In these earlier poems Clizia is present. In "News from Amiata" the poet is writing to her after she has departed. This continues the sequence of the Clizia poems in a logical manner. Montale is now struggling to reconstruct the values of his civilization in the face of his despair, and he is reconstructing the symbols of Christianity and *stilnovismo* to make it possible to express his love to his Jewish beloved through poetry in a time when it seems impossible to say, "I write you from here, from this ugly spot, yet the universe makes all beautiful." This, then, is the "News" from remote Mount Amiata, and the bitter and ironic nature of the title is now apparent. This is not "news" in the shallow, immediate sense of information or gossip but a deeply personal meditation captured in a carefully constructed self-examination of experience, written in the isolated countryside village, home of a famous heretic. It is written to the secret and unnamed beloved. We are allowed to overhear the lament.

The Second Canticle

Since Montale refers to his three greatest books of poems as "three canticles, three phases of a human life," *The Occasions* marks the emerging maturation of the poet as he learns the costs of love and loss. While it was anticipated in *Cuttlefish Bones,* the story of Clizia now begins to unfold in *The Occasions*. A sequence of poems can be discerned in relation to Irma Brandeis in Italy in the 1930s, most particularly her culminating visit in 1938. There was obviously a country excursion in "Toward Capua," anxious trysting in a Florentine interior (in an apartment in the Oltrarno neighbourhood), and a trip to the Siena Palio and the nearby country home of the Vivante family (that generated the poem "Palio"). Brandeis attended the Palio in August 1938, about three months after Hitler's state visit to Italy and a month after the Fascists published their anti-Semitic manifesto. While she was not present for Hitler's visit to Florence, eventually evoked in great detail in Montale's "Hitler Spring" (see chapter 6), "New Stanzas," in which her character does appear, depicts something very much like the scene described in this later poem. "New Stanzas" recreates her in a secluded Florentine interior, with the Fascists and Nazis parading in a dangerous and demonic street scene outside. Her presence in Italy after Hitler's visit to Italy is clearly the basis of "Palio." "News from Amiata" is set in the time of afterward and recollection, during the war. This and other, later poems of recollection corroborate the larger pattern of meditation about these volatile moments in Montale's life and Italian history in general.

It is extremely important to consider how the *tu* (you), the absent lover, has changed and matured overall by the end of *The Occasions*. In this book she is generally still a woman, now identified as I.B., the unnamed person to whom the poems are dedicated.[150] We first see her as Irma, travelling in a horse-drawn carriage in "Toward Capua," sporting a star-spangled scarf. With "The Motets," Montale introduces the senhal of Clizia indirectly and already gives her some of her mythic characteristics. He does not specifically name her in these poems, which are short, fragmentary preludes of the expanded meditations that follow in much longer poems. Clizia is, however, named in the short story "Two Jackals on a Leash," which contains a specific reference to the Dantesque sixth Motet, "The hope of seeing you again forsook me" (*La speranza di pure rivederti / m'abbandonava*). The story also concerns the visit of the beloved to Modena, and the Motet is quoted in it, giving the impression that the poem was authored by the fictional character Mirco and not by the poet himself. With the publication of Montale's love letters to Irma, we know for certain that Montale mailed several of his Motets to her in the 1930s.

While Clizia is still a mere human being in most of *The Occasions*, certain poems already point to her later incarnation as a goddess. We have the first intimations of her great powers of winged flight in the Motets, "The Pico Farnese Elegy," and "Palio." Her moral force, visible in her unusually penetrating eyes, seems to already have supernatural power in "New Stanzas." Later, various images associated with her – her jewels, bangs, and so forth – begin to take on a life of their own. The first hints of Clizia's special powers are already evident here.

Montale takes great pains to evoke an apprehensive vision of a calm but threatened European civilization. This is especially clear in the French setting of "Boats along the Marne," and in the Florentine "Bellosguardo Times," in which Florence is viewed from a hill-top perch. The most sensual of the poems is the mysterious "Bellosguardo Times." Then the love story intensifies in "New Stanzas" and "Palio." The political dangers to the poet and the beloved become apparent in these works. "News from Amiata" brings the whole into focus, as the poet begins with the rhetorical structure of a love letter and then constructs a profound meditation on the forces of Eros, war, and religion. He is alone now, having lost his beloved Irma, and the war is about to begin. When he published *The Occasions* (dedicating the whole book to "I.B."), Montale could not have been certain that Irma Brandeis would ever read his "News from Amiata," his unsent letter in the form of a published poem, and all the other works inspired by her in the collection. But she did. In January 1941 she borrowed the book of poems that had been dedicated to her from the Sarah Lawrence College library in faraway Bronxville, New York.[151]

5 Hitler and Mussolini at the Opera

It was near sundown on a June day and rather than the great crowd, well ordered and unaware, I once again see the doubt and the consternation on Montale's face, seated at the Giubbe Rosse.

– Carlo Bo

The Spectacle of Fascism

The Occasions was Montale's first Clizia book. *The Storm and Other Things* was the second. Between the two came the Second World War and its aftermath. Eugenio Montale never saw Irma Brandeis again after meeting her in Florence in the summer of 1938, but the character of Clizia continued to grow in his mind throughout the war and afterwards. Another image that stayed with him, haunting his thoughts for many years, was the spectacle of Adolf Hitler in Italy in May 1938 when he came to draw Mussolini into an irrevocable alliance with the Nazis.

Fascism, which was invented in Italy, led to an imitator of demonic power, Hitler, who far exceeded the potency and reach of its initial instigators. By the late 1930s Mussolini had been intimidated by the rise of German military might. While historians maintain that many Italians were not eager for war, Mussolini, unlike the cunning Francisco Franco in Fascist Spain, allowed himself to be manipulated into confronting the Western powers. The diplomatic vacillation in Italian foreign policy before the war was one of the great uncertainties of the era. Until 1938 it was unclear even to Mussolini and his closest advisers whether Italy would be a mediator between Hitler and the Western democracies or go to war, with Germany as a staunch ally.

Much was at stake when Hitler visited Italy in the spring of 1938. The balance of power appeared to hinge on whether Italy would side with the Axis powers and abandon France and England, its former allies in First World War. Which way would Mussolini go? Even after Hitler's visit it was unclear to many, and the evidence indicates that Mussolini himself did not know. However, the 1938 state visit of Hitler and his Nazi entourage turned out to be decisive in propelling Italy towards war. This was the third personal meeting of the two dictators, and from this point forward they were committed allies, intending to divide Europe and the Mediterranean between them. While there was still some hope that Mussolini would be a mediator after Hitler had left Italy, the ensuing treaty with Germany locked him in place. Since Italy was not really prepared for war or was not as determined to have one as was Germany, the so-called Pact of Steel, signed the following year, functioned less like an agreement and more like a pair of steel handcuffs, allowing Hitler to drag Italy into war.

By the late 1930s Italy had actually been weakened by the Ethiopian war and the burden of supporting fellow Fascist Francisco Franco in Spain.[1] Mussolini had not prepared efficiently for imperial conquest, differing greatly in this respect from his German counterpart, who had successfully accomplished an enormous military modernization and build-up in the 1930s. While Mussolini was a master of propaganda and media, he was strangely unsound in technical matters. The fact that he was seriously unaware of many of the tactical issues of modern warfare ultimately made him far less effective than was Hitler, and it contributed to his undoing.[2] Hitler's burgeoning military power made him a threat to Italy's northern borders, especially since Italy had claimed new territories from Austria as a result of its role in the Allied victory in the First World War. In 1938 Hitler was as much a potentially dangerous enemy as he was a natural friend and collaborator. The state visit was prepared as a cultural statement as well as a political event. One of the largest acts of cultural propaganda ever undertaken, it remains a kind of inverted portrait of European values, a Dante's *Inferno* of a world turned upside down.

Hitler left Berlin on 2 May 1938, accompanied by a large assembly of top aides, which included Ribbentrop, Goebbels, Hess, and Himmler. A retinue of journalists in uniform travelled with them.[3] His train appeared at the Brenner frontier station at 8:00 a.m. on 3 May and arrived in Rome at around 8:30 that night, when his train pulled into a specially constructed station at Ostia on the southwestern side of the city. The station was bedecked with two frescoes on the walls. At one end was the Italian fasces; at the other, an image of Germania swathed in scarlet robes with a huge swastika on her chest. The vivid description by a reporter for the *London Times* brings out the implications in a compelling manner:

> Last night Herr Hitler arrived in Rome ... and was accorded one of the most elaborate and magnificent receptions of which there is record even in the annals of the Eternal City. Side by side with King Victor Emmanuel (Signor Mussolini had already been with him in the train) the Führer was driven slowly past the floodlit monuments of ancient greatness which formed the identical background of Roman triumphs two thousand years ago, but which were specially embellished for this twentieth-century occasion. The night arrival gave the opportunity of applying modern inventive genius to classic grandeur, and the honoured guest proceeded down the new Via del Impero between an avenue of flaming candelabra, past an illuminated Colosseum, and so by Trajan's column, metamorphosed into a shaft of light against the darkness. At a cost of several millions of pounds Rome has been turned into a city of festival. The provision of a new stadium to seat 50,000 spectators was almost an incident on the preparatory labours. A new stage has also been built ... for a special performance of part of *Lohengrin*.[4]

The passage makes a striking connection between the ruins of the Roman Empire – with its ancient symbols of imperial power, the processional trajectory of the ancient Roman triumph, and the modern display of power, complete with technologically improved props – and one of the most famous operas of the nineteenth century, Wagner's *Lohengrin*. It was one of Hitler's favourites. The opera performance came a few days later after a steady stream of parades and banquets.

Hitler's visit was probably one of the most widely publicized events of the 1930s, and the Fascist organizers used the latest media and propaganda to project their desired message. The press recorded the impressive use of flood-lights, arc lighting, and search-lights on ancient monuments and various aspects of the procession. The flood-lights illuminated a "pageant of colour," made bolder with innumerable brightly burning candelabra. The whole was carefully conceived, intricately complex, and well executed, and it was done at great expense. The staging of the political event was reminiscent of the staging of a scene for a great opera, complete with an elaborate mise-en-scène and many extras. It was only natural that the staged diplomacy of the Hitlerian visit would eventually flow into the fictional world of a staged nineteenth-century opera.

On the next day (4 May) the dictators witnessed an outdoor parade of young Fascists marching in the ancient Roman *manipuli* plan of thirty-three in a group. Then came troops, tanks, motorcyclists, cavalry, and an aerial display. During the ensuing outdoor festivities the austere dignity of martial ceremony was interrupted for an instant by an unintentionally humorous performance of the Wedding March from *Lohengrin.* From one of the stages on the field two thousand trumpets played the famous march. One onlooker, hindered by a bad view, became concerned that the two dictators were getting engaged and asked perplexedly, "They aren't exchanging rings or anything like that, are they?"

On Thursday, 5 May, Hitler made a trip to Naples, where he viewed a massive demonstration of the prowess of the new Italian navy. A total of 190 ships, including 85 submarines, took part in the show of force in the Bay of Naples. He was greatly impressed, as was the Western press. After the display Hitler attended a banquet hosted by the king of Italy in the royal palace. Later they went to the San Carlo Opera House to hear a performance of excerpts from Verdi's *Aida.*

Hitler dined with Galeazzo Ciano, Mussolini's son-in-law, at the Villa Madama on the final night of his stay in Rome. After supper he attended a gymnastics exhibition presented by the youth of the Fascist academies of physical instruction. Then he went back to the opera. Evolving naturally from the pomp and ceremony of Hitler's arrival and subsequent activities in Rome, the performance of the second act of *Lohengrin* was held in a specially designed stadium at the Mussolini Forum. According to Frederick Birchall of the *New York Times,* the performance took place on one of the largest stages in the world at that time. The scale of the production is indicated by the enormous size of one of the props, a tower that was 130 feet high and 65 feet in diameter. The members of the orchestra and chorus were recruited from all of the principal opera houses in Italy.

The world press, massed in great numbers in Rome, anxiously awaited the important toasts that Hitler and Mussolini would make at the Palazzo Venezia banquet of 7 May 1938. The toasts amounted to short self-congratulatory speeches, carefully prepared for national and worldwide dissemination. As the host, Mussolini gave his speech first: "Führer, your visit to Rome fulfills and seals the understanding between our two countries." This common point of view, he explained, is based in "one hundred years of history – from the time when first Germany and Italy raised themselves by Revolutions and by arms to claim their right to national unity – [which] bear witness to the parallel nature of these positions and the solidarity of these interests."[5] Mussolini also mentioned unspecified threats from within the two nations that had had a corroding effect on their parallel nationalistic aspirations. Italy and Germany had "redeemed themselves from the corruption of destructive ideologies in order to create the new regime of the people which is the characteristic of this century."

Hitler returned the favour with a flowery reply: "Duce, with deep emotion I thank you ... I am happy to be here in Rome in which the powerful manifestations of young Fascist Italy are united with the evidence of its incomparably glorious past." Hitler was clearly impressed with Italian culture and history. Then he made a frightening declaration: "The National-Socialist Movement and the Fascist Revolution have created two new and powerful States which today stand for order and healthy progress in a world of unrest and decay ... In this way there has been created in Europe a bloc of 120,000,000 people who are resolved to safeguard their eternal right to live and to defend themselves against all forces which might venture to oppose their natural development." Here Hitler sounded a strange and ominous tone of nationalistic paranoia. Both nations had been persecuted unfairly, in his view, and this common suffering had brought them together. They had been victimized by threats from both within and without. This perceived victimization bound them as much as anything else.

Summarizing the details of Hitler's departure from Rome, Birchall describes the double rows of soldiers stretching all the way from the Quirinal Palace to the train station. In the station there were a "forest of flags" and enough flowers for a greenhouse. This final moment, like every other aspect of Hitler's public visit, was a vast theatrical event with intricate staging carefully planned for each locale as Hitler moved from place to place. Hitler spent most of his stay in the capital. After several days he left for Florence, his last Italian stop before returning to Berlin. While Rome had political and cultural significance as the capital of Italy, Florence was important as the capital of the Renaissance and a centrepiece of Italy's reputation as the cradle of European civilization. This gave Hitler's visit to Italy additional symbolic significance, and it was a crucial aspect of the circumstances that generated Montale's subsequent poetry.

Whereas Rome and Naples had served to demonstrate the contemporary political and social power of a reinvigorated Italy, the visit to Florence emphasized the cultural importance of the Italian past, attempting to link the achievements of the Renaissance to the new alliance of the Fascist regimes. Accordingly the Fascists prepared an intricate procession through important architectural and artistic sites, incorporating the most important museums, palaces, piazzas, and streets in the city. It was a meticulously organized itinerary, prepared at great expense to the hosting Florentines. D. Medina Lasansky, an architectural historian, has retraced the motorized procession in Florence in an impressive scholarly study, recovering forgotten details from city archives and elsewhere.[6] Lasansky has shown that the first part of the tour of the city began at the Fascist-designed train station. Hitler's motorcade then drove through the Piazza del Duomo and the Piazza Vittorio Emanuele II (now the Piazza della Repubblica), passing the huge Strozzi Palace, down the historical and fashionable Via Tornabuoni, and across the ancient Ponte Santa Trinita to the Via Maggio. Hitler later arrived at the Pitti Palace, where he stopped to rest and view the paintings by Raphael, Titian, and other great masters.

In describing Hitler's arrival in Florence on 9 May, the *London Times* refers to what was known at the time as "Hitler weather," which in 1938, contrary to what one might suspect, was considered to be typically pleasant and sunny, not stormy and terrifying. We learn once again about the time of arrival and the circumstances: "Real 'Hitler weather' prevailed today, and in the bright sunshine and with its decorations of banners, tapestries, and flowers Florence presented a brilliant appearance."[7] These banners, tapestries, and flowers turn up in a very different way in Montale's "Hitler Spring," his meditative poem on the historic visit. The reporter gives us a sense of the processional motorcade through the city that followed. "The Führer arrived early in the afternoon and, standing beside the Duce in an open car, drove through the narrow streets to the cheers of the children and the people's shouts of 'Führer-Duce!' 'Führer-Duce!' By the Duomo, almost the only part of the route where a crowd could collect, he was given a welcome which seemed to be heartier than anything he got in Rome."

Hitler's motorcade wended its way to the enormous Pitti Palace, where specially prepared quarters awaited him. After viewing paintings in the Pitti, Hitler crossed the Arno via a secret passageway, the Corridorio Vasariano, to see paintings in the Uffizi Gallery. Afterwards he visited the nearby Boboli Gardens. There Hitler and Mussolini attended a spectacle that had been specially organized for Hitler's visit. It consisted of a combination of activities taken from an assortment of Tuscan festivals. According to Lasansky, it was the first time that these events had ever been brought together for a single occasion: "The men assembled were representatives of the four traditional Tuscan festivals: the Sienese *palio,* Florentine *calcio,* Pisan Gioco del Ponte and Aretine Joust of the Saracen."[8] Almost two thousand people participated in full costume. The festivities incorporated some of the same pageantry that had been used just a few months earlier at the Palio of August 1938, recreated in one of Montale's strongest poems, "Palio" (see chapter 4), to present a very different view of Italian culture at that moment.

As Hitler and Mussolini made their way through the city in their open car, they traversed the same streets that Montale and Irma Brandeis had walked every day. Both the Pitti Palace and the Boboli Gardens are located in the Oltrarno, very near areas that are crucial to Montale's love poems. The Nazi-Fascist procession passed close to Irma's apartment on the Costa San Giorgio, to the Pensione Annalena, and to the Bellosguardo hill. Montale recreated all of these topoi with his characteristic exactitude in his poetry.

Later in the day Hitler and Mussolini visited the thirteenth-century church of Santa Croce, where some of the greatest cultural treasures of Italy are located, including the tombs of Machiavelli, Rossini, Michelangelo, and Leonardo Bruni. In keeping with his affirmation of the Italian borders that had been won at the close of the First World War, Hitler placed wreaths on the crypt commemorating the Italian dead from that war. This was an obvious conciliatory gesture, showing the new German commitment to Italy and her post – First World War borders. Twenty-five thousand Blackshirts celebrated outside in the piazza. Afterwards Hitler and Mussolini were driven up to the Piazzale Michelangelo, where they were treated to one of the most famous and grandest panoramas of Florence.

The main event of the day was a demonstration in the Piazza della Signoria. Trumpeters in Florentine colours heralded the two dictators as they came out on the balcony of the Palazzo Vecchio, where the Medici princes had held forth during the Renaissance. Hitler and Mussolini had to come out on the balcony six times.[9] In a number of Montale's key poems – most obviously "New Stanzas" but many others as well – this type of elaborate display is contextualized to create a horrific world of opposition to the interior world of union with his beloved. The nearness of the threatening celebrations is conveyed in the intricate imagery of the poetry, but the lay-out of the principal settings is still visible today to a casual walker in the city of Florence. Irma's apartment at 54 Costa San Giorgio is just a short distance from all of the locales included in Hitler's itinerary. Perched on a hill that rises over the Arno, and a short walk from the trysts evoked in "Bellosguardo Times," it looks out at the Duomo and the Palazzo Vecchio. Her apartment, a locus for some of the most intimate poems that the poet wrote to her, is almost within view of the Palazzo Vecchio and, therefore, was in especially close proximity to the abuse of culture that occurred nearby.

Eyewitness accounts indicate that the Florentines were more enthusiastic about Hitler than the Romans were, although Lady Una Troubridge, one of the dwindling number of British expatriates still living in the Florence at the time, observed in her memoirs the artificial nature of much of the staged enthusiasm.[10] Harold Acton, too, wrote about the general lack of enthusiasm for the Fascists among the peasantry living in the hills around Florence in the late 1930s.[11] Nevertheless, the greater ardour on display for Hitler's visit to Florence made up for the smaller numbers, since larger crowds reportedly came out to see him in the south. The Fascist government did not leave much to chance. Hitler's visit was declared a national holiday.[12] Following an edict of "civilian mobilization," all Florentines were required to attend the procession of Hitler and Mussolini through the city. The people of the city were assigned different sections in which to assemble along the route.[13] In the evening there was a state banquet at the Palazzo Medici-Riccardi, which had been designed by Michelozzo for Cosimo de' Medici in the fifteenth century. Dinner was served in the Sala Luca Giordano.[14] Then the two dictators went to a reception and concert at the Teatro Comunale. The reception was attended by some of the leading cultural figures in Fascist circles (including Luigi Pirandello, Filippo Marinetti, Giuseppe Terragni, and Giovanni Papini),[15] and then Mussolini and Hitler heard an act from a Verdi opera, *Simon Boccanegra*. Birchall, who was also in the audience, says that the performance was "put on with the utmost artistic skill."

It is easy to guess the reason *Simon Boccanegra* and *Lohengrin* were chosen for performance in excerpt during Hitler's visit. Verdi's *Simon Boccanegra* is set in the late Middle Ages; the character of Boccanegra is modelled on the historical Simon Boccanegra (1301–63), the first doge of the city, who was descended from a powerful Genovese family that had dared to oppose the power of the old aristocracy. Wagner also used a medieval setting for *Lohengrin,* but he preferred a hero with supernatural powers and a mythic context, drawing upon the large reservoir of interrelated literary materials that furnished the characters of heroes, gods, and villains in most of his opera libretti.

In their toasts at the Palazzo Venezia in Rome a few days earlier Hitler and Mussolini had referred to their own sense of natural entitlement, a mythic destiny for their nations. Hitler specifically mentioned the misunderstanding and persecution that had beset the two nations, binding them in friendship. The two operas have plots that fit well with these notions.[16] *Lohengrin,* praised by Hitler in *Mein Kampf,* concerns the travails of a German knight who possesses superhuman powers; the great knight is eventually undone by jealousy and treachery, but only after emerging as the saviour of his people. The overly complex plot of *Simon Boccanegra,* which required revision, also presents a great national hero who is overcome by jealousy and treachery; Simon Boccanegra is eventually poisoned, but not before he has saved the city-state of medieval Genoa. Simon is conceived on a more human scale than is Lohengrin. He makes love to the daughter of his patrician enemy (Fiesco), and he is a prototype of an Italian national leader who seizes power through talent and force, bringing the varied social classes of his era, noble and plebeian, together in a unified and formidable whole. This is what Mussolini had hoped to accomplish in Italy and what he wanted to project to his German counterpart. In the Wagner and Verdi operas chosen for performance during Hitler's visit to Italy in 1938 both mythic Germany and mythic Italy are under threat, at risk because of enemies from within and without. There are external forces waiting to invade, and treacherous figures nearby.

After the opera excerpt from Verdi there was yet another military procession, illuminated by stupendous fireworks. Finally, Hitler left for the train station. The spectators who were gathered there lit three thousand candles. Under their celebratory glow Hitler took leave of his Italian hosts, and his train left for the north at around midnight. By 10 May he was back in Berlin, receiving an almost ecstatic welcome, with an amassed crowd of about 500,000.

Historians generally agree that Hitler was genuinely impressed by what he saw, in spite of the fact that the Italians were not adequately prepared for war. Mussolini fooled him; even worse, he fooled himself and the Italian people. Birchall had the impression at the time that Italy wanted to maintain its alliance with Hitler and yet simultaneously have friendly relations with Britain and France. He was not completely anti-Italian in his extensive coverage. He also suspected that Italy wanted peace at this point. He too was misled.

Hitler's visit to Italy was a disastrous moment in European history. It was marked by an unprecedented reliance on the powers of spectacle. Carlo Alberto Salustri, known by his pen name of Trilussa, summed up the Italian sleight of hand best when he wrote his short but devastatingly bitter *Epigramma* ("Epigram") of 1938: *"Roma de travertino, / rifatta de cartone, / saluta l'imbianchino, / suo prossimo padrone"* (Rome, made of marble, / rebuilt with cardboard, / salutes the house painter, [Hitler's early profession] / her next landlord).[17] The illusion of power led to a self-induced delusion of omnipotence, and eventually war. For the staging of the alliance before a world audience, cultural artefacts from Europe's glorious past and mass propaganda were combined in new ways to symbolize the political and military power of Hitler and Mussolini. It remains a telling example of how easily the message of art can be perverted and manipulated. Montale would confront this distortion in his later work.

The Aryan Italy

After Hitler's visit to Italy the political situation deteriorated rapidly. The Italian racial laws were implemented in 1938. The situation in the country changed quickly, as Mussolini and Hitler decided to make their internal policies parallel as well as to coordinate their foreign policy. Mussolini, who had occasionally toyed with the notion of the Italians as a great Aryan people, had never been particularly anti-Semitic, and two Jewish women, Margherita Sarfatti and Angelica Balabanoff, had even been influential in the formation of Fascist political strategy.[18] In fact, Mussolini, primarily to annoy the British, had even been pro-Zionist for a period of time.[19]

Nevertheless, Mussolini decided to adapt Hitler's anti-Semitic and general racial theories for an Italian application. One pressing motivation was to provide an ideological justification for the Italian invasions of Africa, but Mussolini at this point was quite happy to incorporate some of Hitler's wider notions of racism. On 14 July 1938 the Fascists published the "Manifesto of the Racist Scientists," which contained large sections purportedly written by Mussolini himself and which made it clear that Jews, Ethiopians, and Arabs were to be considered inferior to Aryan Italians.[20] There were ten basic "precepts":

1. Human races exist.
2. Great races and little races exist.
3. The concept of race is a purely biological one.

4. The people of present-day Italy are of Aryan origin, and their civilization is Aryan.
5. It is a legend that great masses of men were transplanted in historic times.
6. A pure "Italian race" is already in existence.
7. It is time for Italians frankly to proclaim themselves to be racists.
8. It is necessary to draw a neat distinction between the Mediterraneans of Europe (Western) on the one hand, and Orientals and Africans on the other.
9. The Jews do not belong to the Italian race.
10. The purely European physical and psychological characteristics of the Italians must not be altered in any way.[21]

In the same month the major newspapers were required to publish articles written by influential professors proving that Italians were Aryans. Soon major Jewish scholars, generals, admirals, and other top people were dismissed. Jews were to be excluded from a variety of professions, including journalism and education. Mussolini himself had to get rid of his Jewish dentist. All of this was required despite the fact that Jews were far less than one per cent of the total Italian population.[22]

Other absurdities followed quickly. Machiavelli's and Boccaccio's works were suddenly declared "unsuitable to the Fascist spirit" and placed on a list of prohibited books. The new laws led to the dismissal of ninety-seven Jewish scholars after their supposed racial impurity had been determined.[23] Some of Italy's best minds were forced out of the country or elected to go into exile. A disgusted Enrico Fermi, concerned about his Jewish wife, Laura Capon Fermi, left Italy directly after receiving the Nobel Prize in Sweden and escaped to the United States, where he joined the faculty at Columbia University and later the University of Chicago. He soon made essential contributions to the Manhattan Project from his new home in America.[24] In September 1938 Mussolini reiterated ideas from the "Manifesto of the Racist Scientists" in a short "Defence of Racist Policy." Although he did not rant in the Hitlerian manner, his words about the Jews were ominous: "World Jewry for the last sixteen years has been an irreconcilable enemy of Fascism. In Italy our policy has resulted in a veritable race on the part of Semitic elements to assault our ship of state."[25]

Irma Brandeis, who had already had some experience translating the Duce's speeches, took a copy of the new anti-Semitic policy with her and wrote about it to Gino Bigongiari from Paris on 27 August 1938.

It is "a document which will make your hair stand on end," she commented. "It comes from an unhappy country."[26] Montale, in turn, was horrified. He wrote to Irma on 14 November, referring to himself by his code name, Mister Gatu, which he knew she would recognize. "I saw Mister Gatu who is horrified by things in Germany and (he said) in Italy, about Jews. He told me he would be very happy, flattered, *honoured,* to marry a Jew. As for me, you know that I think things are running marvelously here and I approve all that is happening. He left me very discouraged."[27] He was afraid of censors and justifiably concerned about getting his severance pay from the Fascists who controlled the Gabinetto Vieusseux. He was formally fired a few weeks later.

The invasion of Albania came in April 1939. Mussolini's communication lines were so poorly set up that the Italian military had to use the public telephone system in order for Rome to keep in touch with the troops.[28] This was one of many indications that the Italians were not adequately equipped for the empire-building war of conquest that he hoped to wage. Ciano, acting on behalf of Mussolini, signed the Pact of Steel in Berlin on 22 May 1939, just a year after Hitler's Italian visit. This agreement locked Mussolini into a forced alliance with Hitler from which there was no escape. Although Mussolini still posed as a peacemaker between the democratic powers and Hitler as late as August 1939, war was inevitable. While Mussolini was trying to function as a go-between, Hitler invaded Poland on 31 August. Mussolini was taken by surprise.[29] It was the beginning of the Second World War.

The Poet as Witness

By 1939 Mussolini had been in power for fifteen years. There had been much ruthlessness, much bravado, much adventurism, but Italy was not prepared for war, and the majority of Italians were not overjoyed about the declaration of war.[30] Acton has observed that the Italians have always tended to be a peace-loving people, even in the era of Mussolini.[31] The streets of Rome were empty on 10 June 1940, the day that Italy declared war on France and England.[32] In other cities, throngs amassed in mob jubilation at the outset, yet there were many who had a sense of the disaster ahead. There was no one more sceptical of Mussolini's militaristic ambitions than Eugenio Montale. Carlo Bo's description of Montale at the Giubbe Rosse is an eyewitness account of the poet's reaction to the news of war on the day it reached Florence: "If I go back to the book of my memories what remains of the croaking voice which announced the Second World War in Piazza Vittorio [Piazza della Repubblica] in Florence? It was near sundown on a June day and rather than the great crowd, well ordered and unaware, I once again see the doubt and the consternation on Montale's face, seated at the Giubbe Rosse."[33]

After he was fired from his post at the library, the dejected Montale turned to his literary pursuits. Even a partial listing of some of Montale's activities at this time conveys a sense of his industriousness as a translator. In 1940 he translated Steinbeck's *In Dubious Battle.* In 1941 he turned to Spanish, translating several stories from Cervantes, some Bécquer (who had attracted his attention while he was writing *The Occasions*), and some work by Ramón Gómez, all for a collection put together by Carlo Bo. However, his dominant commitment was to Anglo-American literature, an interest that would have seemed dangerously subversive in the last years of Fascism. Working with the help of his assistant and collaborator Lucia Rodocanachi, he rendered into Italian Christopher Marlowe's *Faust* and a story by Dorothy Parker. Elio Vittorini edited Montale's translations of Hawthorne, Melville, Twain, Fitzgerald, Faulkner, and others in the following year. Montale translated Melville's *Billy Budd* as a separate project.

In November 1942 Montale's mother, Giuseppina, died at Monterosso. The poet wrote to Giulio Einaudi, describing how his house on the Via Cesare Cabelli in Genoa, with his books and papers, had been destroyed by Allied bombing. It could not have come as a great surprise. Mussolini was unable to protect the port city from the British navy, which had been able to bombard it easily since the beginning of the war. As the war progressed, the Italian coasts were vulnerable to Allied sea and air power. For Montale, this was the era of witnessing and writing. As he himself repeatedly put it, both in his poetry and elsewhere, he was "sitting vigil" in the time of war. He had become Mallarmé's "hero who is no one," defenceless against the unstoppable onslaught of history, while at the same time composing some of his most powerful poetry.

By now Montale was an Americanist scholar in Italy, just as Irma Brandeis was a *Dantista* in New York. He was reading Emily Dickinson, whose poetry he would publish in Italian translation a few years later. One of the poems of which he took particular note was "There Came a Wind Like a Bugle," written about a storm, which he would eventually publish as "La Tempesta" in 1945. Describing a fierce electrical storm, Dickinson finally wonders, "How much can come / And much can go / and yet abide the world!"[34] In the middle of the Second World War Montale must have thought Dickinson's exclamation extremely appropriate.

The war went very badly for Italy, and Mussolini was soon blamed for the disaster. In July 1943 the Allies invaded Sicily and began to bomb Rome. Under orders from the king, Mussolini was arrested and removed from office on 25 July 1943. A Fascist officer, Marshal Pietro Badoglio, was put in place to head the new government, but the war dragged on until Badoglio decided to surrender to the Allies. With the German occupation in September 1943, it became increasingly dangerous for Jewish people and for those who had helped them. While the Fascists had initiated racist policies, they had never enforced them with the efficiency and desperation of the German occupiers. Many Italians, especially Italian Jews, were now dislocated and on the run. While he had his enemies, Bernard Berenson had for the most part been left alone by the Italians at I Tatti because of his huge reputation for championing Italian culture, but even he was finally forced to go into hiding.[35] The composer Luigi Dallapiccola hid with his Jewish wife in Borgunto, a little hamlet in the hills just east of Fiesole. They stayed with Alessandro Bonsanti, who, because he had better Fascist credentials, had replaced Montale at the Gabinetto Vieusseux in 1938 – and yet Bonsanti was also willing to help Italian Jews. Eventually the Germans seized Bonsanti's home, and Dallapiccola's wife had to hide in the city, changing residences regularly.[36] These were the stories of the survivors, however. Others were not so fortunate. In the late fall of 1943 Nazi and Fascist groups raided a number of convents and a Catholic recreation centre, capturing hundreds of Jews who were hiding in them. They all were deported to concentration camps in the north, where almost certain death awaited.[37]

Well aware of the deteriorating situation, Irma Brandeis, safe in New York City, felt regret about the events of the late 1930s: "Arsenio's [Eugenio Montale's] birthday. Ten [years] and plus since we met. And almost 4 years since [the] last letter ... I read from these letters that I must have been to begin with artificial, imbecilic, vain, fearful in ways I am now unable to believe could persist beyond the age of 17 in anyone. With what genius or by what blessing did he see that there was anything at all anywhere in me that he could love ... I hope he is alive. I hope he is alive and safe."[38] Brandeis worked for the Office of War Information during the war, preparing propaganda broadcasts for Italy. When she had gone to the Office to apply for the job, her interviewer, ironically, was Drusilla Tanzi's son, Andrea Marangoni.[39] Marangoni had taken the job that Irma, in the late 1930s, had arranged for Montale at Smith College in the United States, and he had remained in the country to work for the war effort.

As the Allies approached Florence in 1944, conditions continued to worsen for the Italian civilians and the small Jewish population. The desperate Germans were committing atrocities more and more frequently. Perhaps the most horrible story of all was that of Roberto Einstein, a cousin of the great physicist Albert Einstein. Roberto Einstein had been hiding outside Florence with his Jewish-Italian wife, Nina Agar Mazzetti, and his two daughters. On 2 August 1944 the Schutzstaffel (S.S.) found him in his Tuscan hiding place. Einstein was able to elude them by running into the nearby woods, but the Nazis captured his wife and daughters. Hoping to lure him back, they forced his wife to call out to him for help for over an hour. His friends saved his life by muzzling him and restraining him. The Nazis eventually went back to the house, raped Einstein's daughters, and shot the Einstein women, killing them all. Then they set fire to the house. The meaningless nature of this brutality is further emphasized by the fact that it happened only a week before the Allies arrived in Florence. While Roberto Einstein survived physically, he was emotionally destroyed. A year later he took his own life by the graves of his family.[40]

Montale had already lost his publisher and friend Piero Gobetti, who had died prematurely as a result of the brutal beating he had received in 1925. Now the violence came close to him personally once again. Drusilla Tanzi's niece, Natalia Ginzburg, had published actively in *Solaria* alongside Montale and other anti-Fascist intellectuals. She had married the Russian-Jewish scholar Leone Ginzburg, who had been openly anti-Fascist since the early 1930s and was active in the Italian resistance. For most of the war the Ginzburgs hid successfully in the Abruzzi countryside. After Mussolini was removed from power in 1943, Leone returned to Rome to work at Einaudi's newly founded publishing house. But in November 1943 he was captured at the press, where he was preparing anti-Fascist publications. He was tortured and murdered in the Regina Coeli Prison in Rome.[41]

In the winter of 1943 Montale and Drusilla welcomed into their home Jewish writers and friends such as Umberto Saba, Carlo Levi, and others who had been forced into hiding by Nazi activities in Italy. Later Drusilla and Montale went into hiding themselves, seeking refuge for a time with fellow poet Alessandro Parronchi in his country house near

Greve. In September 1944 Drusilla became ill and went to the Palumbo Clinic on the Via Venezia in Florence. Montale wrote a poem about the experience. Titled "Ballad Written in a Clinic," it was his first significant poem about Drusilla, whom he affectionately called *La Mosca* (The Fly). Only much later in his life, after her death, would he turn to her as a subject once again.

It was the beginning of the end for the Fascists. Giovanni Gentile, Mussolini's most important intellectual theorist, had come to Florence to manage the Italian Academy in its new headquarters in the Palazzo Serristori.[42] He was murdered in Florence in April 1944. By that summer it became clear that the Germans would have to withdraw from the city and retrench on higher ground. They decided to blow up all the bridges over the Arno except for the ancient Ponte Vecchio, which, because it was very narrow, was strategically the least important. The beautiful Renaissance-era Ponte Santa Trinita, a site featured in short stories by both Irma Brandeis and Eugenio Montale, was destroyed on 4 August. Montale wrote a short poem, one of his "Florentine Madrigals," about the destruction of the bridge (its epigraph reads "August 11, 1944"). Much of the historic architecture along the Arno was reduced to rubble.

The Allies and partisans entered the city in August. By then Montale was in hiding in Fiesole, anticipating their arrival. By the end of the month the remaining Fascists had been pushed still farther to the north, closer to the hastily formed headquarters that the Germans had set up for Mussolini on Lake Garda. While attempting to escape into Switzerland, Mussolini and Clara Petacci, his favourite mistress, were captured near Lake Como by Italian partisans in April 1945. They were quickly executed. Their bodies were taken to the Piazzale Loreto in Milan and strung up by the ankles. Other Mussolini loyalists were captured and shot soon afterwards.

The war years did not silence Montale's poetic voice. In April 1943, just a few months before the Italians arrested Mussolini and removed him from office, Montale had contacted Gianfranco Contini, who was then teaching in Lugano, Switzerland. Montale wanted his friend to see the fifteen poems that he had composed for a new collection called *Finisterre*. He knew that it would be unsafe to publish them in Italy, so the poems were smuggled across the border to Contini and published in Lugano in a limited edition. These were to form the first part of *The Storm and Other Things*. In addition to a poem about Montale's late mother, *Finisterre* contained a rich collection of new Clizia poems, including "La bufera" ("The Storm"), the poem that was to give the title to Montale's next substantial book.[43] The poet included meditations on Clizia's earrings and bangs, on her flight from Italy, and on the letters he never sent to her. The fifteen poems contain some of the most frightening images of Clizia as a victim of the Nazis or Fascists; she is depicted with a torn wing, a bloodied throat, and – in one of the most disturbing poems – running through the woods as her dress is shredded by the underbrush. Irma Brandeis was becoming more remote in these poems, and Clizia was gradually distilling into something of her own. By the end of *Finisterre* the sacrificing "visiting angel" is more dominant than the woman who inspired her, as she takes on a meaning that helps Montale to express the irreconcilable rift in culture created by the cruelties of the war.

Time would be needed to absorb what had happened. Montale did not publish another major book of poems for more than a decade. Completed long after the war and finally published in 1956, *The Storm* was the third and last of his "three canticles." This third book brought him international standing as one of the greatest poets of the twentieth century.

6 The Storm and the Sun Goddess

It is that part of you that connects with the shipwreck of my people, of yours.
– Eugenio Montale

Unwritten Letters from Land's End

La bufera e altro (*The Storm and Other Things*) is the crisis work of the Clizia Cycle. It is here that the expected catastrophe of the Second World War finally occurs. The Fascist-Nazi *bufera* breaks out, while Clizia, becoming the sunflower that was created in Montale's first book, turns a brilliant yellow, flashing the light of the sun in lovely and defiant protest and eventually burning herself up in the dazzling light. This collection also covers a great expanse of time; it contains poems that originated in the late 1930s and early 1940s and others that were written as late as 1954. *The Storm and Other Things* continues the internal distillation process that was described in the Shakespeare sonnet chosen for the epigraph to the last and greatest section of *The Occasions*. This sustained evolution, which amounts to a remarkably relentless act of sublimation recorded in literary expression, reaches its apogee in the late poems of *The Storm*. By then, what is left of the original passion for Irma Brandeis distills into something else, something idealistic and fine but distinctly different from the earthly obsession of *The Occasions*. *The Storm* contains the most tragic meditations of the Clizia Cycle. The final reflections that come many years later are a rondo of reflection, an old poet remembering his youth, but here Montale is at the height of the meditative powers. Much like the prisoner he describes in one of the last poems of this volume, he is beyond hope, and it is in hopelessness that Clizia undergoes the ultimate metamorphosis in his mind.

A full contemplation of the Clizia Cycle must include an inspection of the list of poems from *The Storm and Other Things* that Brandeis included in the *Quarterly Review,* with, once again, the translated titles that she used: "The Storm," "Two in the Twilight," "Visit to Fadin," "The Black Trout," "Leaving a 'Dove,'" "On Llobregat," "Syria," "In the Greenhouse," "In the Park," "The Orchard," "The Hitler Spring," "The Shadow of the Magnolia," "The Blackcock," "The Eel," and "Little Testament." As in the case of the works chosen from *The Occasions,* this list includes a mixture of logical choices, curious inclusions, and puzzling omissions. Some of the works that Brandeis included were directly inspired by a passion for her; some of them concern a newly created goddess whose thematic purpose in Montale's poetry takes on a life apart from its initial connection to Irma as the woman who inspired her invention; and some of the poems even concern Montale's new interest in another woman.

The Storm and Other Things is divided into seven sections: "Finisterre," "Afterward," "Intermezzo," "Flashes and Dedications," "Silvae," "Private Madrigals," and "Provisional Conclusions." "Finisterre" was originally published by itself as a small book of poetry during the war, in Lugano, Switzerland, and was chiefly written from 1940 to 1942. That little book, also titled *Finisterre,* consists of fifteen poems that in themselves tell a unique chapter of the Clizia story. In "Intentions (Imaginary Interview)" Montale gives a valuable overview of *Finisterre*'s natural progression from *The Occasions*:

> The poems of *Finisterre* ... represent, let us say, my "Petrarchan" experience. I've projected the Selvaggia, the Mandetta, or the Delia (call her what you will) of the "Motets" against the background of a war that is both cosmic and earthly, without an end and without a reason, and I've pledged myself to her, lady or shade, angel or petrel. The motif had already been contained and anticipated in *Nuove Stanze* ["New Stanzas"], written before the war; it didn't take much then to be a prophet. It's a matter of a few poems, written in the incubus of 1940–1942, perhaps the freest I've ever written, and I thought their relationship to the central theme of *Le occasioni* was evident. If I had orchestrated and watered down my theme I would have been better understood. But I don't go looking for poetry, I

> wait to be visited. I write little, with few revisions, when it seems to me I can't not do so. If even so I can't escape rhetoric then it means (at least for me) it's inevitable.[1]

This crucial passage once again displays Montale's remarkable ability for intellectual self-understanding, something that is unusual in great poets. Mandetta was a female character in Guido Cavalcanti's Dolce Stil Novo poetry, Selvaggia is the literary name for Cino da Pistoia's paramour, and Delia is a freed Roman slave who is celebrated in the Latin poetry of Tibullus.[2] Montale has created a similar literary personage for himself in his poetry.

In *The Occasions* Montale had already combined the Dolce Stil Novo pledge of the poet to the undisclosed lady, covered under her various senhals, with the meditation on the last years of Fascism and the war. Two works that best exemplify this combination are the twenty "Motets" and "New Stanzas." Disclaiming any purposeful attempt at obscurity, Montale claims that his difficulty comes from within. He waits for the sounds and images of words to "visit" him; he does not cloak his simpler thoughts in complex words or water them down for easy comprehension.

With *Finisterre* came a Renaissance affiliation. The acknowledged connection of this poetry to Petrarch (1304–74) is yet one more conscious linking that Montale, secure in his originality, openly establishes with great works of world literature. Petrarch, the early Renaissance master, wrote his great sonnets to Laura, *his* absent donna. In writing to Clizia, Montale preserves his great predecessor and supplements his achievement.

Montale said that he printed *Finisterre* a few days before King Vittorio Emanuele III dismissed Mussolini as prime minister. While Mussolini was actually finished by the time that Montale published it in Lugano, the years 1943 to 1945 comprised the era of greatest danger for the opponents of Fascism. The Germans at that point took control of what remained of the Fascist enterprise and then took desperate measures as they began to lose power and declined steadily towards defeat.

Montale also spoke about *Finisterre* in an interview for ERI, the publishing division of RAI (Radiotelevisione Italiana), in 1951.[3] In it he depicts himself as a kind of introspective misfit. He does not deny history or the importance of Fascism, and yet he is unable to create mere reportage as poetry. Montale describes himself here as a "witness" of the twentieth century, a role he refers to quite specifically in the poems, where he portrays his role as a keeper of the "vigil." "New Stanzas," "News from Amiata," "Iris," and "Little Testament" are the most important of the many examples of this concept in the poems of the Clizia Cycle. He sees himself as an observer, not a hero:

> I have lived the events that have tormented mankind through two World Wars by sitting and watching them. There was nothing else for me to do. In my chapbook *Finisterre* (and the title alone is enough to prove it) the last great war in fact occupies the entire background, but only indirectly. Nevertheless my reaction was such that the book would have been unpublishable in Italy. I had it printed in Lugano in 1943. The opening epigraph alone would have been smoke in the eyes of the Fascist censors. It says, "*Les princes* (i.e., the dictators) *n'ont point d'yeux pour voir ces grandes merveilles; leurs mains ne servent plus qu'à nous persécuter ...*" These are the lines of a man who understood slaughter and struggle: Agrippa d'Aubigné. In short, Fascism and war gave my isolation the alibi that perhaps I needed. My poetry in those days had no choice but to become more closed, more concentrated.[4]

Montale turned inward but for very different reasons than, say, Mallarmé, Eliot, or Stevens, all poets with whom he shares important stylistic affinities. The epigraph from Agrippa d'Aubigné helps to illustrate his reasons. Théodore Agrippa D'Aubigné (1552–1630) was a French Huguenot poet, historian, and soldier who served under Henry of Navarre. He described the persecution of the Protestants in works such as *Les tragiques* (1616), which is filled with history, politics, and social critique of the decadent court of Henri III. *Les tragiques* includes a long list of Protestants who died for their faith. With the quotation from d'Aubigné, cited by the poet in the original French, Montale makes it clear that the Fascist dictators of the mid-twentieth century are nothing but persecutors who will one day be punished for their crimes: "The princes don't have eyes to see these grand marvels; their hands only serve to persecute us."

While Donne wrote a poem titled "The Storm," and Dickinson wrote "There Came a Wind Like a Bugle," which Montale translated as "La Tempesta," *la bufera* is also a Dantesque term, used in a variety of ways in *The Divine Comedy.* Montale was an avid reader of these writers, yet none could have predicted the unique poem of 1940 that gave his entire volume its title. The full text of "La bufera" (1940) has a central role in the narration of the Clizia story:

The storm that pours down on the hard
leaves of the magnolia, the long March
thunderclaps and the hail,

(The sounds of the crystal in your nocturnal
nest astonish you, the gold
that is worn from its mahogany, on the page-edge
of cloth-bound books, a grain
of sugar still burns in the shell
of your eyelids)

The lightning flash that candies up
trees and walls and astonishes them in that
eternity of an instant – marble, manna
and destruction – that, engraved within you,
you carry for your sentence and that binds you with
more than love to me, strange sister,

And then the coarse crash, the sistra, the shaking
of tambourines on the pit of thieves,
the tramping of the fandango and above
some groping gesture ...
As when
you turned, and with your hand, clearing
your brow of the clouds of hair,

acknowledged me – and entered into the darkness.[5]

La bufera (the storm) – the first word of the poem and also the first noun in the entire book of poems – is one of the most important images in Montale. It generates a chain of storm images, intoning like a haunting and dissonant sonority over an ominous bass pedal, and generally linked to the war and Fascism. If Monterosso al Mare is one bass pedal in Montale, then the *bufera infernal* of the Fascist years is another, and it exists in a dissonant relationship to the earlier, more consonant harmonies of the Cinque Terre. The primary meaning denoting the natural storm is important as well. Then there is the Dantesque significance of the word. Dante uses both *bufera infernal* and *tempesta* in the *Inferno*

(V, 28), in the famous canto that features the punishment of the lustful.[6] Lust in Dante is signified in sound by an infernal racket. This creates somewhat of an ambiguity about the storm images. We can be sure that Montale was well aware of this, and the terms may also signify his own internal sufferings to some extent.

The storm batters the hard leaves of the magnolia, another crucial image that is part of Montale's personal "ark," collected as one of the precious memories of his Monterosso childhood. The magnolia, a symbol of goodness, safety, and peace, is battered by the assault of the storm. In the second stanza there is the image of the *cristallo* (crystal), which some, including Jonathan Galassi, have linked to *Kristallnacht*, the destruction of the Jewish shops in 1930s Germany.[7] If so, it is a very loose association, but the images of sonic disruption were said by Montale himself to be connected to the vivid, real-life hell of the Fascist and Nazi experience (see the Guarnieri letter below).

Nevertheless, the other images here are very attractive, and parsing the contrasting tones of the imagery unlocks the secrets of the poem. The "you" of the golden light, startled by the crystal, is obviously Clizia. Her nocturnal nest, her resting place, is one of the sure signs of presence in her avian form, illuminated by the gentle but glowing light. The poem contains a wondrous collection of detailed observances of sounds and visual phenomena sited in unlikely, even remote, places. Light doused on mahogany, a grain of sugar in a shell of eyelids – these are the intimate, elegant details that only a poet of Montale's calibre can bring out with such ease. They are also images of a gentle tenderness that suggest the presence of the beloved.

The lightning flash of the third stanza is a very different matter. *Il lampo* is another of the many light images that are signs of Clizia. Clizia is sentenced to a fate, as yet undisclosed but here only evoked through symbols – "marble, manna and destruction." It is indelibly inscribed within her. We learn more of this fate in other poems, but here we know only that it binds her to the poet in a passion that is more than love. Clizia, still unnamed in Montale's poetry, is more than a woman or a lover here. She is already something of the goddess she will become and whose existence has been intimated in "The Motets." Clizia becomes a supra-erotic conception with the culmination of the poems to her. Borrowing from Baudelaire, Montale speaks to her as his "sister." (Clizia also becomes a "sister" in the late poem "The Eel.")[8]

A barrage of unpleasant sound imagery indicates the Nazi and Fascist section of the poem. A great crash, rattling sistra and tambourines, and a grating fandango emanate from a "ditch of thieves." In "The Motets," Baroque dances such as the forlane and the rigadoon, or popular dances such as the tango and the carioca, served to communicate positive and negative connotations. The fandango was originally a lively Spanish mating dance accompanied by castanets and hand-clapping. Montale would have known well the highly stylized fandango in Mozart's *Marriage of Figaro* (1786). After he failed to make a final break with Drusilla, Montale wrote to Irma in June 1939, with feelings of "infinite horror and shame," that his hands were "dancing the *fandango,*" making it difficult to hold a pen.[9] In the poem the fandango seems to be a devilish Nazi dance, and its clamorous qualities have become more important than the amorous ones. Just as the background meaning of musical forms is always important in Montale (fantasia, sarabande, madrigal, motet, et cetera), so are the rhythms of dance (fandango, tango, trescone, sardana, and the like).

The poem ends with overtones of Orpheus and Dante. In classical mythology, despite being warned, Orpheus looked at Eurydice one too many times and lost her forever. Eurydice stepped into the void and left him. Clizia seems to have done the same to Eugenio, at least at this point in the evolution of her story in the poems. Orpheus, whom Rilke treated in his sonnets of the 1920s (which Montale knew and admired), was one of the most famous lovers in ancient literature to have lost a beloved. It is appropriate that he should turn up here. Clizia waves at Eugenio and steps into the darkness: "you greeted me – to step into the darkness" (*mi salutasti – per entrar nel buio*). *Buio* (darkness), along with every shade of shadow and obscurity, characterizes the *Inferno,* whereas *luce,* and all manner of illumination that Dante could imagine, characterizes the *Paradiso.* It is appropriate that Montale's *Bufera* ends in Dantesque *buio.*

Finally, we find in "The Storm" three images that repeatedly evoke the beloved in Montale's Clizia poems: the hand, the forehead or brow, and the hair that covers it. These details are especially important in the poems of the "Finisterre" section (all written in the early 1940s) that follows "The Storm."

We must remember that descriptions of parting take place at many points and in various ways in the poems. They were traumatic moments but special moments that Montale could not forget. They played back in the camera's eye of his mind again and again throughout his life. While all of us have our moments of life indelibly marked in our consciousness, it is important to see how they work out in the mind of a great hermetic poet, for they take on a special power in the expressive language of such writing. Montale's poems contain the motions of going towards the beloved (arrival), her presence, and then going away (departure), as in Beethoven's "Das Lebewohl" Sonata (op. 87). "The Storm," the cornerstone work that begins the third of Montale's three great books, is about parting. In a late letter to Silvio Guarnieri, dated 29 November 1965 (by this time he had married Drusilla Tanzi, and Irma Brandeis had published him in English) Montale spells out rather clearly how the real and the abstract interplayed in his mind here:

> "The Storm" (the first poem) is the war, in specific *that* war after *that* dictatorship (see the epigraph); but it is also cosmic war, the perpetual war of always and of all ... The "sounds of crystal": hail. The location is indefinite, but it's far from me. "Marble, manna and destruction" are the components of a character: if you explain it, you slaughter the poem. "More than love" ... is NOT reducible. The "rattling," etc.: images of war. "As when": separation, as for example in "New Stanzas." "Clearing your forehead": realistic memory. "The darkness" is many things: distance, separation, uncertainty that she's still alive. The "you" is for Clizia.[10]

It is important, here as elsewhere, that Montale points at what is too specific to know as well as what is necessary to disclose. Too much specificity, including biographical or personal information, kills the poem.[11] However, he once again displays his remarkable ability for auto-criticism. He has a meticulously crafted reason for each word he writes, and if he chooses to do so, he can explain himself with great clarity. Montale clearly states that he wants the war to have a double significance. First, there is the very real Second World War, and then there is the larger cosmic war between good and evil.

The Clizia story continues in the next two poems, "Lungomare" ("By the Seashore") and "Su una lettera non scritta" ("On an Unwritten Letter"), both dating from 1940. They are written in the short, compacted two-stanza form common to many of the Motets. In "By the Seashore" the poet gazes at the sea while the wind picks up and the storm takes on force. He remembers a particular aspect of Clizia's appearance, her lovely eyelashes, as he stares at the water.[12] It is easy to imagine the setting as being the same in the next poem of the collection, which also takes place by a stormy seashore.

"On an Unwritten Letter" was written well after the poet had scribbled many "letters" to Clizia that were never sent to her. In "Two Jackals on a Leash" Montale described how many of his poems began as letters that were never sent or that were sent only in his imagination. We have already explored a number of important poems written in this manner, the most substantial of which is "News from Amiata," although there are other candidates for that distinction. Obviously, many phrases in Montale began as words that were intended to be sent to Irma but later turned up in poems to Clizia. Now he adds a slightly new twist to the rhetorical arrangement: a letter that was contemplated but never quite written.

In "On an Unwritten Letter" we meet an "I" who has been looking at the sea all night, scrutinizing the waves, remembering Clizia. Montale himself has referred to this poem as a "poem of absence" and to the war-time backdrop that he intended to create.[13] Clizia has been gone for a long time by now, and the poet is giving in to his almost overwhelming despair. As he looks at the sea, he again remembers the flash of her eyelashes, a beautiful detail that is almost torture to think about now. There is no solace for the poet at this point, not even in prayer. In fact, prayer (*la preghiera*) is a form of torture as is the thought of "the bottle on the sea" (*la bottiglia dal mare*) not reaching the beloved. Meanwhile, waves, empty of her presence, break on the point at land's end (*Finisterre*).[14]

This poem recalls the tormented prayer sequence in "Palio," where the poet is desperate without his beloved. We know that Montale thought of following Irma to America, but he eventually gave up on the idea. He mentions Vigny's "*bouteille à la mer*" in his 1925 essay "Style and Tradition."[15] In September 1933 Montale wrote to Irma, in a mix of Italian and French, that "*mi sento come una bouteille à la mer*" (I feel like a bottle in the ocean).[16] Here it becomes *la bottiglia dal mare,* the same expression, now in Italian. The poet perhaps senses that he will never go to the beloved; all he can do is launch a message in a bottle into the choppy waters. It floats out to sea from the poet's vantage point at Finisterre, land's end, where the breakers crash on the rocks.

Scholars have noted that *Finisterre* not only means "land's end" but also refers to a specific place, the extreme westernmost point in Europe, located in the northwestern province of Spanish Galicia.[17] On a thin strip of land just north of Portugal, facing the open ocean, Finisterre is the closest spot in Europe to North America, where Clizia/Irma resides. The fact that this poem names Finisterre, which points towards North America, makes it especially important. This phrase, tucked into place as the last word of the last line of the "unwritten letter," is the title of

Montale's collection of poems published in 1943, defining the desperate mood of the whole.[18]

The poet also hears Clizia in his dreams. The conflict between the forces of light and the forces of the storm are created in startling contrast as unconscious visions in the poem "Nel sonno" ("In Sleep," 1940). The images of light in this poem are the rainbow and the voice of the beloved. "Iris," a later and more substantial Clizia poem, associates the rainbow with her in a more obvious way. Here it interrupts the sounds of screeching birds. The possibly erotic "groans and sighs," the sinister background descriptions, the intimations of anxiety, all flow together in the dreaming subconscious until the poet hears her voice, which was so important in "The Motets."[19]

The forces of the storm are the "stinging" sound (clearly indicated by the sharpness of the sound image *punge,* from *pungere,* "to sting") of a "cruel gig," danced by the "adversary," who, as Montale specifies, is the same entity as the "silent nemesis" in "Costa San Giorgio," the poem from *The Occasions* about the steep and winding street in the Oltrarno, especially charged with Eros and memory, and near the Pensione Annalena.[20]

Pseudo-Sonnetry

While "In Sleep" gives us a helpful view of the contrasting images that form the two primary symbolic *pedale* in the Clizia Cycle, Montale's next series of poems achieves a new intensity by drawing on imagery already evident in the letters written to Irma in the 1930s. In these love letters, knees (often misspelled as "kneels"), hands, lips, feet, bangs, and earrings are carefully contemplated in one seductive passage after another. Now this intensity is distilled into art. "Gli orecchini" ("The Earrings," 1940) is a major poem in the Clizia Cycle.[21] It is the first in a series of three important Montale pseudo-sonnets in which Renaissance love sonnets and Mallarméan abstractions take on new impetus in an Italian Modernist setting. Montale himself used the term *pseudo-sonnet* in a June 1942 letter to his close friend Gianfranco Contini, the great Italian philological scholar.[22]

These pseudo-sonnets are works that draw on the past and yet at the same time are completely contemporary, pulling the Western tradition into the present moments of the great crises of civilization in the twentieth century. Each has the sonnet length of fourteen lines and a sonnet breadth of conception, compacting dense and complex material into a short space. They are not strictly modelled, however, on either the Petrarchan or the Shakespearean forms. They are not bound together with a strict rhyme scheme, and they do not have the Petrarchan octave or sestet format or the Shakespearean pattern of four quatrains and a couplet. While Montale specifically mentions Petrarch in reference to the poems of *Finisterre,* Shakespeare provides another important model. Montale, who carefully read Shakespeare love sonnets and published three translations of them, experiments playfully here with the sonnet form, just as Stravinsky created neoclassical references to older musical forms in his Modernist voice. "The Earrings" is fourteen lines, like the traditional sonnet, but there is no clear pattern of rhymed quatrains and couplet or octave and sestet.

Both Shakespeare and Montale begin their poems with the image of the mirror. Shakespeare used it in Sonnet 22, which Montale translated. In Shakespeare the "I" looks into the mirror by himself, thinking of time and ageing in relation to the beauty of the beloved: "My glass shall not persuade me I am old / So long as youth and thou are of one date." The first words of Montale's translated version are as follows: *"Allo specchio, ancor giovane mi credo / ché Giovinezza e te siete una cosa."*[23]

The modern poem, "The Earrings," is a totally new creation and in many ways goes beyond the Shakespearean model. As the Montale poem begins, the lover-poet is looking at the mirror, just like the lover-poet is in Shakespeare, but now the mirror is black. There is no trace of what he saw there before, of flashes of earrings in the light and perhaps a dimly lit room. Most of all, the poet can detect no trace of Clizia's flight from Europe, an act that he had previously tied together with such vivid intensity in "Palio," where he overlapped notions of her departure with the gyrations of horses racing around the Campo of Siena. All of that energy has dissipated:

The lamp-black doesn't preserve the shadow of flights
in the mirror (and of yours there is no hint).
The sponge, which the unprotected glimmerings
of the golden circle disperse, has passed.
Your stones, the corals, the strong authority
carrying you off, I sought. I flee
the goddess who won't incarnate herself, my desires
carry on, until in your lightning, they remain unspent.
Outside elytra drone, the crazy funeral
drones on and knows that two lives do not matter.

The tender medusas of the evening return
in the picture frame. Your impression
will come from below: where squalid hands,
twisted, fasten the corals to your earlobes.[24]

At first glance, this poem appears to some to be hermetic pseudo-babble, but with study, everything makes sense. Montale always knows what he wants to say as he tells his secret story.

As a group, the pseudo-sonnet poems seem to have a setting very similar to that of the earlier "New Stanzas," as if the poet is drawing on his memory of the same Florentine apartment. There are similar comparisons of the interior in the company of the beloved with the perilous exterior where the Fascist hordes have assembled. Here, in the first of the poems, the scene is highly reminiscent of "New Stanzas," where so much of the lyric centred on an intense observation of smoke rising from a crystal ash-tray. The major difference is that while the poet is still talking to Clizia, she is no longer actually present in the described scene. The poet refers with greater clarity to such details of the apartment furnishings as the mirror, which, while present in "New Stanzas," is entangled there in a dense metaphorical construction.

Now the poet is more concerned with objects that are much closer to the beloved than the mirror, or than the crystal ash-tray in "New Stanzas." He looks for the corals, jewels that are the mark of Clizia the goddess: "*Le tue pietre, i coralli.*" Clizia is a goddess here: the *iddia,* a "goddess who won't incarnate herself," who refuses to appear in her luscious flesh. This expression may be an early intimation of Clizia as a divine "Christ-bearer," an aspect of her that surfaces with greater clarity in later poems and in Montale's letters. It is also indicative of Montale's developing flirtation with Nestorianism, which appears definitively in the important late poem "Iris."

In "The Earrings" there are two types of flight, hers and his. There is also an important contrast of outside and inside, as in "New Stanzas." Outside, the war rages. While Montale is always anti-Fascist, he is also sickened by the madness of war: "Outside elytra drone, the crazy funeral / drones on and knows that two lives do not matter" (*Ronzano èlitre fuori, ronza il folle / mortorio e sa che due vite non contano*). The phrase *ronzano èlitre fuori* has been identified by Montale himself as denoting warplanes. *Ronzare* is used in the first Motet to indicate a distressing droning sound of dock-side machines in the port of Genoa. It serves a similar function in this poem, where it is used twice. An elytron is "one of the thickened sclerotized anterior wings in beetles and some other insects that serve only to protect the posterior pair – called also wing cover."[25] *Èlytre* is the Italian plural, *elytra* the English. The hard wing cases of beetles are certainly a sarcastic image for the droning warplanes of the era. Those warplanes are one and the same with the droning, insane funeral. This droning, a sound of destruction and death, makes a sharp and carefully constructed contrast with the jewellery images that evoke the beloved: *pietre, coralli,* and *orecchini,* in English "stones," "corals," and "earrings." Once again, aural and visual images combine to convey great symbolic power.

The close-up view of the corals (*coralli*), which appears twice in the text of the poem, is another indication of the earrings, probably details of the jewels installed in them. The central symbology of the poem deals with the ear and the area of the ear. While in some ways we are closer in "The Earrings" to the flesh-and-blood woman than we have been in any earlier poem, something of the process by which Irma is transformed into the goddess Clizia can also be witnessed in the poem. Montale names the beautiful jewellery, warmed by the body of the even more beautiful beloved, but eventually these symbols will become more important than the woman who inspired them.

Metonymy is as important a figure as is metaphor here and in the next poem. It is a useful figure for the troubadour of the twentieth-century trobar clus, for it allows the writer and his secret reader to savour the intimate features that only they would know – the jewel next to the beloved, on her skin, heated by the warmth of her flesh. These minutiae function as talismans that help the poet to reconstruct the lived experience of the moment and preserve it for her. Also, the poetry is densely worded, protective of the very passion encoded within it. It requires a professional reader or an extremely determined amateur to unravel its mystery.

The pattern continues in the second pseudo-sonnet, "La frangia dei capelli" ("The Bangs," 1941). Although this poem, like "The Earrings," is not in strict sonnet form, its fourteen lines establish a Renaissance or Elizabethan frame against which the modern context pulls and pushes to greatly successful effect. The poem begins with the delicate bangs of light-brown hair that hang over Irma's/Clizia's angelic, childlike forehead. The poet addresses her directly, man to woman, imploring her not to disturb those lovely strands of hair:

The bangs that cover
your childlike brow – you should not
divert them with your hand. They too talk

of you, on my road they are all the sky,
the only light with the jades that
encircle your wrist, in the tumult
of sleep the curtain that your pardons
spread out, the wing on which you go waves,
Artemis, transmigratory and unharmed
among the wars of the still-born; and if now
the airy down strews the foundation
with flowers, you make oceanic striations, leaping
downward in one jump, and your troubled brow
blends with the dawn, eclipsing it.[26]

As always, Montale is a great master of detail. Clizia's bangs, charmingly covering her forehead, and a jade bracelet, jewellery around her wrist, recreate the sense of the flesh-and-blood woman. Elsewhere earrings, a lock of hair, or a scarf does the same. They are parts of Clizia or items near or on her, all of which trigger something like a Proustian opening of renewed access to the past and remembered pleasure. Again, a crucial detail preserved in Montale's mind and fashioned into the poem is Clizia's hair, this time celebrated in the observations of her bangs.

At first the speaker is talking rather bluntly, but then the dense poetic language takes on more complexity until it becomes harder to track his beloved *tu*. In a dream vision Clizia suddenly has wings with which she can fly over the wars of the still-born. This is an abstraction for the very real strife of the Second World War. She is Artemis, safe and supreme above the swarming evil forces of the Fascists beneath her. Artemis was the Greek goddess of the hunt, protectress of women, and associated with nature, child-birth, harvest, and the moon. But the poet purposefully creates open-ended zones of meaning for his important symbols. Montale referred to himself as a Zoroastrian, at the banquet given in his honour in Stockholm after he had won the Nobel Prize in 1975: "I am perhaps a late follower of Zoroaster and I believe that the foundation of life is built upon the struggle between the two opposing forces of Good and Evil. I believe that all true poets have always fought in favor of Good, even when they seemed to exalt *les fleurs du mal*."[27]

In the poem Clizia embodies more than the revengeful Greco-Roman goddess who turned Actaeon into a stag and required a human sacrifice of the Greeks before they left for the Trojan wars. Here indeed the forces of good and evil seem to be divided, with Clizia, borne aloft on her wings, as the champion of the forces of good. Here it becomes obvious that everything good, including the whole sky and horizon, is metaphorically linked to her. The bangs are the sky, *tutto il cielo,* the only light, *la sola luce.* This is not the first or the only time we encounter this trope in Montale. The values of the world are recalibrated and measured in relation to his beloved, who is here transformed into a winged goddess. In some poems "all" exists in her, as in the last Motet, where all of life is small enough to fit into the handkerchief of the beloved. In "News from Amiata" nature or life exists to hold her *icona* (image). Similar hyperboles exist in other poems.

At times the struggle between good and evil in the poetry seems Manichean. Both Zoroaster, who lived in the sixth century BC, and Manes, who lived in the third century AD, were Persian. Manes, an intellectual descendant of Zoroaster, taught in Mesopotamia. He also divided the world into a struggle between the forces of good and the forces of evil. This opposition is built into the symbolic structure of many of the Clizia poems of *Finisterre.* Montale is looking for a wider sense of good and evil, a conception that can push out the borders of Christianity to embrace a broader cultural sensibility, reaching out into earlier religions, as indicated by his remarks on Zoroastrianism, Nestorianism, heretics such as David Lazzaretti, and, of course, Judaism (the religious origin of his goddess). Finally he reclaims his Clizia as a Christian heroine, but the larger cultural sensibility is of great importance.

"The Bangs" might also be read alongside Shakespeare's Sonnet 33, which Montale translated and published in Rome in 1944. We should note that there is no way to know when Montale first read Shakespeare, and he may have actually done these translations years before, so it is indeed valuable to think about Shakespeare as a sonneteer who might have exerted some influence on the Italian poet. The Italian version of the Shakespeare, which seems peculiarly abstract to the native English speaker who can read the Montale translation, has intimate details of the lover's brow and sunlight obscured by cloud and shade.[28] In the Italian translation the blending of the sun and light imagery with the notion of the beloved comes through particularly well. In Shakespeare the clouds eclipse the sun, which ultimately has no effect on the lover's determined passion: "Anon permit the basest clouds to ride / With ugly rack on his celestial face." In Montale's poem the lover's brow makes the eclipse and blends with the dawn. The difference is startling. Here the brow is brilliant enough to eclipse the dawn, so there are no reservations expressed about Clizia. In Shakespeare the lover is suffering because he has been tormented by the beloved.

While Montale may have got some images – the mirror, the lover's brow, the eclipse – from Shakespeare, what is most interesting to see is how different the Montale "sonnets" are. They encompass a Modernist's depth of feeling to read against Shakespeare's, and they add the fresh theme of defiance in the face of a great external political and social threat to the modern poet and his beloved. A summation of metonymic images of Clizia in the two poems is helpful. These two pseudo-sonnets, "The Earrings" and "The Bangs," add a great deal of detail about Clizia as she must have been remembered in her human incarnation as Irma. We see the following items as they had remained etched in the poet's mind: earrings, a jade bracelet, bangs, and the forehead or brow. These are the features that spark the recreation of the real woman who inspired Clizia. All of these features of the beloved or the items that she wore are mentioned in the letters that Montale wrote to Irma Brandeis in the 1930s. In addition, we encounter symbols of the woman-become-goddess or -angel: wings, feathers (down), and powers of flight. Something new is going on as the woman is transformed into myth.

The method of projecting the beloved against a background of war, both terrestrial and cosmic, continues in "Finestra fiesolana" ("Fiesole Window," 1941) and "Il giglio rosso" ("The Red Lily," 1942), two very important poems in *Finisterre* that do not have the pseudo-sonnet form. "Fiesole Window" is generally thought to have been written in 1941. However, in an interview published in Lorenzo Greco's invaluable collection of the poet's comments on his own work, Montale says that he waited for the liberating (presumably American and British) troops in Fiesole. From his perch there, perhaps already hopeful so early in the war, he thinks of Clizia's symbols – ivy (a symbol of fidelity and immortality introduced in "Bellosguardo Times") and sunlight.[29] He recreates the context in "Fiesole Window."

Since Montale himself suggests that Guarnieri read "New Stanzas" and "Hitler Spring" in relation to "The Red Lily," the young woman addressed in the poem is obviously Clizia.[30] Although Irma was not precisely twenty when they met, she was certainly in her twenties: "*Il giglio rosso, se un dì / mise radici nel tuo cuor di vent'anni ...*" (The red lily, if it one day / took hold in your heart of twenty years ...)[31] There is a dialectic between the red lily and the mistletoe, and both are extremely rich in symbolic connotations. The red lily is the symbol of Florence, and the banners and towers of the city are depicted in the poem as the rain turns to sunshine. The red lily indicates Eugenio and Clizia's love for Florence and Italian culture. The lily also symbolizes hope and light, overlapping with the powerful iris symbol that became the inspiration and title for one of Montale's major poems. The mistletoe, with both pre-Christian and Christian connotations, stands for healing, feminine power, and rebirth in the dead of winter.[32] For the time being, Clizia seems to have abandoned the lily for the mistletoe. This is another evocation of her departure from Italy before the war.

The scarf image was the first image of Irma to appear in the first Clizia poem, "Toward Capua" in *The Occasions*. It reappears in "The Red Lily." It is a return to an important metonymic symbol of the beloved. On the distant mountaintops "the red lily" (*il giglio rosso*) has already been sacrificed (*sacrificato*) to the "mistletoe" (*vischi*).[33] The poet describes Irma's/Clizia's scarf (*sciarpa*) and, too, hands (*mani*), as chilled in an "incorruptible frost" (*gelo incorruttible*). It is easy to imagine how the scarf and the hands of the beloved were images that played back repeatedly in Montale's thoughts until they found their way into a poem. They were crucial fragmentary details, functioning as gateways to the past and still living in the mind of a man who needed access to his lived experience.

"Il ventaglio " ("The Fan," 1942) is the last of Montale's pseudo-sonnet poems, exactly fourteen lines long, just like the others. It starts with Horace's "*Ut pictura*": "As is painting, so is poetry."[34] After beginning with the familiar phrase, the poet gives up. It as if the lover-speaker of the poem is trying to create the beloved, just as in a picture. He begins to recreate the details – the seductive lips (*le labbra*), the enigmatic looks (*gli sguardi*), the signs (*i segni*) or subtle expressions of love. He remembers the days of trysting, now lost forever. They are distant, as if he is looking at them through a spy-glass in reverse (*cannocchiale arrovesciato*). But then he becomes distracted by something more ominous, the evil spectre of war, explicitly rendered here as a distant vision of men and armour in conflict, with smoke rising around the battle. In the dawn the mists clear, the light changes, and with the arrival of a powerful heroine, the day is "perhaps saved" (*forse salvo*).[35]

The title is an obvious nod to Stéphane Mallarmé, who wrote two famous poems on the idea of a fan waving gently in the warm Parisian air: "Éventail" ("Fan") and "Autre éventail" ("Another Fan").[36] The Asian (Japanese or Chinese) fan was part of the orientalism that fascinated the French of this era. Claude Debussy, captivated by the possibilities of oriental music and intrigued with Mallarmé's poem, set "Autre éventail" to music in an important song. Montale would almost certainly have noticed both the poems and the music.

Mallarmé's wife is the subject whose fan provides the inspiration for the first "éventail." The young daughter, Geneviève, who also happened to sit for the American painter James McNeill Whistler, is the subject and addressee of "Autre éventail." She is the *rêveuse,* the dreamer who plunges the observing father into "a pure delight without end." With each blow of the fan comes a fresh blast of twilight air, until the fan seems to even hold back the horizon. Then the poet feels *vertige,* a type of vertigo or bewilderment of the senses. There is a "shiver of space," which is like a "grand kiss that, mad to be born for no one, cannot spout forth or subside." Space is meaningless in a universe without purpose. In the French poem the fan becomes a wing of flight that generates the universal presence and absence of space, running a long line from its base up along the arm to the laughter in Geneviève's lovely mouth.[37]

Both Mallarmé and Montale see visions of larger things through the very narrow and specific movements of a much-loved female character. In Mallarmé's poem, his daughter moves the fan. In Montale, Clizia generates a similar movement that is most central to the meaning of the poem. In both poems the subtle female movement displaces the horizon, even seeming to open up visions of alternate worlds. The two poets use almost identical words to describe the dizziness that sets in. In Mallarmé much of the meaning of the poem hinges on *vertige,* which occurs at the beginning of the ninth of twenty lines. Montale uses the similar Italian word *vertiginosa* (giddy, dizzy) at the beginning of the tenth line. In both poems the fan becomes a kind of bird wing. But the similarities show the differences, and Montale is able to assert and demonstrate his mastery precisely because of them. Whereas the French poem has a philosophical elegance, based on the implications improvised from the sight of a lovely young French woman waving a fan in the air, the Italian poem uses similar imagery to contrast the sublimity of love and the evil of war, making a much more specific referential point in the moral history of Western civilization as a centrepiece of the meaning.

Montale begins with Horace, as if he were about to compose a pretty picture of the beloved in words, and then abruptly drops him. There is too much at stake for a poem to merely depict a lady with a fan. It is important to note the extremely different ways in which Montale uses Mallarmé's precursor images, and the quote from Horace underscores this difference. When Montale commented on this poem, he singled out its main symbols: "images of war seen or dreamed synthetically (the telescope [or spy-glass]). The fan emerges out of the background, as the earrings did another time. He who has known you cannot really die; or rather, not even death has meaning for him who has known you."[38] While he clearly states his intentions, the fan is never specifically identified in the poem itself, only suggested by Clizia's avian wing movements. Clizia's beating wings divide the world into two visions: love and goodness on one side, evil and conflict on the other.

The phrase "a joust of men and armour" (*una giostra / d'uomini e ordegni*) is a rather blunt image of the Second World War, but it is also rich in allusion. *Una giostra* is another Dantesque term that occurs in the *Inferno.* It means "a joust," and *ordegni* is "armour" or "armaments" and close to our modern English "ordnance," which also has medieval origins.[39] This phrase should be thought of in English as simultaneously communicating a sense of the past and the present, as in a medieval "joust of men and armour" and a modern struggle or conflagration of men and ordnance (signifying modern armour and its explosive power). The medieval references have been mentioned in the scholarly literature on the poem, but there is obviously a contemporary meaning as well, referring to the murderous practices of contemporary warfare.[40] The battle that Montale describes takes place in strong gusts blown by "Eurus," the Greco-Roman god of the east wind. This, following the fragmented quotation from Horace, is the second classical reference in the poem. The victims or losers in the struggle plunge into a *calanca* (a gorge or ravine). There are also *orde* (hordes), a familiar symbol in Montale for the swarms of Nazis or *Fascisti.* Montale has already referred to them as the "*tregenda d'uomini*" (demonic horde of men) in "New Stanzas," and he will do so again in "Hitler Spring." The hordes and swarms of men are tightly related to the notions of storm and tempest in Montale, and it is significant that all of these terms turn up in *Finisterre,* the Petrarchan heart of the Clizia Cycle.

Only the defiant bird-goddess with her beating wings can defy these hordes, and, at the close of the poem, her powerful thunder and lightning blast away at them.[41] In Montale the beloved's beautiful image exists on one side, the carnage on the other, in what he himself once described as a Zoroastrian dialectic of good and evil. Meanwhile dawn now breaks through, reddening the light and smoke. In the last four lines things change in a surprise ending. Irma is no longer a woman, protected by her senhal. She is now the divine Clizia, finally transformed into a kind of omnipotent goddess with feathers on her cheeks. In the "mother-of-pearl light" (*luce la madreperla*) her cheeks "whiten" (*sbiancano*) into plumes, and the poet thinks that perhaps the day is saved (*il giorno è forse salvo*). The fanning movement of Clizia's hand creates great blows of revelation until they generate jagged flashes of lightning and exploding thunder over the hordes of Fascists and Nazis.

Using his unique sensibility for the sounds and images around him, Montale is a master of the telescopic technique of making small details loom large in the mind. He can do the reverse as well, making close and familiar details seem distant and strange. Quite literally, the spy-glass here is *arrovesciato* (turned around), making the objects seem farther away than they really are, not closer. Time has gone by, and it is harder to see the beloved, but things are very much alive in his mind, even more alive than before. It is just like looking through a spy-glass in reverse.

"Separated Personae," "The Ark," and the Dangers of the Night

Montale refers specifically to what he calls the "background of war" in "Personae separatae" ("Separated Personae," 1940), but it is a background that is a symbolic conception, not a literal one. Montale describes "a war seen above all as metaphysical otherness, an almost permanent state of the dark forces that conspire against us ... in common parlance the forces of evil."[42] This ambience applies consistently to the last poems of *Finisterre,* including this poem and "The Ark," "Day and Night," and "Your Flight," which end in a sinister and spectral fantasy. Read together, these short poems from the early 1940s form a sequence. The separated personae are obviously Clizia and the poet-speaker. Here the poet, the persona who narrates, remembers topoi, key locales in which he has been with Clizia, the persona who is supposed to hear him, but she is no longer there, only remembered in the present of the narration. The poet sees himself as he waits for her in the trees. He knows that her form has passed by there, but it has disappeared. The poem closes with a moving dichotomy. In the beloved, light can still find light, can still find itself. Without her, even daytime is darkness.

There is a great spring storm in "L'arca" ("The Ark," 1943), but to create a sense of the flood Montale uses the Italian *la tempesta,* not *la bufera.* This is the term he chose for his translation of Dickinson's "There Came a Wind Like a Bugle," and in many ways this is the closest poem to hers in Montale's work. In both poems a family takes shelter inside the house against a tempest that is raging outside. The *tempesta* has already surfaced in "Palio," where it is one of the threatening signs that Irma/ Clizia sees. The ark obviously refers to the biblical ark of Noah and the flood. Montale does not refer to the flood of the Hebrew Bible, which would have made the biblical reference more obvious. The ark image had been with him since the 1920s as a symbol of key thoughts that he could safely take with him throughout his life.[43] In the short story "Sul limite" ("At the Limit") each person is granted a "private ark" that can be taken even into the hereafter.[44] The ark appeared in the earlier poem "For Liuba, Leaving," where it is used to connote Liuba's Jewish background, and it echoes in Montale's mind. The biblical symbol of the preservation of the pact between God and humanity in the face of destruction is important for Montale as he struggles to save Judeo-Christian civilization in some form that will be meaningful for him and for Clizia.

This ark also carries memories of the house at Monterosso al Mare. The childhood garden and orchard (*orto*) reappear in important images such as the magnolia and willows. In "The Storm," the very first poem of *Finisterre,* the storm pelts the "tough leaves" of the magnolia. It is one of the precious childhood memories of the house on the sea that Montale carries with him as part of his psychological ark. Here it gives shelter to the family pets. Inside, soup is cooking in the kitchen, and the family nannies are at work. Also, the blond willow with bangs suggests something of Clizia. If the storm in "The Ark" is related to the storm of war, then the poem should be read closely with "Hitler Spring" and "Palio." Notions of storm (*bufera*), tempest (*tempesta*), and flood (*diluvio*) are related. The poet's precious memories and the people he loves have been swept away by time, which is as destructive as the biblical flood. The ark, associated with the sunflower and the rainbow, is a symbol of protection from the forces of calamitous destruction. Monterosso and Clizia come together in the great poem "The Orchard," and this relationship is prepared in "The Ark."

In "Giorno e notte" ("Day and Night," 1943) we actually hear the sounds of war, and there are intimations of war-time atrocities. The speaker of the poem begins with charming evocations of the beloved, but then he hears ominous steps in the piazza, followed by screams and weeping from a veranda. There are also threatened cloisters and hospitals, images of the destructive hell of war. The war threatens Clizia, even though the real-life Irma is safe in the United States. The shot booming in the night reddens her throat and shears her wings. Wings, sometimes shattered or torn from fighting her Nazi-Fascist foes, are one of the most important features of the goddess Clizia (see the twelfth Motet), only slightly less important than are her magical eyes. The veranda image is significant because the veranda of the Pensione Annalena turns up in later, less obscure poetry as a site of important interaction between Irma and Montale. Here the veranda serves as a site of Montale's surreality:

> A feather that flies can sketch your figure
> as well, or the sun-ray that plays hide and seek
> among the furniture, the reflection of the baby's
> mirror, on the roofs. Circling the wall
> the trailing mist extends the spires
> of the poplars and below ruffles the knife-grinder's
> parrot on the rickety cart. Then the sultry night
> in the little piazza, and the footsteps, and always this hard
> toil sinking to rise again the same
> for centuries, for instants, in nightmares that are not able
> to find again the light of your eyes in the incandescent
> cavern – and again the same screams and the unending
> weeping on the veranda
> if unexpectedly booms the shot that reddens
> the throat and the torn wings, O endangered
> messenger of dawn,
> and the cloisters and the hospitals destined
> for a cutting blast of trumpets ...[45]

In October 1961 Montale wrote a very important letter to Glauco Cambon, who was then teaching at the University of Michigan. The letter offers a penetrating look into what the poet was attempting to say in "Day and Night" and an even more significant insight into his method in forming the Clizia poems. It is clear that Montale was pleased with Cambon's commentary on his work, and he offers to give still more information to his Italian critic living in America:

> In your very, very intelligent gloss on "Day and Night," published in *Aut Aut* no. 65, you have extracted from the poetry something that in musical terms would be the harmonics [*gli armonici*], the complementary sounds. It does not matter if you treat the more psychological qualities rather than

the sounds or timbre. There is perhaps the possibility of a more practical interpretation that I can propose without contradicting yours. The poetry is part of a cycle – *Finisterre* – that dates from 1940–42, published at Lugano in '43. In the background of the whole cycle is the war, during which I lived in Florence (I've lived in Milan since '48). It would be difficult to see poplars from a Milan veranda, something that is perhaps not even possible in Florence. However, in Florence nature invades the city in a way that it does not in Milan, where I could not imagine the existence of little piazzas with knife-grinders and parrots. Present in all of the little cycle is the droning rumble of the war (understood as a cosmic fact), becoming plainly comprehensible as a "basso continuo" part with weeping and cries on a veranda, as well as a shot that reddens the throat of the endangered *visitatrice* [visiting lady/goddess]. But who is she? Certainly, in origin a real woman, but here and elsewhere, actually everywhere, a *visiting angel* [Montale uses the English words here], less and less material. It is not necessary to attribute the hovering feather to her, as if it had detached in anticipation of her wings (although that is not impossible). The feather sparkling in the mirror and other signs (in other poems) are nothing more than enigmatic announcements of the event that will be achieved: the "privileged" instant (Contini), often the visitation. And why does the *visitatrice* announce the dawn? Which dawn? Perhaps the dawn of a possible redemption, that could be as much peace as a metaphysical liberation. In fact, the *visitatrice* cannot be turned into flesh and bone; she has long since ceased to exist as such. Perhaps she has been dead for some time, perhaps she dies elsewhere in an instant. In her duty as unconscious *Cristofora* [Christ-bearer], she does not consent to another triumph that would not be a failure down here: the distance, the sorrow, vague phantoms reappearing (see "Iris," published in '43 and included in the second edition of *Finisterre* published by Barbèra), that such a presence for the one who receives it would be a memento, an admonition. Her physiognomy is always anxious, altered; her stance is mortal, her courage indomitable: this angel maintains all the earthly attributes, not yet having succeeded in casting them off (cf. "Voice That Came with the Coots," written some years later). Nevertheless, she is already *outside,* while we are *inside.* She, too, was *inside* (cf. "New Stanzas," in *The Occasions*), but then she left (cf. "Hitler Spring") to complete her mission.

If, then, one is to see the nightingale in her – and why not a *robin,* which has a red throat and sings at dawn? – I do not find it difficult. The important thing is that in me the translation from the real into the symbolic and vice versa is always unconscious. I always start with the real. I don't know

> how to invent anything. But when I set about to write (rapidly and with few corrections), the poetic nucleus has had a long incubation in me: long and obscure. *Après coup*, when things are done, I know my intentions.
>
> The realistic datum, however, is always present, always true. In the case of "Day and Night," the barracks, the hospital, and the sounds of bugles (reveille, mess call, leave, etc.) pertain to the outline of a militarized city. Nothing prevents our seeing in this a profile of an endless terrestrial inferno.
>
> I would not rest, dear Glauco, without thanking you for all that you do and will do in your new country [the United States] for furthering the cause of Italian culture. But perhaps you will remember ... all my admiration for your work.[46]

Montale's commentary on his own "Day and Night" is so comprehensive, so exact, that it leaves dangerously little for the critic to do. Montale has laid out what he sees as the fundamental activity of his method. He starts with the real and moves to the symbolic. His symbols, however, fit in a pattern of meaning that is analogous to harmonies in a tonal relationship in music. Once again, borrowings from musical vocabulary (*harmonics* and *basso continuo*) make this clear. The most obvious case of the real transformed into the imaginary is the real woman Irma who has mutated into the symbolic entity Clizia, but this is a general operation used throughout his writing process. Here we see how far Irma's transformation into Clizia has evolved. She becomes a *visitatrice* (a visiting lady-goddess or angel) or a *visiting angel* (Montale uses both English expressions in his letter written in Italian), a supernatural character with an existence of her own. A feather, a ray of light, and the glittering of a mirror are all signs of the Angel Clizia. Finally, Clizia becomes (both in spite of and because of her Jewish origins) an unconscious bearer of Christian symbolism and all that it embodies within the context of Montale's poetry. She is the unknowing salvific Christ-bearer, pagan, Jew, a pan-cultural symbol of good in a pitched battle against evil, and, finally and most important, Christian in her connotations.

Montale makes his symbolizing procedure perfectly clear. Irma has become the visiting angel Clizia and is no longer a material woman, and Clizia is the symbol of something that enables Montale to focus on hope, even at the worst moments of the war. There is the evident contrast of the joy in describing her and the disgust and repugnance in describing war-time Italy and the fallen state of Florence. Most important, Montale lays out a map of a number of the key Clizia poems. The poet himself, a number of times in this letter, describes these poems as part of a *ciclo* (cycle). "Day and Night" exists in a symbolic relationship with "New Stanzas," "Iris," "Voice That Came with the Coots," and "Hitler Spring." Using these as markers, we can begin to see the larger map of the Clizia poems. Even in this extraordinary document the full map is not complete. The cycle extends backward to other poems that have already been written, and forward into the future to poems that will be written later. In his letter to Cambon, Montale does not mention his late poems about the Pensione Annalena (because he has not yet written them), where he may well be contemplating one last time the same veranda that occurs in "Day and Night."

The final poem of the Clizia Cycle in the *Finisterre* sequence is also clarified by the clues that Montale provides for Cambon in his letter, but he does not mention it specifically. Irma's last departure from Italy before the war, which echoes repeatedly in Montale's mind throughout his life, is the subject of "Il tuo volo" ("Your Flight," 1943). Important details in this poem are the lock of Irma's hair that dangles down charmingly, one more image of her jewellery (the amulets), and still another image of her lovely hand, bedecked with gems and silk. We must add these to the growing images of the human aspects of the composite – hands, bangs, earrings, bracelet, scarf – which we slowly put together as we read poem after poem. Here we learn that Clizia's hair (unlike the real Irma's) is ash-blonde (*biondo cinerei*).[47]

How does it fit in relation to the Palio poems and the time scheme of the "Hitler Spring" setting? We can imagine how the image of Irma running from Italy played back in Montale's mind again and again. Clizia's moments of parting and flight take place repeatedly across his writing. Other poems with images of her flight from Italy are "Palio," where it is still fresh in the mind of the poet, and "The Earrings," where it has begun to fade into his memory. Some of these poems are clearly set in the spring or summer of 1938. "Your Flight" is an ambiguous nightmare vision, without a clearly determined date. Here Clizia's flight from the Fascists is treated with a fresh intensity, even though the poem itself was written in 1943. At that time Berenson, Dallapiccola, and other Florentine Jewish residents were forced into hiding, and some did not survive. Montale now imagines the fate of the beloved if she had not taken flight to safety in the United States:

If you appear in the fire (dangling
from the lock of hair and your dazzling
amulets),

two lights contend with you
in the deep ditch that stretches under
the twisting thorns.

Your dress is in shreds, the trampled
shrubs gleam back
and the fish pond swollen with human
tadpoles opens to the hollows of the night.

Oh do not stir up the filthy
edge, leave the burning piles,
the acrid smoke
over the survivors!

If you break up the fire (your ash-
blonde hair
above the wrinkle that so tenderly
has abandoned heaven),
how can your hand of silk
and of gems find your faithful follower
again among the dead?[48]

Consistent with his stated method of composition in his letter to Cambon (great poets are not always so consistent), Montale starts with the real – the lock of hair and the amulets – in the first stanza. In the second his imagination takes off as he imagines the tattered dress and trampled shrubs. Clizia is in a kind of metaphorical dream-flight from the immediate danger of capture, which, happily, did not actually occur. She is running in the woods at night, and her dress is torn to shreds. This is one of the few instances of Montale in which light does not have a positive connotation. The two lights mentioned in the first stanza could now be search-lights, attempting to track her as she flees. While the great bog seems real enough, it is also evocative of the many marshes and mud piles in Dante's *inferno,* and the reference to human tadpoles makes this even more obvious. Hell is both real and symbolic, as the poet states. In the third stanza, burning piles of debris and odorous smoke are disturbing and all too accurate images of the war, more evocative of the actual Holocaust than Montale could have imagined in 1943. In the last stanza he creates an unusual image of Clizia. In other poems she flies back to Italy as an avenging angel with wings, or her wings are lacerated by the great difficulties of her efforts, as they are in the twelfth Motet. Here she appears as a victim, her lovely hand reaching out for her faithful lover, another victim, buried among the piles of the dead. She will be depicted in the last poems as a bird goddess, invulnerable to her enemies, who chooses to consume herself in the brilliant sun.

"A mia madre" ("To My Mother," 1943) is the last poem of *Finisterre,* prompted by the death of Montale's mother, Giuseppina, at Monterosso in November 1942. The images of the cliffs of Mesco, so vital to the setting of *Cuttlefish Bones,* appear after the long series of Clizia poems. The magnolia, prominent on the Montale family property, begins the series, in "The Storm," and reappears in "The Ark." These images from Montale's life in the Cinque Terre provide an earth-bound framing for Clizia's struggle against supernatural evil, a counter-tonality to the diabolical *basso continuo* of the war and the heavenly harmonies of Clizia.

Madrigals of the Wayward Lover

There was a great gap in time between the publishing of *Finisterre* in 1943 and the eventual 1956 republication of it in the larger context of *The Storm and Other Things.* Montale signals this by dividing "Finisterre" from the next section of the book with the word *Dopo* ("Afterwards"). From this point he moves in many ways beyond the war years, and the memory of Irma seems to fade in his poetry for a time. However, there is a final and surprising flowering of the Clizia Cycle that is yet to come in the last poems of the collection.

In order to understand the process that gets Montale to this culmination, it is helpful to trace the wayward path in his poetry that leads once again to Clizia. In "Afterword," the next section of the book, he included two short poems under the distinctly musical title "Madrigali fiorentini" ("The Florentine Madrigals"). It is Montale's first use of this musical term to indicate a poetic form. The musical madrigal, a choral form, was first developed in Italy in the fourteenth century and later flourished, in very different and more intricate incarnations, in the sixteenth century, eventually laying the foundations for Baroque polyphony. The texts of the early madrigals are often short three-line stanzas, with each line normally consisting of seven or eleven syllables, followed by a closing *ritornello* made up of two lines of eleven syllables. The musical madrigal is a more profane genre than the motet, and the texts often deal with amorous or bawdy topics. One of Petrarch's begins, "Nor did

Diana ever please her lover / So much as when through good fortune he saw her naked."[49] Montale, whose choices of musical references and topics are meticulously planned, practises an unrhymed version of a form used by Petrarch (3 + 3 + 2) in his profane madrigals. He is moving away for a time from the more elevated tone that was appropriate for his Motets and towards a new range of subjects.

Historical context is obviously important for the "Florentine Madrigals." The first madrigal has an epigraph, "September 11, 1943," that clearly dates the poem to a little more than a month after Mussolini had been deposed in late July 1943 and after the German occupation of northern Italy had begun. Montale addresses "Herma" in the poem. The closeness in names at least suggests the possibility that Herma is another senhal for Irma.[50] However, the recent publication of *Lettere a Clizia* has brought to light Herma Fusćkar, an attractive, glamorous, and narcissistic young woman who played the piano and married into the Austrian nobility.[51] She, not Irma, seems a better fit for the poem, in which Montale refers to Herma's vanity. At the same time, the poet may have been indulging in some wordplay on the Herma/Irma similarity. In his madrigal Montale refers obscenely to Hitler's mustache as a *baffo buco* (an anus-mustache).[52] The epigraph for the second madrigal, "August 11, 1943," dates it to shortly after the arrival of the Allies in August 1944. The poem juxtaposes an image of a Bedlington terrier and the ruined stones of the Santa Trinita bridge, which had been detonated by the retreating Germans.

While "Intermezzo," the third section of *The Storm and Other Things*, does not concern Clizia, Irma included a prose poem from this section of the book, "Visita a Fadin" ("Visit to Fadin"), in the *Quarterly Review.* Sergio Fadin (1911–42), a Venetian writer, was one of Montale's old friends. Brandeis presumably could have met him through Montale. Another old friend, Sergio Solmi, wrote a preface for Fadin's *Elegies*, which were published in 1943. Fadin died in a hospital on the Ligurian coast, succumbing to a disease that he had caught in Africa while serving in the Italian campaign.[53]

"'Flashes' e dediche" ("Flashes and Dedications") is the fourth section of *The Storm and Other Things.* It marks Montale's new post-war life and features the emergence of new female listeners. Once again, Montale returns to the poetics of snap-shot that were so crucial in his Motets. He is quite clear about this, specifying in a note that they are the "magnesium flashes" of the photograph and that they belong, as a group of poems from a particular phase in his life, to the 1948–54 period.[54] It is noteworthy that Montale prefers the English word *flashes* for this poetry, as in the light-bulb flash of the photographer's camera. In Greco, Montale also specifies that the "Flashes" were to have "madrigalistic intonation."[55] The exploration of the "profane" side of love has the visual qualities of the snap-shot and the musical tones of the secular vocal composition.

There are two other women who now appear in Montale's writing. The first, known only as G.B.H., is someone whom Montale first met in Florence in 1945 and saw again during a trip to England in 1948 with Alberto Moravia and Elsa Morante. She may have been the inspiration for "La trota nera" ("The Black Trout," 1948), "Di un natale metropolitano" ("A Metropolitan Christmas," 1948), and several other important poems of the late 1940s and early 1950s. Regardless of its source of inspiration, Irma liked "The Black Trout" enough to include it in the *Quarterly Review* in Cid Corman's translation. The second and more important female presence in the new poetry is the *volpe* (vixen). She is modelled on Maria Luisa Spaziani, a poet and professor of French whom Montale met in 1949. The Vixen is the feminine antithesis of Clizia. She is the symbol of the earthy, carnal side of femininity. Clizia represents the ethereal and inspirational side, and she becomes that exclusively in the next phase of Montale's writing. The Vixen is the strongly sexual, female presence in "Sulla Greve" ("On the Greve," 1950), "Luce d'inverno" ("Winter Light," 1951–2), "Siria" ("Syria," 1951–2), and other poems in the "Flashes and Dedications" section and elsewhere in *The Storm and Other Things*. Spaziani herself asserted that she was the object of inspiration in "Verso Siena" ("Toward Siena," 1943, revised in 1950).[56] However, the early date of the initial version and the fact that Montale wrote three other poems about the Palio of Siena make it plausible that Clizia had some significance in the gestation of the poem. It begins with a pained outcry against the torment of memory. At its close, God hurls lightning at "his rebel." This is an indication of the continued penchant for religious questioning in many of the Clizia poems.

In some poems Clizia and one of Montale's new muses (G.B.H. or the Vixen) appear together, as the poet contemplates two sides of the feminine in symbolic form. One particular instance is "Lasciando un 'Dove'" ("Leaving a 'Dove,'" 1948), which, as Montale indicates, takes place at Ely Cathedral in Cambridgeshire, England. In this poem Montale says good-bye (temporarily) to the Clizia senhal. He admits that he "loved the sun, the color of honey" (*ho amato il sole, / il colore del miele*). Now a new love begins. He asks for "the brunette" and begs for "the fire that smoulders" (*il fuoco che cova*).[57] The sun image refers to Clizia. The Vixen and G.B.H. (who prefigures the Vixen) are usually symbolized with dark, sensuous images. "Eastbourne," another poem with an English setting, was one of the first Clizia poems of the 1930s. Now, many years later, the poet is turning away from Clizia, in an English setting once again.

"Sulla colonna più alta" ("On the Highest Column," 1948) takes place in the Great Mosque of Damascus, a site more extensively described in Montale's travel piece "On the Road to Damascus."[58] The mosque, formerly a church, is sacred for both Muslims and Christians. Staring at the three prominent minarets, Montale recalls the legend that Jesus appeared atop the eastern tower to do battle against the Antichrist before the Last Judgment.[59] In the poem the Vixen and Clizia are polar opposites, in a contest before "Christ the judge." Clizia, a Jewish woman now transformed into a kind of winged angel, flies down from the mountains of the Anti-Lebanon, her wings once again encrusted with ice. She has powers of transformation, turning all to mistletoe (an image associated with her in earlier poems). Divine law will be uttered through her. While they are from the heart of the Arabic world, the Middle Eastern images are important for the Jewish evocations of Clizia.

"Winter Light" has a visceral quality that is not evident in most of the Clizia love poems. Here the poet has assumed some of Clizia's avian qualities, descending from the sky to engage in lovemaking with the Vixen. A scratch on his throat and bite marks on his breast are signs of their coupling. The poet finds a reawakening in his knowledge of the Vixen, who generates elements of excitement and danger that are not elicited by the more aerial Clizia. A similar sense of renewal is evident in "Syria," another Vixen poem, in which the poet, speaking to the Vixen, claims, "I found my voice again through you."

Montale compares Clizia and the Vixen one more time in "Incantesimo" ("Incantation," 1948–54). An incantation is a magical spell that is sung, and the title is extremely apt in that the poem has a remarkable incantatory power in the Italian. Here the poet speaks about a woman named Diotima, a cunning reference to Hölderlin's code name for his beloved Susette Gontard. Montale now addresses another woman who has newly taken up the role of his customary female listener. The context indicates that the listener is the Vixen. Montale, commenting in Greco, says, "Diotima is Clizia, the cicadas were in an Italian garden, but they help to prepare the evocation of Galilee."[60] If so, the poet, describing her to the Vixen, speaks with compassion for both of his loves. In this poem Clizia and the Vixen, while distinctly different, have certain divine qualities in common.

As Arrowsmith and others have noted, Diotima means "God-honouring."[61] This is close to *Cristofora* (Christ-bearing), a concept that is crucial in Montale's notion of apotheosis for Clizia. Galilee, like the Mosque of Damascus, is a Middle Eastern image that has importance because it symbolizes a place in the land of Clizia's ancestry. Galilee (from the Hebrew word for "circle") is the area of what is now northern Israel. The poet predicts that the Vixen's *amore profano* (profane love) will be borne there, as it becomes worthy of a spiritual connection to her "God":[62] All around the world fades (*il mondo stinge*), but this new and powerfully profane love will be incandescent (*incandescente*) in the "lava" that carries it all the way to Galilee.[63]

By 1962, some thirty years after her original meeting with Montale, Irma Brandeis was determined to give a thorough sampling of his work, regardless of personal considerations. She included in the *Quarterly Review* "Leaving a 'Dove'" (in which the poet leaves her for another), "Syria," and "Sul Llobrogat" ("On the Llobrogat," 1954), all love poems obviously written to either G.B.H. or the Vixen.

The Rainbow, the Iris, and the Two Shipwrecked People

Since the rival female characters who appear in "Flashes and Dedications" seem to be so important to the poet, the intensity of the Clizia poems in the next section of *The Storm and Other Things* is surprising. Eleven poems are gathered under the title "Silvae" ("Undifferentiated Matter," 1944–50). It is a strangely humble title, given that these late poems have the greatest power and density of all the poems in this collection. The poetry is even more important than the fragmentary snap-shots that precede it, and the poems are longer, bringing the collection to a climax. Cary has explored the etymology of *silvae* extensively. The word means "forest" or "woods," bringing to mind an outdoor topos of some sort. Both Quintilian and the Renaissance humanists used the title to indicate an unrelated collection of assorted poems.[64] The original title of this section was "L'Angelo e la volpe" ("The Angel and the Vixen"), which indicates that the contest between the two continues in these poems. Angelo Jacomuzzi emphasizes the *religiosità*, the intense religious tone of the "apocalyptic" language in the great Clizia poems of this period.[65] With the dense symbolic texture of this difficult writing, Irma has truly been transformed into the quasi-Christian symbol Clizia. The "Silvae" section contains the poems of Clizia's final and most brilliant flowering and the richest and most challenging symbolism of the whole cycle.

The first poem in "Silvae" is "Iride" ("Iris" or "Rainbow," 1943–4). "Iris" is one of Montale's strongest poems, and the iris is one of his most intricately complex symbols, overlapping in a number of ways with the sunflower and other Clizia symbols. The title has many contexts in Italian; its various meanings include the flower known as iris, the rainbow, the iris of the eye, the general iridescence of light, and more (*arcobaleno* is another word for "rainbow" in Italian). In keeping with Montale's poetic practice, there is a generally unified "harmonic" area of meaning to the Italian word that connects it to other related Clizia images. The Italian critic Giuseppe Savoca contextualizes *iride* as representing the "absent-present *Iride*-Clizia, the woman angel," while Arrowsmith calls the word "polysemous" and preferred the translation "Rainbow" to "Iris."[66] The English word *iris* is almost as complex as the Italian *iride* and closer to the original language. It also includes notions of rainbow, for the mythological Iris was a personification of the rainbow. Like Clizia she had wings. For these reasons I prefer to translate the title as "Iris," following Galassi rather than Arrowsmith. Most important of all is that *iride* is obviously a Clizia word, because it is semantically linked to *luce* (light), *girasole* (sunflower), and related words. There are thus two flowers closely associated with Clizia, the sunflower and the iris, but the iris also has larger associations with the rainbow, the eye, and light in general. The rainbow, another phenomenon of light, is yet another senhal sign of Clizia. Finally, as we have seen, Montale associated the iris with Irma's eyes in the 1930s. In late July 1938 he wrote to her, "I saw once the iris of your eyes swimming and loosening shape and colours. It was in Genoa."[67]

In his notes to the Mondadori edition Montale included a clear guide to the personalities in the late poems of *The Storm and Other Things*:

> "*Silvae.* 'Iris': the character is that of 'The Red Lily' and the whole series of *Finisterre.* She comes backs in 'Hitler Spring,' in various *Silvae* (also with the name of Clizia) and in 'Little Testament.' We had already met her in many poems in *The Occasions,* for example in the *Motets* and in 'New Stanzas.' 'Iris' is a poem that I dreamed and then translated from a non-existent language. I am perhaps merely the medium rather than the author. The figure of 'The Ballad Written in a Clinic' was another woman [the Fly]; still another woman again [the Vixen] was the one in *'Flashes' and inscriptions* and the *Madrigals.*"[68]

La Mosca and the Vixen had become important symbols by the time of "Iris," and in this passage Montale quite clearly expresses where they are to be found, but Clizia is a character who connects a vast body of his work. In his "Imaginary Interview" (1946) Montale specifies in his own self-criticism how Clizia evolved into her appearance in "Iris." She may be the same character, but she is now recast as a dream vision and is far removed in appearance, purpose, and ability from the original woman who inspired her creation:

> But in key, terribly in key, among the new additions is "iride" ("Iris"), in which the sphinx of "Nuove Stanze" ("New Stanzas") who had left the east to illuminate the ice and mists of the north returns to us as the continuation and symbol of the eternal Christian sacrifice. She pays for all, expiates all, and he who recognizes her is the Nestorian, the man who knows best the affinities that bind God to incarnate beings, not the silly spiritualist or the rigid and abstract monophysite. I dreamed [it] twice and rewrote this poem: how could I make it clearer, correcting and interpreting it arbitrarily myself? I feel it's the one poem which merits the charges of obscurity recently brought against me.[69]

The "key" (Montale, as is his custom, uses the musical term *chiave*) links the new creation with all the tonally related symbols that evoke her in a clear harmonic relationship, yet Clizia's incarnation as a goddess in "Iris" is very clearly expressed here. According to Montale's own words, he may already have been contemplating Clizia as a supernatural figure, a figure he claims to have conceived as a sphinx as early as in "New Stanzas," yet the intimacy of the beautiful woman in the Florentine interior is as strongly conveyed in that poem as, in this poem, is the notion of a bird-like figure who moves from east to north to shine light on the mists and so forth. Now, returning to the poet and to Italy, she becomes a new sort of sacrificial symbol, and one with a newly ripened Christian significance. She makes, as the poet wrote to Cambon, her "vague, ghostly reappearance" in "Iris." She has become a Christian goddess, a "Christ-bearer," sacrificing herself for the common good. Finally, she came to him, as he says repeatedly, in a frequent dream.

There is a catch, however. Only another character in the dream poem itself, the Nestorian, understands what Clizia is doing, and Montale clearly identifies himself as the Nestorian in this passage of self-criticism and in the poem. Elsewhere he states quite explicitly that the Nestorian of *The Storm and Other Things*, like the sad-sack Arsenio of *Cuttlefish*

Bones, is another projection of himself.[70] Nestorianism is named after Nestorius, the patriarch of Constantinople in the early 400s. When one of Nestorius's priests questioned the notion of Mary as *Theotokos* (God-Bearer), Nestorius found himself at the centre of a great controversy. He supported his priest, and he gave sermons arguing that Mary's humanity should be underscored and that she should be described merely as *Christokos* (Christ-Bearer). This emphasis on Mary as the mother of a man, not of God, led to great alarm and to Nestorius's eventual downfall and exile. Subsequently Nestorianism came to be understood as the belief that Christ was essentially two entities, one human and one divine. It is not clear, however, that Nestorius ever expressed this view himself. The "monophysite," whom Montale describes disparagingly, believed fiercely that Jesus had only "one nature" that brought together in one entity both the human and the divine. Monophysitism, too, was later condemned as a heresy.[71]

The *Oxford Companion to English Literature* reminds us that the sphinx "had the head and breasts of a woman, the body of a dog, the tail of a serpent, the wings of a bird, the paws of a lion, and a human voice."[72] Clizia by now is no longer a mere woman, although she is still completely feminine. She too has wings, leonine qualities, jewel-encrusted surfaces, and a penetrating gaze that focuses like a laser beam on the evil forces around her. In spite of this assembly of features, I am quite sure that Montale imagined Clizia as an attractive sphinx. At times her womanly qualities, including her lovely voice, come to the fore. At other times her goddess attributes are more important.

Clizia until now had been generally very much a woman like Irma, and we can imagine the Clizia figure with her lover in a place of shelter, inside (*interno*), while outside (*esterno*) the tregenda is gathering. Her apotheosis is consistently prefigured or even indicated in a number of earlier poems, even among "The Motets" in the 1930s. This transformation is much more obvious in "Iris," as Montale points out in his own criticism. However, the woman who inspired the goddess peeks through even here, and the poem vacillates between depicting the goddess as woman or the woman as goddess. At times the human or the divine significance dominates. As usual, Montale can point to a basis for the poem in his actual life. The goddess appeared, after all, in her supernatural form in a dream that the poet had twice:

> When suddenly San Martino slips its embers
> downward and stirs them at the bottom of the dark
> blast furnace of Ontario,

crackling the green pine cones in the ashes
or the vapours from an infusion of poppies
and the bloody Face on the shroud
that separates me from you;

this and little else (if your sign
is little, a wink, in the struggle
that pushes me into an ossuary, shoulders to
the wall, where celestial sapphires
and palms and storks on one leg don't block
the wretched vision of this poor
lost Nestorian);

it is that part of you that connects with the shipwreck
of my people, of yours, or that a fire
of ice brings to mind the soil
that is yours and that you don't see; and I don't have
another rosary between the fingers, no other flame
if not this one, of resin and of berries,
invested in you.

*

Another heart is not similar to yours,
the lynx does not resemble the beautiful tabby cat
that hunts the hummingbird in the laurel;
but you believe them equal to you if you venture
beyond the shade of the sycamore,
or is it perhaps that mask on the white towel,
that effigy of purple that has guided you?

Because your work (that is a version
of His) might flower in other light,
Iris of Canaan you melt away
in that cloud of mistletoe and holly
that your heart conducts
into the night of the world, further than the mirage
of the desert flowers, your relatives.

If you appear, bring me back here, under the pergola
of dried-out vines, near the wharf
on our river – and the ferryboat does not turn around,
the sun of San Martino dissolves, black.
But if the you returning is not you, your earthly story

is changed, you don't wait
for the ferry prow,

you did not see, neither yesterday nor tomorrow;

because His work (that transforms
into yours) *must be continued.*[73]

The poem "Iris" is divided into two sections. In the Italian the first three seven-line stanzas are one long sentence, punctuated with three semicolons. The second half also has three stanzas, with three lines trailing after the last stanza, forming a kind of coda. If the poem is based on a written-out dream, as Montale claims, then it is logical to assume that real-life events overlap with surrealistic distortions in the text. In the first stanza we find the first of two references to San Martino, the Italian term for Indian summer. St Martin's Day occurs on the first of November. This was, in 1938, the time of Montale's most desperate letters, written after Irma had returned to the United States (Montale lost his job a month later, in December). Whether or not the poem is set in November 1938, the seasonal connection to this time of great anxiety in Montale's past is important because the poem is a reconfiguration of a dream. The seasonal setting of the poem is clear – the transitional moment between summer and autumn. The heightened fertility of summer and the ripeness of fall will soon transform into the decay and the death of late autumn and early winter. The natural rhythm of the seasons captures the larger cosmic rhythm.

The Ontario furnace is not an industrial image but instead Lake Ontario, churning up the energy of fall, which is also expressed in the "crackling of pine cones." Montale, who was extremely fond of the rhetorical device of metonymy, often turns to jewellery, clothing, and even vast geographical regions that are next to Clizia's location in order to suggest her presence. This is one of his most baffling and perhaps striking uses of the device. Why Ontario? Ontario is at least closer to Clizia than he is. The most terrifying image of the stanza is the "bloody Face on the shroud." It is part of the dream that Montale says he recreates in the poem. Is it Christ? It is generally assumed to be the towel that Saint Veronica handed to Jesus on the road to Calvary.[74] Jesus's visage left a permanent imprint on the linen towel (or *sudarium*), and the saint was able to carry it to Rome, where she used it to cure the emperor Tiberius. In the poem the towel separates the speaker and the beloved: "*il Volto insanguinato sul sudario / che mi divide da te*" (the bloody Face on the shroud that separates me from you).

In the second stanza, which flows directly from the first, with the two sections separated by a semicolon, the war (indicated by *lotta,* meaning "struggle" or "strife") has pushed the poet-speaker into a slaughterhouse or ossuary (*ossario*), with his shoulder to the wall. It is in this crucial moment in his poetry that Montale calls himself a *povero Nestoriano smarrito* (a poor lost Nestorian). The lost Nestorian recalls the lost prisoner of "Palio." Now, however, a deeper spiritual crisis has emerged. The watcher, the keeper of the vigil, has become a heretic, unable to sustain his belief in light of what he has seen. Culturally Catholic, thoroughly immersed in the grand breadth of his European Christianity and its rich cultural achievements, Montale has been rocked by the cruelty and anti-Semitism of the war years, and shaken in his faith. The poet-lover speaking to Clizia here is closely autobiographical. Yet he needs to preserve and redeem. Accordingly, he reconfigures himself, at least within the context of the dream poem, as a heretic.

In the third stanza Montale explicitly refers to the shipwreck of both his people (the Italians) and Clizia's people (the Jews). While Mallarmé liked the shipwreck image (for him, *naufrage*), he never spoke of something so obvious and direct as the suffering of the Jewish and Italian peoples in relation to it. Without detracting from the French master, we must look once again at the great power in Montale's allusion precisely because he is tying his writing to the tragedy of history, something that Mallarmé did not want to do. Both the speaker's people and the hearers' people are desperate shipwrecks in the mid-1940s. The Jewish people left in Europe were about to be destroyed, as, to some extent, were the Italians, lost in their own self-made catastrophe and about to face the brutality of the Nazis in the last years of the war. The storm and flood references implied in the notion of a shipwreck connect to the various ark symbols in Montale's work.

Montale turns to another way of encoding Irma Brandeis in his verse here. He uses a pair of senhals for her Austrian-Jewish family name. The images *fuoco* (fire) and *gelo* (ice) are obviously the German *Brand* (fire) plus *Eis* (ice) translated into Italian. Together, these are the components of the name "Brandeis," as has been suggested by Rebay, Clodagh Brook (more recently) and others.[75] This *Brand* plus *Eis* causes the poet to think of the soil that is hers but that he has never seen. This land is Palestine, which by 1948 would become modern Israel.

While Irma has now been sublimated into Clizia as goddess, Montale has moved on in his emotional life. Accordingly, the sign of another woman, the lynx, appears in the fourth stanza. Commentators have supposed the lynx to be Drusilla Tanzi Marangoni, who is usually symbolized as La Mosca (The Fly) and who is the subject of "Ballata scritta in una clinica" ("The Ballad Written in a Clinic," 1945), a long poem also included in *The Storm and Other Things.* If the lynx is not Drusilla, then the *mosca uccello,* a somewhat unusual Italian expression for "hummingbird," certainly suggests her presence. This nuance is of course lost in translation.

The fifth stanza is the stanza of redemption. Clizia's work and His (God's) work become allied, even the same. This is the first of two important allusions to the *canzone* from Dante's *Vita Nuova,* where Dante writes that speaking to Beatrice and speaking to God amount to the same thing.[76] However, there is a Middle Eastern reference here that is certainly not in Dante. Montale drops the sunflower senhal for another flower here. Clizia is the "Iris of Canaan." This can only be a reference to her Jewish background. The iris is traditionally connected to "the power of light,"[77] a power always characteristic of Clizia. In Greek culture Iris was the feminine messenger of the gods. Another of the various references to mistletoe (the fourth) in *The Storm and Other Things* now appears. It unites with the iris to connote Clizia's female power and salvific mission. She will heal and redeem. Holly and desert flowers, perhaps also indicative of the Middle East, round out the Clizian bouquet.

Sublimated Eros and Clizia's now divine purpose overlap in the sixth stanza, where, upon sight of the iris-rainbow, the poet seems to be recalling a forgotten trysting place by a river landing. Cambon, who also detects a secret trysting place here, compares this passage to Dante's ecstasy when he sites Beatrice on top of Mount Purgatory in the *Purgatorio.*[78]

San Martino comes back at the end of the poem, but its sun breaks up into blackness. If Clizia would come back, her "earthly history" would be transformed into something else, not the young woman who was in his arms by the river. It is too late for that. The poem ends with a Dantesque couplet declaiming, for the second time in the poem, that His (God's) work is now transformed into Clizia's. Clizia is now the unconscious Christ-bearer that Montale describes in his self-explanatory letter to Cambon. This is the poem in which Clizia is transformed into a goddess, if a quasi-Catholic one – a Christ-bearer perhaps – and Montale identifies himself as a Nestorian. It is one of the culminating peaks of the Clizia Cycle.

Love in the Garden

Irma Brandeis included two Arletta poems from "Silvae" in the *Quarterly Review.* "Nella serra" ("In the Greenhouse," 1946) and "Nel parco" ("In the Park," 1946) contain rich imagery of Monterosso once again. Most notable are the lemon trees and the magnolia, two crucial symbols in longer poems. It is surprising that Montale would still have been writing about his first love at such a late juncture, and it is surprising that Brandeis would have chosen to publish these two poems. The poet James Merrill translated them for the *Quarterly Review.*

"L'orto" ("The Orchard," 1946), however, is a strong Clizia poem, which some critics see as another climactic moment in Montale's poetry. *Orto* is a very important word in Montale, and the most important orto of the many gardens in his poems is the one beside the family home in Monterosso. There is another orto scene in "The Ark," where we see a large sheltering magnolia and the nearby Monterosso house, replete with pets and nannies. In "L'orto" this lost sheltering world and Clizia come together. *Orto* in Montale is sometimes translated as "orchard" and sometimes as "garden." To an Italian, however, the orto suggests a utilitarian area, cultivated for food in the family kitchen, while the *giardino* is generally decorative, intended for visual pleasure. In English, *orchard* suggests a larger cultivated area, as in a grove of fruit trees, and *garden* something smaller. In both languages there is, in the larger sense, the "Garden of Eden." In one of his essays Montale writes that the orto could be any "kitchen garden" or "vegetable patch" known to Italian families: "*L'orto* ... several square meters not always protected with shards of broken bottles in which a family finds everything, I say everything that is necessary for its sustainment."[79] He also made a distinction when he wrote to Irma on 7 September 1938 to describe his childhood home in Monterosso: "*Una pagoda a tre piani con grandi palme davanti, un giardino in decadenza e un orto.*" (A pagoda of three floors with great palm trees in front, a decorative garden in decay and a kitchen garden.)[80]

English strains to make the distinction. In the poem the meticulously observed details once again give Montale's verse a visceral sense of being in the scene, not simply reading a description of one. In spite of what Montale says about the small Italian kitchen garden, the obvious model for his orto is the ample area for gardens, plants, and trees at his Monterosso home, where the considerable property was sealed off by stone walls with broken bottles on top (see again the famous early poem "To Rest at Noon Pale and Engrossed," discussed in chapter 2, for another view of the broken bottles on the wall), for it is this topos that is indelibly recorded in his mind and which had been a source of imagery since *Cuttlefish Bones.* Following Montale's explanation in his letter to her, Irma translated "L'orto" as "The Orchard" ("The Garden" might have been a better choice) and placed it in the *Quarterly Review* just before Maurice English's translation of "Hitler Spring" in the same issue.[81] Once again, we have Irma's words disseminating in English a poem that, as she knew perfectly well, was inspired by her, is about her, and even addresses her. Her translation is powerful and clear, one of her strongest efforts on behalf of Montale:

I do not know, messenger
in descent, whom my god cherishes
(yours too, perhaps), if in the crab-tree grove
where the fledgling wrens mourn
languishing at nightfall,
I do not know if in the orchard
where the acorns rain and where beyond the wall
the hornbeams shed their airy garlands and point out
the foamy border of the waves, a sail
between crowns of rock
submerged or darkblack or more gleaming
than the first star that breaks –

I do not know whether your muffled step,
blind nightmare whereby from the day I saw you
I have grown toward death,
I do not know whether your step
that makes my veins throb
to its approach here in this labyrinth
is the same step that overtook me in another summer
before a gale grazing the upthrust peak of Mesco
shattered my mirror ...

I do not know whether the hand grazing my shoulder
is the same hand that once
at the celesta keyboard answered calls
from other nests and from a thicket long since burned.
The hour of torture and lament

that struck down on the world,
the hour you fore-read clear as though by book
fixing your hard crystal glance
full to the depths where acrid veils
of soot rising on flashes from the forge-room
barred from view
the handiwork of Vulcan,
the day of Wrath which more than once the cock
proclaimed unto the perjured,
did not divide you, undivided soul,
from the inhuman anguish, did not fuse you
within the cauldron, heart of amethyst.

O mute lips dry
from the long journey down the pathway made of air
that bore you, O limbs
I cannot tell apart from mine, O fingers slaking
the thirst of the dying and kindling those that live,
O purpose exceeding your own compass, having formed
the hand of the dial and expanding
into human time, into human space, in rages
of incarnate demons, in brows of angels
sped down in flight ... If the force
that turns the disc *already cut*
were another, your destiny bound up with mine
would show a single groove.[82]

Montale begins the first two thirteen-line stanzas with *Io non so* (I don't know) and repeats the phrase five times within the poem. The anaphoric effect of the repetition, creating a hypnotic musicality that comes through in English as well as in the Italian, conveys the doubt and anguish of the poet-speaker. He is talking to "her" about his God, and *forse* (maybe) hers. Here there are two Gods, two ways of knowing God, Christian and Jewish. Clizia once again is the *messaggera* (messenger). The root meaning of the word *angel* is "messenger" in both Italian and English. Clizia is the angel-messenger, the "visiting angel" that Montale described in his letter to Cambon.

Brandeis's determination to get the poem right in English is underscored by the fact that she actively sought advice on how to translate it from Cambon, the same scholar who had prompted Montale to clarify the symbolic design of his poetry with such precision. Cambon wrote to Brandeis, accurately describing the meaning of the word *messenger* in the poem, but totally unaware that he was writing to the actual woman who had inspired it: "One clue should come from what I called Montale's *Dolce Stil Novo* ... attitude to the addressee of this and many other poems: she is a '*donna angelicata,*' an angelized woman. The beginning of the poem, in fact, presents her as 'messenger' of God, retranslating into current Italian the original meaning of the word 'angel.'[83]

In the second stanza the highest peak of Cape Mesco, the same rocky peak that has been so important in earlier poems, appears once again, locating the orchard quite clearly as the one outside the family homestead in the Cinque Terre. The orchard, part of which still exists today, connected the houses of the two Montale cousins. The placement of the home and the orchard is significant. They are near the beach of Fegina and just outside the old town of Monterosso. During Montale's childhood his home was one of the last houses to the northwest of the town and closest to the bleak rocky peaks of the Punta del Mesco, which in turn thrusts dramatically outward into the sea to block the sight of Levanto and other points to the north.

The poet combines his vision of Clizia with his ark of memories of Monterosso, binding them together in his mind. He describes a remembrance of a wonderful light touch that remains, although he seems unsure whether it is Clizia or some other gentle touch from even further back, in his adolescence (Arletta or Paola Nicoli). The rhetoric of the poem makes it clear that the poet-speaker is addressing Clizia, and his torment and doubt end incisively when he begins to contemplate the evils of the Second World War. This was a time of "torture and lament" unleashed on the world, and Clizia is praised for her clarity of vision. She saw its implications clearly, more so than anyone. Clizia has a *duro sguardo di cristallo,* a "hard crystal gaze" (in Brandeis's translation). Her purity of vision takes on a cold clarity, but this vision also has a divine quality. Sometimes depicted with twin beams of light, Clizia's crystal gaze is related to the jewellery that she wears in other poems. The image emerges from an evolution of metonyms taken from her eyes, jewels, hair, and earrings, stretching to the more elusive symbols of dazzling light, Iris, and rainbow. All become symbols of *luce* as she becomes an angel-messenger from God, and her work and His combine in Montale's mind. In opposition to this symbol, Montale refers quite clearly to the "inhuman anguish" of the era. Clizia was a voice that championed "the perjured" Jews and other victims. She withstood the demonic work of Vulcan, the diabolical wrath and destruction, and the heat of the cauldron.[84] These are symbols for the Nazis and Fascists.

The last stanza answers the pronouncements of uncertainty that begin the poem. Echoing the many words of praise in the love letters for Irma's eyes, lips, hands, knees, and feet, the poet now addresses the lips, limbs, fingers, and purpose of the beloved in his poem. The parallelism of these nouns gives the lines a symmetrical deep structure, firmly etched within its grammar.[85] This stanza, therefore, has an incantatory drama that rivals the musicality of the opening lines, with their riveting cry of *io non so* (I don't know). While Clizia's lips, limbs, and fingers seem human, she once again is airborne, flying from the United States back to the beloved, from divine time and space into "human time and space." Her wings, described in other poems, are not mentioned here, but judging from other Montale works, it is logical to assume that the goddess has her own means of transportation and does not need an airplane. The poem closes with an indication that Clizia's destiny and the poet-lover's are separate yet together. Her disc has already been cut (as in a phonograph record). The italics giving emphasis to the notion that Clizia's fate was determined earlier are indicated in the original typed Italian manuscript and perhaps mark her Jewish-American origin as distinct from Montale's Catholic-Italian orientation.[86] If things were different, there would be only one groove for the two of them. This notion of a cut disc, encoding the life and purpose of Clizia, is reminiscent of the striking image of the "cut furrow" or "etched trace" at the end of "Palio." Both indicate the poet's notion of Clizia's clear purpose.

The coastal region of Liguria steadily pushes its way back into the last poems of *The Storm and Other Things*, particularly in the "Silvae" section. The next poem in the series, "Proda di Versilia" ("Coast of Versilia," 1946), concentrates exclusively on Liguria. Even the two palm trees in front of the family home at Monterosso appear in this poem. While the Florentine setting is still important, Montale brings together various sites of primal experience in his life, melding important cityscape, landscape, and sea-scape. Thus, the Ligurian coast is of vital importance in all three of Montale's great books. Similarly, Montale's erotic life generates a more elaborate symbology, as Clizia and the Volpe interact in a new diversity. Nothing essential is taken away as new things are added.

The next poem in "Silvae" is "Ezekiel Saw the Wheel." The use of the English title alone is a purposeful reference to the Old Testament prophet Ezekiel and to the well-known American Negro spiritual. In his criticism Montale expresses his admiration for the combining of "word and sound" in African-American spirituals, and it is not surprising that he wanted to co-opt some of that musicality for himself.[87] In a letter to Irma in the 1930s he makes specific reference to the spirituals and to the internationally famous Paul Robeson, even borrowing repeatedly from one of Robeson's most frequently recorded tunes, the lullaby "My Curly Headed Baby," to begin his letters to her (see chapter 3). At one point he even asks her to send him the sheet music for the tune.[88] This is important new information pointing to Clizia as the addressee of the poem. Arrowsmith says that Clizia's and Ezekiel's stories are blended in "Ezekiel Saw the Wheel," noting also a reference to Ezekiel in Dante's *Purgatorio.*[89] Both Clizia and Ezekiel warned of coming destruction in an age of moral decay. Initially Ezekiel's prophecies were warnings from within Jerusalem. Later he gave hope to the Jews during their Babylonian exile. The Negro spiritual speaks of Ezekiel's visionary sightings of the divine message, a wheel floating in the air above him. Similarly, with her firm "crystal gaze," Clizia warns of the destruction to come in Europe, and after her exile to America she offers a symbol of light and redemption in Montale's poems.

Nevertheless, Montale's rarefied European hermeticism makes this poem difficult and very much within his tradition. It is one of his most impenetrable works. The "vein of onyx" (*una vena d'onice*) is certainly a purposeful echo of the "nails of onyx" in one of the most difficult Mallarmé sonnets, the famous "Sonnet en yx."[90] The image of the *burrasca* (yet another word for "storm") is in line with the *bufera, tempesta,* and *tregenda* images of the Nazis and Fascists. As a bird goddess, Clizia might well have the claw (*il tuo artiglio*) that stretches out to reach the poet in the last line. If so, she has become a very remote symbol, with her pure, icy stare, her wings, her claws, and so forth. She has now evolved far from the human being who wore jewellery, smoked a cigarette, read and translated John Donne with the poet, or made love. This is the person we encounter in earlier poems, poems such as the early Motets or "Bellosguardo Times," the more Petrarchan poems of *Finisterre,* or the last, very late poems about Irma/Clizia that were written near the end of Montale's life (to be discussed in chapter 8). Clizia is now a kind of sphinx – sun goddess, just as Montale himself described in his self-criticism. In most cases in the poems of Clizia's most intricate evolution, the goddess still has some of her human attributes. In "Ezekiel Saw the Wheel" the poet recalls her gossamer hair, and he tries to suppress a memory of her lovely voice. In this dense, elusive poem little is left of what was once a beautiful young woman.

"Hitler Spring" and the Sunflower Goddess

Montale noted the bizarre paradox implied in linking Hitler and spring-time in Florence, long before Mel Brooks's comic masterpiece *The Producers,* which features a group of ingenious frauds (played by Zero Mostel and Gene Wilder) who stage a musical, *Springtime for Hitler and Germany,* that is so bad that it seemingly has to fail. They have intentionally written the title song, as well as the entire production, to be in such bad taste that the show will undoubtedly be a disastrous flop, thus allowing the shady producers to escape with all the money raised by the backers. They think they have a certain failure and a fool-proof scam, for what could be more tasteless and ridiculous than a grand theatrical tune about Hitler in spring-time? The audience reacts with the expected shock and disgust until someone starts to laugh. Unpredictably, the guaranteed flop is suddenly a hit. The film, released in 1967, was subsequently adapted by Brooks for a musical comedy (and a musical within the musical) that opened on Broadway in 2001. The musical has since been adapted for a new film treatment.

The madcap exaggeration of the two films and the Broadway musical make all the more obvious the poignant irony captured in Montale's "Hitler Spring," but it also makes it more difficult to see that Montale's poem is one of the twentieth century's most important poems. Montale, too, laughs with his ironic title, but his laughter is bitter and sarcastic. Montale wrote the great poem about the strange moment in history when Hitler and Mussolini met in Florence for a propagandistic celebration of their binding alliance. In this poem it is spring-time for Hitler in Florence in May 1938. The sun shines; the flowers are in bloom. The crowds cheer, and the international press naively talks of "Hitler weather" – warm and balmy, with plenty of sunshine. Hitler is at the end of his week-long tour of Italy. He has participated in the huge festivities in Rome in his honour. He has seen works of art and attended operas. On the way back he steps off the train for one last celebration with Mussolini and for more opera and art.

There were huge implications for Hitler and Mussolini in the Florence of May 1938. Two main strands of Western history collided on the day that Hitler's train pulled into the station. The first was the rise of Fascist dictatorships in the twentieth century. This, sadly and undeniably, was one outcome of European cultural history, springing most obviously from the emergent nationalism of the nineteenth and early twentieth centuries. With his hosting of Hitler in Italy, Mussolini bound his fate inexorably to Hitler. The other strand was the history of European humanism itself. Regrettably, Florence, a jewel of Western civilization and the chief site of the Renaissance, was chosen for a historic meeting of the two dictators. Montale captures in his poem the irony, the paradox, and the bitter moral implications of Hitler's visit to the seat of humanistic culture. Shortly after his culminating visit to Florence, the last stop on his Italian tour, Hitler plunged the world into war. Montale's poem is one of the great poems of the twentieth century, not only because of its quality but also because it addresses in a single poem, with an unequivocal moral stance, the collision of the worst and the best of European culture. For this reason it is equal in importance to similar works by T.S. Eliot, Paul Celan, Anna Akhmatova, and other major poets.

"Hitler Spring" is also a poem of culminating importance in the Clizia Cycle. By this late point in *The Storm and Other Things* Montale has written many of the important poems in his cycle. He has consistently spoken to Clizia in poem after poem, but he has never actually called her by name in any of the many poems in which he addresses her. "Hitler Spring" is the first poem in which Clizia actually is named. Here, however, she has gained a new symbolic identity totally apart from her initial inspiration. She has been fully sublimated from woman to goddess. This is a poem written to her incarnation as a goddess of hope and justice. In "Hitler Spring" Clizia, while still Jewish in her origin at this late date in the cycle, has been transformed into a classical sun goddess and a Christianized symbol as a feminized Christ-bearer.

Irma Brandeis, who knew better than anyone what this poem meant, included "Hitler Spring" in the *Quarterly Review,* using Maurice English's translation.[91] For the purposes of analysis I prefer my own:

Nor did she who turns to see the sun ...

Dante (?) to Giovanni Quirini

The thick white cloud of crazed moths
whirls around the dim street lights and parapets,
and spreads a shroud on the ground which crackles
like sugar under your feet; the imminent summer now releases
nocturnal frost contained
in secret caves of the dead season,
in the gardens of Maiano displaced to these sands.

Scarcely a moment ago the ambassador from hell rushed past us on the street

among the Fascist war cries of cutthroats, a gulf of staged mysticism lit
and adorned with hooked crosses took him and swallowed him whole;
the windows are closed, poor
and inoffensive, although they too are armed
with the cannons and toys of war;
the butcher has bolted up his shop that once bedecked
the snouts of slaughtered kids with berries,
the festival of mild-mannered executioners yet ignorant of blood
is transmuted into an obscene country dance of broken wings,
the larvae on the flood plain, and the water that follows
to eat into the shores; and no one is innocent any more.

Was it all for nothing, then? ... and the Roman
candles, to San Giovanni, that slowly whitewashed
the horizon, and the vows and the long good-byes
strong as a baptism in the lugubrious waiting
of the canaille (but a gem furrowed the air, setting loose
over the ice floes and seacoasts of your native shores,
the angels of Tobias, the seven, the seeds
of the future) and the heliotropes born
from your hands – all burnt and sucked
by a pollen that hisses like fire
and has peaks racked with blizzard winds ...

Oh the wounded
spring is still a festival that freezes itself
in death this death! Yet see
on high, Clizia, it is your destiny, you
who preserve an unchanged love through change,
until the hidden sun that you carry in you
blinds itself in the Other, and destroys itself
in Him, for all. Perhaps the sirens, the alarms
that greet the monsters in the night
of their demonic gathering, they already mingle
with a sound, which unloosed from the sky, falls, conquers –
with the breath of a dawn that tomorrow for all
returns, white but without wings
of terror, to the parched river beds of the south.[92]

The poem, obviously too dangerous to have been published in *Finisterre* in 1943, is a meditation on the 1938 meeting of Hitler and

Mussolini in Florence and the processional entrance of the two dictators into the heart of the city. The setting is rather clear: evening by the banks of the Arno at the Comunale of Firenze. In the usual Montale manner the white clouds of swooping moths disorient us, creating an odd and impertinent juxtaposition with the parapets and street lamps.[93] Montale left a note verifying this setting for the collected edition of his poems: "*Hitler e Mussolini a Firenze. Serata di gala al Comunale. Sull'Arno, una nevicata di farfalle bianche*" (Hitler and Mussolini at Florence. Gala evening at the City Hall. Along the Arno a snowfall of white moths).[94] In a 1961 interview with the Italian actor and writer Giansiro Ferrata he commented more substantially on what instigated the poem and on the complex symbology that makes it work:

> "Hitler Spring" is a very difficult poem. In Florence, the day on which the meeting of the Führer and the Duce took place; on the Arno a downpour of white moths, in an enormous quantity: it was a true snowfall, crackling under the feet. Naturally this is remembered as a sad sign.
>
> And then there is also Clizia, who left (Clizia was a Jewish woman who left for America).
>
> Clizia was not named Clizia; it is but the symbol of the woman changed into the sunflower: here the "hidden sun" that is carried in herself. In this moment, while the horde descends on the world and also on Florence, there is also, however, a streaming star, a gem that cuts the air and sets loose the angels of Tobias, the seeds of the future. All this is synthesized in very few words, naturally.
>
> Let us try, in closing, to see if we can read this "Hitler Spring," which bears an epigraph, a verse from Dante, to Giovanni Querini [*sic*]: "Nor did she who turns to see the sun" (it is always the woman "changed into the hidden sun").[95]

In "Hitler Spring" Montale uses his richly figurative voice to get at the implications of a precise moment in Italian history.[96] With remarkable effectiveness he employs his hermetic language, filled with metaphorical and metonymic elaboration, as a vehicle for a more forceful and resounding expression, purposefully avoiding a simpler, journalistic style of description or narration. In this poem, as in many of Montale's best works, the poet's language moves in dense chunks, carving out blocks of semantic space by moving against the pressure of reality – or, I should say, against the pressure of his subject. It connotes symbolic ideas, sending out blocks of meanings into the mind. It seems not to describe easily recognizable events or situations or emotions. Yet Montale can use his style to comment on very specific events, and he does so with a unique intensity that he could not achieve through conventional writing.

The meaning of the poem can be entered from two crucial lines, lines that explore the concept of mutability explicitly and even use Italian cognates of the word – *mutare, tramutata, mutata.* The Latin root for Italian and English is the same: "*muto, muta*" (change). We find the lines in the second stanza: "the festival of mild-mannered executioners yet ignorant of blood / is transmuted into an obscene country dance of broken wings" (*la sagra dei miti carnefici che ancora ignorano il sangue / s'è tramutata in un sozzo trescone d'ali schiantate*). Here even the innocent among the Italian hosts, those who are merely shopkeepers or butchers, become part of the larger dance of evil. The *trescone* is an Italian folk dance, which here serves to communicate the demonic atmosphere. The image of torn wings is associated with Clizia elsewhere in the cycle, and her injuries generally result from the struggle against evil. Here there is also a more specific association with the trampling of humanism and individualism, values represented by the city of Florence in general.

The fourth stanza contains the beautiful lines in which Montale finally calls out to Clizia by name:

> … Guarda ancora
> in alto, Clizia, è la tua sorte, tu
> che il non mutato amor mutata serbi …
>
> (Yet see on high,
> Clizia, it is your destiny, you
> who preserve an unchanged love through change ...)

This line is a quotation buried in the climax of the poem. It goes with the epigraph, which comes from the same source – a sonnet that is sometimes attributed to Dante. Montale almost certainly found the sonnet in the edition of Dante's *Rime* published by his friend Gianfranco Contini.[97] Dante may have sent this sonnet to the Venetian poet Giovanni Quirini. In context the lines that Montale borrows are:

> Né quella ch'a veder lo sol si gira
> e'l non mutato amor mutata serba,
> ebbe quant'io già mai fortuna acerba.

(Nor did she who turns to see the sun
and preserves an unchanged love through change,
ever have such bitter fortune as I.)

Whether by Dante or someone else, this is a medieval love poem, a sonnet that reworks an Ovidian myth, and both earlier texts are rewritten in the work of the modern poet. Montale chooses to emphasize two aspects of Clizia's name at this late point in the Clizia Cycle. First, he underscores her connection to Dante, Irma Brandeis's chosen subject of study. Second, he brings out the classical origin of her most important senhal. In so doing, he meticulously constructs echoes of both the Ovidian myth and the Dante sonnet in his own work.

Ovid's Clytie (Clizia) was the jealous nymph who loved the sun god Apollo.[98] When Apollo left her for another beauty, Leucothoe, Clytie pined away and went on a hunger strike. Staring at the sun in longing, following its movement across the sky, she eventually turned into a sunflower:

Where once her face had been; she was a flower,
Rooted, but turning always toward the sunlight,
Changed, but forever keeping love unchanging.[99]

The nymph Clytie did not turn away from the sun, and she changed into a sunflower. Her transformation preserves her unchanged love, for the sunflower always turns with the sun's change in position and never turns away from it. Irma Brandeis read and commented on Montale's great poem on the sunflower in *Cuttlefish Bones,* first becoming entranced with it in the 1930s and then writing criticism about it later in the decade. Before long she was transformed, like the Ovidian Clytie, into the symbol that had originally attracted her attention. She resented the intimations of jealousy in the Ovidian myth (more suitable for her rival, she thought): "I am tired of being asked whether I am, told that I am, Clizia in E.M.'s poems. Those who do so seem not aware of Clitie [Clytie] as Ovid tells her. She is a villainess, a woman suspended in love, and vengeful. She brings about the death of her innocent rival and is cursed by the god whom she continues to love in her heliotropic transformation. This is not my story. It resembles far more that of Xenia's except that Xenia succeeded in all she desired: blaming me, slandering me, returning herself to favor both in respect to her rival and to herself."[100]

In her bitterness Irma forgets that the sunflower, with its unique beauty, is the topic of one of Montale's most compelling poems, indeed one of the loveliest poems written in the entire twentieth century. Moreover, she assumes that Drusilla's code-name must be Xenia, when it is actually La Mosca (The Fly). The error is understandable because Drusilla was the chief addressee of the late series of twenty-eight "Xenia" poems, and Drusilla is explicitly referred to with her senhal of the Fly in these poems. *Xenia* actually means "hospitality," or "caring for the foreigner," in Greek, and, in any case, the "fly" did offer "hospitality" to the poet in that she took him into her home and supported him for many years, refusing to let go of him in her battles with Irma.[101] Far more important than any of these things within the world of Montale's poetry, Irma, not the hospitable fly, now becomes his "divine one," definitively dominating his literary imagination. It is Irma whom he has turned into Clizia, the sunflower goddess. Clizia, in her glorious incarnation of fire and light, now becomes the saviour of the world. The transformation, which has slowly taken place over many earlier poems, is finally accomplished in "Hitler Spring," the poem in which Montale's Clizia-goddess is named for the first time in his verse.

"Hitler Spring" is a poem that depends upon intertextual references to other works, some by Montale himself, many by others. Its first inklings are in the poem within the love letter that Montale wrote in English to Irma Brandeis in April 1934 (quoted in full in chapter 3). In that poem the dualistic antagonism of good versus evil is already evident, with Irma (as Lady Bat) on one side of the equation and Mussolini and the Fascists (chanting "Blood blood! / Birth copulation and death!") on the other. Further explanation of the connection between Clizia and the Dante epigraph to Quirini can be found in Montale's "Two Jackals on a Leash," the same short story, published in the *Corriere della Sera* in the winter of 1950, that helps us decipher "The Motets" (see chapter 4). In the story, the narrator reveals that the true identity of the unnamed woman is not really Clizia, but that her model can be "found in a sonnet of uncertain authorship which Dante, or someone else, sent to Giovanni Quirini."[102]

As we have seen, the fictional Mirco in "Two Jackals on a Leash" sits in a café and writes poems that the real-life poet, Montale, actually published in his "Motets," his series of enigmatic love poems in *The Occasions*. Montale's little narration also helps to explain "Hitler Spring," shedding light on various connected symbols: the epigraph, the myth of Clizia, Irma, the sunflower (*girasole*), and the heliotropes springing from her hands. They all resonate together as part of the same metaphorical equation. The botanical, the observed everyday object, the flesh-and-blood woman, and the mythic character commingle. Even the epigraph contains the disassembled roots of the Italian word for sunflower: *gira* (from *girare,* "to turn") plus *sole* (sun) equals *girasole* (sunflower).

The layers of culture, history, politics, and personal experience are carefully crafted and undeniably present: the myth of Apollo and a possible image from Plato's *Phaedrus* (shattered or broken wings); Dante's idealized romantic love, with its medieval adulation of unrequited passion; the broadest possible cultural view of Judeo-Christianity (including the story of Tobit, the feast of San Giovanni); Hitler and Mussolini in the social and historical specificity of 1938; and Clizia as Irma Brandeis. All of this blends in the mind of the poet-speaker, who meditates on these matters at some unspecified later point of narration. Time, history, love, religion, and intellectual knowledge all fold one into the other and are contemplated in the poet's mind as he searches for the implications of that instant in 1938 by the Arno River.

This is a poem of four irregular stanzas of irregular lengths (seven, twelve, eleven-and-a-half, and thirteen-and-a-half lines), written in free verse. The sequence of speech acts is of interest. Montale's customary poet-speaker is unnamed. He addresses Clizia through the course of the poem, moving from narration of the past event (Hitler in Florence) to a rhetorical question ("Was it all for nothing, then?") to conversational but direct address ("the ice floes and seacoasts of your native shores," "the heliotropes born from your hands") to the exhortation in which he finally names the beloved ("Yet see on high, Clizia"). Each stanza has a specific job and a specific shape that helps the job get done. The first stanza sets the stage. The second presents a vision of the Fascists swooping through the crowds and juxtaposes the mundane, relatively innocent world of everyday Florence. That world, we learn, is corrupted through a process of transformation or mutability (*mutazione*). The third stanza questions religion and all its teachings, its thousands of years of myth, morals, and ritual. Catholicism, Judaism, Christianity in its broadest possible sense – all are subtly evoked here. The fourth stanza responds to the great drama of the second stanza. The Hitleriana stanza is answered by the stanza of love. Here Clizia, goddess of the sunflower, emerges. The quote from Dante appears. Here change answers the change of the second stanza. Clizia's inner, concealed sun emerges and combines with an implied resurrection of humanity. It is an unspecified resurrection, part Judeo-Christian, part pagan (let us not forget that Apollo is the god of sun and light), part pantheistic. There are two kinds of change. One is from innocent into demonic. The other, achieved in the last stanza, absorbs both the angelic and the demonic into something larger, which we can describe as the redemption of humanity.

Let us take a closer look at the four stanzas, one by one. Years earlier, Montale began his self-reflective poem of modern despair, "Arsenio," with the phrase "*I turbini sollevano la polvere*" (Whirlwinds lift the dust). The word *turbini* had puzzled Irma Brandeis when she was reading "Arsenio" to prepare for her *Saturday Review* article on Montale in 1935–6, and she asked him about it in one of her letters. Now, in "Hitler Spring," using the same Italian word, he describes a whirling pack of crazed moths.[103] In "Arsenio" the immediacy of sensation makes all the more poignant the painful isolation of the modern individual. In "Hitler Spring" the same immediacy of sensation tells us about the banality of evil. The natural phenomena of the universe are as pungent and beautiful as ever. The natural world in which human beings live and move is as indifferent to the historical events in "Hitler Spring" as it was to the alienation of the young poet in "Arsenio." (We should remember that Arsenio, like the Nestorian, is an autobiographical masque for Montale.) May, the time of Hitler's Florentine appearance, is as cruel for Montale as April for Eliot in this respect.

Telescoping and foregrounding, so typical of the modernist poet, conveys this point of view effectively. The crazed moths flutter and cavort around the street lights and stones of the old city. They move in a flash of energy. The poet hears the crackling sounds of the insects as they are crushed underfoot. As spring comes, the air blows in mutable gusts, released from cold recesses in the caves near the little hillside towns of Maiano and Fiesole. The air flows over the orchards and gardens in the Tuscan hills, down through the charged site of historical and social significance, the city hall, past the spot of the observer-speaker, and finally to the low-lying flood plain by the riverbanks of the Arno (although Montale does not specify exactly where along the Arno this area is located).

The second stanza is the stanza of demonic mutation. Hitler, the ambassador from hell, zooms past, urged on by roars of Fascist approval against a background of "staged mysticism." He is absorbed in a sea of "hooked crosses" or swastikas. Montale obviously wants to blend the two with the phrase *croci a uncino.* Once again, details of everyday life are used to create a sense of the banality of evil. Carefully selected images evoke much more through their metonymic powers of suggestion. Closed shop windows, toy cannons, and other symbols of misguided patriotism, all these tell us of the people and things around and nearby. A butcher shop is tainted by Hitler's visit and is bolted shut. Once the scene of an innocent slaughter of kids, decorated with berries and flowers for the feast of San Giovanni, now it is *tramutata* (transmuted), changed into something obscene. Three seemingly unrelated images evoke this change: the obscene dance of broken wings (either symbolic of Clizia and her kind or, as Arrowsmith suggests, taken from Plato's *Phaedrus*),[104] dried larvae, and water that eats away at the shores (recalling the awesome sea of *Cuttlefish Bones*). It ends with the devastating words "no one is innocent any more."

By comparison, Frederick Birchall's account of exactly the same event, which he wrote as a reporter on the scene for the *New York Times*, seems dry, although it helpfully describes what transpired on that day: "A crowd of 200,000 massed in the square before the station and in the city's streets, gave the procession a rousing welcome as it proceeded to the Pitti Palace. The streets were so adorned with flags, at windows, on roof tops and festooned between houses, that the sky was almost hidden."[105] Montale's imagery penetrates deep into the culture of Italy and vividly records the experience of being there. Reading the two texts (the poem and the reporter's description) against each other is a great lesson in what the symbolic language of poetry can do and what journalism cannot.

"Was it all for nothing, then?" So begins the third stanza. Implied in the question is the larger cultural achievement that Florence represents. This includes the entirety of the great outpouring of learning and artistic expression that took place there and inspired the whole world. The fragments of religion come quickly. San Giovanni is the patron saint of Florence. The Piazza del Duomo, site of Filippo Brunelleschi's great dome, is really the Piazza di San Giovanni. Brunelleschi's dome is the most conspicuous visual symbol of the entire Florentine Renaissance, and it is visible from every important vantage point of the city in the surrounding hills. The festival in San Giovanni's honour, which combines both sacred and secular, popular and elite, elements of Florentine cultural life, is evoked through the zoom lens close-up of Montale's modernist hermeticism.[106] Candles stretch light across the horizon, even whitewashing it. The poem suggests that rituals of religion are practised by untutored masses, a passive crowd of followers who are now tainted by the Nazi and Fascist hordes that have mingled with them. The poet-speaker is wondering whether all of this has been rendered pointless by what took place in the city in May 1938.

Yet there is hope in "the gem" that "furrowed the air," a sure sign of Clizia, whose characteristic wings and jewels are by now well known from other poems. The furrowing gem recalls the cut furrow of Clizia's gyrations high up above the crowd in the 1938 poem "Palio," another indication of her powers of flight. Other jewels are the ring in "Palio" and the earrings and bracelet from the pseudo-sonnets in *Finisterre* (1943). Clizia, more of an active agent in "Hitler Spring" than she was in "Palio," now sends the angels of Tobias into action, and they slip through the air, fertilizing the icy shores.[107]

Tobias is the son of the Jewish patriarch Tobit. Both are figures from the Apocrypha, with varied importance in the Jewish, Roman Catholic, and Greek Orthodox literatures.[108] Clizia and Tobit are similar in that they share a clarity of inner moral vision. Tobit, who also resembles Antigone in many ways, dared to honour the unburied dead, defying a state decree against doing so. He is blinded by bird dung as a result of his good deeds. He sends his son Tobias away. Tobit regains his sight when Tobias returns from his adventures. Applying a special ointment made from the gallbladder of a magic fish, Tobias cures his father. The Angel Raphael, one of the seven angels summoned by Montale, helps and protects this suffering family. Tobias then marries Sara, who was formerly tormented by a demon, and the story ends happily.[109] In spite of the hopeful interlude, which incorporates Clizia as well as some similarly virtuous characters from the Apocrypha, the third stanza ends ambiguously. Although Clizia peaks in the poem here as a generator of heliotropes, it all ends in imagery of parched flora, flames, and blizzards.

Also, the name Brandeis is once again carefully crafted into the wordplay of the poem. Expanding on the very clear reference to Irma's family name in "Iris," the whole of the third stanza is filled with yet another use of the traditional opposition of fire and ice that has been used in European love poetry over many centuries. Montale knew that Petrarch used this contrast to describe his Laura. Even more important, the dubious Dante sonnet from which he borrows also contains it. By coincidence, Irma Brandeis's family name also features the fire and ice imagery. The *Brand* (fire) and *Eis* (ice) in "Brandeis" point covertly to Clizia's original identity and the Austrian-Jewish origin of her family name.[110] While Clizia is finally given her name in the cycle, Montale leaves a secret but perfectly clear path back to her origins in Irma Brandeis.

In the last stanza Montale describes what happens in Florence in May 1938 as a *tregenda* of *mostri,* a "demonic gathering" of "monsters," expanding on the *inferno* references in the second stanza. The use of *tregenda* (which might also be translated as "hellish horde" or "Witch's Sabbath") clearly aligns the demonic imagery of the poem with the *tregenda d'uomini* (the demonic horde of men) of the earlier "New Stanzas" in *The Occasions.* The *tregenda* is also associated with "pandemonium," or infernal racket. It should also be remembered that Pandaemonium was the capital of Hell in Milton's *Paradise Lost.* Unpleasant noise, swarming crowds, and hell are linked elsewhere in the great poetry of the world.

In this fourth and last stanza the spring-time is wounded, while Clizia is changing, transforming, absorbing both good and evil through her love. The poet's love for her remains unchanged because of this mutability. Here the second line from the medieval sonnet that is attributed to Dante is to be found. Once again, the embedded line is "an unchanged love preserved through change" (*e'l non mutato amor mutata serba*). The sunflower/Clizia/beloved carries a sun within her, which, dazzled by divine light, breaks up and becomes one with a greater light, making her one with a new, universal whole. This change is a *mutazione* of ecstatic decomposition and recomposition. The fantastic sense experiences described here are reminiscent of the *Paradiso.*[111] Light becomes sound as the senses converge, just as they do in the *Paradiso* when Dante ascends into heaven. A divine tone, heavenly music in defiance of the tregenda, descends from above and overwhelms the pandemonium of evil, reducing it to nothingness. It will return peace and reconciliation to the world. The sound/sun will shine again, the terrors of war forgotten in the inevitable transformation of historical unfolding. Evil is inconsequential and finite. Good evolves into the future.

Scholars are not sure of the exact date when Montale wrote "La primavera hitleriana," offering a variety of views on its composition. He may have made an early draft in the late 1930s or early 1940s. In the authoritative *Opera in versi,* Rosanna Bettarini and Gianfranco Contini refer to a typed manuscript, conserved by Montale's friend Alessandro Parronchi, that had been marked "1939–1946" at the foot of the first page.[112] It did not appear until the publication of *The Storm and Other Things* (1956), while in many aspects of style and content it seems connected to "Palio" and "The Pico Farnese Elegy," which appeared in *The*

Occasions.[113] In spite of the difficulty of the language, it would have been dangerous to publish the poem in the Fascist era. That fact alone underscores one of my main points, which is that such difficult and even hermetic poetic language need not be divorced from social and historical circumstance. Montale was a great master in the art of bringing these diverse aspects of literary expression together in his poetry.

In his varied critical writings Montale tends to deny his connection to the French, but stylistically he bears a family resemblance to several French writers. In his poetry we often find a succession of images that suggest meaning by amassing contrasting associations, a preference for paratactic juxtaposition over sequential explanation, the interjection of semi-conscious states, the tendency to magnify small details into huge importance, sudden shifts in syntax and semantics (the broken lines are one example), and dense blocks of language that are so thick you can barely get your mouth around them. All of this is familiar to any Mallarmiste.

Nonetheless, Montale was right in setting himself apart from old notions of "pure poetry" and *ermetismo* (hermeticism), as he does in various essays and interviews. He was able to make his High Modernist style speak directly to the human condition in a manner that was far removed from the original intentions of those who instigated its development in the late nineteenth century. In this direct connection to his era Montale is far closer to Dante, whose great poem is filled with fierce commentary on the history and politics of his time. Montale sensitively captures the clash of staged cultural artefact and true cultural wisdom, the irony and ambiguity of hellish events in spring-time, the paradox of the demonic actions of human beings as they take place in the fine spring weather. And yet he is able to present a larger view of his subject, meditating on the process of events in mutable history, predicting that even the darkest moments in "Hitler Spring" must pass into something new and perhaps even hopeful.

Italian Birds, the Shade of the Magnolia, and the Eel

Montale saw "Voce giunta con le folaghe" ("Voice That Came with the Coots," 1947) as a critical part of the Clizia sequence. This poem is written to Montale's father, who is dead and thus cannot respond. Montale also refers to Clizia. His pointed use of *buio* (darkness), *ombra* (shade), *la via* (the road), and *vermene* (verbena) gives this poem a markedly Dantesque flavour. Here once again Montale's early life, including his memories of his family at Monterosso, combines with the symbolized incarnation of Clizia. The poem continues the gradually developing practice in *The Storm and Other Things* of blending the Clizia/Florentine experience with the Monterosso culture and background, effectively combining *Cuttlefish Bones* and *The Occasions* in a new synthesis. Clizia's otherworldly form is as evident in "Voice That Came with the Coots" as it is in "Hitler Spring." Playing upon his remodelled motif of Beatrice in the *Paradiso,* Montale introduces Clizia here as an *ombra fidata* (trusted shade) who accompanies him to his father's tomb at the family grave site, perched high above the sea at Monterosso, with boats passing in the distance. Her womanly attributes, including her bangs and forehead, are to some extent evident, and her eyes, often possessing an inhuman power of penetration in some poems, are here merely ardent.

Montale describes Clizia's condition in this poem quite specifically in his letter to Cambon (quoted above). She is an immortal character with womanly or "earthly attributes" that she has not yet discarded. Without this key information it would also be plausible to read this Monterosso-based poem as part of Montale's Arletta sequence, an ambiguity that might still be kept in mind. But by now Clizia is in an altered state, having been transfigured into a Dantesque immortality in "Hitler Spring." Continuing the pattern of "Hitler Spring," Clizia has a fire burning within, giving her a "disembodied" form, until she is consumed by the solar light of "Him" (God). Her salvific role as an unconscious Christ-bearer is as clearly indicated in this poem as in any of the late Montale poems of *The Storm and Other Things.*

From her unique perspective as Montale's most important secret reader, Irma Brandeis decided to publish two of James Merrill's translations of Montale poems in the *Quarterly Review:* "L'ombra della magnolia" ("The Shadow of the Magnolia," 1947) and "Il gallo cedrone" ("The Blackcock," 1943). Owing to Merrill's own prominence as one of the best American poets of the late twentieth century, his translations mark an important point of Montale's entry into the mainstream of American literature. "The Blackcock" is one of the many fine Montale poems that deal with birds. Since it concerns a wounded bird, often a sign of Clizia, it is indirectly related to the Clizia Cycle, but it probably is based on an incident from Montale's youth in Monterosso.

Far more important to the Clizia Cycle, "The Shadow of the Magnolia" brings together *The Occasions* and *Cuttlefish Bones* with even greater clarity than does "Voice That Came with the Coots." This is a poem that begins the last moments of the last movement, after the modulations and just before the return to a long *pedale* in the home key. This is a home key in more than one sense because the magnolia symbol takes us back to Monterosso and Montale's deepest boyhood memories of home. *Cuttlefish Bones* thus has a resounding symbol in these last moments of *The Storm and Other Things.* One of the most persistent symbols of Monterosso is the magnolia tree, and as the poet recalls its charms, he says good-bye to Clizia.[114] Galassi points out the original subtitle, "Altra lettera non scritta" ("Another Unwritten Letter"), which contextualizes this poem specifically with the earlier poem by that title in the *Finisterre* collection and with poems of similar title and intent.[115] While the Motets were the first, this is one of the last of the many Clizia poems conceived as an unwritten or unsent letter to the beloved. Although Montale could write to the goddess symbol that he made for himself within the privacy of his poetic world, actual communication with the original human being who inspired the writing of the poetry was possible only years afterwards.

The magnolia makes an early appearance in "Bellosguardo Times" and turns up in a significant symbolic position in "The Storm," "In the Park," and "The Ark." Here it is a Japanese magnolia that once possessed purple buds but now, past its high season, has lost them. A cicada on top of the magnolia, vibrating intermittently, marks the autumnal moment. "The Shadow of the Magnolia" expresses the resigned and final good-bye to the beloved goddess – or so Montale thought when he wrote it. The poet-speaker addresses Clizia directly, saying her name at the beginning of the sixth line:

The shadow of the Japanese magnolia
thins out now that the purple buds
have fallen. Up top a cicada vibrates
intermittently. It is no longer
the time of the unison voice,
Clizia, the time of the unlimited God
that consumes and replenishes his faithful.
Spending oneself was easier, to die
with the first flutter of the wings, at the first meeting
with the enemy, a trifle. Now the harder way
starts: but not you consumed
by the sun and firmly rooted, and pure soft
fieldfare flying high above the frozen
banks of your river – not you fragile

fugitive in whom zenith nadir cancer
capricorn remain indistinct
since the war could be in you and in he who loves
on you the stigmata of your Spouse, you brush off
the shiverings from the ice ... The others withdraw
and fold. The file that carves
sharply will become quiet. The empty rind
of the one who sang will be soon be pulverized
glass under foot, the shadow is black and blue –
it is autumn, is winter, is the heaven
that leads you and in which I hurl myself, a mullet
jumped to dry land under the new moon.
Goodbye.[116]

Merrill's version reads fluently in American English, with a musicality of its own. He chooses to substitute "Sunflower" for the direct address to "Clizia," obscuring the fact that Montale calls her by the name Clizia in the original (for only the second time in the complete poems). Subsequent translations have corrected this. Arrowsmith and Galassi have brought out the crucial Catholic references to stigmata in the original as well. For the sake of precision in describing the overall development of the Clizia myth, I have created my own translation.

All the renderings bring out the main point of the poem, which is quite clearly stated in the Italian. The fight against Fascism required a unified voice in order to defeat it. As horrible as the fight was, some good did come of that unity. One way or the other, that era is over, the poet tells Clizia: "Henceforth / begins the harder path" (*Comincia ora / la via più dura*). In the new era, lacking the obviously evil common enemy from before, things are in some ways as frightening as ever for Italians and Europeans and for human beings in general. Arrowsmith has singled out the vicious political divisions, the fragmentation of society in industrialized Italy, and the long shadows of the geopolitical situation in the post-war nuclear era as some examples of Montale's new concerns.[117] But Clizia is still consumed by the sun, as she was in "Hitler Spring." She remains something more, something that can resist the uncertainties and impurities of this new era as well. Clizia, or Clizia's "shade," is now drawn to some new purpose in the autumnal season described in the poem. While the others fold under the new pressures, she is still the poet's fire-and-ice angel, the *fuggitiva fragile* (fragile fugitive) still soaring high above, Christ-like, displaying the *stimme* (stigmata or wounds) of her *Sposo.* Clizia is "married" to God. Montale was well aware of the vast range of religious and mystical poetry (Saint John of the Cross, John Donne, and others) that includes amorous and sometimes surprisingly sexual imagery to describe religious ecstasy.

At the close of the poem the poet says good-bye to Clizia in a one-word line. Galassi mentions the pun in the word *addio,* which contains the Italian for "to God" (*a* + *dio*). Clizia is fading in the poet's mind now. It is the late 1940s in post-war Italy, and Montale and the Italians have moved on to other matters.

In his note Arrowsmith says that Clizia is by now a Christian convert.[118] In my reading, Montale makes her Christian or, rather, incorporates her into Christianity in the broadest possible sense of cultural Catholicism. (Christians might well claim Clizia as Christian, while Jews might just as easily claim her as Jewish.) In his effort to reconfigure his very personal vision of Christianity, Montale makes Clizia into a Christian symbol, but by clear implication he pushes back the borders of that tradition to encompass more of its usable past. Clizia's meaning comes from the pagan mind of Ovid and the Judeo-Christian world of the Bible, blending the classical world, the Middle East, and early Christianity. Her American background, symbolized in other poems, is also important. Clizia is intercultural and pan-religious, or religious in a deeper sense that enables Montale to transcend the hypocrisy of the Fascist decades and the particular evils of the war era. He incorporates Clizia's Jewishness into his Catholic culture and his Catholic culture into her Jewishness, all based on the classical background of the Ovidian Clytie. Once again, Montale was continually searching for a subtle, even elitist, view of modern religion, but it was a view that embraced more of the history of the world.

Montale is one of the great sceptics in world literature, but the ramifications of his vision make culture as a whole, including both Catholic and Jewish culture, warmer, greatly expanded, more inclusive, more humane. A long process of sublimation – involving a complex mixture of love, anger, and desperation – had caused him to adopt and absorb Irma Brandeis's transformed memory into his Italian culture. Whatever the actual Irma would have thought of her Christian status, this Clizia is no longer Irma, and her earthbound existence is also no longer. She has been, to use Montale's own phrase, finally disincarnated. She is Clizia the immortal goddess, who wears "the stigmata" of her "spouse." She is a part of the Christian culture she was meant to save. The poet, transformed by another surprising metaphor into a mullet leaping towards the moon, rises to give her a parting salute. "The Shadow of the Magnolia" is perhaps the most important companion poem to "Hitler Spring," clarifying the sequence of the Clizia Cycle. Clizia's death and transfiguration is now complete. It is one of the culminating poems of the collection, moving the Clizia poems to a form that is all their own within the work of Montale.

"L'anguilla" ("The Eel," 1948) offers another important perspective of Clizia. It is generally considered to be one of Montale's greatest poems, famous among Italians for its symbolic evocation of Italian vitality. The eel swims upstream into the waterways of the countryside, struggling for its existence as it zigzags with the energy and force of its own nature as its best champion. There is an eel in "The Lemons," the great *art poétique* of *Cuttlefish Bones*, and there are still others in "The Motets," where there is an eel fisherman. In "The Lemons" rugged boys fish for eels in stagnant pools of water, and those pools now reappear in "The Eel."

Now the eel has evolved into a more complex symbol. It undulates in a variety of bodies of water, signifying the unique vivacity of the Italian soil and the Italian spirit. It is an unusually sentimental and humanistic symbol in Montale. The *élan vital* of the eel swimming upstream seems Bergsonian in conception, as has been noted by several commentators.[119] The eel also connotes the female life force that has powered so many of Montale's great modernistic re-creations of the Dolce Stil Novo. The eel is not masculine or phallic; she is feminine, even in the amazing chain of metaphors at the heart of the poem: "The eel, torch, whip / arrow of Love on earth" (*L'anguilla, torcia, frusta / freccia d'Amore in terra*).[120] Juxtaposed and separated by commas from its comparators, the eel, we learn, *is* a torch, *is* a whiplash, and *is* an arrow of love on earth. It has all of these contradictory qualities, expressed through metaphor. It is also plausible that the *frusta* (whip) image has something to do with the defiant liberal spirit of Scannabue's *frusta letteraria* (literary whip), a phrase that gave Gobetti the title for his short-lived journal of the 1920s, and perhaps the Dantesque *fersa* (lash, whip) in the early Clizia Motet of the 1930s.

In his comments to Silvio Ramat, Montale himself seems to wonder whether the poem was written for Clizia or for the Vixen.[121] While he truly needed a woman or muse as a secret reader in order for him to write his poetry, even he may not have known which was which all the time, in every line, in every poem. There is no literary law or ethic that requires a great poet to know such things. Some expert readers see qualities of both the Vixen and Clizia in the eel. The animal vitality of the female eel seems typical of the Vixen. However, the eel displays the ability to swim through the ice-cold Baltic seas of the north to the southern waters of Italy and then to struggle upstream, flashing reflections of light in the water. This defiant energy seems typical of the *Brand* plus *Eis* of Clizia. The poem, too, ends with images of the "iris/ rainbow" that are so crucial in other Clizia poems. The iris image aligns this poem with the poem "Iris" and other symbols that are important for evoking the luminosity of Clizia (jewels, hair, sunflower, clothing, dazzling colours, sunlight, and other qualities). Thus it would be logical that some aspect of Clizia is indeed a part of the poem's conception, combined with other female forces.

Montale once again displays his virtuosic ability to make large things suddenly small and small things suddenly large from the perspective of the poet's eye. The lashing of the eel in the water now frames the larger image of Clizia or the sky and sun, just as the delicate Japanese fan frames the horizon in his "Fan," or in Mallarmé's short poem "L'autre éventail" ("The Other Fan"). Similarly, the smoke rising over the ash-tray generates pictures of war-time combat in "New Stanzas"; the fluttering moths set the stage for Hitler's visit to Florence in "Hitler Spring"; or, many years before, in Montale's early poem "To Rest at Noon Pale and Engrossed," the shards of a broken bottle on a stone wall seem to imply the vast pointlessness of the universe. Once again, the tiny shapes the large, forcing an entirely fresh view of things. But here the implications are enormous. Clizia is "shining virginal / among the sons of men." She sounds like the innocent Susannah in Wallace Stevens, who bestows upon her a "constant sacrament of praise." Finally the poet asks the eel: Can you fail to see her (Clizia, the rainbow/ iris) as a sister?

Whether or not the eel combines elements of the Vixen and Clizia, the last five lines of the poem make it part of the Clizia Cycle. Here Montale suddenly says that the eel and the "brief rainbow/iris" (*l'iride breve*) are linked. They are twins, in fact, symbols of a resurgent life force that will enable Italy to rebuild itself once again and overcome its calamitous past. The eel, deep in the mud, must shine "amidst the sons of man" (*in mezzo ai figli dell'uomo*). But the *iride breve,* the "rainbow/iris" sign of Clizia, is its "sister," and the eel should understand this obvious truth.[122] "The Eel" is the penultimate poem in Brandeis's *Quarterly Review,* in a translation by John Frederick Nims. It has a prominent place in Montale's oeuvre and in Brandeis's reading of his work. This poem ends the great sequences of "Silvae" in *The Storm and Other Things*. Thus the image of the *iride* (iris or rainbow) begins it and ends it. The *iride* is a Clizia symbol. Surely the masterly verbal musician Montale knew that beginning and ending his profound meditation of poetry with the same image would be like ending in a key or tonality in music. He intoned the primary *chiave* of his Clizia Cycle one more time.

The Last Testament of the Witness

With his "Madrigali privati" ("Private Madrigals," 1946–9) Montale returns to his repertoire of suggestive musical titles. Madrigals have a secular basis, once again, and the poet's attention turns to the Vixen, the lady of the earth, in a series of exuberant poems. The poet writes to her openly in the "Private Madrigals," repeatedly calling the Vixen by name. "Se t'hanno assomigliato / alla volpe" ("If They've Compared You / to the Vixen," 1949) is an obvious Vixen poem that is often read in conjunction with "The Eel." Both poems are exactly thirty lines. "If They've Compared You" is more obviously a poem that celebrates a specific woman, rather than using the vitality of the feminine to say something more abstract. The Vixen is easy to see and hear in this poem. Her quick movements refresh the ground as she darts along her path, and her "almond eyes" send out luminous waves. In a striking image the poet scratches a permanent mark into her forehead. Similarly, "Per Album" ("For an Album," 1953) has a frank and exuberant sexuality, inspired by the Vixen, that is not characteristic of the Clizia Cycle.

In "Da un lago svizzero" ("From a Swiss Lake," 1949) Montale explicitly names his new lover/reader. The poem begins with the words *Mia volpe* (My Vixen) and spells out *Maria Luisa Spaziani* in a perfect acrostic pattern using the first letter in each line. Spaziani, a young poet and professor who knew French literature well, had already prompted Montale to write an earlier madrigal poem about Rimbaud. Now Montale refers to himself as the *poeta assassinato*, clearly an allusion to Guillaume Apollinaire's "Le poète assassiné" ("The Poet Assassinated," 1916), a late prose work that anticipated Montalean statements about the threatened status of the poet in the callous modern world, as well as his "La chanson du mal-aimé" ("The Song of the Poorly Loved," 1903). Obviously, Montale has now cast himself in the role of the misunderstood elder poet-statesman for the charming younger female poet who fascinates him. In "Anniversario" ("Anniversary," 1950?) he tells his Vixen that he has remained on his knees before her since the day she was born.

The excursion away from Clizia, however invigorating, is once again a short one. The poet returns to her in the "Conclusioni provvisorie" ("Provisional Conclusions," 1953–4), the disturbing end of both the single book *The Storm and Other Things* and the trilogy of books that began with *Cuttlefish Bones* in 1925. It is an unresolved coda, filled with disquieting harmonies that echo in poetic time and space. The "Provisional Conclusions" are made up of two great post-war poems, "Piccolo testamento" ("Little Testament," 1953) and "Il sogno del prigioniero" ("The Prisoner's Dream," 1954). These poems take us into the post-war years and the new set of self-constructed horrors that threatened humankind in the second half of the twentieth century. Montale, in his finale, finds himself not in the medieval *Paradiso* of Dante but in a modern world of tragi-comic uncertainty. It is now the mid-fifties, ten years after the Fascist defeat. Modern Italy has taken shape, and the cold war has arrived. And the poet is uneasy.

"The Prisoner's Dream" evokes both a war-time concentration camp (though with a bit too much light-heartedness for Auschwitz) and a post-war Gulag.[123] An unnamed and never-ending purge is under way, and the poet protagonist has a choice: he can have a *mestolo,* a ladle with which he can eat, or, if he does not cooperate, he will be served up in the very next batch of pâté. The poet, who cannot tell dawn from night in the dark prison, hears the cries from the endless beatings, and he wonders whether he will attend the coming feast as *farcitore* or *farcito* (stuffer or stuffing). Treachery seems to be the only way out. Since Montale does not specifically spell out the context, the poem is indicative of all post-war purges, including those of Eastern Europe and the Chinese Cultural Revolution (which had not yet taken place). The poet still speaks to a female listener, and it is about her that he dreams as he waits in his solitary cell. She could be Clizia, the Vixen, or some other unnamed "you." He dreams that he is sleeping safely at her feet.[124]

"Little Testament," as translated by Ben Belitt, is the last poem in Brandeis's issue of the *Quarterly Review.* It therefore has a culminating importance in her careful shaping of Montale's poetry for English-speaking readers. Arrowsmith and Galassi have pointed out a winking reference to François Villon (1431–?), the French poet and thief who also wrote "Testaments."[125] Even more important, *testamento,* a word of Hebrew origin, evokes the activity of witnessing, which has been a consistent theme of all three of Montale's great books. Those three collections are a testimony of the witness, the poet who sat vigil. Once again the poet casts himself as a witness but now to a very different scene.

Montale himself refers to Clizia's presence in "Little Testament" in relation to other Clizia poems.[126] It is the last poem in his trilogy that he specifically wrote in the context of Clizia. While the poem could easily be read as concerning Clizia and what she symbolizes, its rhetoric seems to indicate that the poet is speaking to someone else, most probably the Vixen. Clizia has been condensed into a series of light images, first an intermittently flashing presence in the poet's mind (the *traccia madreperlacea,* the mother-of-pearl trace, recalls the *madreperla,* the clear image of mother-of-pearl luminosity in "The Fan"), and then, once again, a rainbow. While she may have been reduced from both her womanly and divine forms to a mere token of flickering or coloured light, her luminosity is still important. In Montale's quasi-Zoroastrian conception of good and evil, the light symbolizes hope. Hope is not to be found, however, in the officialdom of post-war culture. Both church (*chiesa*) and factory (*officina*) nourish clerics; just the colour is different in each case, red for the former and black for the latter.[127]

Calvino has described Montale as a "poet ... little inclined toward anything official."[128] It is the artifice and plasticity of the emerging modern world that Montale objected to as much as anything else. His post-war political views were deemed old fashioned by many, and perhaps, with his roots deep in the nineteenth-century humanism of Croce, this critique is understandable. Although Montale refused to join the Fascists in the 1930s, he distanced himself from the leftist partisans who used violence to wrest back control of the country in the mid-1940s. He already had criticized the excessive actions of church ideologues after the war, in his little madrigal entitled "Le processioni del 1949" ("The Parades of 1949," 1949). Now well along what he had described (in "The Shadow of the Magnolia") as the "harder path" of 1950s post-war culture, Montale witnessed a renewed warring of ideologies and a nuclear era that threatened the very existence of the world. The Marxists for him were merely another orthodoxy; he saw them as simply another group of clerics, dressed in red. The older power was that of the Church, and its clerics dressed in black. Thus Montale echoes the old title of Stendhal with a twentieth-century meaning that the French writer could not have predicted. (In Stendhal's *The Red and the Black,* red is a symbol for Napoleon's military, while black is for the clergy.) In "Little Testament" it is clear that, in Montale's view, communism and the church are a threat to the freedom of the individual. As Alvaro Valentini has pointed out, it was a snobbish but proud position that Montale explained in greater detail in "Né in Dio né in Marx"

("Neither in God nor in Marx"), a 1956 essay he included in *Auto da fé.*[129] In his introduction to a Swedish translation of his poems Montale states that his work offers "the testimony of a writer who has always rejected the clericalism that afflicts Italy today in its two opposing forms ('black' and 'red')."[130]

Only the light of the rainbow offers some hope of *varco,* some hope of a way out. The poet claims he can leave this light as "testimony" (*testimonianza*) of a "faith that was fought for" *(d'una fede che fu combattuta).* This faith was a kind of hope, burning very gradually, slower even than a slowly burning log in the hearth.[131] This recurring celebration of the importance of the rainbow points backward to the great poem "Iris," the dream vision in which Montale establishes the Nestorian sceptic and heretic. That heretic survives in the troublesome post-war climate, but Clizia is more remote now than she was in "Iris," where she was already becoming difficult to trace. Even the vigorous abandon inspired by the Vixen is nowhere evident here. Only the rainbow is left as testimony.

"Little Testament" names the great rivers of three cities: the Thames, the Hudson, and the Seine. The rivers stand metonymically for the three great cities they penetrate: London, New York, and Paris. Each river runs through the heart of a threatened seat of civilization, just as the Marne suggested the vulnerability of Europe in Montale's pre-war poetry. But now there is a new threat, a new Lucifer, casting a long shadow from the *Inferno.* The sardana, a famously nationalistic Catalan folk dance in 6/8 time, now "becomes infernal" (*si farà infernale*). A shadowy Lucifer appears – standing at the prow of a ship as it sails down the three great rivers (presumably in the sequence listed by the poet) – all the while furiously whipping his "semi-mutilated coal-black wings" (*l'ali di bitume semi-mozze*). Finally, Lucifer says, "It is time" (*è l'ora*).[132]

The sardana in "Little Testament" is a diabolical dance, in this way similar to the trescone in "Hitler Spring" or the Nazi fandango in"The Storm," offering a crucial clue to both mood and meaning as do the dances in the other Montale poems. Many commentators have pondered the significance of the ombroso Lucifero (dark Lucifer) that Montale warns about in this poem of 1953. The purposeful ambiguity makes the image more effective. The next coming of shadowy Lucifer could signify nuclear war, other post-war horrors, such as resurgent Fascism, or even, sadly and prophetically, post–cold war terrorism. The main point is that New York, Paris, and London (and by implication Rome, Milan, and Florence) are not safe, even after all that has happened (including the two world wars that Montale survived). In the twenty-first century, alas, Montale's poem seems prophetic. Of course, as an Eliot translator, Montale knew well the highly similar passage in "The Wasteland," and the effect is similar. Eliot's poem dates from 1923, during the early years of Fascism and just before Montale published Cuttlefish Bones. Eliot's poem, too, was strangely prophetic, as only a major poem can be, predicting the wasteland of the mid-twentieth century:

Falling towers
Jerusalem Athens Alexandria
Vienna London
Unreal[133]

But now Montale is writing after the Second World War, and the world seems as frightening as before. "It is time," proclaims Montale's Lucifer. But he does not say exactly what is coming.

One imagines the poet in the mid-1950s, recalling the tumultuous period of the 1930s and the decisions he made at that time and now looking at the coming threat of the cold war and the spectre of nuclear holocaust. He remembers Clizia once again, sees reflections in the mirror (recalling the mirror of the pseudo-sonnets in *Finisterre*), refractions of light brought to mind from long ago at 54 Costa San Giorgio, and by the magical procedure of his metaphor he concludes that some essence of her rainbow light can be pulverized into fine powder or crushed glass, portable enough to carry in a tiny compact that may belong to his new lover (or is she Clizia?). Clizia's jewels, earrings, and locks of hair stay in his mind. The tiny details of Clizia, the things next to her, the things that she possesses, are symbols of her charm, just as is the brief rainbow in the sky. Once again, these are the metonymic talismans that evoke what she was at that earlier seminal moment of his life, enabling her memory and her meaning in his mind. All of that past is blended with the present and the future, which now is terrifying in new ways.

7 The Poet and the Modern Beatrice Spread Their Myth around the World

Her eyes ... were grey and queerly lit from within, as by some dangerous electricity.

– Mary McCarthy

The Second Profession

Montale took refuge in the Tuscan coastal town of Forte dei Marmi in the summer of 1945. He sat for hours on a terrace at the Pensione Bertelli, staring at the sea and the pines by the Versilian shore. Encouraged by two friends, Raffaele De Grada and Ernesto Treccani, the poet began to paint, at first in oils, then in pastels and mixed tempera.[1] It is not unusual for an artist to be talented in more than one area. Arnold Schoenberg and William Blake were gifted painters. Eugène Delacroix was a skilled diarist, Michelangelo was a poet, and Cellini and Fuseli were writers. Montale's efforts in the visual arts amount to something more than a hobby. Working chiefly in a post-Impressionist style, he was quite talented. He had a sure sense of colour and abstraction. He was also a gifted cartoonist. Montale's visual sensibility and unusual powers of observation are evident not just in his verbal mastery but also in a variety of visual formats.[2]

Out of hiding in the first months after the war, Montale launched a number of new activities. In 1945 he joined the liberal Partito d'Azione. He assumed the co-directorship (with Leo Valiani) of a newspaper, *L'Italia libera,* and wrote theatre reviews for *La Nazione del Popolo,* yet another Florence paper. He collaborated with Alessandro Bonsanti, Arturo Loria, and Eugenio Scaravelli to found a short-lived bi-weekly, *Il*

Mondo. In March 1945 Montale gave a speech, "Fascism and Literature," which was published in *Il Mondo* that April, articulating for public viewing many opinions already evident in the letters he had written to Irma Brandeis in the 1930s. The speech outlined the cultural failures of Fascism. The poet described its "neo-barbarian babble and acrobatics."[3] Montale had outlasted his nemesis.

The end of the Second World War meant an immediate renaissance of Montale's literary fortunes. In December 1945 Professor Alessandro Levi, who had joined Montale as a signatory to Croce's anti-Fascist manifesto twenty years earlier, called the poet to tell him that Mario Borsa wanted him at the *Corriere della Sera*.[4] Montale was being given an opportunity to write for Italy's leading newspaper, based in Milan. He began what he referred to as his *secondo mestiere* (second profession) in 1946 when he started to write consistently for the *Corriere della Sera* and for the *Corriere d'informazione,* its companion publication. For the next twenty-seven years he worked almost full time as a cultural journalist. Montale wrote widely, and while he did not earn a living as a creative writer, his journalistic work in many respects afforded him an outlet for exploring his lifelong interests in poetry, music, and the visual arts. As the British poet and essayist Stephen Spender has noted, Montale's prose writing for the newspapers is generally in the French or Italian tradition of the *feuilleton,* a short journalistic prose piece that functions as a kind of learned cultural appetizer for the lay reader.[5] Montale wrote a wide array of concise, insightful articles, often illuminated with characteristic brilliance and wit but rarely encumbered by analytical detail.

At this time he wrote "The Shadow of the Magnolia" in which he says good-bye to Clizia against the back-drop of his Monterosso home, blending two of the most important symbols in his poetry. But the separation was only temporary. He was never able to truly say good-bye to Clizia. While bringing together the symbolic bases of his past poetry, the poem, an early expression of Montale's concerns about the post-war world situation, also points out important themes that he will treat in the future.

Montale's opportunities in journalism blossomed quickly in the late 1940s, bringing to an end the long Florentine period of his life. In 1947 he authored twenty-one articles for the two Milanese papers. He accepted a full-time editorship at the *Corriere della Sera* in 1948. This required that he leave Florence and move to Milan. It became increasingly difficult to find time for sustained attention to his poetry. Montale makes it clear that Milan was not a city that he chose; it chose him.[6] Nevertheless, Milan, which has always been a dynamic urban centre, had its attractions. While it lacks the charm and the visual culture of Florence or Rome, it is the economic powerhouse of Italy, which makes it an important cultural centre in its own right.

The British Council invited Montale to visit England in 1948 along with the novelists Alberto Moravia and Elsa Morante. They travelled to London in March. There Montale participated in a reading with Herbert Read, Moravia, Louis MacNeice, and C. Day Lewis. He also called on T.S. Eliot at Faber & Faber (Eliot had first published him in 1928). In his account of that meeting Montale includes a vivid description of the thoroughly anglicized American poet: "tall, elegant, already a little stooped, blue eyes behind two thick lenses, he was a type of English *gentleman,* just as Italians love to describe."[7] At a travel agency in London he saw a young Italian woman to whom he referred only as G.B.H. He had originally met her in Florence in 1945. Furnishing the inspiration for several important poems of the late 1940s and early 1950s, she obviously accompanied him on some of the English trips.

"Intentions (Imaginary Interview)" appeared in *La rassegna d'Italia* in January 1946. Densely packed into only a few pages, it is perhaps the single most important piece of combined self-criticism and autobiography in all of Montale's prose writings. Montale begins with his early years, describing in some detail his extensive musical studies with Sivori, his extensive readings of Croce, Gentile, Émile Boutroux, and Henri Bergson, and his early attempts at poetry, describing how he found his poetic voice. He recounts how the character of Clizia was projected into his poetry in *The Occasions,* and he extends his self-analysis all the way to *Finisterre,* his most important published work at that time.

Montale was still unsure of himself, caught between the calling of the artist and the professional journalist. In a letter to his friend Giuseppe de Robertis in the winter of 1949 he wrote, "Unfortunately ... I have not resolved the problem of finding a profession that gives me a means of support without distracting me from the work that is more truly mine."[8] Nevertheless, Montale, by now an important critic as well as a great poet, wrote a number of short but penetrating pieces on Italian culture in the late 1940s. These included an essay on Italian "decadence," and another on the Cinque Terre, analysing in prose the sea-scape he had treated so extensively in his poetry. He wrote a series of essays on Eliot – "Eliot e noi" ("Eliot and Us") in 1947 and another piece in 1948 when Eliot was awarded the Nobel Prize. Montale was among Eliot's most perceptive European readers. He understood Eliot completely, tracing his origins in French Symbolism, noting his snobbery, and dissecting his use of pastiche in "The Wasteland." He even heard the hidden sound of Whitman in Eliot's disjunct verse.

Widening his journalistic range, he wrote on Rilke (whose poetry has a close affinity with his), Aldous Huxley, and Toscanini, the great anti-Fascist conductor who had fascinated Irma Brandeis in the 1920s. In 1949 Montale authored a series of travel writings, and more pieces on literary topics, such as "Saroyan a Milano in viaggio per l'Armenia" ("Saroyan in Milan on the Way to Armenia"). He also wrote a playful essay on the interaction of poetry and music in vocal music, "Le parole e la musica" ("Words and Music"). In "Tornare nella strada" ("Returning to the Street," but translated by Galassi with the English title "The Second Life of Art"), which appeared in the *Corriere della Sera* in May 1949, Montale examines the interrelation between the work of art and its resonance in everyday life, outside of its original context. The initial consumption of the work is not enough. It must echo somehow in the mind and in a manner that is close to personal experience. He mentions Clizia as an example: "I cannot meet certain persons – Clizia or Angela or ... *omissis omissis* – without seeing once again the mysterious faces of Piero and Mantegna or having a line of Manzoni ... flash in my memory."[9] Here, for a brief moment, Montale's secret symbology appears in the newspaper as he ponders how life and art blend in unpredictable ways.

Quaderno di traduzioni (*Translation Notebook*) came out in September 1948, featuring Italian translations of Hardy, Shakespeare, Dickinson, and others.[10] Montale's study of English and American writers had continued after the war, and his translations of Dickinson, Shakespeare, and Gerard Manley Hopkins were of special importance in the formation of his forthcoming collection, *The Storm and Other Things*, which appeared in the mid-1950s. Montale himself noted his intrigue with Hopkins's "sprung rhythm." He admired how it caught Hopkins's religious ecstasy, creating thick chunks of syncopated counter-rhythms that chopped the natural iambic or trochaic flow of English verse. This may have influenced Montale's formation of the disjunct rhythms that were housed within the long lines of his last poems in *The Storm* and even the lengthier poems in *The Occasions*.[11]

In 1949 Montale met Maria Luisa Spaziani at the University of Turin. He soon fell in love with the young poet, whose name is inscribed acrostically in the short love poem "From a Swiss Lake." His description of Spaziani in relation to himself helps to clarify her impact on his life. "She was a young woman with ... a very different personality from Clizia, a personality of the earth. In front of the Vixen I was like Pafnuzio [Athanael], the priest who goes to convert Thais but who is conquered himself. In her company I felt like an abstract man beside a concrete woman: she lived with all the pores of her skin."[12] It was obviously a revivifying experience to know her. Spaziani inspired a small but brilliant output of erotically charged poetry, but her presence, however inspiring, did not generate a sustained effort and scope equal to that of the Clizia Cycle.

Montale was never able to completely abandon Drusilla Tanzi ("La Mosca"), whom he had known since the 1920s, living with her for most of the time, and whom he would eventually marry in 1962. The steady pattern of long summer breaks with Drusilla by the shore at Forte dei Marmi continued throughout the 1950s and early 1960s.

In the meantime Irma Brandeis had taken up a lively career of her own as a scholar and professor of literature. After a teaching stint at Sarah Lawrence College, she became increasingly active as a freelance writer and journalist. She at one time hoped to work for the *New Yorker* magazine. Before the war she had published eight short stories in the *New Yorker* and one in *Harper's Bazaar.* For a while she had hoped to continue, publishing one more short story, "Ladies in the Dark," in the *New Yorker* in 1943.[13] She even tried her hand at writing a novel late in her life. Brandeis's *MacGregor's Island,* set on a small coastal island in Maine, concerns the unrequited love of a young woman for a brilliant Italian-Jewish scholar. Though filled with sharply etched psychological insight, it remains unpublished.[14]

In 1944 Brandeis took a teaching position at Bard College in Annandale-on-Hudson, New York. She taught there until 1979 and continued her association with the school in various ways until her death in 1990. In the late 1940s she also began teaching at the New School in lower Manhattan. She gave courses on Dante, creative and expository writing, and French literature there for many years. Meanwhile, at Bard, she became friendly with a number of distinguished literary colleagues, including the poets James Merrill and Theodore Weiss. Weiss was chair of the college's Literature Division in the mid-1950s and hired the novelists Saul Bellow and Mary McCarthy as well.[15] It is commonly assumed that Irma Brandeis was the model for Domna Rejnev, one of the main characters in McCarthy's *Groves of Academe.* Not coincidentally, Domna has qualities that are reminiscent of Montale's Clizia:

> Domna Rejnev was the youngest member of the Literature department. A Radcliffe B.A., twenty-three years old, teaching Russian literature and French. To deter familiarities, she wore a plain smock in her office that gave her something of the look of a young woman scientist or intern ... Her dark, straight, glossy hair was worn short and loose, without so much as a bobby-pin; she kept ruffling an impatient hand through it to brush it back from her eyes. She had a severe, beautiful, clear-cut profile, very pure ivory skin, the color of old piano-keys; her lips, also, were finely drawn and a true natural pink or rose. Her very beauty had the quality, not of radiance or softness, but of incorruptibility; it was the beauty of an absolute or a political theorem ... She wore dark suits of rather heavy, good material, cut somewhat full in the coat-skirts: the European tailor-made. Only her eyes were an exception to this restraint and muted gravity of person; they were grey and queerly lit from within, as by some dangerous electricity; she had a startling intensity of gaze that never wavered from its object, like that of a palmist or a seer. (37–8)

McCarthy, who changed Domna's academic background from Irma's Barnard to Radcliffe, creates a character of austere beauty, a quality found in Clizia, and even in Dante's Beatrice. Indeed, McCarthy needs to move into metaphor to truly evoke Domna's unique beauty to her satisfaction. It is the beauty of an "absolute" or "political theorem," remarkable for its "incorruptibility" (in this, somewhat like Montale's mythic heroine). Obviously, Domna's short bangs, her beautiful skin, and especially her amazingly penetrating eyes are highly reminiscent of Clizia. Both Italian poet and American novelist found similar qualities in the unique beauty of Irma Brandeis.

Montale made a brief trip to New York in July 1950 in honour of the opening of the Rome – New York air route. There is no indication that he saw Irma Brandeis during the visit, and he was purportedly anxious to avoid meeting her again at that point. Later that year he travelled with Glauco Natoli, an Italian professor of French, to Brittany. There he probably visited the coastal town of Dinard, which later gave him the title of his book of short prose fiction, *The Butterfly of Dinard*.[16]

Montale was by now well established at the *Corriere della Sera.* Over the next two years he wrote approximately two hundred articles on world literature, art, architecture, and music. His enormous range in itself illustrated his long-standing Crocean belief in the "fundamental unity of the arts."[17] It is possible, however, that some of the material signed by Montale in the late 1940s and 1950s was actually authored by a ghost writer named Henry Furst, whom Montale had known since the era of the Caffè Giubbe Rosse in the 1930s. Montale spent a great deal of time with Furst in the 1930s, often commenting in his letters to Irma on Henry's eccentricities. Montale reviewed Furst's book of poems *Songs of Tokimarne* in 1937, and in 1938 he wrote to the French poet Valéry Larbaud about Furst's considerable talents.[18] It was common practice in Italian journalism to use a lesser-known apprentice for assistance in the authoring of short articles; Montale himself had served in that capacity early in his career. Furst was a polymath, fluent in French, German, Italian, Arabic, and English. He was an American and was well versed in American literature. In the early 1930s he taught Italian at Vassar College and worked as a librarian in the Casa Italiana at Columbia University. There he met the young Mario Soldati, who later rose to prominence as a film director and novelist. Furst and Irma Brandeis had mutual acquaintances, among them Lauro de Bosis. All of this made Furst a logical choice for an assistant who could help prepare articles on foreign literature or even ghost-write some of them. What was particularly strange about the relationship is that Furst had once worked as Gabriele D'Annunzio's secretary and had even fought with D'Annunzio at Fiume. Eventually Furst became a Fascist sympathizer, startling Montale with his anti-American statements before the Second World War and later joining Mussolini at Salò.[19]

Montale went to Paris in May 1952 to read his short essay "La solitudine dell'artista" ("The Artist's Solitude") at the International Congress for Cultural Freedom. In the mid-1950s Paris was the capital of existentialism, where Sartre had called for the political *engagement* of the artist. Montale, while speaking the argot of the French intellectuals of the day, stood his ground in his address. He argued that in an era of mass communication, in which everyone would be a sort of artist, the true activity of artistic communication would come only from seclusion. It was a paradox, yet it was the only way for poetry to survive in the modern world. "My premise, then, would be this: that the artist succeeds in communicating only through isolation and that a polemical or propagandistic kind of *engagement* cannot be of interest in this regard."[20] Thus the poet does not flourish merely as a direct proponent of a political or social cause, however apparently noble or correct. True poetic communication is far more private, delicate, and unpredictable.

This is a theme he would develop in the decades to come. After his lecture Montale wrote to Giorgio Zampa about his Parisian experience: "I've been in *Lutetia* [Paris] for 15 days and I've talked for the second *entretien,* with some success. I've seen Camus, Supervielle, Adrienne Monnier, Doeblin, Faulkner, Peyrefitte and Frénaud and others, many others ... I've had many cocktails and many dinners."[21]

Montale made another trip to Paris, in April 1953, to attend the opening of Samuel Beckett's *Waiting for Godot.* It was fitting that Montale, whose literary career was now resurgent, should witness the first performance of Beckett's most important work. As a young man, Beckett had published a translation of Montale's "Delta," one of the last poems in *Cuttlefish Bones,* in Edward Titus's Paris-based literary review, *This Quarter.*[22] Beckett was friendly with James Joyce, who had worked for Montale's old friend Italo Svevo. Beckett probably knew of Montale long before Montale had heard of him. While in Paris, Montale also interviewed Georges Braque and Constantin Brancusi and met Albert Camus.

The world of poetry was changing. One exponent of that change was Pier Paolo Pasolini, about whom Montale first writes in a short article, "La musa dialettale" ("The Dialect Muse"), in the *Corriere della sera* in January 1953. Montale recognizes Pasolini's then uncollected verse as "among the most interesting today" but worries about a certain decadence implied in the young poet's use of Italian dialect.[23] It was a criticism that was not forgotten. A year later Montale comments on Pasolini's *La meglio gioventù* (*The Best of Our Youth*). In that review Montale notes the vivid popular expression in Pasolini's work, which incorporates Friulian dialect with Pasolini's own translations into modern Italian and which features a dedication to Montale's longtime friend and ally Gianfranco Contini. Sections of the work concern the impoverished conditions of the *contadini* of Casarsa, the peasant classes of the northeastern Italian province, in the post-war era. Montale was far more impressed with Rina Sara Virgilitto's writing, which he treats in the same article. Far closer to Montale's own introspective style, Virgillito was writing poetry with roots in myth and, at the same time, a modern voice "nourished by a more alive sensibility of our era." He obviously prefers her collection of poems, *I giorni del sole* (*The Days of the Sun*), to the work of Pasolini, a brash young Marxist who was determined to uncover the neglected underlayerings of Italian letters.[24] Also, in 1954, Montale reviewed a new Italian edition of Wallace Stevens's poetry, translated by Renato Poggioli and entitled *Mattino domenicale ed altre poesie*. In one brilliant sentence Montale probes Stevens's famous but elusive poem, which Stevens had published in *Harmonium* in 1923: "The poem 'Sunday Morning' is a portrait of a woman prismatically decomposed, which has cosmic implications and celebrates an absolute pantheism."[25] The irreligious religiosity of this great Stevens poem has always been an interpretive problem, and Montale zooms in on this key issue with penetrating insight. It is notable, too, that Montale focuses on the female character in the poem. In the mid-1950s Montale was still prismatically decomposing his own female figure, his Clizia, and constructing her most superhuman incarnation, which appeared in 1956.

Seventeen years younger than Stevens, Montale was the last of the great poets who wrote in the post-Symbolist mode. Active in the twentieth century but with roots in the nineteenth, these poets worked from the opacity of language outward into the world. Each word of the poet was to be savoured and to be, as Montale preferred to put it, "vertical" in its nature. The perfume of evoked meaning was paramount in Montale's poetry, as opposed to the forward thrust of prose. Pasolini was writing in a new line, politically engaged, fertilized directly by the popular culture, even reaching outward to endangered dialects to show the raw energy of expression in the untutored voices of the poor and marginalized. By 1971 Pasolini was almost militant in his condemnation of the senior poet's preoccupations, horrified by what he saw as the bourgeois self-absorption of Montale, who, he thought, rambled on endlessly about his love life, fancy hotel rooms, and other insignificant detail. For Pasolini, Montale was not a writer of pure poetry but a writer of narcissistic preoccupation.[26] But the older poet had the upper hand. Soon after this attack, in 1975, Montale won the Nobel Prize for literature. In his acceptance speech at the Stockholm ceremony Montale recounts how, by reading his own pre-composed obituary (what the Italians call a *coccodrillo*), he learned that Mayokovsky had admired reading his poetry. He also describes how Walter Pater, a fin-de-siècle aesthete, rescued an exquisitely subtle work by Joachim du Bellay, which may have been inspired by a forgotten Venetian Latinist known as Naugerius. Poetic art is not elite by intent but by occurrence: "Art is always for everyone and for no one. But what remains unpredictable is its true 'begetter,' the person for whom it is written."[27]

The "begetter" is the lover/reader. In 1938 Montale had used exactly the same word when he wrote to Irma Brandeis that she was "the only begetter of my life." Poetry begins in Eros and intimacy and extends from its writing to its first intimate reading and then to other intimate readings. The bittersweet but faintly hopeful message of his Nobel Prize speech is that this intimacy, so characteristic of the densely worded style he favoured, might save poetry. The revolutionary poet will not triumph by singing to the masses. Poetry will move from the writer to the particular reader, from human mind to human mind, spanning unpredictably across cultural and linguistic boundaries. According to Montale, this is how poetry can survive.[28]

Beatrice, Writer and Critic

Irma Brandeis returned to Florence in 1955 to work on a critical study of Dante.[29] She described what it was like to be in Italy once again in a letter written to her Bard colleague Ted Weiss and his wife, Renée:

> The first month was not so bad (not, at least once I had recovered from the shock of being here at all and from a wild bus-trip down the Tyrrhenian shore to Florence). I kept my eyes to myself, got my exercise by walking to and from the National Library in this modest condition, and read as much as I could read. Very boring mostly. I threw over the criticism finally and tried just to learn a few things. At night, when the streets were full of wonderful moving, roving life, and all the American visitors were taxiing to the opera or to the Cathedral Square for a drink, I stayed home and read a Latin grammar. (I thought in a week or so I should read Virgil without a pony. I did not.)
>
> I came here – to a place and people I knew before the War – and fell instantly into a swoon, woke in an Italian trance, and have not, after ten days, recovered at all. I have a room with a view from which all those countryside backgrounds of Renaissance paintings were made. There is a garden filled with lemon trees and ilex and morning glories and palms and marigolds and cactus. And there are people, this family, so damned marvellous and beautiful that I have to stop and laugh for joy and incredulity, just mentioning them. I don't want to write a book on Dante; I want to write a play.[30]

The letter, dated 28 October 1955, was written at the Villa Solaia in Malafrasca (near Siena). In the 1930s it was the home of Elena and Leone Vivante, two young intellectuals from Montale's circle. Since the Vivante family was part Jewish, Montale had written to Irma with great concern about their affairs just before the outbreak of the Second World War. Brandeis had visited the Vivante home before the war (in 1934 and for the last time in 1938) in the company of Montale and some other Italian friends. Clearly stimulated by her return to this Tuscan setting situated just north of Siena, she offers a vivid description of the Mediterranean plants and flowers on the grounds of the Villa Solaia that are also reminiscent of the richly symbolic images in Montale poems, which she knew well.

Although she complains about the boredom of writing criticism (her lifelong fascination with creative writing is evident in her letter to the Weisses), Brandeis's Dante project eventually evolved into her fine book *The Ladder of Vision* (1961).[31] It has been an admired work in the world of Dante scholarship for many years. She also translated Leopardi's famous lyric poem "L'Infinito" ("The Infinite") for Weiss's *Quarterly Review* (vol. 8, no. 1 [1955]) in the mid-1950s, an important collaboration that led to her later Montale project for the journal.

By the time Brandeis returned to Italy, Montale had already amassed a distinguished record as a cultural essayist. In 1950 he had written on Eliot again and an article on Ernest Hemingway, "Un americano a Venezia" ("An American in Venice"), in which he recounts Hemingway's long involvement with Italy, stretching back to the First World War. In 1951 Montale reminisced about Piero Gobetti, the socialist editor who had been beaten to death by Fascists in the 1920s. In the early 1950s Montale also produced essays on Camus, Auden, Pound, Constantine Cavafy, and a wide variety of French poets (including Gerard de Nerval, Jacques Prévert, and his late friend Paul Éluard, for whom he wrote an obituary). Also in the mid-1950s he drew on his massive knowledge of Italian literature to write short pieces on writers such as D'Annunzio and Giovanni Pascoli, and a long series of articles on foreign artists, including Stravinsky, Malraux, Brancusi, and Braque. Many of these columns required travel so that he could personally conduct interviews with his subjects.

The definitive moment of Montale's career as a poet came in June 1956 when the publishing house Neri Pozza in Venice released a small edition (only one thousand copies) of his *La bufera e altro* (*The Storm and Other Things*). Even though it was now more than a decade after the war – and eighteen years since Irma Brandeis's last, dramatic, pre-war visit to Florence – the new book contained some of the greatest Clizia poems. *The Storm and Other Things* includes the war-time "Petrarchan" poems of the 1943 *Finisterre,* which Montale had explicated in the "Imaginary Interview" he wrote just after the war. The new book also added the culminating apotheosis of Clizia in the last poems of the collection, including the climactic "Hitler Spring," in which he named Clizia openly for the first time in his poetry. He saw it as his best work, and many Italian critics agreed.[32] He won the Marzotto Prize for his poetry later that year. In 1957 Mondadori republished *The Storm and Other Things* in a large national edition.

After the appearance of the third part of his trilogy it seems that Montale gave up writing serious poetry for a substantial period of time. Instead he concentrated on his career as a musical and cultural journalist. In December 1956 he published *Farfalla di Dinard* (*The Butterfly of Dinard*), a collection of short fiction pieces that are stylistically somewhere between a short story and a prose poem.

Montale's activities in journalism in the late 1950s offered him ample opportunity for travel and first-hand experience with some of the major figures in European cultural life. Between 1956 and 1960 he wrote more than five hundred articles, although he may have had considerable unacknowledged assistance with some of them. The result was an impressive list of reviews of operatic performances (including perhaps every major opera presented at La Scala during this period) and music festivals; obituaries; incidental reportage on cultural matters; and book reviews. Even with the assistance of a ghost writer or two, it must have been a vast project just to organize all of the material. Most of the pieces contain informative but unsensational accounts of Italian cultural life, but many are spiced with flashes of Montalean wit and insight. Often, one of Montale's short pieces will offer a glimpse into his poetics or related artistic and aesthetic problems.

One of five invaluable essays that Montale wrote on Ezra Pound, a report in 1958 on his release from a mental hospital (Pound had been incarcerated there for twelve years) and his imminent return to Italy offers an unusual perspective – an anti-Fascist Italian poet evaluating the career of an American poet who was famous for his importance in developing literary Modernism and infamous for his anti-Semitic and anti-American ranting on Italian radio during the war. Montale had known Pound in the 1920s and 1930s and had commented on their meetings in his letters to Irma. For him, Pound was not "crazy," unless it could be established that all the great poets were crazy. However, he regretted Pound's general lack of interest in modern Italy, and he criticizes, both here and elsewhere, Pound's tendency to view Italian culture mainly as a usable treasure trove of artefacts from a now defunct but glorious past. Finally, Montale is blunt in characterizing Pound's

Radio Rome broadcasts of the war era as "authentic and sad mental decadence."[33]

In two pieces from 1959, "Il secondo mestiere" ("The Second Profession") and "Le magnifiche sorti" ("The Magnificent Destinies"), he continues to develop his long-standing meditation on the alienation of the artist in modern life. For Montale there was no post-war panacea for the artist. Mass culture, whether communist or capitalist, created unsatisfactory conditions for the survival of poetry. State sponsorship and censorship in Stalinist countries compromised the poet. In capitalist countries, economic censorship was just as sterilizing.

While he was writing little or no poetry during this period, in 1960 he did publish *Accordi* (Chords) and *Musica sognata* (Dreamed music), small assemblages of older poems dealing with musical topics, some of them originally written many years earlier for *Cuttlefish Bones.* Further indication of his stature came in 1961 when the University of Milan gave him an honorary doctorate. In 1962 the first poems of *Satura* ("Satire" or "Stage Medley") appeared, in a private edition printed for the wedding of two friends. Scheiwiller published *Accordi & Pastelli* (Chords and Pastels), a collection of Montale's paintings and drawings. The musician Margherita Dalmati, director of the Istituto Italiano di Cultura in Athens, invited him to Greece.[34] His speech on Benedetto Croce, given at the Teatro Eliseo in Rome in December 1962, was a clear testament to Croce's enduring importance in his intellectual formation.[35]

In the meantime, thanks to Irma Brandeis, Montale was about to get some much-needed exposure in the United States. Theodore and Renée Weiss had been editing and publishing the *Quarterly Review of Literature* since the 1940s, devoting special issues to both American and foreign poets. Among the European poets featured in these special issues were Valéry, Leopardi, and Hölderlin. Now their attention turned to Montale. For some time Brandeis had been collaborating with Weiss, who was also her colleague at Bard College, to bring out a special number of the *Quarterly Review* completely devoted to Montale's work. According to Weiss, Brandeis was always discreet, as "enigmatic as the Mona Lisa," when asked about her relationship with Montale.[36] Her correspondence with Weiss about Montale is friendly but completely professional. Montale himself assisted in the preparation of the review issue of his own work, corresponding with Weiss from Italy.

While Brandeis was undertaking editorial responsibility for the Montale project, she was also translating the poet, including a number of key works that had been inspired by her or written to her. Throughout much of 1960 she had an engaging correspondence with Glauco Cambon, who was also in touch with Montale at that time. Cambon was extremely helpful in answering the detailed queries that resulted from her efforts to translate "The Orchard," a crucial work in the Clizia Cycle in which Clizia appears as an "angel messenger." In June 1960 Cambon wrote to her with great concern when the fate of the Montale issue seemed to be temporarily in question. He was unequivocal in his convictions about the significance of the poetry: "I feel sad about the kind of 'prudence' that suggests to curtail the Montale issue. Does anybody doubt he is one of the two or three greatest living Western poets?"[37] He went on to explain the complex nature of the angelic and demonic character of the angel messenger in "The Orchard," tying Clizia directly to Beatrice, something that would have been of great interest to Brandeis for more than one obvious reason:

> True, there is a demonic aspect to the lady in the Montale poem, but: in the first place it has to do with the essence of love; in the second place, Beatrice and the donna gentile of Convivio both have such connotations – destructiveness, death, fire, along with the sustaining – creative attributes. See Sonnet No. I from *Vita Nuova,* and canzoni *Donne ch'avete intelletto d'amore,* and *Amor che ne la mente mi ragiona.* Also, see *Paradiso:* Beatrice's smile cannot be sustained by Dante, etc. Finally, despite the troubling traits of the angelic lady, she is definitely *against* the really demoniac forces of our world: war, totalitarianism, betrayal of our civilization.

In her lively letters to Weiss about the volume in preparation, Brandeis displays her intimate knowledge of Montale's culture, including her acquaintance with his old literary friends, stretching back many years. All of this invaluable expertise poured into her collaboration with Weiss to bring about the Montale issue.

> I wrote Paolo Vivante, as I promised, and he answered "I really don't feel like writing the preface on Montale. My admiration for his poetry is great; and I don't want to do injustice to it; you would be far better suited to do the job. Besides I am rather steeped in my usual homeric researches; and two intellectual works at the same time are too much for me." So much for the indolent Sienese. I *can't do it.* Shall I write and ask Nicola Chiaromonte whether he can suggest someone? Or – and I think this a rather good idea – shall I write to an old friend of Montale's, Camillo Sbarbaro, a little-known poet, who is living very much retired on the north

> Mediterranean coast absorbed in his studies? I could sound Paolo out on his suitability, for Paolo has seen him more recently, and I not for 20 years. The thing is that he has known Montale all along since their youth. (He could write in Italian, for us to translate.) Or – should I ask Paolo to hunt for some already published superb piece covering the ground you want, and try to get permission to translate it in the Quarterly?[38]

In her letter Brandeis claims that she has not seen Montale for some twenty years, which would take her back to the late 1930s, when some of the strongest of the Clizia poems were written. It is impossible not to wonder why she so overtly states that she could not write the introductory essay for the projected collection, even underlining her statement for emphasis. It is a rare moment of exposed emotion in the otherwise completely discreet correspondence extending throughout her intense period of collaboration with the Weisses. Did she feel, even at this late date, that she was too close to the subject? Did she know that eventually it would become clear that in fact she actually was the subject of many of the poems? She critiques young William Weaver (later to become a famous translator of Italian literature), who had sent his version of "News from Amiata," but there is absolutely no mention of the fact that this poem, a particularly desperate Montalean outcry of despair, was written directly to her.

Weiss's letter of 3 August 1960 is an obvious indication of how much he depended on Brandeis for the whole project.

> This Montale letter (following) arrived yesterday, in reply I suppose to my 2nd airmail to him. We're happy to gather that he approves of our project in general and in particular too. My letter asked him for permission to use his poems and the Valéry piece (I named the poems we so far have), inquired about the possibility of a new poem we might translate and feature, and suggested that he might suggest any other poems he thought ought to be included in a representative issue like ours. Unfortunately not all our Latin and best good [*sic*] will help us through some of the details of his letter; there's no one around here, at least that we've thought of yet, to translate for us. We'll wait, and eagerly, to hear from you.[39]

Weiss copied out by hand the whole of the letter from Montale, which he hoped that Brandeis would translate. Montale had written to endorse the project, suggesting the addition of "Hitler Spring," "The Prisoner's Dream," "Bellosguardo Times," "New Stanzas," "Voice That Came with the Coots," "Separated Personae," "Eclogue," "Moiré," and some of the "Motets."[40] With a few exceptions, these are almost all crucially important poems in the Clizia Cycle (and have already been examined in detail in earlier chapters of this study). He suggests that Weiss leave out "Buffalo" and "The Lemon Trees," two famous poems from *Cuttlefish Bones.* He also suggests one Vixen poem, which begins with the phrase "If they've compared you," and he points out that this poem had already appeared in English translation in George Kay's *Penguin Book of Italian Verse.* While he apologizes that he does not have any new poems for Weiss, he mentions that he has a forthcoming volume of short prose stories, *The Butterfly of Dinard.*

Weiss, who had a good sense of what Montale actually meant, appealed to Brandeis with some desperation: "What, pray tell, do we reply to this? Is it – he – helpful? Has he some new short stories? Do you know them? How does one get hold of them?" Brandeis wrote back to assist and comfort her friend. Later she intervened with the Italian publishers to straighten out permissions for their volume, and she translated Weiss's own words into Italian when he needed to clarify similar issues himself. Weiss carefully inspected every line of her Montale translations, challenging her, in spite of her mastery of the Italian, with gentle criticisms and queries. She took it well, writing back to defend her versions. They worked harmoniously together up until the last moment, hoping to beat out a similar project to publish a volume of Montale poems at New Directions and another one under consideration at Indiana University Press.

Their long-standing effort came to fruition. The entire 1962 issue of the review (volume 11, number 4) was dedicated to Montale, with ample selections from his three great books. Irma Brandeis is listed as guest editor at the top of the table of contents page. In late October of 1961 Weiss wrote to Brandeis to congratulate her, telling her that "all the effort, hardship of preparing the no. has been more than worth it." With good-natured understatement he gave her the credit she clearly deserved: "and you as the Mama will have to take much – if not all – of the 'blame.'" While they collaborated on their project, Ted Weiss never suspected that his guest editor was in fact the model for Clizia, the subject of many of the poems.

During the period in which she was writing her study on Dante, Brandeis was obviously involved with furthering the cause of Montale's poetry, and the work of the two poets clearly intermingled in her mind. A project such as the Montale issue, which involved some of the best poets and translators of the day, takes long preparation. Brandeis included essays by Sergio Solmi, whom Montale had known since the First World War, and Glauco Cambon, one of his most probing English-speaking critics. The first comprehensive collection of Montale's poetry to appear in English, this publication gave Montale crucial visibility in the English-speaking world, leading to the steady rise in his international reputation that culminated in the Nobel Prize of 1975. Montale and Brandeis were in touch, at least through intermediaries, for professional reasons and perhaps for other reasons as well. Regardless of the other details of their personal lives, their bond had weathered many decades, and now a common literary purpose connected them.

While Brandeis worked on Montale's poetry, her book on Dante found its way into the scholarly world. The early reviews of her *Ladder of Vision* were for the most part very good.[41] Not one of the reviewers could have known how remarkably close the author, the modern Beatrice intensely active on behalf of her Dante, was to her subject.

Brandeis's *Ladder of Vision* argues for the structural and thematic unity of Dante's *Divine Comedy*. It is a series of close textual readings of key passages in Dante, bringing out the overall symbolic organization by moving from the analysis of a specific passage to larger generalizations. It is very much in keeping with the critical vogue of the 1950s. Whereas today a provocative Dante critic might wish to show the cultural voices in Dante as a discordant polyphony, Brandeis, following Erich Auerbach, Charles Singleton, Étienne Gilson, and others, intended to show precisely the opposite. To launch this agenda Brandeis presents an epigraph from the writings of Saint Bonaventura on the title page of her book: "Since, then, one must climb Jacob's ladder before descending it, let us place the first step of the ascent far down, putting the whole of this sensible world before us as it were a mirror through which we may pass to God ..." She begins by taking on Croce's challenge of the 1920s, articulated in his *Poetry of Dante* (1922), in which the Italian philosopher argued that the disunity of *The Comedy* was far greater than had previously been perceived. For Brandeis, Dante's *Comedy* is completely unified in form and content, as coherent as a Beethoven sonata or a Mozart symphony. She offers intricate readings of specific passages that are designed to show it as a complete theophanic system, with each step upward from hell to heaven analogous to a rung on a ladder, and with each rung intended to mirror some aspect of Dante's personal vision of divinity.[42]

Montale's letters and late Clizia poems indicate that Irma had been already reading Bonaventura and other scholastic philosophers in the 1930s and that she discussed Bonaventura's writings with him at that time. (He refers specifically to her interest in Bonaventura in the poem "Brooding" and also in Thomas Aquinas in his letters.) Bonaventura was born in Bagnoregio, near Orvieto (and Viterbo), in 1221. He was cured of a dangerous childhood disease by St Francis of Assisi. His mother is purported to have then exclaimed, "*Buona ventura,*" and changed his name.[43] He rose to become a professor of philosophy and theology at the University of Paris and eventually became head of the Franciscan order. He wrote in the era of the Scholasticists, reconciling Aristotlean thought and medieval notions of the human soul, arguing for the primacy of spirituality over intellect. His most important work is *Journey of the Mind to God* (1259). He appears in the twelfth canto of the *Paradiso,* where his own purity of spirit puts him in a position to comment on various types of corruption or heresies among the orders of the Church. In her study Brandeis contends that the notions of a structural hierarchy of spirituality that Dante encountered in the writings of Bonaventura and St Thomas Aquinas were crucial in the formation of *The Comedy.*

One of the longest chapters in *The Ladder of Vision* is devoted specifically to Beatrice. Here Brandeis gives special attention to the heart of the thirtieth canto of the *Purgatorio,* where, two-thirds of the way into *The Comedy,* Beatrice makes her first entrance. It is a pivotal moment. Dante has at last climbed to the top of Mount Purgatory before his ascent into heaven. He is in the Garden of Eden and beside the waters of the Lethe, a scene uniting, in Dante's powerful imagination, both biblical and classical imagery. Beatrice finally appears, wearing garments rich in symbolic meaning. Her white veil stands for faith, her green cape stands for hope, and her flame-red dress symbolizes charity. She is adorned with a crown of olive boughs, signifying her wisdom.

Dante turns to speak to Virgil, quoting his own words: "*conosco i segni de l'antica fiamma*" (I know the signs of the ancient flame). Brandeis points out that Dante's words are taken from Virgil's *Aeneid* (IV, 23).[44] This indicates a complex signification of the meaning of the flame that Dante carefully constructed. In the original Virgilian context the flame indicated a distinctly carnal passion. In Dante the passion may have been carnal at first, but it has been sublimated into something more, distilled over time through the tempering effects of faith, hope, charity, and wisdom. But Virgil has disappeared. The great confidant and guide through the first two-thirds of *The Comedy* is no longer available to comfort Dante as he faces his beloved for the first time. Beatrice now speaks to him:

Dante, perché Virgilio se ne vada,
non pianger anco, non piangere ancora;
ché pianger ti conven per altra spada. (*Purgatorio,* XXX, 55–8)

(Dante, though Virgil's leaving you, do not
yet weep, do not weep yet; you'll need your tears
for what another sword must yet inflict.)[45]

Beatrice calls Dante by name. It is the first utterance of his name in the entire *Comedy*, and the only time it is used. This underscores the significance of the passage.

Brandeis had studied the views of Charles Singleton, whom she had even published in her slender but informative anthology *Discussions of "The Divine Comedy,"* which also appeared in 1961 and is full of important commentary on Dante. In the excerpt from his criticism that Brandeis published, Singleton argues that when Beatrice finally emerges on top of Mount Purgatory at the end of the *Purgatorio,* she occupies what appears to be the logical dramatic place in *The Comedy* for the entrance of Christ. Beatrice comes instead, ready to conduct Dante through repentance and forgiveness in preparation for his ascent into heaven: "At last there is someone in triumph upon the chariot at the center. What in so many ways was called for is now delivered. A pattern is fulfilled. It is not Christ who comes. It is Beatrice – Beatrice who comes as Christ."[46] While Singleton stops short of maintaining that Beatrice replaces Christ or is equivalent to him, he explicitly states that she is analogous to Christ.

Irma knew well her own reconfiguration as Clizia, the Christ-bearing female goddess in Montale's poems. It is not surprising that she would find similar overtones in her great literary model. But Clizia has a significance that Dante never could have anticipated. A Jewish symbol as well as a Christian one, she has a sacrificial significance in Montale's poetry that stands for the six million human beings sacrificed in the Holocaust.

Both Clizia and Beatrice are *trashumanar* (transhumanized). Brandeis finds this concept in Dante's poetry:

Trasumanar significar per verba
non si porìa; però l'essemplo basti
a cui esperïenza grazia serba. (*Paradiso,* I, 67–72)

Brandeis gives her own prose translation of the passage: "To pass beyond humanity may not be told in words, wherefore let the example satisfy him for whom grace reserveth the experience."[47] Brandeis, who elsewhere translates *trasumanar* as "transhumanized," here translates the Dantesque word as "to pass beyond humanity." She analyses the term from various points of view in the course of her study, showing Beatrice's changing appearance as Dante is increasingly able to perceive her "transhumanization" with greater accuracy, as they both move up the ladder towards the summit of heaven. She shows how Beatrice becomes "more beautiful" when she and the Pilgrim ascend to Venus, in the eighth canto. Then in the fourteenth, her appearance is so lovely that she defies Dante's powers of memory. When they get to Jupiter, in the eighteenth canto, the clarity and joy he perceives in her eyes is so overwhelming that it surpasses all previous visions of her.[48] Finally, she tells Dante that her radiant eyes are merely symbolic of the larger magnificence of heaven:

Vincendo me col lume d'un sorriso,
ella mi disse: 'Volgiti ed ascolta;
chè non pur ne' miei occhi è paradiso' (*Paradiso*, XVIII, 19–21)

(Overcoming me with the light of a smile,
she said to me: "Turn and listen,
for not only in my eyes is Paradise.")[49]

With each planet Beatrice grows more omnipotent, closer to divine knowledge and beauty. But in the final enactment of sublimation Dante must clearly perceive paradise beyond Beatrice's increasingly beautiful eyes, and in her own words addressed directly to her admirer Beatrice herself encourages this transformation.

The *Paradiso,* written in the great age of religious faith, is remarkably abstract in its conception. In the twenty-eighth canto Dante, in an ingenious coinage, observes that Beatrice is "*quella che 'mparadisa la mia mente*" (she who imparadises my mind), but her beauty is only a gateway to his higher vision of divinity. Finally, in the thirtieth canto Dante observes that only God, as the maker of Beatrice's beauty, is able to fully perceive it. She is ultimately subsumed in celestial light and song as she finally takes leave of Dante and assumes her rightful seat alongside Rachel, Sarah, and Rebecca in canto 32. With each step up the ladder of vision Dante demonstrates, through a series of examinations given by the saints, his knowledge of faith, hope, charity, and wisdom in relation to love. Ultimately he is ready to perceive that the love of Beatrice and religious love are one and the same, and Beatrice's luminosity, like Clizia's, is incorporated in the light of divinity.

While she was writing about Dante and Beatrice in her critical study, Brandeis was well aware that she herself had inspired a twentieth-century reincarnation of Beatrice and that the character she had inspired also had undergone a process of transhumanization. Reverberations and echoes abound. Brandeis brings out aspects of Dante's Beatrice that are highly similar to her own treatment in Montale's work. For example, light, a symbol of Beatrice's divine perfection, serves a similar function for Clizia. Brandeis, who inspired the winged sun goddess of the 1940s, describes a familiar incarnation in the medieval poem in *The Ladder of Vision:*

> Light continues to stream from Beatrice's eyes in the pilgrim's as the two rise upward on the first stage of the journey into the *deiform realm* ... As they progress into heavenly things, Beatrice's image increases in splendour, and combines attributes no lady ever united before. She is at once brilliant, holy, wise and bewitching. She is a prism filled with divine light and an acute dispenser of that light, capable of manifesting its smallest mote in discursive language. At the same time the old spell of her beauty, far from shrinking in this high place, increases at every upward step.[50]

Brandeis argues that the combination of sacred and profane love was typical of the culture that spawned Dante, but she insists that the uniting of the erotic and the intellectual was Dante's original conception.[51] This obviously proved to be a fruitful model for Montale in the 1930s. Brandeis, reading Dante, finds in Beatrice a moral clarity that makes her seem cold and reserved: "Her disconcerting sternness makes even the attendant angels compassionate ... Beatrice is stern because she sees with terrible heavenly accuracy, and exercises her power of truth without palliative or delay."[52] Beatrice's clarity of vision and austere manner are qualities she shares with Clizia, who as a character in Montale's great poems of the 1930s and 1940s stares down the Fascist hordes with supernaturally endowed eyes and unswerving strength.

It would have been intriguing to hear Brandeis comment on the similarities and differences between Dante's Beatrice and her own treatment in Montale's poetry. On this topic she is, of course, silent in *The Ladder of Vision.* Brandeis eloquently describes Beatrice's increasing magnificence and beauty as she moves up the ladder of vision to the highest realms of Dante's heaven. Clizia is far more threatened in Montale's poetry. Her wings are torn. Her brow is frozen. She needs to flee for her life and then return. While Montale modelled Clizia after Beatrice, he expresses in Clizia's torment a rift at the centre of culture that could only be a part of the modern world.

Montale and Dante

Montale's everyday life was not spent in the company of the woman who inspired the divine Clizia, in spite of her exalted role in his poetry. He had remained with Drusilla Tanzi-Marangoni since the end of the war in spite of his various dalliances with other women. In 1962 he finally decided to marry her. In May they had a religious wedding in the parish of Sant' Ilario a Montereggi, just outside Fiesole. A civil marriage in Florence followed in late April 1963. Drusilla was now officially Drusilla Montale at last. But it was only for a short while. Just a little over three months later, in August, Drusilla fell and broke her leg. She died in Milan on 20 October 1963.

In 1964, in his role as journalist, Montale accompanied Pope Paul VI on his trip to Jerusalem, arriving at last in the Israeli landscape that he had evoked in his imagery of Clizia. His subsequent article "On a Divided Jerusalem" appeared in the *Corriere della Sera* and later in his collection of prose writings *Fuori di Casa* (*Outside the House*).[53] Roberto "Bobi" Bazlen died the following year. A critic and literary gad-fly, Bazlen had been part of the same Jewish Triestine circle as had Italo Svevo. A close friend of Montale's for much of his life, Bazlen had worked in and around Italian publishing. Many years before, in Genoa, he had introduced the poet to the writings of Svevo, Kafka, Robert Musil, and others. He appears as a character in one of Montale's short stories.[54] Bazlen had also been Montale's confidant during the crisis years of the late 1930s when Montale was wrestling with the question of whether to leave Italy and Drusilla Tanzi for America and Irma Brandeis.

The year 1965 marked the seven-hundredth anniversary of Dante's birth. For some time the International Congress of Dante Studies had been organizing events that were to take place over a period of eight days, stretching from 20 to 27 April in Florence, Verona, and Ravenna. Many foreign luminaries were invited to speak or contribute essays, among them T.S. Eliot (who did not attend),[55] Nicholai Rubinstein of the University of London, the French poet and diplomat Saint-John Perse (who had been awarded a Nobel Prize in 1960), the eminent Catholic philosopher Etienne Gilson, and prominent American scholars such as Charles Singleton and Robert Clements. They journeyed to Italy to participate in the festivities with important Italian academics such as Gianfranco Contini, Bruno Nardi, and Raffaello Ramat. In his sweeping opening address Saint-John Perse spoke on Dante's significance for Tuscany, Italy, Europe, and the West, expounding upon the poet's surprising relevance at the end of the twentieth century. In a special volume prepared for the congress Singleton articulated his theory of the unity of *The Comedy*, arguing in almost mystical tones that the poem is "christocentric" and that "what we seek is full experience of the great Poem in all the concrete and vivid detail of its unfolding structure, which is its poetry, verse by verse, tercet by tercet, canto after canto."[56]

Saint-Jean Perse opened the scholarly conference in Florence, and Montale brought the sessions of 24 April to a close with his speech. The organizers thus had two great modern poets frame the many presentations given at the Dante Congress. Montale read his essay "Dante ieri e oggi" ("Dante, Yesterday and Today") in the Palazzo Vecchio, which is just a short distance from his old base at the Palazzo di Parte Guelfa, the pre-war home of the Gabinetto Vieusseux.[57] One of his more extensive pieces of criticism, Montale's essay is a vitally significant document for several reasons. First, it offers a glimpse of one of the greatest modern Italian poets reading the unmatched medieval poet. But there is a subtext. The essay is also a summing up of Montale's own work, and the echoes of Irma Brandeis's writings on Dante are intentionally brought into his own reflections on the towering giant of all the Italian poets. He borrows Brandeis's ideas on Dante and quotes her in his essay. This act brings into play an unspoken and unwritten aspect of the speech. His poetic incarnation of Irma Brandeis into Clizia demands comparison with Dante's transhumanization of Beatrice.

Montale makes it clear that his reading of Dante has gone on all his life, he is familiar with all aspects of Dante's oeuvre, keenly aware of the complex history of six hundred and fifty years of Dante reception, stretching from Dante's own era to the modern period, and he is also familiar with the vast body of contemporary Dante criticism in several languages. In addition to Irma Brandeis he cites Gianfranco Contini, Erich Auerbach, Ernst R.R. Curtius, and Singleton. In a surprise twist Montale argues that Dante is not as far from "today" as we might think, because he sees a new Middle Ages and "new barbarousness" in the contemporary technological culture. A cultural elite keeps poetry alive in the modern era, just as it did in Dante's time, and he points out the error of assuming that the Middle Ages was devoid of art or science.[58] He hails Guido Guinizzelli, Guido Cavalcanti, and the Dolce Stil Novo poets for the development of the donna salutifera. The figure of "the lady who heals and redeems ... is the most evident theme of the entire school."[59] While Beatrice appears as a very similar type of Dolce Stil Novo character in Dante's short poems and in the *Vita Nuova,* Dante takes their innovations further in the vast architecture of the *Commedia,* making Beatrice, his donna salutifera, a figure of almost ultimate religious salvation who is encountered first in *Purgatorio* and then in *Paradiso,* giving off and bathed in glowing heavenly light in a variety of increasingly intense gradations.

While reading Brandeis and Montale on Dante, it is hard not to notice that when Montale describes "Beatrice's process of transhumanization," he is referring to a procedure already analysed in Brandeis's criticism, and a procedure that in many ways resembles Clizia's transformation in his own poems.[60] While he denies ever having read Bonaventura, Montale sounds a bit like him when he describes Beatrice as "the necessary intermediary in Dante's ascent to God." Similarly, his own Clizia is a necessary intermediary in the redemption of his own religion and culture. She too has divine powers, blazing light beams from her endowed eyes and flying over oceans to rescue him. Consumed by her divine love, she finally burns herself up in the light of the sun in "Hitler Spring." Even as Montale speaks of Dante's transhumanization of Beatrice, he knows full well that he has achieved a similar fictional process for Irma Brandeis. Clizia is Montale's "necessary intermediary" even at this very late juncture in his life.When Montale refers specifically to Brandeis's scholarship, towards the end of his lecture, only he and she could have understood the rich irony of the fact that the congress was meeting in Florence, the site of their initial trysts of the 1930s and the setting of many of his strongest poems, including *Finisterre* and "Hitler Spring." As he introduces her interpretations of Dante, he critiques Eliot: "As metaphors are not as frequent in Dante as Eliot would have us believe, and in fact become increasingly rare as the poem progresses, we thus reach a limit or an insufficiency in Eliot's proposed reading of the *Commedia.* Irma Brandeis has devoted herself to an analytic study in the sense I have indicated ... in her book *The Ladder of Vision* (1961), which is the most suggestive study I have read on the theme of the stairway which leads to God, and which is entrusted for good reason to the patronage of St. Bonaventura."[61]

He then quotes in its entirety the exact Bonaventura epigraph that Irma chose for her book, thus underscoring the essentially instructive nature of the great poem. More important, Montale takes some of her ideas and summarizes them, showing that he read Irma Brandeis's book very carefully (especially her chapter on Beatrice):

> Once he has passed the stage where he is content with an ingenuous reading, the reader's interest grows rather than diminishes as the tangle of symbols becomes more problematic. Precisely by basing her case on the literal, Miss Brandeis makes us feel how vivid and concrete the presence of Beatrice is throughout the poem and how the passages from the *Song of Songs*, St. Matthew, and the sixth book of the *Aeneid* are structurally necessary in order to make possible – and, I would add, credible – the apparition of the lady dressed in the three colors of faith, hope, and charity, who can arouse the poet who has not forgotten his earthly love, and make him say to Virgil: "Less than a drop / of my blood remains which does not tremble / I know the signs of the ancient flame."[62]

He borrows much of her analysis, including her references to Dante's sources. Montale quotes from the same passage of the thirtieth canto of the *Purgatorio* that Brandeis examines in her chapter on Beatrice. Thus, as Montale addressed the Dantisti in Florence, Irma was present in his mind and in spirit but not, as far as I know, in the flesh.

Reconsidering Dante while quoting Clizia, Montale is aware of another undercurrent of meaning that only he can probe and project. At the height of purgatory and just below the threshold of heaven Dante needs to make amends. He had for a time forgotten Beatrice for another *donna gentile* (often said to symbolize "philosophy"), and she is annoyed with him. Beatrice, who now identifies herself, chastises Dante for his wayward behaviour. When he recognizes her, he weeps. Even the angels ask her to be compassionate with him. But he needs to repent, precisely because of his great talent, which, she explains, can be used for good or evil. While Dante married another woman in his actual life, his love for Beatrice is a part of the moral order of his fictionally constructed universe – far more important, in fact, than his love for his own wife, who is never mentioned. In the next canto the repentant Dante is immersed in the waters of the Lethe for a final purification. Once he has been cleansed, all is forgiven, and Dante is prepared to ascend, under Beatrice's guidance, to the *paradiso*. But before they go on, Beatrice offers a long series of important prophecies about Florence and Italy.

The irony is only too apparent. In spite of his dalliances with other women and in spite of his long-standing relationship with Drusilla Tanzi, Montale made Clizia a vivid and concrete moral presence throughout his poetry. Now, standing before the assembly of scholars in 1965, he explains how Beatrice is just such a concrete moral presence in Dante, and he cites Irma Brandeis, the scholar who inspired him, in explaining his point. In elucidating how Dante's earlier combining of Eros and ethos informed the character of Beatrice, Montale is also explaining how Dante and Beatrice in turn made possible the character of Clizia in his poetry. The poet, as straying lover, quotes his beloved in speaking about another poet as straying lover, a poet who just happens to be arguably the greatest of all Italian writers. Nevertheless, the historical and epistemic differences that separate Montale from Dante are also important to him. Montale observes that "the *Commedia* is the last miracle of world poetry." In Dante's era, the end of the Middle Ages, it was possible to make a coherent encyclopaedic structure. In his view, Byron's *Don Juan* and Goethe's *Faust* are brilliant but failed attempts at a similar all-encompassing coherence in the nineteenth century.

Brandeis notes that Dante constructs an atemporal and static structure for *The Comedy*. After 1,300 years Statius is still in the sixth terrace of purgatory, while Forese Donati, Dante's old friend, gets there in only four years.[63] There is no seniority, and judgment is more important than temporality. Through this system the Pilgrim makes a linear progression.

While Montale had obviously studied Dante all his life, he was unwilling to structure his own poetry in a similar system; instead he merely gathers up juxtaposed moments of past, present, and future, available at all times, in a floating time-space continuum of consciousness in his poetry. Caught inextricably in the web of passing time, the poet reaches out in different directions to explain his plight. Similarly, Dante's *inferno*, *purgatorio*, and *paradiso* are available all at once for continuous reference in his modern poetry. They are available as regions of demarcated human experience, making every moral success or failure redolent with cultural reference. In the modern era an immense gathering of notions, assembled in literary collage, is all that is possible for the poet, whose isolated stream of his own consciousness is now the main narrative thread. He views this as true for his own work and for others who were influenced by Dante. He cites Pound's dense and rambling *Cantos* as an example of the fragmentary nature of the modern experience.[64] Dante is unique in his position as the last comprehensive poet.

Montale writes with a keen awareness of his vantage point as a Modernist poet contemplating the vast gap that separates him from his great medieval precursor. In *The Ladder of Vision* Irma Brandeis had already described this chasm: "The reader of Dante's *Comedy* has acutely the sense of being in touch with an inviolate conviction that the world is meaningful: not a tale told by an idiot, but the utterance of a noble god ... In the middle of the twentieth century, when such a conviction is not ours any more and we have become expert at saying why, this is all the more moving to us."[65] Montale, who envied the cohesive world vision that Dante presented so unreservedly in 1300, was also an admirer of Samuel Beckett, and, like Beckett, he was keenly aware of the Modernist vision of the senseless nature of the human condition. It was his Modernist scepticism that kept Montale from going quite as far as Singleton in his adulation of the great poem. In his last remarks he observes that Singleton once maintained that Dante's *Comedy* "was dictated by God and that the poet was only his scribe."[66] He pokes gentle fun at the great scholar (which he also does in the late poem of 1979 "Clizia Says"), insisting that he can comment on such information only "secondhand," but should Singleton turn out to be correct, he would "not object." Singleton also proved to be an important link between Irma Brandeis and Montale. Brandeis, who should have been present at the Palazzo Vecchio as an honoured guest, did not attend the congress, but she did learn about Montale's historic Dante lecture, in which her own ideas played such a significant role, shortly after he had presented it to the audience of distinguished scholars who had assembled to hear him. As she confesses in an unpublished letter to Glauco Cambon, Charles Singleton told her about it just after the Dante congress.[67]

While 1965 was not as spectacular a year for Montale's own literary fortunes as it was for Dante's, it was a good time for him in many respects. Many of the translations from the special Montale issue of the *Quarterly Review of Literature,* including those by Irma Brandeis, were reprinted in a book entitled *Eugenio Montale: Selected Poems.* It was published by New Directions, a small New York publishing house that specializes in modern European writers in translation. Mysteriously, Irma is not listed as editor of the book, and no other editor is cited. Only Glauco Cambon, who expanded his piece from the *Quarterly Review,* is listed, as the author of the introductory essay. Although the *Quarterly Review* issue and the New Directions book are similar, there are some substantial differences. New translations were added to the book, and some from the *Quarterly Review* were omitted or replaced. The copyright page indicates that "certain of these translations were first published in the special Montale issue of the *Quarterly Review of Literature.*" For the book, Irma Brandeis discreetly stepped aside to allow Cambon greater prominence.

While D.S. Carne-Ross touted the international importance of Montale as a poet, he gave the book a mixed review in the *New York Review of Books* in October 1966: "The New Directions volume unfortunately does little to suggest Montale's stature. Mr. Glauco Cambon's introduction is too Italianate in manner and reference to be very helpful to the English-speaking reader; and the translations, apart from those by Lowell and a couple by G.S. Fraser, are mostly less than adequate. Prose versions would have been much more satisfactory."[68]

In December 1965 Richard Harrier wrote a letter to the editors to point out the significance of the earlier *Quarterly Review* issue on Montale, which Carne-Ross had ignored in his account of the history of translations of Montale into English.[69] Irma Brandeis also responded to Carne-Ross in a letter to the editors in January 1967. She did not describe her role in the preparation of the Montale volume or defend her translations, but she made her role as Montale's long-time American ally quite clear, citing her own pieces on the poet from the 1930s and 1940s:

> Mr. Carne-Ross ... appears confidently to suggest that the English-speaking countries were unaware of Montale between the Praz translation in *Criterion* (1928) and the publication of Edwin Morgan's volume in 1959. He perhaps forgets that before the War closed off literary communications between Italy and these countries for a period of years, the published poetry of Montale had barely reached its second volume – namely, the 1939 *Le Occasioni.* But he forgets or is unaware of other hints that Montale was not unknown. To mention a few: translations of two poems by Samuel Putnam and S.B. Beckett in the April-May, 1930 issue of *This Quarter*; a critical summary in the *Times Literary Supplement* of June 21, 1934; an article of mine with two accompanying translations in the *Saturday Review of Literature,* July 18, 1936; a biographical and critical entry in the *Columbia Dictionary of Modern European Literature,* 1947. No great shakes, these things? Perhaps; but surely hints and beckonings to the great shakers.[70]

Whatever the status of their personal relationship, Brandeis was a consistent supporter of Montale's poetry. Her beauty and American audacity may have first captivated the poet in the 1930s, but over the years her writing, her criticism, and her thought penetrated deeply into the mind of the poet, becoming an essential part of his artistic expression and, eventually, his trajectory into the larger realm of world literature.

8 Clizia Becomes a Woman Again

Time which changes human beings does not alter the image which we have preserved of them.

— Marcel Proust

Fleas and Saints by the Window Overlooking the Garden

There is every indication that Montale thought he had said good-bye to Clizia in *The Storm and Other Things*, the last book of his great trilogy, but he was wrong. Clizia's reappearance in Montale's last poems is a fascinating occurrence and an intriguing demonstration of how memory can trump time in the poetic imagination. In these short, sparse, direct poems, written near the end of his life, we see Clizia with greater clarity than ever. She is no longer a fantastic sun goddess, created in an intricate embellishment of the imagination, symbolized by one meticulous detail after the other, and armed with a great power that can surmount the evils of Fascism. There has been a reverse metamorphosis. Now she is a lovely young woman once again, charming and bright, with a penetrating intellectual curiosity.

While these last Clizia poems date from the late 1970s, Montale returns in them to the crucial period in his life that gave rise to many of his great poems. Thus they give us one more set of Montalean "flashes" recollected from forty years earlier, offering a last glimpse at the magical and bittersweet moments before the war. Eugenio Montale died in Milan in 1981. Irma Brandeis died in New York in 1990, outliving Montale by less than a decade. When she read these final poems, she surely recognized the main characters and the unmistakable setting.

In them Irma and Eugenio are once again young, beautiful, and in Florence. As the poems offer few clues, the reader has to gauge not only who is speaking to whom but also the time of poetic utterance, whether it be the 1930s and 1940s, the 1970s, or, as the narrative of each poem progresses, a combination of the two. Taken together, the poems are like fragments from a novella, with carefully crafted loci in place and time, and shards of remembered dialogue. They add significant detail to the hidden Clizia story that runs throughout most of Montale's poetry. They also contain some of Montale's last reflections on the irrevocable onslaught of time.[1] In the last years of his life he makes no heroic pronouncements about how his verse will preserve the memory of the beloved. Imagining a coming flood of biblical proportions, he wonders whether Clizia's various artefacts might better preserve some residue of her than might his poetry. Or he imagines his writing being swept away, along with the memory of them both, in another type of flood, the flood of time that will rush forward after their death. The act of writing is no guarantee of eternity.

The poetry of the post-trilogy Montalean manner is less ornamented with densely detailed imagery. When Montale stopped writing, something changed within him. A new type of poetry emerges in the 1960s and afterwards. Gone are the rich allusive phrases, and gone, too, much of the elusiveness. The new style is brief, conversational, and ironic. It is far easier to understand than his early poetry of the trobar clus. Montale's new style began a decade earlier, in the generally non-Clizia poems of *Satura* (1971). Written between 1962 and 1970, these poems include sequences of poems entitled "Botta e riposta" ("Thrust and Parry"), which contain important reflections on Montale's conception of memory (including his enigmatic poem on his use of the I/You rhetoric in all of his poetry), and one poem that links his Jewish heroines – Gerti, Dora, and Clizia (discussed in chapter 4). The most important work of this period is *Xenia,* a remarkable series of poems that commemorate Drusilla Tanzi.

Every word in Montale has important connotations. In ancient Rome the *satura* was a type of coarse theatrical presentation with music, frequently put on as a kind of warm-up act before the presentation of a comedy.[2] As an earthier, primal form of entertainment, something like an ancient Roman version of vaudeville with somewhat rough and even lewd satirical elements, the satura was very different in tone from the motet, the madrigal, or the trobar clus. Montale points in a very fresh direction with this title. It indicates the irony, sarcasm, and self-mockery that now come naturally to him. The concept of "thrust and parry" also indicates the new style. *Xenia,* a strange title for the small and late volume about "La Mosca," means "hospitality to the foreigner" in Greek. Montale, connoisseur of Italian works, certainly also knew its botanical meaning: "a particular case of hybridization between two varieties that provokes several fruits in a plant with the characteristics of one parent and others with that of the other."[3]

Every now and then there are flickers of Clizia, even during the long period that Montale's principal literary concerns are elsewhere.[4] In "L'Eufrate" ("The Euphrates," 1969), a poem included in *Satura,* the poet-speaker refers to a span of thirty years, wondering what his secret listener has seen during that lengthy period. This time frame would take the poet and his listener precisely back to 1939, the era of Clizia. The poet admonishes his beloved not to tell him what appears to be something he has heard from her on many occasions: "*Non ripetermi che anche uno stuzzicadenti, / anche una briciola o un niente può contenere il tutto.*" (Don't claim yet again that even a toothpick, / even a crumb or a nothing can contain the all.)[5] Here the idea of the small thing containing a code explaining the large, so frequent in many of the great Clizia poems, seems to be linked to Clizia herself. Similar notions are expressed in "The Motets," "New Stanzas," the pseudo-sonnets, "News from Amiata," "Iris," and "The Eel."[6]

In such poems as the first of Montale's "Due prose veneziane" ("Two Venetian Prose Pieces," 1969) and "Senza salvacondotto" ("Without Safe Conduct," 1969), which are also in *Satura,* we detect further traces of the Clizia story. "Two Venetian Prose Pieces," as the title indicates, is set in Venice. It has three characters: the poet-speaker; Clizia; and an unnamed person – a woman who came to Italy, presumably from America and especially to visit Venice. Making distinctions with customary musical references, Montale explains that this unnamed woman preferred to hear only Gesualdo, Bach, and Mozart. Montale's "I" compares this to his own preference for a "horrid operatic repertory and worse." Judging from the poem, Clizia, the unnamed second woman, and Montale travelled together to Venice. They took separate rooms. Montale slept alone in one room, the women in the other. The trio made visits to the Church of San Marco, the Café Florian, the Riva degli Schiavoni, and the Trattoria Paganelli, recommended by a Tuscan painter.

Now we have the additional benefit of Montale's letters and Brandeis's journal, both of which indicate that Montale was recollecting places and events that were part of their actual Venice experience in the summer of 1934.[7] In an extremely detailed "diary" of the Venice visit in late July 1935 he even mentions Paganelli, the same trattoria named in the poem, where they had a "bad dinner." From his recollections we can see that Irma and he were travelling with others, that they indeed had some romantic interludes interspersed with arguments (instigated by Irma's recent discovery of her rival, Drusilla), and that they met with a number of artist and writer friends.[8] Brandeis's journal corroborates most of Montale's recollections.

Then the narrative of the poem suddenly moves back to Florence, the site of many earlier Clizia poems. The poet is presumably with Clizia. He refers again to the Oltrarno (the sanctified topos in Montale's poetry), the special neighbourhood of Florence located across the river from the cathedral and the Palazzo Vecchio that contained the revered haunts of the Pensione Annalena, the Costa San Giorgio, and the Costa Scarpuccia, and the area near the Bellosguardo hill. We see an unnamed "we" (presumably a pair of lovers, the speaker and the addressed) walking from the lower areas of the Oltrarno up the sloped streets *(rampe)* to the Piazzale Michelangelo, which offers a spectacular and justifiably famous view of the city, and the poet recalls the "miraculous reveries" (*mirabili fantasmi*) they "had invented" (*avevamo inventato)* while walking up the *rampe*, eventually leaving the Oltrarno neighborhood and coming to "the great piazza" (*al grande piazzale*).[9] Montale never identifies the third personage hinted at in the poem. After the Florentine interlude he cuts abruptly to Venice, where the poem indicates that the heat was ghastly at the time of the visit, and pigeons and photographers were everywhere. Clearly tourism was alive in Italy in 1934: "It was, it seems to me, in '34" (*Era, mi pare, il '34*). Clizia, her friend, and Montale did not fit in. The poet quips that they were too young and perhaps even too bizarre for such a city that caters to "tourists and aging lovers" (*turisti e amanti anziani*).[10] The letters contextualize the bittersweet Venetian interlude described in the poem, and Montale even approximated his feelings for Irma in his 1935 record of the events in a mix of Italian, English, and percentage points: "30% happiness, 30% *disperazione*, 30% dullness etc."[11]

Clizia turns up as the addressee again in "Without Safe Conduct." This late poem contains important details. First, it is one of the few poems in which Montale bluntly refers to the Nazi gas chambers (*al forno crematorio*). In addition, it is obviously autobiographical; the speaker of the poem, the *io* (I), is quite clearly Montale. Also, the poem begins by mentioning someone named Hannah Kahn, a Jewish friend of Irma Brandeis, not the mythical Clizia. According to the poem, Kahn visited Montale several times, and it appears that even though she was an American, she was in some danger. From the poem we can construct a picture of Montale hiding in a Florentine basement, sharing his food and companionship with her. The poet begins by wondering if Hannah could have escaped the Holocaust ovens, and then he describes her visit, recounting how she called on him in a "subterranean hole-in-the-wall" where he was "vegetating" (presumably a basement apartment near Drusilla). Because she spoke about Irma (who is the obviously intended private listener to the speaking poetic voice), he "invites" Hannah "to supper" (*l'invitavo a cena*) in a local "dive." He finds Hannah a bit boring, suspecting that Irma did as well, but admits that she probably did see them together in the 1930s walking "on the Scarpuccia" or on the Costa San Giorgio, which the poet once again refers to as "the street of the Golden Idol" (*quella dell'idolo d'oro*). According to the poem, Hannah was "not indiscreet," knowing that the situation for Jews was dangerous. He closes his brief vision of Hannah's visit by wondering if she had been swallowed up by the vortex of the war years, worrying that it may have been "difficult for her to save herself" (*difficilmente poté / salvarsi*) in the dangerous era of the Italian racist laws and the war.[12]

The real-life Hannah Kahn (later Hannah Kahn Barsky, Barnard class of 1926)[13] had collaborated with Irma Brandeis on her translation of Tobia Nicotra's Toscanini biography, and she had also translated Gaetano Mosca's *The Ruling Class*.[14] Kahn's English translation of Mosca has a preface by Arthur Livingston, who was one of Brandeis's professors at Columbia. Clearly Hannah knew Irma as early as their student days at Columbia in the 1920s. Jean Cook, executrix of Brandeis's estate, has found a letter from Kahn to Brandeis in one of the journals from the 1930s. In the letter Kahn indicates that Brandeis has requested that she look up Montale in Italy: "Of course I shall see Montale, if you want me to. Only I don't see that it will do any good. It's so hard for me to judge him – I have seen him only once, you know, and even then I do believe it was a strain for him. How could it help but be, when he knew that I was going to report to you everything he said, and when, besides, he realized that we could talk neither as intimate friends (since, really, I know nothing of your relationship to him), nor as utter strangers. But if you are worried about his state of mind, his health, of course I shall go around to the library to see him and tell you what I can."[15]

We now know that Montale knew Hannah as early as 1933 and that he consistently refers to her in his letters to Brandeis with the code name "David." He describes a September 1935 dinner with her in great detail in one of the letters. It took place a little over a year after his last stormy encounter with Irma, which had almost ended in a permanent rupture. Montale even recorded what Hannah ordered for supper: "She had *tagliatelle verdi, fegatini* with *salade,* fruits and a bottle of white Val d'Arbia. She spoke (I understand her better than you), she ate like a bird and I knew she was rather pretty, clever and so on. *L'ho riaccompagnata verso le 10 e mezza ad Annalena ma non ebbi il coraggio di salire* [I walked her back to the Annalena at around 10:30, but I didn't have the courage to go up]."[16] The next day Hannah visited Montale at the Gabinetto Vieusseux, and he showed her a well-known propaganda photograph of a shirtless Mussolini standing in a cornfield, which Montale facetiously describes as "the naked cardinal in the corn."

While I have been able to find no evidence that Hannah Kahn was in Italy in the 1940s, that is the time of the poem's setting implied by the title and other detail. The poem projects a scenario indicating the truly great danger for Italian Jews in Florence between 1943 and 1945, and, at the very least, its temporal moment could also be construed as sometime after the racial laws of 1938. If the poem reflects what actually happened in life, Kahn arrived and welcomed help, like the others who had come to the Florence apartment building where Montale was staying with Drusilla Tanzi. Probably because she did not want to get Montale in trouble, she kept quiet. As an American, Kahn may not have been in the same grave danger as was an Italian Jew, but who could have been sure of that in the 1940s? Based on a real or imagined event, the poem underscores what could have happened to Irma Brandeis had she remained in Italy throughout the war years. Nevertheless, Irma, as transformed into her Clizia guise, had miraculous powers, her *passepartout* (master key) that enabled her to survive and even defy her enemies. The poet sees no similar gift in Hannah Kahn.

Towards the end of the poem Montale refers to the winding streets of the Costa Scarpuccia and the Costa San Giorgio, giving us yet one more glimpse of the Florence of Irma and Eugenio, one more evocation of her apartment at number 54. In "Costa San Giorgio," an earlier poem in *The Occasions,* and one of the first poems of the Clizia Cycle, the image of the golden idol of the "conquistadores" served as a focal point, allowing Montale to voice his general frustrations with religion. It reappears here with no explanation, almost as a private reference that only Irma Brandeis could have known.

Other poems that refer to Clizia in *Satura,* either directly or possibly indirectly, are "Le revenant"[17] ("The Ghost," 1968), "L'angelo nero"

("The Black Angel," 1968), and "Gli uomini che si voltano" ("Men Who Turn Around," 1969). At one point in "The Ghost" the speaker in the poem declaims to his unnamed listener, "*sei stata forse la sua Clizia senza saperlo*" (you may have been his Clizia without knowing it). It is unclear from the context whether the poet is addressing his own Clizia or somebody who has taken on that role for another poet-speaker, but perhaps Montale is talking yet once more to *his* Clizia in this poem. We cannot be sure. In "L'angelo nero" ("The Black Angel"), an angel-messenger with wings reappears, recalling the winged Clizia, but this one is consistently described as black, dark, or ebony, whereas Clizia is customarily associated with light, the sunflower, and the sun itself. However, this could be yet another transformation of Clizia. In "Gli uomini che si voltano" ("Men Who Turn Around") the poet could be wondering what Clizia looks like in the present moment, so many years after the fact.

In the short collection entitled *Diario del 71 e del 72* (*The Diary of '71 and '72*, 1973) one poem, "A C." ("To C.," 1971), may concern Clizia and even be dedicated to her, as the letter of the title indicates, and just as, many years before, *Le occasioni* was dedicated to I.B. (Irma Brandeis).[18] The mention of suicide in this poem might be a reference to Drusilla Marangoni's threatened suicides in 1938, which we know about from some of Montale's most troubled letters, and the image of the pressing passage of the hours anticipates some of the reflections on time in the very late Clizia poems that Montale will write just a few years later.

Another collection, *Quaderno di quattro anni* (*The Notebook of Four Years*, 1977), shows more signs of Clizia. In a very short poem in the *Quaderno* entitled "Due destini" ("Two Destinies," 1973) the poet writes, "*Clizia fu consumata dal suo Dio / ch'era lei stessa*" (Clizia was consumed by her God / which was the same as herself), thus recapping some of the same notions already expressed in "Hitler Spring," but the poet is not speaking to Clizia directly here. He is comparing her to another muse, a "Celia" who was reduced to a skeleton by *termiti* (ants).[19] "Una lettera che non fu spedita" ("A Letter Never Sent," 1975) recreates the motif of an intensely written poem that was originally conceived in the form of a letter, so common to the great poems of *Le occasioni* ("News from Mount Amiata" and others), but now a newly ironic and playful voice emerges without the desperation of tone so vital to the poems of the late 1930s. Judging from later poems that name her directly, Clizia could well be the listener addressed at the beginning of this poem about yet another "unsent" letter in which Montale writes, "*Consenti mia dilettissima che si commendi / seppure con un lasso di più lustri / il mirifico lauro da te raccolto"* (Consent, my extremely beloved one, to let me praise you, despite the lustrous expanse of time, for the wonderful laurel you picked). Even more significant, the poet tells his beloved listener that "it doesn't matter" to either of them if her name remains unknown and *nell'ombra* (in the shadow), and yet she is the one *che era e sarà folgorata dal sole* (who was and will be burned up by the sun). This is still very reminiscent of the sun-goddess in "Hitler Spring."

Of all these, "L'eroismo" ("Heroism," 1975) offers the freshest perspective on Clizia in which she seems very unlike her earlier apotheosis. In this poem Montale describes a conversation with Clizia, bringing her back into play with startling immediacy. It is an important statement of his anti-militaristic views, in which he distances himself once again from the nationalism of earlier writers such as D'Annunzio, his famous predecessor. Both Montale and D'Annunzio were veterans of the First World War, but Montale's "Heroism" is tellingly different from anything D'Annunzio could have written. D'Annunzio is known for celebrating the macabre slaughter of war as an act of glory. "Heroism," by contrast, is a short anti-war poem, possibly based on Montale's own war-time experience, in which the poet contemplates the humanity of his enemy with considerable compassion. He describes a German prisoner who became a friend for a time because he happened to possess a copy of a book by the great German poet Rainer Maria Rilke:

> Clizia suggested to me that I join the guerrilla fighters
> in Spain, and more than once I imagined myself
> dead at Guadalajara or an illustrious survivor
> barely standing upright after years in prison.
> But nothing of that sort happened: not even the torrential
> words of a politico redeemed by glory
> and prestigious posts bestowed upon me by fate.
> But where have I fought, I who didn't love
> the mob of crazed soldiers and fugitives?
> Some things I remember: *my* prisoner,
> who had in his hand a copy of Rilke, and we were friends
> for a few seconds, and the wearily useless
> thumping of bombardment and the fastidious
> clicking of snipers.
> Rather little and even useless for her, someone
> who didn't love homelands and had one only by happenstance.[20]

The context of the poem clearly is the late 1930s, and the subject of discussion recalled in it seems to have been whether or not the poet should leave Italy to fight against the Fascists in the Spanish Civil War (1936–9). The poem remains a remarkable antithesis to the excessive love of war and death celebrated in D'Annunzio's writings, and records once again Montale's sense of himself as an anti-heroic "witness." His level of "heroism," or rather his lack of it, remains a disappointment for Clizia in the poem, but she too remains as suspicious of nationalism as does Montale, perhaps because her Jewish-American status makes her only a descendant of recent immigrants to the United States.

While these glimpses of Clizia's ongoing importance in Montale's imagination are intriguing, the last truly important Clizia poems are in the very last book of poems published in Montale's lifetime, *Altri versi e poesie disperse* (*Other Verses and Dispersed Poems*, 1980). It appeared a few months before his death in 1981.[21] More than any of the later collections, *Other Verses* adds new details that enhance our comprehension of the earlier Clizia poems and clarifies the importance of the impact of the Clizia era on the poet's life. Clizia is once more a symbol for Irma Brandeis. No longer a goddess, she is now a senhal for a real woman. We encounter the former goddess, newly metamorphosed into a young woman, in the short poem "Clizia nel '34" ("Clizia in '34"). Here we find Clizia at the Pensione Annalena, where she has appeared in earlier poems. Now she is stretched out on a chaise longue on the veranda, looking out over the *giardino.* The poem is an obvious flashback to Irma Brandeis as she was in 1934, alluring, brilliant, and young. The extremely late date of the poem, 5 January 1980,[22] and the vividness of description of the scene are compelling proof of how Irma had indelibly marked the poet's imagination. Most of the Clizia poems were written in the late 1930s and early 1940s. It is now forty years later.

In the poem, Clizia and the poet are back at the beginning of their love affair, just shortly after the time Irma first came to Florence. Montale was the young director of the Gabinetto Vieusseux, and we may imagine the poet-speaker to be Montale himself. He has come to call on his Clizia, who is staying at the well-known base for culturally minded foreign visitors. As usual, he finds Clizia stretched out on the chaise longue on the veranda that looks out over the garden there. In fact, she is almost always stretched out like that (*sempre allungata*), often with a book in her hand. He suspects she is reading about "vaguely known saints" (*santi semisconosciuti*) and baroque poets of "scanty reputation" (*scarsa reputazione*). The poet ends by describing his deep feelings for her, back then in 1934 as in the time in which he is writing the poem, as something more than love, an ideation of passion perhaps. He calls it "veneration" (*venerazione*).[23] The poet claims here that this is the overarching emotion that he has "always" (he repeats the Italian word *sempre*) felt for Clizia. Not love, but veneration.

Judging by this and other poems written about life at the Pensione Annalena, Clizia was often relaxing on a favourite veranda chair. The memory of her on the chaise longue on the pensione's veranda is as strong as the evocations of the madeleine pastry in Proust. The Italian word *sempre* (always) gives the sense that Irma was "always" like that or, at least, often like that when Montale saw her. That is how she persisted in his imagination, living on in his mind's eye decade after decade until his death. One would like to think that somehow and in some way, perhaps in another dimension, she still is.

Clizia and Montale were reading John Donne (1572–1631), the metaphysical poet and one of the various figures "of scanty reputation" championed by Eliot and Richards in the 1930s. In the original, the Italian word for "reputation," *reputazione,* makes a striking rhyme with *venerazione,* "veneration," which is the last word of the poem.

These poems are reflections of reflections in the mirrors of time. For example, we read about the lovers reading about other lovers in "Le pulci" ("The Fleas," 1974). Montale refers explicitly here to John Donne's "The Flea," a poem about what he calls "the golden 1600s." Donne's poem dates from around the turn of the seventeenth century. Judging from other poems and information, I can say with some confidence that Irma and Eugenio obviously read the Donne poem and translated it together, probably in the garden of the Pensione Annalena sometime between 1933 and 1938. An interest in translating English poets into Italian would have been entirely in keeping with the international literary interests kindled at the Gabinetto Vieusseux, offering a professional bond that would bring the young lovers together.

John Donne and Ann More were antecedents of Eugenio and Irma, just as Dante and Beatrice were. Anne and John Donne were as tormented by circumstance in the 1600s as were Irma and Eugenio in the 1930s. In 1597 John Donne was appointed secretary to Sir Thomas Egerton, Lord Keeper of the Great Seal. While working for Egerton, Donne became a familiar and trusted house guest, but he made the mistake of falling in love with Lady Egerton's niece, the beautiful seventeen-year-old Ann More. Donne married Anne secretly, without the requisite family approval. For his transgression he was thrown in jail for several weeks and was dismissed from his post, thus beginning a long period of financial hardship. He summed up this experience with one of the most famous of his many puns: "John Donne, Ann Donne, Undone."

A poem can be written years later about a specifically loved and remembered experience, or a specifically detested one, for that matter. When he is writing in 1980, Montale composes in a much more straightforward style than he did when he mythologized about Irma in earlier decades, as if everything he now describes had just happened yesterday, not almost fifty years before. He sees with vivid accuracy the lovely Irma and himself as young Eugenio translating Donne in the Pensione Annalena of the 1930s. As a result we do too. Details from the past give Montale access to his memory by recreating a fragment from the texture of lived experience. One fragment of the texture is the texts that he had read with his beloved. The Donne poem unlocks a door to the past. Montale's recollection of the shared reading of Donne so long ago is incorporated into "The Fleas." It is an irreverent reading. The speaker in Montale's flea poem begins by asking his listener if she has ever had a flea mix his blood with hers, creating a *frappé* (Montale uses the French word). This mixture, he assures his lover, would guarantee their "immortality" (*immortalità*). This is because, back in the 1600s, when Donne's lover was bitten by a flea, the same one that had already bitten him, something of their essence had combined in nature through the mixing of their blood within the flea, and they became immortalized. Now in the twentieth century, the era of what Montale describes as "full time" (*tempo pieno*), the same thing could happen again, but it might even take less effort on the part of the modern flea because time has now grown shorter and the centuries are nothing but "feathers in the wind" (*piume al vento*).[24]

In the original poem by John Donne the flea pierces the skin, sucking out blood, mixing its blood with that of the other lover. Its actions can be construed as sexual, through a "conceit," a figure standing for the act of making love:

Mark but this flea, and mark in this,
How little that which thou deny'st me is;
It suck'd me first, and now sucks thee,
And in this flea, our two bloods mingled be;
Thou know'st that this cannot be said
A sin, nor shame, nor loss of maidenhead,

Yet this enjoys before it woo,
And pamper'd swells with one blood made of two,
And this, alas, is more than we would do.[25]

Donne's poem was irreverent, too, daring to argue with contorted and seductive pseudo-logic that the commingled blood in the flea is more of a consummation than marriage or sexual intercourse. Then the poem doubles back on itself, admitting that the flea, after all, is innocent, committing only a minor transgression in sucking a drop of blood. If the beloved would just give in to the poet, she would lose no more honour than she did when the flea bit her.

In Montale's poem there is more than one flea, in fact many fleas (*le pulci*), making the connotation very different than in Donne's original poem. If we compare Donne's other passionate love poems ("The Sun Rising" is an excellent example) to the poems of Irma and Eugenio in Florence, we can see that the Clizia poems are more ethereal, drawn with a deft hand of intimation, whereas Donne's poems are obviously written with a more direct carnal passion. This type of passion can be found in Montale's Vixen poems but rarely in the Clizia Cycle, where Montale's admiration for Clizia rivals Dante's devotion to Beatrice. Montale's poem argues that in the era of Donne, things were slower and grander. In the modern age of *tempo pieno* (full time), things are faster, more desperate. Fame is more easily attained now, as time seems to go by with ever greater speed and intensity. In fact, time is racing by with such great speed that it seems to be disappearing – *il tempo si raccorcia* (time is growing shorter). As Montale reflects on his great love of the 1930s, he compares the simpler world of Donne to twentieth-century chaos.

We know from his prose writings that Montale was distressed by the post-war horrors of mass political movements, the bomb and other new instruments of murder, a vast political propaganda machine, and a disturbingly dehumanizing technocratic society. Clizia makes Irma immortal, an achievement with ironic implications for both Montale and Brandeis. Now it takes less time to become "immortal," but there is less time in general. In fact, time is running out (as the poet also says in his charming and bittersweet Nobel Prize speech). Montale treated this topic with more detail and similar reverence in "Previsioni" ("Predictions," 1977), another poem written in this late era.

Time is not a simple linear process in Montale. Time exists in the emotional range of memory, from the distant past, continually affecting the present. Moreover, the present changes the past, as in the actions described in "Hitler Spring." In his verse and criticism Montale is keenly aware of modern notions about the relativity of time and space, and the absurdity of history, but he is an uneasy Modernist. Like Stevens, he regrets the inevitable modern loss of the intensity of religious passion and thought. In "Tempo e tempi II" ("Time and Times II," 1979) the poet regrets how Einstein's relativity took away the anchoring self-identity of an individual with the possibility of a "meaning ahead." These are recurrent themes in his poetry, and while they were already present in the dense mid-century poems, they are more apparent in the more direct poetry of the later years.

John Donne's wife, Anne, turns up in another poem, "Prosa per A.M." ("Prose for A.M.," 1980). We can surmise that here Montale is again talking to Clizia. In the second stanza he refers explicitly to "the sweet Ann More" (*la dolce Anne More*) who in 1617 did not survive the last of her many pregnancies and died at the young age of thirty-three. But the ordering of time and space seems questionable in this poem. Clizia and the poet both "regress" and "advance" to go back to the era of Ann More, an era of slower and grander time.

In "Rimuginando" ("Brooding," 1979) the "I" thinks of the many years that have passed, and then he remembers "C" who is obviously Clizia, identified not just by the letter "C" but also by her fascination with Saint Bonaventura. He adds a little prayer, "May God protect her" (*che Dio la protegga*).[26] Clizia is described here, as she is elsewhere in Montale, as a student of various obscure saints. He remembers her interest in Saint Bonaventura (*San Bonaventura*), the Franciscan theologian whom Brandeis treated in some depth in her study on Dante, which Montale admired. The Dantesque *selva* (woods) appears also in the second line of the *Inferno*, and therefore Montale is hinting at Clizia's scholarly inclinations by including it again in his poem. The poet is not talking to her in this poem, as he is in so many others. Instead he is thinking about her and meditating, speaking to himself. He is returning from a boring play, possibly one he actually attended in his work as a critic. This poem, written years after the trauma of the thirties, is most important because of its sense of time and the vast span of time it encompasses, at least on the limited scale of a human life. In Montale's mind, all past, present, and future are in a state of relativity. The 1930s are just as near as *battibaleni* (the twinklings of an eye). The past implodes on the present and is in fact already the future. Before we realize it, even the future has passed.

In Montale's great "Hitler Spring" all of Western civilization is on trial. The import of the present overwhelms the meaning of the past and the implications and promise of the future. In "Brooding" the situation is reversed. Now all the trauma of the 1930s is only a wink away, as if it happened a few seconds ago, and the implications of the past (particularly the traumatic era of that decade) are already future. Montale comments in this poem on the absurdity of life and the big bang theory. The "first causes," the "explosion of the ridiculous," guaranteed the insane nonsense of the universe. The origins of life seem without purpose. Time and history stretch from random gases, to Dante, to May 1938, to the boredom of the current moment of the critic in the audience, attending the "performance" (*lo spettacolo*) perhaps in the late 1970s. It is uninterrupted and proceeds from prehuman understanding, to sense and meaning imposed by human culture, to the absurdity of the 1930s, and beyond to who knows what and if. This is an example of the pessimistic side of Montale, who is often sceptical about the future of humanity. Montale's impish pessimism was anticipated years earlier at the end of Italo Svevo's wonderful comic novel *Confessions of Zeno* (1923), a work that Montale had championed early in his career: "When all the poison gases are exhausted, a man made like all other men of flesh and blood, will in the quiet of his room invent an explosive of such potency that all the explosives in existence will seem like harmless toys beside it. And another man ... will steal that explosive and crawl to the center of the earth with it, and place it just where he calculates it would have the maximum effect. There will be a tremendous explosion, but no one will hear it and the earth will return to its nebulous state and go wandering through the sky, free at last from parasites and disease."[27] Here Svevo predicted the atomic age that later horrified Montale, understanding in the 1920s the destructive power of a human race that seemed determined to terminate itself in a final man-made big bang that would echo the big bang that supposedly started the history of the universe.

A similarly senseless human condition appears in Montale's "Lo spettacolo" ("The Performance," 1979), a late poem in which God and purpose seem to be as absent from the universe as is the author in Pirandello's *Six Characters in Search of an Author.* "The Performance" gives us a more extensive view of the Montalean sense of the absurd. Here the existence of the universe seems like a bad performance of a play, and the author has abdicated along with the prompter in his box.

The absurdity of a purposeless universe turns up in "Clizia dice" ("Clizia Says," 1979), another poem that shows how fresh in Montale's mind is the encounter with Irma in Florence almost fifty years before:

> Although a half-century has elapsed
> it will be easy to find again
> the bay window by which we stayed for hours
> picking fleas off the monsignor of the fleas.
> On the roof a nightingale shouted himself hoarse,
> but not with success. As for the argot
> of the people's festivals or
> of the comedies or farces living only
> in oral traditions, all would be easily explained,
> if we had with us, as happened
> one day, a master of humble sermon
> (as well as the bronze master of the Patrology).
> But when will that day be and where will we be?
> If there exists a heaven and in it many languages,
> his fame as interpreter will grow
> in varied circles and the "puzzle" will be
> worse than the inferno of us deaf mutes.[28]

The poet-speaker's time is different from the time of the scene first described in the poem. It is now almost half a century later, and the narrator begins by commenting on the vast expanse of years separating him from the events he describes. The poem starts with a description of the large windows in the Pensione Annalena, which opened generously onto the veranda and the garden, where the lovers sat together to study and perhaps translate Donne in the 1930s. Montale still remembers the nightingale singing on the roof, indicating that their window would have been on the veranda level or above.[29]

The delightful play on words inherent in the Italian *spulciando,* which is lost in all translation attempts, includes the double meaning of defleaing (somewhat sarcastically identifying Donne's poem "The Flea") and the activity of close scholarly examination. In his note for the poem Montale clearly indicates that he is referring to Donne, who is "in fashion today." The poet also specifies in a note that the "master of humble sermon" is the scholar Charles S. Singleton.[30] Singleton (1909–85) was a famous translator of Dante and the foremost American Dante scholar at the time of Montale's own 1965 lecture on Dante. Brandeis published some of Singleton's material on Beatrice in her 1961 anthology of Dante criticism, and Singleton and Montale gave presentations at the same 1965 Dante conference.[31] Singleton's six-volume prose translation of *The Divine Comedy* (1970–5) features extensive commentary and massive erudition (too massive for some). As a young scholar, Singleton had researched the popular musical culture of the early Italian Renaissance. Montale plays with these aspects of Singleton's career in his poem.

The poem suggests that both Eugenio and Irma were in the company of the great Singleton. It is logical to assume that Irma would have wanted to attend the 1965 conference, along with many other American Dante scholars, and that the meeting with the famous scholar, described mysteriously in the poem as having taken place "one day," happened then, but I have found no evidence that she was there. Instead there is evidence that Singleton, having heard Montale's Dante lecture at the conference – a lecture in which Brandeis's ideas on Dante were quoted conspicuously – reported to Brandeis about the lecture after the fact (see chapter 7). The actual meeting of the three probably took place much earlier, in the summer of 1934, when all of them were in Florence.[32] Another late poem, "Sono passati trent'anni, forse quaranta" ("Thirty Years Have Passed, Maybe Forty," 1979), is dedicated "to Charles Singleton." Obviously addressing the American scholar, it indicates that Montale knew Singleton in the 1930s while he was in the middle of his love affair with Irma Brandeis. Either way, the poet goes on to imagine the company of the "master" of erudition at some later point beyond the initial meeting described in the poem. Montale ironically posits that if heaven exists, Singleton would be in Dantesque *paradiso,* his fame growing in Dantesque circles, but the confusion that his learning would cause would be a comical *inferno* of multilingual babble, a cacophony much worse than that of the "deaf mutes" below. "Clizia Says" also refers to another scholar, the "bronze one of the Patrology," included in Clizia's book containing writings of the church fathers. It is perhaps once again Saint Bonaventura, who was obviously of life-long interest to Irma Brandeis.

The *giardino* of the Pensione Annalena is a particularly effective stimulant for Montale's memory. The lovers take refuge in it in the 1977 poem "Predictions," another late work that is based on recollections of the Annalena. As in "Clizia Says," the lovers in "Predictions" escape into the familiar *giardino,* here recalled as a hanging garden (although the poet claims he is not sure about this), to get away from the chattering of a new boarder who accosts them with unwanted bawdy gossip (*fanfaluche erotiche*).[33] The Clizia/Irma character in the poem then talks about "poet's women" (*donne dei poeti*) who are rendered in "illegible lyrics" (*illeggibili carmi*). Clearly, the woman speaking in this poem knew this was going to happen to her and she is concerned about her fate, whispering that she knows she will be joining these other "poet's women" in Montale's "illegible lyrics." The poet responds by arguing that the bullet is unaware of who shoots it. The woman in the poem, whose name is "C," responds wittily that "we are not on a target range" (*Ma non siamo .... ai baracconi*), pointing out, too, that her poet does not have a gun in his baggage.[34]

Irma clearly knew even in the 1930s that she was in the company of a major poet. Here we can see that she also knew she was likely to appear as a female character in her poet's verse. She makes her "predictions" about what might become of her, as suggested by the title. She hides her anxiety with sarcasm, claiming that she does not want to end up as one of the many women who become personages in mediocre poetry. However, she was to be the focal inspiration for one of the great poets of the twentieth century and not merely a romantic stimulant to shore up a poet with a lack of talent. Montale remembers that he was stunned into silence by the remark, and then retorts with his own predictions by saying that the poem is equal to a bullet. It has a trajectory of its own, even a life energy of its own. Equating author and reader with shooter and target, he says that the poem does not know the author or where it is supposed to go. It has autonomy. But the poet's donna, Irma, gets the last word in the poem. In this poem, at least, art is no more important for her than life itself.

"Predictions" is essentially a dialogic exchange between the two characters in the Pensione Annalena, and once we know the context, it reads easily, almost like conversational prose excerpted from a novel. In the first part the narrator speaks directly to the beloved ("we escaped," "you spoke," et cetera). In the last four lines Montale makes the conversation seem to recede into the past by referring to Irma in the third person and calling her "C." for Clizia. Clizia rejects his metaphor, claiming that a firing range (shooting gallery) and firearms make a bad analogy for describing their literary fortune. Montale is describing a conversation from their youth in which the participants are wondering what literary fate will evolve from their passion. He looks back into the past and with full knowledge ponders what *became* of it. Through the medium of his poem the poet has carried out a continuous conversation with Clizia for his entire literary life.

The Absent or Present Lover and the Reality of Memory

The internal-external contrast, found in the poem "Interno/Esterno" ("Inside/Outside," 1976), was of great significance in earlier poems, especially the pseudo-sonnets. The interior was a refuge of love and safety, and the exterior a precinct of madness and danger. This contrast occurs in "Café at Rapallo," the poem in *Cuttlefish Bones* that is dedicated to the crepuscular poet Camillo Sbarbaro. With the late poem "Inside/Outside" the conception finally merits a poem with its own title. Here, however, the memory is "the internal," carrying fragments of a life within the mind as the body moves through the external world:

When reality decomposes
(if it ever even existed) and a few of its parts
encrust themselves upon us,
then an ether smell not from a hospital
warns us that the chain is broken off
and that memory is a piece of eternity
that roves by itself
perhaps waiting to reintegrate itself with us.
And for that reason I see you
turning around on the pier, your back to me, to board
the transatlantic ship that will return you
to New England
or we are together on the veranda of
the "Annalena"
to pick fleas from the rhymes of the venerable
itchy John Donne,
you setting aside the wild abysses
of Meister Eckhart or someone similar.
But today the telephone rings and a voice
I struggle to recognize says hello.
I want to speak to you, it adds, after thirty years.
My name is Giovanna, I'm Clizia's friend,
and I left with her. I can't add anything
and even to say *arrivederci* would be ridiculous
for the two of us.[35]

This poem corroborates the possibility of a seaside parting of devastating finality, perhaps at or near Sottoripa, the arcade at the port of Genoa, which is a setting that turns up in the much earlier Motets, the pivotal short works in *The Occasions* in which Irma first emerges and then takes on greater and greater importance. Here Montale refers quite specifically to the ocean liner that will carry Irma to New England. If we couple this with the Motets, we imagine Eugenio and Irma on the dock, counting the minutes before final boarding. The motet poem concerns the moments before the beloved leaves. Here the beloved is already on the ship. The Genovese portside area of Sottoripa in the Motets has been attributed to a scene of parting inspired by another woman, Paola Nicoli. However, this late poem to Clizia is another argument for reading the Motets as completely about I.B. Or perhaps Sottoripa was a place of loss for Montale more than once in his long life. Paola was an early loss. Irma's departure was a more profoundly resonant loss that occurred a few years later at the same or a similar spot in Sottoripa. Both Brandeis and Montale record that the poet wept after their 5 September 1933 tryst at the Hotel Bristol near Sottoripa. Neither says whether they were tears of joy or sorrow. Irma left for the United States shortly afterwards.

Montale's contemplative lines on memory examine the elusive connection between lived experience and what he describes here as *la realtà* (reality). Some things that happen to us are unforgettable, permanently recorded in our consciousness and embedded still deeper in the recesses of our mind. These are the moments that, in Montale's words, "encrust themselves upon us." We never lose them although we lose much of the context around them. While the rest falls away into the irretrievable past, the adoring poet can never forget Clizia on the dock before leaving or on the chaise longue on the Annalena veranda, reading John Donne. That is why these images still play back repeatedly in his mind at the time of this writing near the end of his life, so many years after he witnessed them. He remembers her as she left him on that day of parting before the war, as she perhaps waved to him from the ship and turned away from the dock, her form receding into the ocean liner that carried her to New England and safety. The instant of such parting and loss is a moment in life that a man does not forget. It is the instant of the last time he sees a woman whom he loves or loved. It plays back, intolerably or happily, in his mind again and again.

Is the memory as real, at the moment in his life when he recalls it years later, as it was the day after it happened? Is a memory real? The poet gives us a fascinating answer. For Montale it is "encrusted" (*s'incrosta*) or "inlaid" in the mind, and that fracturing from the moment of experience and subsequent retention in the interior life of the individual has a reality of its own. This entity is like floating molecules with a unique odour, and memory allows it to live and possibly even reform or reconstitute itself (*rintegrarsi in noi*) in us and at specific instances in our lives. These events are captured and retained deep in the mind, and we take them with us through life. The rest is merely external and drops away. Memory keeps alive the image from so long ago. Repeatedly the poet sees Clizia, turning away from the dock, on the ocean liner that transported her to New England and far away from him. It is the *chronotopos,* the spot on the space and time continuum where loss begins. Absence starts at point zero, and presence must be created in the poet's mind from that instant. Afterwards he reconstructs her in his mind.

Montale cuts from this recurring scene of dockside loss with cinematic abruptness. Suddenly another flashback comes. In this poem, as in several other late ones, we see the veranda of the Pensione Annalena on the Via Romana. Here, yet one more time, Montale recalls how the couple translated Donne into Italian at the Annalena. He again resorts to his sarcastic reference to Donne, recalling how the two of them were "picking the fleas" from Donne's rhymes. In this poem we find out a little more about their reading. Perhaps tired of their intellectual pursuits or simply infatuated with each other, they have set aside the works of the German mystic Johannes Eckhart (1260–1327?) and other related writers. One imagines the rooms of the pensione, the veranda, the garden, and the dockside setting of departure and loss as places of magical permanence for Montale; he replays a variety of sensory messages in his mind, decade after decade, until as a very old man he writes his last poems.

This "inlaid" lived experience, etched permanently in Montale's mind, is prompted by an external event, a strange phone call that comes thirty years later. Something alive, floating in time and space, recomposes itself in the poet. It is like an internal ruin lodged in memory. A phone call brings it alive. The broken chain (*la catena interrotta*) is hooked together for an instant. The caller is an unspecified person named Giovanna, who may be Giovanna Calastri (1913–74), the niece of the proprietor of the Pensione Annalena during its hey-day in the 1930s. Giovanna Calastri sailed with Irma Brandeis to the United States and later decided to emigrate.[36] In the poem Giovanna says that she travelled with Clizia on the ocean liner back to New England on that day of the final parting many years ago. Montale closes the poem by indicating that he has been left speechless by this call. It seems ridiculous after all this time even to utter *arrivederci*.[37]

"Poiché la vita fugge ..." ("Since Life Is Fleeing ..."), written in January 1980, begins with a line typical of a carpe diem and may have been taken from one. Then something goes wrong, almost immediately, in fact, when the very noble first words of the poem, "*Since life is fleeing*," give way to the very irreverent and modern second line, "and the one who attempts to put it in reverse" (*e chi tenta di ricacciarla indietro*), which sounds like the driver of a car who wants to change gear or change direction. But this person is "trapped" in a "primordial web" and cannot put things in reverse, and he wants to know how he can get beyond the locality of his physical limitations, beyond the objects (*gli oggetti*) that appear to be "imperishable parts" (*non peritura parte*) of the self.[38]

This is similar to the pseudo-sonnet "The Fan," which begins with a Latin quotation about painting and poetry ("*Ut pictura ...*") and then turns into one of the most dramatic Clizia poems. Despite the nod to the carpe diem rhetoric in this late Montale poem, the lover does not try to seduce the beloved and ask her to give in to sexual desire because life is fleeting. A typical carpe diem would have been written that way, as in Robert Herrick's line "Gather ye rosebuds while ye may" or Andrew Marvell's "The grave's a fine and private place / but none, I think, do there embrace." Here the opportunity for lovemaking has long since been lost, and we know that the author of the poem has only a year left to live. The question, instead, is whether the poet can hold on to some aspect of what he was, which includes some residual aspect of the passion he once felt.

The opening line is in italics in both the Zampa edition and the authoritative earlier edition edited by Bettarini and Contini, indicating that it is a fragment, but no note in either edition specifies a source. Probably Montale left no definitive clue. Another source was almost certainly Petrarch's *canzoniere,* where a sonnet begins:

> Life flies and will not be delayed an hour,
> And, by forced marches, Death pursues apace,
> And present deed, and matters past, as well
> As what's to come – all these make war on me![39]

The Petrarch poem, included in the "poems written after the death of *madonna* Laura," is not a carpe diem but a poem of despair. The poet, mourning the loss of his beloved, is exhausted; his "pilot is tired out," and his "mast and sails" are unusable.

Montale is near the end of his life, and unlike Petrarch he will precede his lover in death. While not as pessimistic as Petrarch, he is at least philosophical. Montale's poem argues that some residue of ourselves may be retained in our favourite possessions or in things that were closely associated with us. Objects of dress, furniture, earrings – these are some of the details that years later are still charged with the memory of the beloved. Again they are encrusted on us (*s'incrosta su di noi*). A new item emerges that we have not seen before, lodged in the poet's memory all this time. It is the *piccolo scaffale,* the little bookcase that "travelled with Clizia" (*viaggiava con Clizia*). It is this little bookcase that housed Clizia's collection of metaphysical poets of "questionable reputation" and reference books on the saints. It was perhaps shipped back and forth to Italy as she did her research. This bookcase now is no longer merely filled with admirable if pedantic books but is a wonderful thing in the memory of the poet, something that he hopes will stay afloat on the crest of the waves after the coming flood (*il diluvio*) of destruction has submerged absolutely everything else.

Montale hopes that Clizia or some bit of her can conquer oblivion if he cannot. Perhaps her little bookcase will continue to float on the waves after everything else has been engulfed by the flood. This thought is like a reverse Shakespearean sonnet. In Shakespeare the lover fears that the beloved's charms will be destroyed by time. By the turn of logic that often comes with the final Shakespearean couplet, we are told that the poet's pen will preserve the charms of the beloved because they have been distilled in words. Montale turns this upside down. Montale's "I" instead argues that he hopes the beloved will survive in some way, but existence is meaningless for him because he is certainly heading for oblivion. The "I" is not even sure that his voice exists, but he is at least grateful that *una E maiuscola* (a capital E) exists so that he can at least express it. Time and "the voice" will soon dissolve, but not the hope that something of Clizia will survive.

Then Clizia's sunglasses, one more lovely metonymic detail, are, in Montalean terms, reconstituted from the ether of memory. Here Clizia puts aside her sunglasses (*occhiali affumicati*) with Donne's poetry close at hand. He specifically mentions, again, Donne's poem about "the fleas" (*le pulci*). This recollection remains as an instant of happiness, of simple pleasure, remembered for a lifetime, obviously. Recalling it with great pleasure and intensity forty years later, Montale seems to feel that the blissful moment so long ago is sustenance enough as he prepares for the *gran tuffo,* the fatal "big plunge" (*al gran tuffo*).

Montale questions the meaning of pleasure, just as Stevens questions the notion of pleasure in "Note toward a Supreme Fiction." If happiness existed for a moment, can its existence in that moment ever be completely lost? Are a few hours of happiness any less important than many years of happiness? What if the former is truly sublime and the latter only mild and mediocre? At the close of the poem Montale asks his long-gone lover the following question: "We were happy for one day, an hour, an instant / and can this be obliterated?" (*Fummo felici un giorno, un'ora un attimo / e questo potrà essere distrutto?*)[40]

We know that Montale reviewed Wallace Stevens's poems in the 1950s, and it is a fair guess to surmise that he read him in the 1960s and 1970s as Stevens's international reputation increased. Stevens, in his great passage from "It Must Give Pleasure," the third and last section of "Notes toward a Supreme Fiction," voices a similar observation. If "there is an hour / Filled with expressible bliss," writes the American poet, then "There is a month, a year, there is a time / In which majesty is a mirror of the self."[41] A moment of pleasure is just as real as is an hour of it. A day is just as real as is a year, and so forth. Montale goes the other way around, from the large to the small. The lovers were happy for "a day, an hour, an instant," but the occurrence is undeniable. The poet ends by describing some (unnamed philosophers, perhaps) who claim that everything starts up again (*tutto ricominicia / eguale*), just as if it is a copy (*come copia*) of what has gone before. He does not believe it, however. His instant of happiness, remembered for his whole life, was unique and it is that uniqueness which is a comfort.

The precision of time and place in these late poems is remarkable. While "Credo" ("I Believe") was written in 1978, its epigraph gives the date as "1944," as if the speaker were writing to the reader, to the unnamed "you," during the last months of the war. Once again, poetic time is not the time of the actual authorship of the poem. The context makes it another Clizia poem. In 1944 Eugenio must have been thinking of Irma, and he may have known that she was newly employed at Bard College. Now, in 1978 and in the last few years of his life, he knows full well what happened. In 1944 he would have written with renewed hope because Mussolini had been removed from power and pushed out of Rome in 1943. But this was also the worst period of all, the time of arrests, deportations, and massacres under the Nazi reoccupation of northern Italy. Very few letters from Florence could have reached the United States until after the Nazi withdrawal, and order had been slowly restored. This poem certainly falls within the many poems in the epistolary genre sent or intended for Clizia, but the "letter" is thirty-four years late:

1944

Perhaps through some mistake in the law
of retribution
it was possible for a sneeze at Via Varchi 6, Florence,
to be able to eventually arrive at Bard College, NJ.
Was it love? Not what, following a horrendous shock,
has populated the sky with stars and planets.
No such force of god with a beard and hair,
who had been dethroned by the social set at the Rotary Club,
but who is worthy of surviving their intrigues.
I believe true the miracle that between life and death
there exists a third status that sets us among its own.
May a god (but with a beard) protect you,
my divine one. And the rest, the fibs
in which we are bottled up, are less
than nothing.[42]

Montale knew that Irma Brandeis had begun teaching at Bard College in 1944, and he placed that date at the top of the poem to clearly emphasize the year of its setting. He playfully puts the college in New Jersey, when it actually is located in a picturesque setting on the east bank of the Hudson River in New York State, some one hundred miles north of New York City. Via Benedetto Varchi 6 can be found on a small Florentine street in a residential neighbourhood. Montale had moved there with Drusilla Tanzi in 1939, and it was his principal address through the war years. Perhaps following Donne's conceit about the flea, Montale is describing germs carried in his sneeze, unleashed as he prepares to seal up an envelope containing the letter to Irma in the United States.

Most of the poem is a jocular commentary on organized religion. The poet wonders whether God has a beard and hair. This seems a comical proposition to the speaker of the poem, but the notion of God with a beard and hair is much less ridiculous than the actual intrigues of human beings who babble about "God," depicted here as Rotary Club members. He had first described Irma as his "Goddess" in a love letter written in November 1935. Clizia, who had been Montale's goddess in the personal religion that he developed in his earlier poetry, is once again referred to as *la mia divina* (my divine one) in this poem from 1978. This is a reference to Clizia's earlier role in Montale's imagination, but it is now playful and tender, a return to the charming irreverence of the letters from the 1930s. He hopes that the anthropomorphic god will protect her after all. He also called to Irma as his "goddess, his divinity," in the last message he wrote to her before he died, a message written a short time after he had written "I Believe."

Last Rememberings: 1938 in 1978

While the Annalena poems give us a last glimpse of the poet and Clizia in Florence, there are a few late poems that offer another look at the lovers in the Italian countryside. Some are about the Palio, and one is about a brief visit to the Etruscan ruins at Luni, near the Ligurian coast. "Nel '38" ("In '38," 1978) is another Palio poem, written many years after the great Palio poem in *The Occasions.* Its title indicates that this Palio, which is featured as the central image of the 1978 poem, took place in 1938, although Irma may have gone to Siena and its Palio a number of times in the 1930s. The Palio of 1938, on either 2 July or 15 August, clearly took place after Hitler's May visit. This poem concerns what transpired after the Palio, during the *Dopopalio,* when Clizia and some friends stopped to take the typical photographs (*le foto d'uso*) that people often make as a record of such an outing. The speaker in the poem claims he stills has one, but it has turned a sullied yellow (*giallo sudicia*) over the many years and has broken up almost in pieces (*quasi in pezzi*). But he sees something wonderful in the picture. It is Clizia's incredible face (*il tuo volto incredibile*). After saying this, he writes one word, in a line all by itself: "marvellous" (*meraviglioso*). In the next line, he gives the year in which the photograph was taken, which also contains the title of the poem: "it was in '38" (Si era nel '38). "Si era nel '38" (It was in '38) is repeated twice, emphasizing the importance of the date in Montale's mind. The photograph of Irma's "incredible" and "marvellous" face is also a "marvellous" door that opens up the past. It is like the one that Montale described years before in the eighteenth Motet. Or, since the poet does not specify, perhaps it is the same photograph. The unnamed "they" stands for the group of friends and mutual acquaintances who kept the two in touch, at least through indirectly delivered news, and who possibly referred to her shift politically "to the left," which is mentioned towards the end of the short poem (though nothing particularly remarkable about Irma's political views has emerged in my interviews or other research). The poet closes by saying that he is not worried about her views, one way or the other, because "Being / doesn't have opinions, or not many" (*l'Essere / no ha opinioni o ne ha molte*).[43]

One of the surviving photographs taken during Irma and Eugenio's last trip to the Palio is included in Franco Contorbia's *Montale: Immagini di una vita*, a remarkable book of photographs, poems, and excerpts from Montale's writings, covering every aspect of the poet's life and also featuring an introduction by his close friend Gianfranco Contini.[44] It may well have been on the same roll of film as the photograph that inspired the eighteenth Motet, written some forty years earlier. Also, Montale repeatedly discusses his efforts to develop the snap-shots from this roll of film in his letters of 1938.[45] The photograph reproduced in Contorbia's book, surely one of these images mentioned in the 1938 letters, perhaps inspired "Quartetto" ("Quartet," 1979), yet a third Palio poem. The figures in the snap-shot are, from left to right, Paolo Vivante, Elena de Bosis Vivante, Irma Brandeis, Leone Vivante, Camillo Sbarbaro, and Montale.[46] These are the people who also populate "Quartet":

In a yellowed photograph
from forty years back
dug out from the bottom of a drawer,
your face severe in its sweetness
and your servant next to you; just behind is Sbarbaro,
bryologist and poet – and Elena Vivante,
grande dame of us all: gathered here to see
four nags whipped until they bled
in a shell-shaped piazza
in front of a crazed mob.
And the date? Forty years ago, I said, perhaps zero.
I don't believe in time, in the big bang, in anything
that measures the events in a before and in an after.
I imagine that to someone and something belong
the attribute of being. On that day it was you.
But how much, and how? And here re-sprouts
the execrable notion of time.[47]

Elena Vivante was the charismatic daughter of the poet Adolfo de Bosis. Her husband was the Jewish-Italian philosopher Leone Vivante, an enthusiast of English poetry. Elena's American mother had been thrown in jail by Mussolini in the early 1930s. Her brother, Lauro de Bosis, was a poet and one of the well-known early anti-Fascists. Lauro, who had written a long poem about Icarus, made a dramatic solo flight over Rome in 1931 during which he dropped anti-Fascist leaflets. He then flew out over the Mediterranean Sea and disappeared, probably because he ran out of fuel.[48] Elena and Leone Vivante lived in the hills in the Villa Solaia, at Malafrasca, a small town just outside Siena. Sbarbaro was the respected senior poet and Montale's old friend who was treated in "Café at Rapallo," the much earlier poem from *Cuttlefish Bones.*[49] Here Montale refers to Sbarbaro's expertise in bryology, the study of mosses, which is somehow quite fitting for a Crepuscularist poet. All of the figures in the photograph were part of the closely knit circle of remaining liberal intellectuals in Tuscany before the Second World War. Brandeis wrote a description of Elena, Leone, Paolo, Sbarbaro, and other Italian friends from this period of 16–18 August 1938 in her journal: "Sbarbaro coming to meet us at the café in Siena, with his frightened bird look; and telling me 'you are a mystery for everyone – they are wondering who you are – M[ontale] said simply he was bringing "a person."' Lello [Leone Vivante] came to get us, hidden behind driving goggles, silently piling us and our things in the sweet automobile. There was an instant warmth of friendliness – as tho all this were simple and expected. There was a cold wonderful mist as we drove out of Siena and through that miraculous invisible landscape."[50]

In "Quartet" Montale uses much simpler language to recreate the energy of the Palio than he did in the earlier and greater poem from the late 1930s. The contrast is useful in getting a good sense of his new style. It is also helpful to get one last account from him of the horses racing around the famous shell-shaped piazza of Siena (here described as *una piazza-conchiglia,* literally "a piazza-shell"). He once again recalls the poor quality of the horses in the race (they were "nags" in "Palio"), here whipped until they bled, and the crazed mob (*una folla inferocita*), ominously dangerous for reasons that went beyond the horse-race, and which Montale associated with the threatening hordes, the tregenda of Nazi-Fascists. As in many of these late poems, the poet seems to be questioning the working of time. Defying reason, he now says succinctly that he refuses to believe in it. But if someone deserves to have existed, to have claimed a phenomenological space in the flow of time-space, it would be his beloved Clizia, and no other. On that day in 1938 she existed. He cannot forget her. Nothing else is sure.

Two other short poems, "Luni e altro" ("Luni and Other Things," 1979?) and "Ho tanta fede in te" ("I Have Such Faith in You," 1979?), give us a last look at the poet and his Clizia in the Italian countryside near Florence.[51] While "Luni and Other Things" was probably written in 1979, the epigraph places it in 1938. The narrator here speaks directly to Clizia (clearly a code word again for the humble Irma and not the goddess) and refers to the couple as an unnamed "we." The poem once again recalls precursors in literature worthy of this literary couple: Orpheus and Eurydice, Petrarch and Laura, Dante and Beatrice, Shakespeare and his young man, John Donne and Ann More. The date in the epigraph makes it clear that the poem is set, like so many others, in that last moment of tenderness before the storm. The poet is remembering vivid details from the distant past. Montale imagines that the two are together again, driving through the Italian countryside in a coastal area he knows well. They are driving alone and pause by the ruins of Luni: "We stopped the car / in the shade of several ruins" (*Arrestammo la macchinia / all ombra di alcune rovine*).[52] The poet imagines "*la jeunesse dorée*" who must have disembarked at Luni centuries ago. He and Irma, more modest than the great visitors of the past, must be content with less, paupers by comparison, though they are also visitors. The listener to the poem, obviously Irma, responds by saying, "too much of this reflection," admonishing the poet to get back in the car and drive on. She has had enough of "illustrious cadavers" (*cadaveri illustri*). The poet agrees, and they leave, moreover, "without any nostalgia" (*senza nessuna nostalgia*) for the glamorous past.

Luni is located just south of La Spezia, near the Magra River (see "The Return"). It is where Liguria ends and Versilia begins. There are ruins of an amphitheatre, at least one temple, and a circus there. Populated long before the arrival of the Romans, Luni was once a thriving Etruscan city in eastern Liguria with a port on the Gulf of Spezia. Dante mentions the region, and the entire area was understood by Montale to be part of ancient Lunigiana.[53] We can imagine Irma and Eugenio driving there after the Palio and on the way back to Florence in 1938, possibly alone together for the last time. Since Luni is very near the Cinque Terre region of Montale's boyhood, so crucial to every word of *Cuttlefish Bones,* it would be easy to envisage a last tour of the coastal area before Irma's return to the United States. Brandeis also mentions the Bocca di Magra in her journal. Galassi reminds us that Petrarch used the ruins of Luni to point out the transitory nature of human achievements and that Dante refers to it in a similar way in the *Paradiso*.[54] This could be a key to understanding the poem. In terms of the external world, this special moment of togetherness in 1938 was as transitory as Luni. But it survives internally, in the poet's mind. It is an especially remembered moment among their few moments together, but one that took place on a site pregnant with the rich residue of a vast cultural history.

This is yet another instance when the poet seems to accurately recall an actual conversation from forty years earlier. The crisp dialogue seems too plausible to be invented, as if it had echoed intact in Montale's inner ear for years (though this is impossible to prove). The female speaker in the poem is Clizia/Irma, talking frankly, with a sharp and no-nonsense wit that deflates the balloon of the poet's abstract and philosophical reflections. He is pondering the vast history of the Luni ruins, and Clizia cuts him off, just as in "Predictions" when she tells him that she is tired of his analogies connecting his poetry and bullets fired from a gun. The poetic "I" engages in cultural chatter, imagining, for example, the *jeunesse dorée* (gilded youth) of antiquity disembarking at the ancient port city, and he continues to ramble. Clizia has had enough and wants to move on. Nevertheless, the Etruscan ruin set in the background against the personal rupture to come makes for an ominous and beautiful effect. Was their love a beautiful ruin, too? Was European civilization to be a ruin? The juxtaposition is compelling. However, Montale does not offer a definitive answer.

Both "I Have Such Faith in You" and "Luni and Other Things" were written shortly before Montale's death in 1981. "I Have Such Faith in You" is dedicated specifically to "C," as are, in one way or another, whether openly acknowledged or not, so many of Montale's poems.

In November 1933 Montale had used the word *fede* (faith) to describe his feelings for Irma. The phrase *ho fede in te* (I have faith in you) appears in a letter written in early December of that year.[55] The phrase resurfaces one more time, forty-six years later, in this poem written in 1979. It begins with the poet asserting that his love for her will last until a lightning bolt destroys the planet on which human beings live, which implies, certainly, a vast expanse of time extending into the future: "I have so much faith in you / that it will endure" (*Ho tanta fede in te / che durerà*). He admits that this is very much the "nonsense" (*sciocchezza)* that he once told her, and he imagines that then, at what for the earth will be the end of time and maybe even space, he and she will sit down together to discuss, one last time, a few controversial verses of the divine poem (*del divino poema*).[56] It would be logical to guess that the "divine poem" to which Montale refers is Dante's *Commedia*, a lifelong passion of both the poet and "C." It is also probable that the controversial verses mentioned here are the same ones that were discussed in the Annalena in the 1930s, along with the metaphysical poets, the writings of the saints, and the philosophical works of Eckhart. The poet describes the world as an "immense dump" (*immenso cascame*) here, but he would at least like to *imagine* an afterlife where his conversations with his beloved listener can continue. His faith in "C" also grants him faith in himself: "I have so much faith in me" (*Ho tanta fede in me*), he insists. It is she who has, without meaning to do so, rekindled this faith in himself. This reigniting of faith occurs without explanation, capable of bursting forth out of "every wreckage / of life" (*ogni rottame / della vita*), though we may be trapped, and even ignorant of knowing that we are trapped or giving meaning to it. Finally, the poet proclaims, in the last lines, "I have so much faith that it sets me on fire" (*ho tanta fede che mi brucia*). He is certain that whoever may see will know that he is "a man of ashes" (*un uomo di cenere*). No one will notice that this was a miraculous "rebirth" (*rinascita*).[57]

"Faith" (*fede*) – with the poet describing himself as Clizia's "faithful follower" (*il suo fedele*), and the notion of the "faithful" (*i fedeli*) – was an important concept in "Your Flight" and "The Shadow of the Magnolia" in the 1940s and in "Little Testament" of the mid-1950s. Montale also writes of Clizia's unchanging *fedeltà* (fidelity) in " Bellosguardo Times," one of the early Clizia poems in *The Occasions*. The notion returns at the end of his life. Montale's faith, rekindled by Clizia, led to a last personal *rinascita* (renaissance), a most Italian concept.

Taken together, the late Clizia poems make it obvious that Irma Brandeis remained prominently in the poet's mind until the end. Rarely seen footage, filmed for Italian television, of the ailing poet, old and feeble, reading these last poems to Clizia, documents the authenticity of the feeling behind them.[58] The intensity of experience is measured in the carefully rendered details, the exact recollections of the pensione's veranda, the chair, the garden, the bookcase, the sunglasses, the specific poetry, and the poets read and discussed. All of the distinctly recollected details are remembered fragments of events that took place more than four decades before the time these last poems were written. Most significant, they are different from the earlier poems, where the remembered Irma is less important and the constructed Clizia is more important. They are closer to the kind of autobiographical reconstruction that, as interdisciplinary research connecting neuroscience and the humanities has revealed, involves the combinatory effects of emotional, semantic, and episodic memory to form an explicit recollection of the past.[59] The poet's last letters to the scholar Rosanna Bettarini (and the drafts of his poems that he gave her, in which he refers to Irma directly as Clizia and his "sunflower") make this mysterious final metamorphosis even clearer.[60]

Montale's sharp memory and warm tone in these final poems of the Clizia Cycle show how a person can resume an internal conversation many years later with someone who has left a lasting mark, someone who was loved intensely at an earlier point in life. The more intense the love, the more possible it is that the lover still lives inside the mind and that the final parting seems as though it happened just yesterday. Even though the conversation with the beloved was interrupted some thirty or forty years ago, that conversation begins again as if nothing has happened, as if no vast expanse of time has passed. Mad people often speak to characters who are not there. Poets and artists are only a little less than mad, in this sense, because their imaginations are so alive and skilful in reconstructing the past. And who can say that people who talk to their lost loves as if they were still present are truly mad? If the idea of the person and the conception of the lost love endure in the mind or in a poem after the loss, does the idea of the beloved not have a life of its own, a life that continues in spite of the flood of time that sweeps us all away?

Montale's poetry answers that question.

Coda: Montale, Brandeis, the "I," and the "You"

The eternal dispute between the public and the private, between curiosity and delicacy ... the greatest of all literary quarrels.

– Henry James

The squirming facts exceed the squamous mind.

– Wallace Stevens

The true paradises are the paradises that we have lost.

– Marcel Proust

In the end, which is more important – the context that gives rise to the work or the work as a discrete set of structures and symbols? The cry of the occasion, or the poem itself? Caught in the love triangle of the 1930s, Montale remained with Drusilla Tanzi Marangoni. He married her many years later, in 1962, and they remained married for only a few months near the end of her life. In the meantime he had found other amorous interests in his life, some of whom also became symbolic characters in his poems. The idealistic, somewhat Manichaean, symbolic world that Montale created in his poems is far different from the life that he actually lived. The actual women in his life were not exact equivalents to his brilliantly constructed constellations of symbolic images (arranged in *chiavi*). Yet life does fertilize art, and Montale, the self-proclaimed "witness," worked with what he could observe. It is naive to think otherwise. As examples, Montale's Clizia and Mary McCarthy's Domna have qualities that are reminiscent of the actual Irma Brandeis, and an abundance of critical and historical information enables us to see striking similarities between the procession of Mussolini and Hitler through Florence, or the Fascist Palio of 1938, and the dazzling poems that Montale creates about these events. So when more can be known, I believe we should know it.

In spite of several glamorous affairs in the 1920s and 1930s, Irma Brandeis never married. By all accounts, she was an ascetic professor in her later years, living at Bard College in a very small house that she called "Casa Minima," which is still on the campus to this day. She was a dedicated teacher and colleague. Instead of a family, Irma enjoyed a close circle of colleagues and friends, many of them former students. Perhaps because she never married, she was easily hurt if she did not hear from one of her close friends for a period of time. Her correspondence with Renée and Ted Weiss indicates how seriously she took her friendships and how easily she could feel abandoned by them. In 1979 she was still unsure about what to do with her many love letters from Eugenio Montale. In August of that year she decided to write to the Gabinetto Vieusseux about her literary treasure and her personal relation to it:

> I have every note and letter that E.M. wrote me – between 1933 when we met, and 1939, when the war made it as impossible as it was already useless to speak of ourselves further. Nothing more. We never saw one another again. In 1950 he wrote to offer me copies of what he had published during the war years: I could not respond as he asked (with an unsigned postcard saying "yes" and addressed to his office), so those books never came to me.
>
> I have thought I should continue to keep all these letters, and they are very many; and have thought I should destroy them all. Tonight (in August of 1979) trying to imagine another pair of eyes reading them, it seems to me I must in decency destroy some – perhaps a great many. The story is, after all, brief; and what we have both withheld of it has lost its importance except to me.
>
> In 1931 Leo Ferrero read me some of the poems in the *Ossi di Seppia.* I cannot say here what they meant to me then. But in 1933 I went to the Vieusseux Library and asked to see E.M. There was a disastrously stupid meeting which should have ended our acquaintance. I do not remember how we overpassed that. We saw each other every day, and wrote to each other every week when I came back to the US in September, to my teaching job. In 1934 I returned to Florence and learned for the first time of Mosca's existence. From the moment she learned of mine, and that we

> wanted to marry, she was implacable. She promised to kill herself. Her love for him saw no reason not to torture him – and so she did. She wrote me a vile letter which I hope to attach to these others. She forced him to write me a parting letter – and he did so, warning me of it beforehand and asking me to disregard it, to understand it as necessary to prevent her death. She exacted a promise that he would not see me again, and in 1938 he would have kept that promise had a mutual friend not interceded. When I came home at the end of that summer, I knew we would not see one another again as well as I knew that there would be war.[1]

Several years later Irma finally travelled back to Florence, placing her letters under seal at the Gabinetto Vieusseux for two decades.

The more that is known about Montale and Brandeis, the greater is the enigma of the poetry. Although there is a massive amount of material in print on Montale's poems, the great Italian biography has yet to be written. While the articulate but slender biographies of Testa and Nascimbeni are filled with valuable information, and much (but not all) correspondence has been made available, we still do not have a portrayal in print that offers a fully developed picture of Montale. Brandeis's life and work, too, both merit further study and critical evaluation. She was, after all, a poet, translator, fiction writer, and critic who had formative influences on some of the great poets of the twentieth century. In addition to Montale, she knew James Merrill, Robert Lowell, and Anthony Hecht (who also was her student). She is rumoured to have played a key role in influencing Merrill to become a poet. Certain aspects of the relationship between Montale and Brandeis remain puzzling.

In the interaction of poetry and its interpretation, and its attendant interrelationship with biography and history, which is more important? Does meaning come chiefly from the work itself? Does the poetry transcend the occurrence of their actual lives, as Irma and Eugenio almost certainly thought? Or does the historical circumstance, especially in this case, make the poems more important than the specificity of the immediate relationship between the two? What is gained by setting the great Clizia Cycle against the biographical and historical circumstances that generated it? For me, it is important to gauge this unique body of work against the background of history and biography. Interpretation, never complete or final, is always a negotiation with authorial intent, and consequently there is no reason to avoid new information that might change us. Following my meeting with Montale's friend, poet and translator Rina Sara Virgillito, I began my search into Montale's relationship with his long-lost American muse. Using dashes of "microbiography" (newly revealed letters, memoir, and other materials), and even journalistic inquiry (interviews with Montale's friends, Brandeis's caretaker, and Montale's first American publishers), I began to sense my subject, finding my way into the works of the poet from an American vantage point very much like that of Brandeis. I have traced the symbolic trajectory of the Clizia poems across the long span of Montale's work, a trajectory that emerges here for perhaps the first time in its complete unfolding. History and biography help us to see that trajectory with greater clarity, but the poems themselves remain the most important feature. Montale's creation of a myth stemming so directly from the experience of his personal life may have been part of the impulse to write a new kind of "autobiografiction," a tendency that was common among many of the early Modernists.[2] Nevertheless, the poems are a symbolic construction that projects something larger and more lasting than the details of the private life as it actually was lived. Clizia is, after all, a sublime literary creation, stretching across almost all of Montale's poetic expression. Irma is something else again – an actual person whose life in America took her far away from Montale. In the end, the reader must decide whether the poetry commands attention, and to make that decision, the reader must finally turn back to the works themselves.

Poetry was always connected to Montale's fascination with women and their fascination with him, right up until the end of his life. A *Posthumous Diary* appeared in 1991, written to flatter Annalisa Cima.[3] Over a period of ten years beginning in 1969, Montale (then in his seventies) would present the young Annalisa (in her late twenties) with a short poem every time he saw her. By 1979 he had eighty-four poems, which he divided up into little packets. The understanding was that these short poems would be slowly released to the public, to be published after his death. If we compare the very moving High Modernist poems to Irma to the playful high jinks of the poems for Annalisa, it is easy to wonder which was truly characteristic of the real Montale. Was poetry for him always a means of seduction? At one point he even told Maria Luisa Spaziani, who appears in the Montale oeuvre as "the Vixen," that one of the Clizia stories ("Clizia at Foggia") was 99 per cent about her[4] (perhaps, for him at that moment, it was). A contemporary feminist reading of Montale might detect a trace of misogyny in his female symbols, fashioned into something other than the human (vixen, fly, lynx, or sunflower goddess). Even Clizia, a jealous Ovidian nymphet, had negative connotations – a slightly cruel symbol for a woman who lost out to a jealous rival. Regardless of how he treated the women in his life, Montale will not attract his reader because he conducted his life in an immaculate manner, and he was not obliged to leave a neatly organized set of signposts for his lovers or critics.

One important Montale scholar, Dante Isella, has questioned the authenticity of the posthumous poems. Nevertheless, other commentators have judged them to be authentic. Some, including Paolo De Caro, have even detected signs of Clizia in them.[5] The poems include a number of familiar Clizia Cycle symbols, such as Mount Amiata, the testament (*testamento*) of the witness or vigil keeper, the bottle (*bottiglia*) in the ocean, the woman as angel-messenger, the rainbow (now *arcobaleno,* not *iride*), the storm (*forti temporali, bufera*), flight (*volo*), seashores (*prode*), and the groove or track (*sentiero*). While they seem devoid of their originally charged Clizian context, they are simply too numerous to be mere coincidence. Once again the anti-hero appears, no longer simply a witness but now an old man, too cowardly to turn down the Nobel Prize, as he had proclaimed earlier to his female listener (newly modelled on Cima) that he would do. Aside from the possible presence of Clizia in the symbology of the poetry, she is present at least indirectly. Luciano Rebay, the most widely known of the Clizia hunters among the Montale critics, is a character in two of the poems, which are short fantasies about New York City, his academic home. In one poem he is referred to as "Re-bay," king of the bay, a playful reference to the New York City harbour. Marco Forti and Angelo Marchese, two of the Italian critics who wrote books uncovering the myth of Clizia, appear in the *Posthumous Diary* as well.[6]

Then there is the mysterious case of Montale's last letter to Irma. In his memoir, *A Different Person,* James Merrill recounts how Irma Brandeis brought up the topic of Montale in the early 1980s when he visited her at her house near the Bard campus. "I heard from Montale, did I tell you? Oh, sometime last winter. Here let me show you."[7] She brought out a sheet of stationery with a short message from Montale, his characteristically cramped handwriting scrawled in the middle of the page, and showed it to Merrill. The letter is the last of so many sent and so many written but never sent, all of which echo and overlap with a grand trajectory of poems that span almost fifty years. It was found, forgotten, lodged in a book in Brandeis's home after her death. The original is now in the Gabinetto Vieusseux, where Irma deposited her correspondence in 1983, to be kept under seal for twenty years. First published by Luciano Rebay, it has now been published again, as the last of the 156 extant letters from Montale to Brandeis. It is written half in English, half in Italian:

> Irma,
> You are still my Goddes [*sic*],
> my divinity. I prie [pray] for you,
> for me. Forgive me, please.
> *Quando, come ci rivedremo?*
> *Ti abbraccia il tuo*
>
> [When, how will we see each other again?
> I embrace you, your]
> Montale[8]

Irma wrote the date in the lower right-hand margin: "about June 15, '81."[9]

She still had hopes of seeing Montale again. "I'm flying to Milan at the end of the month. I had thought in spite of everything to see him. But now I hear from G. … that there's talk of his marrying his housekeeper. Under those circumstances a meeting is out of the question."[10] While it is understandable that an eighty-year-old man might be tempted to marry a caretaker (Eliot married his secretary), Irma's passions were still strong on the subject of Montale. But it was too late to see him anyway, for he had only a short time left. On 12 September 1981, almost exactly three months after she had written on the letter, Montale died. He was buried on 14 September, next to Drusilla at San Felice a Ema Cemetery, just south of the city of Florence.

Irma Brandeis died on 29 January 1990. She was buried in the Bard College cemetery; near her are her closest friends, colleagues, and students. Next to her grave are the graves of Elizabeth Stambler and Bill Wilson, her colleagues in the Department of Literature and Languages. Bill Wilson's wife, Anyss, a former student, is also nearby. Hannah Arendt and her husband, Heinrich Blücher, colleagues at both Bard and the New School, are buried just a few feet away. After Brandeis's death her friends, among them the poet James Merrill, endowed the Irma Brandeis Chair in Romance Languages in her memory.

We should remember that Montale once wrote a poem about his critics in which he maintained that all of his intimate *tus* (*yous*) are one and that he had purposely misled his critics, trapping them in a net. Rather than becoming caught up in that net, it might be better to understand that the energy of love is behind all of the poems. Love is not proper. Love does not stay within artificial boundaries. Life is always messier than the exquisite pattern that can be found in art. Eros is one of the unpredictable aspects of our being. The great Dante Alighieri wrote all of the *Comedy* to a woman who was not his wife, and his daughter, so overwhelmed by her father's obsession, felt compelled to change her name to Beatrice, the name of this beloved woman, and eventually entered a nunnery. His life was not as ordered as his tautly structured masterpiece.

Shortly before Montale's death, Irma Brandeis wrote an entry in her journal that makes it perfectly clear that she understood the literary possibilities suggested by her adventure with her Italian poet: "What a novel there would be in the E.M. story in the style of H. James!! The woman who falls responsively in love with a young poet, learns after 2 years that there is a life-or-death obligation to another woman, bitterly accepts the separation yet feeling his anguish more than her own, makes another (truncated) life for herself and keeps perfect silence about her role in his life even when his growing fame and her presence in his poems brings inquiries and guesses. Many years later the 'other' dies. They are old now, but she is sure that he will speak to her, want her friendship, express a concern for her life."[11]

The raw material for a sentimental film version of the Clizia story is obvious. The first setting would be the breathtakingly scenic and mysterious Cinque Terre on the Italian Riviera. Then the scene would move to pre-war Florence, with Brunelleschi's Duomo in the background. The unsurpassable visual beauty of Italy is at times overshadowed by ominous hints of the true implications of Fascism. Later come trysts in the hills outside Florence, by the sea at Bocca di Magra, in the countryside near Naples, and elsewhere. Then the Fascists come out in greater force. The marching hordes, the ringing bells of the towers of Florence and Siena, the diabolic entrance of Hitler on parade in Florence, the spectacle of the Palio (with the sinister undertones of the summer of 1938) – all these appear in the poems, as read by a narrator with an Italian accent, and recreated impressively for the camera. This serves as the background for a beautiful love affair between an American woman and a handsome Italian poet. The Italian, of course, is in love with the beautiful American, who happens be Jewish. He defies the anti-Semitism of the 1930s and the racial laws, at great risk to himself. After the Fascists fall, the camera eye could cut to a scene featuring a rush to an amorous embrace in America or, still better, on the Bellosguardo hill in Florence. A post-war reunion in Italy follows, with throbbing music in the background. Or perhaps there could be a sentimental reunion that takes place many years later, just like the one Irma herself imagined.

None of this happened. Instead, Montale's infatuation with Irma became an idea that burned in his mind in spite of the twists and turns of life. Instead, the real drama was internal. After a time, that idea had a life and purpose of its own. In the meantime he chose to stay with Drusilla, finally marrying her in 1962, near the end of her life.

In the case of Montale, what was love in 1938 was sublimated into something else as the years passed. The great theorist of sublimation is still Sigmund Freud, who wrote one of his most penetrating works during the same Nazi-Fascist era that provoked some of Montale's best writing. *Das Unbehagen in der Kultur,* the famous title known in English as *Civilization and Its Discontents,* was published in 1930, five years after *Cuttlefish Bones.*[12] In *Das Unbehagen in der Kultur,* Eros, for all its unpredictability, is superior to Thanatos, the death instinct. Freud made these the twin poles of human nature. Eros is a defying light, a light in the night, illuminating our hope as a species. Another, perhaps better, translation of the title might be "The Uneasiness in Culture" because the word *Unbehagen* conveys a sense of psychological anxiety not captured in "discontents" and because translating *Kultur* as "culture" captures the conflicting processes of social life rather more efficiently than does the relatively static term "civilization." Freud's great pessimistic essay concludes with one hope for humanity, based in the life force of Eros. (The life force, eroticism, and the love of children are all bound up together, in Freud's view, and it is his hope that they may cause the human race to overcome its destructive instincts.) Around the same time that Montale was about to celebrate Clizia in his verse, Freud was arguing that the love of children is an outgrowth of Eros, and there is the hope that in the end it will have to triumph over our urge to murder one another (and the urge for self-destruction) if the human race is to survive. Montale and Freud made Eros the focal point of hope for the human race at almost the same moment in human history.

So it is fitting that one of the greatest of the twentieth-century poets would find his subject through his initial experience of Eros and, through sublimation during his vigil of many years, find a way to turn his lover into a goddess and in the process discover a new and intense voice that enabled him to address some of the critical junctures in the troubled history of modern civilization. In the greatest poems of his Clizia Cycle – poems such as "News from Amiata," "Palio," and "Hitler Spring" – Montale's sense of humanity, following his initial passion for

Irma, compels him to confront the European civilization that he knew so well. He combines the heritage of his European Christian civilization with his love for Irma in a new and modern synthesis. It is the combination of his imaginative passion and his great talent for syncretism that enables him to redefine his culture in a modern myth, one of the most resounding myths of twentieth-century literature.

The message of his poems is larger than the cry of the occasions that prompted them.

The Original Italian Poems

Twenty of the original Italian poems discussed in detail in this book are shown below. While the full cycle of Clizia poems extends into many other Montale writings, these are the most important works of the Clizia Myth. The texts are taken from Eugenio Montale, *Tutte le poesie.*

Portami il girasole (Bring Me the Sunflower)

Portami il girasole ch'io lo trapianti
nel mio terreno bruciato dal salino,
e mostri tutto il giorno agli azzurri specchianti
del cielo l'ansietà del suo volto giallino.

Tendono alla chiarità le cose oscure
si esauriscono i corpi in un fluire
di tinte: queste in musiche. Svanire
è dunque la ventura delle venture.

Portami tu la pianta che conduce
dove sorgono bionde trasparenze
e vapora la vita quale essenza:
portami il girasole impazzito di luce. (34)

Mottetti (The Motets)

Lontano, ero con te quando tuo padre
entrò nell'ombra e ti lasciò il suo addio.
Che seppi fino allora? Il logorìo
di *prima* mi salvò solo per questo:

che t'ignoravo e non dovevo: ai colpi
d'oggi lo so, se di laggiù s'inflette
un'ora e mi riporta Cumerlotti
o Anghébeni – tra scoppi di spolette
e i lamenti e l'accorrer delle squadre. (142)

*

La speranza di pure rivederti
m'abbandonava;

e mi chiesi se questo che mi chiude
ogni senso di te, schermo d'immagini
ha i segni della morte o dal passato
è in esso ma distorto e fatto labile,
un *tuo* barbaglio.

(a Modena, tra i portici,
un servo gallonato trascinava
due sciacalli al guinzaglio). (144)

Nuove stanze (New Stanzas)

Poi che gli ultimi fili di tabacco
al tuo gesto si spengono nel piatto
di cristallo, al soffitto lenta sale
la spirale del fumo
che gli alfieri e i cavalli degli scacchi
guardano stupefatti: e nuovi anelli
la seguono, più mobili di quelli
delle tue dita.

La morgana che in cielo liberava
torri e ponti è sparita
al primo soffio; s'apre la finestra
non vista e il fumo s'agita. Là in fondo,
altro stormo si muove: una tregenda
d'uomini che non sa questo tuo incenso,
nella scacchiera di cui puoi tu sola
comporre il senso.

Il mio dubbio d'un tempo era se forse
tu stessa ignori il giuoco che si svolge
sul quadrato e ora è nembo alle tue porte:
follìa di morte non si placa a poco
prezzo, se poco è il lampo del tuo sguardo,
ma domanda altri fuochi, oltre le fitte
cortine che per te fomenta il dio
del caso, quando assiste.

Oggi so ciò che vuoi; batte il suo fioco
tocco la Martinella ed impaura
le sagome d'avorio in una luce
spettrale di nevaio. Ma resiste
e vince il premio della solitaria
veglia chi può con te allo specchio ustorio
che accieca le pedine opporre i tuoi
occhi d'acciaio. (184–5)

Palio (The Palio)

La tua fuga non s'è dunque perduta
in un giro di trottola
al margine della strada:
la corsa che dirada
le sue spire fin qui,
nella purpurea buca
dove un tumulto d'anime saluta
le insegne di Liocorno e di Tartuca.

Il lancio dei vessilli non ti muta
nel volto: troppa vampa ha consumati
gl'indizi che scorgesti; ultimi annunzi
quest'odore di ragia e di tempesta
imminente e quel tiepido stillare
delle nubi strappate,
tardo saluto in gloria di una sorte
che sfugge anche al destino. Dalla torre
cade un suono di bronzo: la sfilata
prosegue fra tamburi che ribattono
a gloria di contrade.

È strano: tu
che guardi la sommossa vastità,
i mattoni incupiti, la malcerta
mongolfiera di carta che si spicca
dai fantasmi animati sul quadrante
dell'immenso orologio, l'arpeggiante
volteggio degli sciami e lo stupore
che invade la conchiglia
del Campo, tu ritieni
tra le dita il sigillo imperioso
ch'io credevo smarrito
e la luce di prima si diffonde
sulle teste e le sbianca dei suoi gigli.

Torna un'eco di là: 'c'era una volta ...'
(rammenta la preghiera che dal buio
ti giunse una mattina)

'non un reame, ma l'esile
traccia di filigrana
che senza lasciarvi segno
i nostri passi sfioravano

Sotto la volta diaccia
grava ora un sonno di sasso,
la voce dalla cantina
nessuno ascolta, o sei te.

La sbarra in croce non scande
la luce per chi s'è smarrito
la morte non ha altra voce
di quella che spande la vita',

ma un'altra voce qui fuga l'orrore
del prigione e per lei quel ritornello
non vale il ghirigoro d'aste avvolte
(Oca e Giraffa) che s'incrociano alte
e ricadono in fiamme. Geme il palco
al passaggio dei brocchi salutati

da un urlo solo. È un volo! E tu dimentica!
Dimentica la morte
toto coelo raggiunta e l'ergotante
balbuzie dei dannati! C'era *il* giorno
dei viventi, lo vedi, e pare immobile
nell'acqua del rubino che si popola
di immagini. Il presente s'allontana
ed il traguardo è là: fuor della selva
dei gonfaloni, su lo scampanìo
del cielo irrefrenato, oltre lo sguardo
dell'uomo – e tu lo fissi. Così alzati,
finché spunti la trottola il suo perno
ma il solco resti inciso. Poi, nient'altro. (187–9)

Notizie dall'Amiata (News from Amiata)

Il fuoco d'artifizio del maltempo
sarà murmure d'arnie a tarda sera.
La stanza ha travature
tarlate ed un sentore di meloni
penetra dall'assito. Le fumate
morbide che risalgono una valle
d'elfi e di funghi fino al cono diafano
della cima m'intorbidano i vetri,
e ti scrivo di qui, da questo tavolo
remoto, dalla cellula di miele
di una sfera lanciata nello spazio –
e le gabbie coperte, il focolare
dove i marroni esplodono, le vene
di salnitro e di muffa sono il quadro
dove tra poco romperai. La vita
che t'affàbula è ancora troppo breve
se ti contiene! Schiude la tua icona
il fondo luminoso. Fuori piove.

*

E tu seguissi le fragili architetture
annerite dal tempo e dal carbone,

i cortili quadrati che hanno nel mezzo
il pozzo profondissimo; tu seguissi
il volo infagottato degli uccelli
notturni e in fondo al borro l'allucciolìo
della Galassia, la fascia d'ogni tormento.
Ma il passo che risuona a lungo nell'oscuro
è di chi va solitario e altro non vede
che questo cadere di archi, di ombre e di pieghe.
Le stelle hanno trapunti troppo sottili,
l'occhio del campanile è fermo sulle due ore,
i rampicanti anch'essi sono un'ascesa
di tenebre ed il loro profumo duole amaro.
Ritorna domani più freddo, vento del nord,
spezza le antiche mani dell'arenaria,
sconvolgi i libri d'ore nei solai,
e tutto sia lente tranquilla, dominio, prigione
del senso che non dispera! Ritorna più forte
vento di settentrione che rendi care
le catene e suggelli le spore del possibile!
Son troppo strette le strade, gli asini neri
che zoccolano in fila dànno scintille,
dal picco nascosto rispondono vampate di magnesio.
Oh il gocciolìo che scende a rilento
dalle casipole buie, il tempo fatto acqua,
il lungo colloquio coi poveri morti, la cenere, il vento,
il vento che tarda, la morte, la morte che vive!

*

Questa rissa cristiana che non ha
se non parole d'ombra e di lamento
che ti porta di me? Meno di quanto
t'ha rapito la gora che s'interra
dolce nella sua chiusa di cemento.
Una ruota di mola, un vecchio tronco,
confini ultimi al mondo. Si disfà
un cumulo di strame: e tardi usciti
a unire la mia veglia al tuo profondo
sonno che li riceve, i porcospini
s'abbeverano a un filo di pietà. (190–2)

La bufera (The Storm)

Les princes n'ont point d'yeux pour voir ces grandes merveilles, Leurs mains ne servent plus qu'à nous persécuter ...

– Agrippa d'Aubigné, *À Dieu*

La bufera che sgronda sulle foglie
dure della magnolia i lunghi tuoni
marzolini e la grandine,

(I suoni di cristallo nel tuo nido
notturno ti sorprendono, dell'oro
che s'è spento sui mogani, sul taglio
dei libri rilegati, brucia ancora
una grana di zucchero nel guscio
delle tue palpebre)

il lampo che candisce
alberi e muri e li sorprende in quella
eternità d'istante – marmo manna
e distruzione – ch'entro te scolpita
porti per tua condanna e che ti lega
più che l'amore a me, strana sorella, –

e poi lo schianto rude, i sistri, il fremere
dei tamburelli sulla fossa fuia,
lo scalpicciare del fandango, e sopra
qualche gesto che annaspa ...
Come quando
ti rivolgesti e con la mano, sgombra
la fronte dalla nube dei capelli,

mi salutasti – per entrar nel buio. (197)

Gli orecchini (The Earrings)

Non serba ombra di voli il nerofumo
della spera. (E del tuo non è più traccia)
È passata la spugna che i barlumi
indifesi dal cerchio d'oro scaccia.
Le tue pietre, i coralli, il forte imperio

che ti rapisce vi cercavo; fuggo
l'iddia che non s'incarna, i desiderî
porto fin che al tuo lampo non si struggono.
Ronzano èlitre fuori, ronza il folle
mortorio e sa che due vite non contano.
Nella cornice tornano le molli
meduse della sera. La tua impronta
verrà di giù: dove ai tuoi lobi squallide
mani, travolte, fermano i coralli. (202)

La frangia dei capelli (The Bangs)

La frangia dei capelli che ti vela
la fronte puerile, tu distrarla
con la mano non devi. Anch'essa parla
di te, sulla mia strada è tutto il cielo,
la sola luce con le giade ch'ài
accerchiate sul polso, nel tumulto
del sonno la cortina che gl'indulti
tuoi distendono, l'ala onde tu vai,
trasmigratrice Artemide ed illesa,
tra le guerre dei nati-morti; e s'ora
d'aeree lanugini s'infiora
quel fondo, a marezzarlo sei tu, scesa
d'un balzo, e irrequieta la tua fronte
si confonde con l'alba, la nasconde. (203)

Giorno e notte (Day and Night)

Anche una piuma che vola può disegnare
la tua figura, o il raggio che gioca a rimpiattino
tra i mobili, il rimando dello specchio
di un bambino, dai tetti. Sul giro delle mura
strascichi di vapore prolungano le guglie
dei pioppi e giù sul trespolo s'arruffa il pappagallo
dell'arrotino. Poi la notte afosa
sulla piazzola, e i passi, e sempre questa dura
fatica di affondare per risorgere eguali
da secoli, o da istanti, d'incubi che non possono
ritrovare la luce dei tuoi occhi nell'antro
incandescente – e ancora le stesse grida e i lunghi
pianti sulla veranda

se rimbomba improvviso il colpo che t'arrossa
la gola e schianta l'ali, o perigliosa
annunziatrice dell'alba,
e si destano i chiostri e gli ospedali
a un lacerìo di trombe ... (209)

Il tuo volo (Your Flight)

Se appari al fuoco (pendono
sul tuo ciuffo e ti stellano
gli amuleti)
due luci ti contendono
al borro ch'entra sotto
la volta degli spini.

La veste è in brani, i frùtici
calpesti rifavillano
e la gonfia peschiera dei girini
umani s'apre ai solchi della notte.

Oh non turbar l'immondo
vivagno, lascia intorno
le cataste brucianti, il fumo forte
sui superstiti!

Se rompi il fuoco (biondo
cinerei i capelli
sulla ruga che tenera
ha abbondonato il cielo)
come potrà la mano delle sete
e delle gemme ritrovar tra i morti
il suo fedele? (210)

Iride (Iris)

Quando di colpo San Martino smotta
le sue braci e le attizza in fondo al cupo
fornello dell' Ontario,
schiocchi di pigne verdi fra la cenere
o il fumo d'un infuso di papaveri
e il Volto insanguinato sul sudario

che mi divide da te;

questo e poco altro (se poco
è un tuo segno, un ammicco, nella lotta
che me sospinge in un ossario, spalle
al muro, dove zàffiri celesti
e palmizi e cicogne su una zampa non chiudono
l'atroce vista al povero
Nestoriano smarrito);

è quanto di te giunge dal naufragio
delle mie genti, delle tue, or che un fuoco
di gelo porta alla memoria il suolo
ch'è tuo e che non vedesti; e altro rosario
fra le dita non ho, non altra vampa
se non questa, di resina e di bacche,
t'ha investito.

*

Cuore d'altri non è simile al tuo,
la lince non somiglia al bel soriano
che apposta l'uccello mosca sull'alloro;
ma li credi tu eguali se t'avventuri
fuor dell'ombra del sicomoro
o è forse quella maschera sul drappo bianco,
quell'effigie di porpora che t'ha guidata?

Perché l'opera tua (che della Sua
è una forma) fiorisse in altre luci
Iri del Canaan ti dileguasti
in quel nimbo di vischi e pugnitopi
che il tuo cuore conduce
nella notte del mondo, oltre il miraggio
dei fiori del deserto, tuoi germani.

Se appari, qui mi riporti, sotto la pergola
di viti spoglie, accanto all'imbarcadero
del nostro fiume – e il burchio non torna indietro,
il sole di San Martino si stempera, nero.

Ma se ritorni non sei tu, è mutata
la tua storia terrena, non attendi
al traghetto la prua,
non hai sguardi, né ieri né domani;

perché l'opera Sua (che nella tua
si trasforma) *dev'esser continuata.* (247–8)

L'orto (The Orchard)

Io non so, messaggera
che scendi, prediletta
del mio Dio (del tuo forse), se nel chiuso
dei meli lazzeruoli ove si lagnano
i luì nidaci, estenuanti a sera,
io non so se nell'orto
dove le ghiande piovono e oltre il muro
si sfioccano, aerine, le ghirlande
dei carpini che accennano
lo spumoso confine dei marosi, una vela
tra corone di scogli
sommersi e nerocupi o più lucenti
della prima stella che trapela –

io non so se il tuo piede
attutito, il cieco incubo onde cresco
alla morte dal giorno che ti vidi,
io non so se il tuo passo che fa pulsar le vene
se s'avvicina in questo intrico,
è quello che mi colse un'altra estate
prima che una folata
radente contro il picco irto del Mesco
infrangesse il mio specchio, –
io non so se la mano che mi sfiora la spalla
è la stessa che un tempo
sulla celesta rispondeva a gemiti
d'altri nidi, da un fólto ormai bruciato.

L'ora della tortura e dei lamenti
che s'abbatté sul mondo,

l'ora che tu leggevi chiara come in un libro
figgendo il duro sguardo di cristallo
bene in fondo, là dove acri tendìne
di fuliggine alzandosi su lampi
di officine celavano alla vista
l'opera di Vulcano,
il dì dell'Ira che più volte il gallo
annunciò agli spergiuri
non ti divise, anima indivisa,
dal supplizio inumano, non ti fuse
nella caldana, cuore d'ametista

O labbri muti, aridi dal lungo
viaggio per il sentiero fatto d'aria
che vi sostenne, o membra che distinguo
a stento dalle mie, o diti che smorzano
la sete dei morenti e i vivi infocano,
o intento che hai creato fuor della tua misura
le sfere del quadrante e che ti espandi
in tempo d'uomo, in spazio d'uomo, in furie
di dèmoni incarnati, in fronti d'angiole
precipitate a volo ... Se la forza
che guida il disco *di già inciso* fosse
un'altra, certo il tuo destino al mio
congiunto mostrerebbe un solco solo. (251–2)

La primavera hitleriana (Hitler Spring)

Né quella ch'a veder lo sol si gira ...

– Dante (?) a Giovanni Quirini

Folta la nuvola bianca delle falene impazzite
turbina intorno agli scialbi fanali e sulle spallette,
stende a terra una coltre su cui scricchia
come su zucchero il piede; l'estate imminente sprigiona
ora il gelo notturno che capiva
nelle cave segrete della stagione morta,
negli orti che da Maiano scavalcano a questi renai.

Da poco sul corso è passato a volo un messo infernale
tra un alalà di scherani, un golfo mistico acceso

e pavesato di croci a uncino l'ha preso e inghiottito,
si sono chiuse le vetrine, povere
e inoffensive benché armate anch'esse
di cannoni e giocattoli di guerra,
ha sprangato il beccaio che infiorava
di bacche il muso dei capretti uccisi
la sagra dei miti carnefici che ancora ignorano il sangue
s'è tramutata in un sozzo trescone d'ali schiantate,
di larve sulle golene, e l'acqua séguita a rodere
le sponde e più nessuno è incolpevole.

Tutto per nulla, dunque? – e le candele
romane, a San Giovanni, che sbiancavano lente
l'orizzonte, ed i pegni e i lunghi addii
forti come un battesimo nella lugubre attesa
dell'orda (ma una gemma rigò l'aria stillando
sui ghiacci e le riviere dei tuoi lidi
gli angeli di Tobia, i sette, la semina
dell'avvenire) e gli eliotropi nati
dalle tue mani – tutto arso e succhiato
da un polline che stride come il fuoco
e ha punte di sinibbio ...

Oh la piagata
primavera è pur festa se raggela
in morte questa morte! Guarda ancora
in alto, Clizia, è la tua sorte, tu
che il non mutato amor mutata serbi,
fino a che il cieco sole che in te porti
si abbàcini nell'Altro e si distrugga
In Lui, per tutti. Forse le sirene, i rintocchi
che salutano i mostri nella sera
della loro tregenda, si confondono già
col suono che slegato dal cielo, scende, vince –
col respiro di un'alba che domani per tutti
si riaffacci, bianca ma senz'ali
di raccapriccio, ai greti arsi del sud ... (256–7)

L'ombra della magnolia (The Shadow of the Magnolia)

L'ombra della magnolia giapponese
si sfoltisce or che i bocci paonazzi

sono caduti. Vibra intermittente
in vetta una cicala. Non è più
il tempo del'unìsono vocale,
Clizia, il tempo del nume illimitato
che divora e rinsangua i suoi fedeli.
Spendersi era più facile, morire
al primo batter d'ale, al primo incontro
col nemico, un trastullo. Comincia ora
la via più dura: ma non te consunta
dal sole e radicata, e pure morbida
cesena che sorvoli alto le fredde
banchine del tuo fiume, – non te fragile
fuggitiva cui zenit nadir cancro
capricorno rimasero indistinti
perché la guerra fosse in te e in chi adora
su te le stimme del tuo Sposo, flette
il brivido del gelo ... Gli altri arretrano
e piegano. La lima che sottile
incide tacerà, la vuota scorza
di chi cantava sarà presto polvere
di vetro sotto i piedi, l'ombra è livida, –
è l'autunno, è l'inverno, è l'oltrecielo
che ti conduce e in cui mi getto, cèfalo
saltato in secco al novilunio.
Addio. (260)

L'eroismo (Heroism)

Clizia mi suggeriva di ingaggiarmi
tra i guerriglieri di Spagna e più di una volta mi sento
morto a Guadalajara o superstite illustre
che mal reggesi in piedi dopo anni di galera.
Ma nulla di ciò avvenne: nemmeno il torrentizio
verbo del comiziante redimito di gloria
e d'alti incarchi mi regalò la sorte.
Ma dove ho combattuto io che non amo
il gregge degli inani e dei fuggiaschi?
Qualche cosa ricordo. Un prigioniero *mio*
che aveva in tasca un Rilke e fummo amici
per pochi istanti; e inutili fatiche

e tonfi di bombarde e il fastidioso
ticchettìo dei cecchini.
Ben poco e anche inutile per lei
che non amava le patrie e n'ebbe una per caso. (549)

Clizia dice (Clizia Says)

Sebbene mezzo secolo sia scorso
potremo facilmente ritrovare
il bovindo nel quale si stette ore
spulciando il monsignore delle pulci.
Sul tetto un usignolo si sgolava
ma non ebbe successo. Quanto al gergo
delle sagre del popolo o a quello
delle commedie o farse vive solo
in tradizioni orali, se con noi fosse
come un giorno un maestro del sermone umile
nonché del bronzeo della patrologia,
tutto sarebbe facile. Ma dove
sarà quel giorno e dove noi?
Se esiste un cielo e in esso molte lingue,
la sua fama d'interprete salirebbe
in altri cerchi ancora e il puzzle sarebbe
peggiore che all'inferno di noi sordomuti. (713)

Interno/Esterno (Inside/Outside)

Quando la realtà si disarticola
(seppure mai ne fu una) e qualche sua parte
s'incrosta su di noi
allora un odore d'etere non di clinica
ci avverte che la catena s'è interrotta
e che il ricordo è un pezzo di eternità
che vagola per conto suo
forse in attesa di rintegrarsi in noi.
È perciò che ti vedo
volgerti indietro dall'imbarcadero
del transatlantico che ti riporta
alla Nuova Inghilterra
oppure siamo insieme nella veranda
di "Annalena"

a spulciare le rime del venerabile
pruriginoso John Donne
messi da parte i deliranti abissi
di Meister Eckhart o simili.
Ma ora squilla il telefono e una voce
che stento a riconoscere dice ciao.
Volevo dirtelo, aggiunge, dopo trent'anni.
Il mio nome è Giovanna, fui l'amica di Clizia
e m'imbarcai con lei. Non aggiungo altro
né dico arrivederci che sarebbe ridicolo
per tutti e due. (716)

Credo (I Believe)

1944

Forse per qualche sgarro nella legge
del contrapasso
era possibile che uno sternuto in via Varchi 6 Firenze
potesse giungere fino a Bard College N.J.
Era L'Amore? Non quello che ha popolato
con un orrendo choc il cielo di stelle e pianeti.
Non tale la forza del dio con barba e capelli
che fu detronizzato dai soci del Rotary Club
ma degno di sopravvivere alle loro cabale.
Credo vero il miracolo che tra la vita e la morte
esista un terzo status che ci trovò tra i suoi.
Che un dio (ma con la barba) ti protegga
mia divina. Ed il resto, le fandonie
di cui siamo imbottiti sono meno
che nulla. (721)

Quartetto (Quartet)

In una istantanea ingiallita
di quarant'anni fa
ripescata dal fondo di un cassetto
il tuo volto severo nella sua dolcezza
e il tuo servo d'accanto; e dietro Sbarbaro
briologo e poeta – ed Elena Vivante
signora di noi tutti: qui giunti per vedere
quattro ronzini frustati a sangue

in una piazza-conchiglia
davanti a una folla inferocita.
E il tempo? Quarant'anni ho detto e forse zero.
Non credo al tempo, al big bang, a nulla
che misuri gli eventi in un prima e in un dopo.
Suppongo che a qualcuno, a qualcosa convenga
l'attributo di essente. In quel giorno eri tu.
Ma per quanto, ma come? Ed ecco che rispunta
la nozione esecrabile del tempo. (718)

Poems in the Clizia Cycle[1]

Verso Capua (Toward Capua)
Mottetti (The Motets)[2]
- Lo sai: debbo riperderti e non posso (You know this, I must lose you once again, and cannot)
- Lontano, ero con te quando tuo padre (Far away, I was still with you when your father)
- La speranza di pure rivederti (The hope even of seeing you again)
- Il saliscendi bianco e nero dei (The black and white swooping of)
- Ecco il segno; s'innerva (Here is the sign; it is traced out)
- L'anima che dispensa (The soul that scatters)
- Ti libero la fronte dai ghiaccioli (I liberated your forehead of icicles)
- Infuria sale o grandine? Fa strage (Does it storm hail or brine? There is a slaughter)
- Il fiore che ripete (The flower that repeats)

Tempi di Bellosguardo (Bellosguardo Times)
Costa San Giorgio (San Giorgio Street)
Eastbourne
Elegia di Pico Farnese (The Pico Farnese Elegy)
Nuove stanze (New Stanzas)
Palio (The Palio)
Notizie dall'Amiata (News from Amiata)
La bufera (The Storm)
Lungomare (By the Seashore)
Su una lettera non scritta (On an Unwritten Letter)
Nel Sonno (In Sleep)
Gli orecchini (The Earrings)

La frangia dei capelli (The Bangs)
Finestra fiesolana (Fiesole Window)
Il giglio rosso (The Red Lily)
Il ventaglio (The Fan)
Personae separate (Separated Personae)
L'arca (The Ark)
Giorno e notte (Day and Night)
Il tuo volo (Your Flight)
Lasciando un "Dove" (Leaving a "Dove")
Sulla colonna più alta (On the Highest Column)
Incantesimo (Incantation)
Iride (Iris)
L'orto (The Orchard)
Ezekiel Saw the Wheel (original title given in English)
La primavera hitleriana (Hitler Spring)
Voce giunta con le folaghe (Voice That Came with the Coots)
L'ombra della magnolia (The Shadow of the Magnolia)
L'anguilla (The Eel)
Piccolo testamento (Little Testament)
L'Eufrate (The Euphrates)
Due prose veneziane (Two Venetian Prose Pieces)
Senza salvacondotto (Without Safe Conduct)
Le revenant (The Ghost)
A C. (To C.)
Due destini (Two Destinies)
Una lettera che non fu spedita (A Letter Never Sent)
L'eroismo (Heroism)
Clizia nel '34 (Clizia in '34)
Le pulci (The Fleas)
Rimuginando (Brooding)
Clizia dice (Clizia Says)
Previsioni (Predictions)
Interno/Esterno (Inside/Outside)
Poiché la vita fugge ... (Since Life Is Fleeing ...)
Credo (I Believe)
Nel '38 (In '38)
Quartetto (Quartet)
Luni e altro (Luni and Other Things)
Ho tanta fede in te (I Have Such Faith in You)
Botta e risposta I (Thrust and Parry I)

Poems Published by Irma Brandeis (Clizia) But Written Before Montale Knew Her

I limoni (The Lemon Trees)
Caffè a Rapallo (Café at Rapallo)
Meriggiare pallido e assorto (To Rest at Noon Pale and Engrossed)
Portami il girasole (Bring Me the Sunflower)
Là fuoresce il Tritone (There the Triton Surges)
Casa sul mare (House by the Sea)
I morti (The Dead)
Incontro (Encounter)
Il balcone (The Balcony)
A Liuba che parte (For Liuba, Leaving)

Notes

Works frequently cited have been identified by the following abbreviations:

DMH	Translation by the author.
IBJL	Brandeis, Irma. "Journals and Letters." Edited by Jean Cook. Unpublished manuscript. The Italian version of this material has been published as *Irma Brandeis (1905–1990), una musa di Montale: Passi diaristici ed epistolari scelti, trascritti e introdotti da Jean Cook.* Edited and with an essay by Marco Sonzogni. Balerna, Switzerland: Edizioni Ulivo, 2008.
IO	Montale, Eugenio. *Le occasioni.* Edited by Dante Isella. Turin: Einaudi, 1996.
JGCP	_____. *Collected Poems, 1920–1954.* Translated by Jonathan Galassi. New York: Farrar, Straus, and Giroux, 1998.
LC	_____. *Lettere a Clizia.* Edited by Rosanna Bettarini, Gloria Manghetti, and Franco Zabagli, with an introductory essay by Rosanna Bettarini. Milan: Mondadori, 2006.
Op	_____. *L'Opera in versi.* Edited by Rosanna Bettarini and Gianfranco Contini. Milan: Einaudi, 1980.
QR	Brandeis, Irma, ed. Montale Issue. *Quarterly Review of Literature* 11, no. 4 (1962).
SLA	Montale, Eugenio. *The Second Life of Art: Selected Essays.* Translated by Jonathan Galassi. New York: Ecco Press, 1982.
Tp	_____. *Tutte le poesie.* Edited by Giorgio Zampa. Milan: Mondadori, 1996. All quotations from the original Italian poetry are from this edition.

WAO _____. *The Occasions.* Translated by William Arrowsmith. New York: Norton, 1987.
WAS _____. *The Storm and Other Things.*Translated by William Arrowsmith. New York: Norton, 1985.

1. The Clizia Myth and the Secret Cycle

1 From *The New Princeton Encyclopedia on Poetry and Poets* (ed. Preminger and Brogan), s.v. "trobar clus and trobar leu": "controversy between troubadours defending the t.c ('enclosed, hermetic poetry') and those extolling the t.l. ('light' or 'easy poetry') is found ca. 1160–1210, with later echoes, and seems to have centered on some poets' desire to write for a select audience of connoisseurs. The *clus* manner is characteristically allusive, oblique and *recherché* in vocabulary and rhymes."

2 Joseph Cary's definition of *senhal* is succinct: "the Provençal troubadour's term for the protective pseudonym that at once screens his *donna* from unseemly publicity and celebrates her virtue." Cary, too, notes that Montale was aware of the frequency of senhals in Dante. See Cary, *Three Modern Italian Poets*, 303. For a short but essential study on the importance of women (*donne)* as hearers or muses, with or without the senhal, see Giusi Baldissone, *Il nome delle donne: Modelli letterari e metamorfosi storiche tra Lucrezia, Beatrice e le muse di Montale,* and especially, for Montale studies, see 7–12, 55–71, 107–16.

3 Translation by David Michael Hertz (hereafter referred to as DMH). Montale, *Tutte le poesie,* ed. Giorgio Zampa (hereafter referred to as Tp), 283.

4 *La bufera e altro* has only been published in English as a separate work with the title *The Storm and Other Things,* in the translation by William Arrowsmith, and I use this English translation of the title for this reason. However, Jonathan Galassi chose the wittier *The Storm, Etc.* for his complete translation of the work in his *Collected Poems, 1920–1954* (hereafter referred to as JGCP).

5 Montale, Tp, liii, and JGCP, 538.

6 While researching at the Gabinetto Vieusseux in Florence in April 2002, I discovered Paolo De Caro's *Journey to Irma.* De Caro similarly proposes a *ciclo di Clizia* in his very original research. While Montale himself speaks of a *romanzetto* (novella) and a *ciclo* (cycle) in describing his own poetry at various points in his life, De Caro gives an important chart of the cycle and does much to "reconstruct" the "*romanzo*" (novel) about Irma buried in the poems. However, there are significant differences in our readings,

and his work to date concentrates more on uncovering Brandeis's life and influence on Montale and less on his reading of the important Montale poems. While he places more emphasis on the impact of Brandeis's own writings on Montale's than I do, I have learned much from the valuable biographical information about Irma Brandeis that he has gathered.

7 Montale, *The Second Life of Art: Selected Essays*, trans. Jonathan Galassi (hereafter referred to as SLA), 138–9. For the original Italian text see Montale, *Il secondo mestiere, Prose*, vol. 2, 2668–90. Erich Auerbach fleshes out the connection between Dante and Guinizzelli in his classic study, *Dante*, 24–68. This work, first published in German in 1929 under the title *Dante als Dichter der irdischen Welt*, has recently been republished in English translation. See also Guido Guinizelli, *The Poetry of Guido Guinizelli.*

8 The identity of Montale's Secret Reader was carefully hidden for many years. The scholarly world should be grateful to Luciano Rebay for clearly uncovering Irma Brandeis as the model for Clizia. He was originally directed to Clizia's identity by Montale himself. Professor Rebay, while based at Columbia University, has written a stream of scholarly articles on Clizia in Italian since the 1960s (see the bibliography). Rebay eventually turns up as a character in a late Montale poem, in a winking reference by the master himself. Others, especially in Montale's closest circles, probably knew Clizia's true identity from the beginning. I suspect that Montale had long since divulged his secret to the composer Luigi Dallapiccola and his wife, Roberto "Bobi" Bazlen, and above all to the distinguished Italian philologist and editor Gianfranco Contini. The Vivantes, a lively intellectual family based near Siena, and the poet Camillo Sbarbaro – who knew Irma and Eugenio in the 1930s – also must have known Clizia's identity and kept discreetly silent.

9 Cambon, who wrote one of the strongest early critical works on Montale in either English or Italian, brings out the interrelations of Jewish, Catholic, and even Nestorian symbolism in Clizia with great perspicacity. See Cambon, *Eugenio Montale's Poetry*, 117–18, 123–4.

10 In addition to the poems of the Clizia Cycle, these references to the Middle East also exist in poems that are not about Irma but about other Jewish female personae (Gerti in "Gerti's Carnaval," Liuba in "For Liuba, Leaving," and Dora in "Dora Markus").

11 Irma Brandeis, ed., Montale Issue, *Quarterly Review of Literature* 11, no. 4 (hereafter referred to as QR), 232.

12 Instead, it was the other way around. Both Joyce and Montale were great proponents of Svevo's writing.

13 Montale, *Lettere a Clizia*, ed. Bettarini, Manghetti, and Zabagli (hereafter referred to as LC), 29, 198, and passim.

14 Montale's essay on Chaplin, published in *Solaria*, is available in SLA, 20–4. See also Biasin, *Montale, Debussy, and Modernism*, 69–117.

15 Irma Brandeis to Glauco Cambon, 25 August. There is no year indicated on the letter. The envelope is dated 1979. Glauco Cambon Correspondence, Archives and Special Collections, Thomas J. Dodd Research Center, University of Connecticut, Storrs.

16 Glauco Cambon Correspondence, Archives and Special Collections, University of Connecticut, Storrs.

17 The editors of this excellent edition are Rosanna Bettarini, Gloria Manghetti, and Franco Zabagli. Bettarini is a professor of Italian literature at the University of Florence and co-editor of *L'opera in versi*, the authoritative edition of the Montale poems; she also worked closely with Gianfranco Contini. Manghetti is director of the Archivio Contemporaneo "Alessandro Bonsanti" at the Gabinetto Vieusseux. Zabagli, an archivist, is also based at the Gabinetto Vieusseux. The edition contains 155 letters from Montale to Irma Brandeis written in the 1930s, one short letter from Montale to Brandeis written in June 1981, and two letters written by Brandeis, one of them addressed to Montale and dated 21 February 1935 and the other addressed *al lettore da I.B.* (to I.B's reader) and written in August 1979. The second letter accompanied her collection of letters from the poet when she deposited them in the Archivio Contemporaneo. Bettarini contends that the second letter was "*mai spedita*" (never sent), possibly because it was included in the package sent to the library in 1983 (LC, xliii).

18 Steiner, *In Bluebeard's Castle*, 77.

19 Eliot, *Notes towards the Definition of Culture*, 70.

20 LC, 15. DMH translation from the Italian.

21 Biasin, *Montale, Debussy, and Modernism*, 3–68. For an insightful essay on the evident musician's sensibility that Montale displayed towards sound in his poetry, see Stefano Verdino, "Il Mancato Lotario" in Iovino and Verdino, *Montale la musica e i musicisti*, 53–68.

22 Montale writes the following about the Debussy performance: "Concert. Last night concert at the Carlo Felice Theatre ... Here is a resume ... Debussy, 'Les collines d'Anacapri' and 'Ménestrels': descriptive and impressionistic music, filled with disconnectedness, colors and meters. First it leaves you almost indifferent, if not hostile; but then it remains imprinted, as if in a nightmare; and you would like to hear it over and over. 'Les collines' ends with a white key, dissonant and jarring like the cry

of a lost bird. 'Ménestrels' is, or is taken to be, ironic, music." As quoted in Biasin, *Montale, Debussy, and Modernism*, 18–19.

2. Murder, Manifestos, and the Poems of the Cinque Terre

1 There are a number of readily available books in English that offer authoritative accounts of this era. An excellent overview is offered in Mack Smith, *Modern Italy.* See also Adamson, *Avant-garde Florence*; Di Scala, *Italy*; and Lyttelton, *The Seizure of Power*. The most respected biography of Mussolini in English is still Mack Smith, *Mussolini.* See also De Felice, *Mussolini,* for a widely known revisionist account of the Italian dictator.

2 I spoke with Dr Luca Tortorolo, a direct descendant of Montale, in the family's Monterosso house in April 2002. His grandfather and Montale's father, who were first cousins, had built adjoining houses. His grandfather's house has remained in the family, whereas the Montale house has been divided into condominiums. Dr Tortorolo explained the eventual family tension over Montale's interest in the arts. Montale had quarrelled with his father about his chosen avocation as a poet. Father and son broke apart over the issue and were never fully reconciled.

3 Nascimbeni, *Montale,* 33–40.

4 Ibid., 36–8.

5 Ibid., 17, 21–22. Contorbia, *Eugenio Montale,* 40.

6 Woodhouse, *Gabriele D'Annunzio,* 173; Mack Smith, *Modern Italy,* 177.

7 As described in Lyttle, *Il Duce,* 46–7.

8 Mack Smith, *Modern Italy,* 224–5.

9 Di Scala, *Italy,* 214.

10 D'Annunzio proclaimed that "Dalmatia belongs to Italy by divine right as well as human law." See Mack Smith, *Modern Italy,* 279.

11 Ibid., 292–3; Ledeen, *The First Duce*, vii–viii.

12 Nascimbeni, *Montale,* 48, 54.

13 Pier Vincenzo Mengaldo has shown the lexical relationship between D'Annunzio and Montale in an essay of dazzling erudition. See Mengaldo, *La tradizione del novecento da D'Annunzio a Montale,* 13–107. For a more general description, see Jared Becker, *Eugenio Montale,* 4–6.

14 See the very interesting study of fame by Leo Braudy, *The Frenzy of Renown.*

15 One such D'Annunzian hero was Corrado Brando, the main character of the 1906 play *Più che l'amore* (*More than Love*). Brando was a kind of Italian Übermensch who would commit crimes, including murder, to fund his ambitious and "noble" colonial projects. See Montale's remarks

on D'Annunzio in SLA, 4, 90. See also Woodhouse, *Gabriele D'Annunzio*, 226–7.

16 Mack Smith, *Modern Italy*, 329.

17 Lyttle, *Il Duce*, 82.

18 Ibid., 82–7.

19 Tannenbaum, *The Fascist Experience*, 282.

20 Croce had inherited a fortune that enabled him to write as an independent scholar, but he also believed in public service. He was a member of the Italian senate in 1910 and minister of education in 1920–1.

21 Rizi, *Benedetto Croce and Italian Fascism*, 90.

22 Ward, *Antifascisms*, 54. See also Papa, *Storia di due manifesti*, 97–102.

23 Delzell, *Mussolini's Enemies*, 91. The Italian text for this passage can be found in Croce, "La protesta contro il 'Manifesto degli intellettuali fascisti,'" 489–90.

24 Montale mentions his meetings with Croce in his important essay "Aesthetics and Criticism," delivered in Rome in 1962. Translated and reprinted in SLA, 118–19.

25 SLA, 128. Montale reiterates this remark elsewhere, calling Croce "our last great writer who had faith in man" (SLA, 132).

26 An excellent survey of the "Revolt against Positivism" launched by Croce, Henri Bergson, Alfred North Whitehead, and others can be found in Wellek, *Concepts of Criticism*, 256–81. "Aesthetica in Nuce," one prominent Croce essay mentioned by Montale, widely read in the Anglo-American world as the entry on "Aesthetics" in the 14th edition of the *Encyclopedia Britannica*, gives a sense of Croce's eminence in the early twentieth century. Montale lists other favourite Croce titles as follows: *Sul carattere lirico dell'arte, Breviario di estetica, Il carattere di totalità dell'espressione artistica, L'Arte come creazione e la creazione come fare, Aesthetica in nuce, La poesia.* See Montale, *Il secondo mestiere: Prose*, vol. 2, 2527.

27 SLA, 121, 128–30.

28 Ibid., 130–1.

29 All of this material, paraphrased or quoted, can be found in SLA, 130–1. Montale quotes here the little-known Genovese Tommaso Ceva, a seventeenth-century Jesuit poet and mathematician.

30 SLA, 130–1.

31 Croce, *Philosophy, Poetry, History*, 763. See also Montale's late essay on Freud and Croce, "Freud e Croce: Due grandi nemici di tutti gli 'ismi,'" in Montale, *Il secondo mestiere: Prose*, vol. 2, 2779–82.

32 René Wellek points out Croce's hostility to Modernism in his excellent survey of twentieth-century Italian criticism. See Wellek, *A History of Modern Criticism*, vol. 8: *French, Italian, and Spanish Criticism, 1900–1950*, 187–223. See also Becker, *Eugenio Montale*, 8–10.

33 Nascimbeni, *Montale*, 55.

34 Montale never forgot his friend Gobetti. Writing later in his "Intentions (Imaginary Interview)," Montale said that Gobetti was not happy with him when he sent a political article for *Rivoluzione liberale*. Gobetti thought that a poet should not involve himself with politics. Montale said that Gobetti was wrong (SLA, 296). Montale also commented that he was considered an engaged poet because of his alliance with Gobetti (SLA, 317).

35 SLA, 295–6.

36 Ibid., 4–5.

37 Ibid., 4.

38 Ibid., 6.

39 Ibid., 7–8.

40 For an introduction to the study of cultural value and commodification, see Bourdieu, *The Field of Cultural Production*. See the earlier work by Norbert Elias, including *The Civilizing Process* and *The History of Manners*, and *Norbert Elias on Civilization, Power, and Knowledge: Selected Writings*. See also Ron Rosenbaum, *Explaining Hitler*, 201–20.

41 As quoted in Delzell, *Mussolini's Enemies*, 27–9. See also Mack Smith, *Modern Italy*, 329.

42 Delzell, *Mussolini's Enemies*, 29. Montale recalls his last visit to Gobetti's house in *Il secondo mestiere: Prose*, vol. 1, 1693–4. See also David Ward, *Piero Gobetti's New World*, 22.

43 SLA, 16. Montale also mentions here others who died for their anti-Fascist position: Leone Ginzburg, Eugenio Colorni, Giaime Pintor, and Giorgio Labò.

44 Mack Smith, *Mussolini*, 70, 90.

45 Montale finds in Svevo's characters an important series of models for the anti-heroic persona he will later develop in his own poetry. He was also aware of James Joyce's importance in promoting Svevo's reputation in France. See Montale, "Omaggio a Italo Svevo," in *Il secondo mestiere: Prose*, vol. 1, 72–84.

46 DMH. Tp, 30. My approach to this poem was anticipated in many ways in an insightful article from the late 1960s. See Vasili Bertoloni Meli, "Eugenio Montale: *Ossi di seppia*," 539–41.

47 SLA, 298. This important essay is available in the original Italian in Montale, *Il secondo mestiere: Arte, musica, società*, 1475–84. The French spelling is in Montale's original text.

48 Biasin, *Montale, Debussy, and Modernism*, 66–7.
49 Balakian, *The Fiction of the Poet.*
50 *Montale racconta Montale*, with Gabriella Sica and produced by Gianni Barcelloni, RAI Educational Video 755, Einaudi Tascabili. The video clip, along with several other remarkable excerpts from RAI Television interviews, is also available on the web at http://www.rai.tv/dl/RaiTV/programmi/media/ContentItem-d8690164-b500-4ee1-a5ba-8a234924ae98.html?p=0.
51 See Cook, "*Etendre, simplifier le monde.*"
52 Mallarmé, *Selected Prose Poems, Essays, and Letters*, 39–40.
53 Ibid.
54 Trans. DMH. Montale, *Il secondo mestiere: Arte, musica, società*, 1499. This statement is excerpted from a letter to Glauco Cambon. It is an important document in Montale studies, and it is quoted in full in chapter 6.
55 Preminger and Brogan, *The New Princeton Encylopedia of Poetry and Poetics*, s.v. "hermeticism."
56 See Wellek on I.A. Richards in *History of Modern Criticism*, vol. 5, 221–38 and on the early Richards in his *Concepts of Criticism*, 265. Two important early Richards works, surely known to Brandeis, were *Principles of Literary Criticism* (1924) and *Practical Criticism* (1929).
57 Gianfranco Contini, who gave Montale important information about Dante, also displays a sophisticated knowledge of the poet's French connections, as do the most sensitive Montale experts in Italy. See Contini, *Una lunga fedeltà: Scritti su Eugenio Montale*, 33–4, 39, 79.
58 QR, 244.
59 Rebay says that Montale met Nicoli in Florence in 1929–30, which would make her an unlikely candidate for the female presence in *Cuttlefish Bones.* Other scholars, including Zampa, feel differently, arguing that she indeed competes with Arletta for Montale's attention in his early poetry. See Montale's own statement on his *donne* in Greco, *Montale commenta Montale*, 33. See also Rebay, "Sull' 'autobiografismo' di Montale," 75, and Montale, Tp, xxviii.
60 Pipa, *Montale and Dante*, 8, 18.

3. Love in Fascist Florence

1 SLA, 14. While it must be read as a companion piece to the anti-Fascist and Crocean essay of 1925, Montale wrote his essay on Fascism after the fact, publishing it first in 1945, two years after Mussolini's fall from power .The whole essay is pertinent. See SLA 12–19.

2 Mack Smith has an incisive account of doings at the Fascist academy. See *Modern Italy*, 360–2.
3 Ibid., 389.
4 SLA, 13–14, 17.
5 SLA, 15.
6 Ibid., 12; Pipa, *Montale and Dante*, 10. This is a notion that Montale also reiterates elsewhere; see his essay "Is There an Italian Decadence?" SLA, 75–81.
7 SLA, 17.
8 Etlin, *Modernism in Italian Architecture*, 591.
9 Cannistraro and Sullivan, *Il Duce's Other Woman*, 428–49.
10 Nascimbeni, *Montale*, 74, 83. See also Pini, *Incontri alle Giubbe Rosse*, 91.
11 Vittorini as quoted inTannenbaum, *The Fascist Experience*, 263.
12 The Chaplin article, "Report on Cinema," is available in English in SLA, 218–20. Eliot's "A Song for Simeon" appeared in *Solaria* in 1929.
13 As quoted in Tannenbaum, *The Fascist Experience*, 195. The argument here, with some qualifications, is roughly summarized from page 295 of *The Fascist Experience*.
14 Moravia and Elkann, *Life of Moravia*, 81.
15 Alberto Moravia notes that Drusilla was related to Ginzburg (*Life of Moravia*, 198–9). Her first husband was an influential art critic. Nascimbeni (*Montale*, 73) quotes Montale's letter to Svevo about his initial meeting with Drusilla. Natalia Ginzburg, born in Palermo in 1916, was the daughter of Giuseppe Levi and Lidia Tanzi. Montale and Drusilla Tanzi married much later, in 1962. They are buried together in the little cemetery at San Felice a Ema. Drusilla's brother, Silvio Tanzi, was a musicologist and composer.
16 Nascimbeni, *Montale*, 72–3.
17 Ibid., 76. See the chronology in Tp, lxv, for the formal letter of appointment.
18 Adamson, *Avant-garde Florence*, 27–8.
19 The Vieusseux family ran the library until 1919. At that point it became a foundation, with a board headed by the mayor of Florence or one of his representatives. Other noted directors were Tecchi and Alessandro Bonsanti. Over time, the Gabinetto evolved into an elite scholarly library located in the Palazzo Strozzi. Today the Gabinetto Vieusseux is a research library housing 500,000 volumes.
20 For further reading on Louis Dembitz Brandeis see Strum, *Louis Brandeis*, and Paper, *Brandeis*.
21 De Caro has done the most to excavate facts about this branch of the Brandeis family. See De Caro, *Journey to Irma*, 36. While De Caro has added

new information, the pioneer in the exploration of the Brandeis connection has been Luciano Rebay. Jean Cook fleshed out many further details for me during our many conversations and interviews.

22 Rebay, "Montale, Clizia e l'America," 171–202. See also 198n38.

23 For her telling insights into the background of the Brandeis family and much information on the life of Irma Brandeis in general, I am grateful to Jean Cook, executrix of Professor Brandeis's estate. Ms Cook, for all practical purposes, also has served de facto as Professor Brandeis's literary executor.

24 The fine old Steinway is today in the home of Frank and Ruth Oja in Annandale-on-Hudson, New York. Frank Oja is a retired professor of sociology from Bard College. Ruth Oja is a former student of Irma Brandeis. Irma writes about her father's piano playing in "Journals and Letters," ed. Jean Cook (hereafter referred to as IBJL), 99.

25 There are intriguing entries for Frederick Brandeis in Claghorn, *Biographical Dictionary of American Music*, and Slonimsky, *Baker's Biographical Dictionary*, 7th ed. Czerny, who had befriended the aristocracy in post-Napoleonic Europe, chased Frederick Brandeis out of his studio because he was greatly offended by Brandeis's liberal views.

26 De Caro, *Journey to Irma*, 39. Livingston and Bigongiari published a wide range of translations and critical pieces, stretching from Dante to modern Italian literature and politics.

27 Information courtesy of the Barnard College Archives and Columbia University Transcripts Department.

28 IBJL, 40.

29 Irma Brandeis's employment application for her job at Sarah Lawrence College indicates that she worked as a secretary and literary assistant to Mrs Gano Dunn from 1928 to 1930. Sarah Lawrence College Archives.

30 Trans. DMH. This is first of twenty poems, crucial to the study of the Clizia Cycle, translated into English in the commentaries, and reprinted in the original Italian in the back of this book on pages 311–27.

31 "Tanzt die Orange: Die wärmere Landschaft, / werft sie aus euch, dass die reife erstrahle / in Lüften der Heimat!" See Rilke, *Sonnets to Orpheus*, 130–1.

32 Mrs Weiss made this remark in conversation in Princeton, New Jersey, in July 2003.

33 De Caro has tracked down a literary profile of Montale that was published in the Columbia University *Casa italiana* bulletin in 1932. Since the bulletin was published by Irma's teacher Dino Bigongiari and several colleagues, it is likely that she read it as well. See De Caro, *Journey to Irma*, 78. Also, De Caro conjectures that Irma Brandeis actually met Montale as early

as 1932 in a pensione on the Costa San Giorgio, near the Arno River (76, 77). The generally accepted chronology puts the meeting at the Gabinetto Vieusseux in the spring of 1933, but Sarah Lawrence College shows that she taught there until June of that year. Their meeting most likely took place some weeks after the semester ended in June with the commencement ceremonies for the college. *Lettere a Clizia* and Brandeis's "Journals and Letters" offer clear indications that the meeting was in July 1933.

34 Brandeis's "Hospital Solarium" was written in 1926 and published in the *New Yorker* on 1 October 1932. The five-stanza poem, which includes some witty rhymes, later appeared in the Barnard College alumnae magazine. A copy was provided to me by the Sarah Lawrence College Archives. "MacGregor's Island" was completed in the 1980s. The manuscript, never published, is in Jean Cook's archival materials.

35 IBJL, 74.

36 Ibid., 75.

37 Brandeis documents her accomplishments in translation in a detailed letter of 21 September 1932. In this letter, addressed to the dean of Sarah Lawrence College, she is applying for employment as an Italian instructor. Sarah Lawrence College Archives.

38 Hannah D. Kahn is probably the Hannah Kahn mentioned in Montale's late poem "Without Safe Conduct." Kahn also translated another Italian book, Gaetano Mosca's *The Ruling Class.* Arthur Livingston, Irma Brandeis's Columbia professor, wrote an introduction for the book.

39 In a memorandum prepared for President Constance Warren in 1942 Brandeis's employment record at Sarah Lawrence College is described in detail. From 1932 to 1935 she taught Italian two days a week, and her maximum salary was $1,300. Beginning in 1935 she had a three-year contract to teach both Italian and French, earning as much as $2,600 in 1936–7. A second three-year contract began in 1938. From this point she taught Italian two days a week and French two days a week, earning a maximum salary of $2,900 in 1940–1. Finally, she had a one-year contract during the 1941–2 academic year to teach full-time in French and Italian at $3,000. See the Sarah Lawrence College Archives.

40 Her dates of attendance in the graduate school at Columbia were 1934–8, 1940–1, and 1943–4. Information courtesy of the Columba University Transcripts Department.

41 IBJL, 49. Brandeis wrote from the Annalena in March 1931.

42 Jean Cook gives the address of the apartment as 54 Costa San Giorgio. It is a strange fact that the street is named Costa San Giorgio at the top of the hill, near the Forte di Belvedere, and Costa di San Giorgio at the bottom of

the hill, where it runs into the Via Romana. Montale obviously preferred Costa San Giorgio for his title.

43 Lewis, *The City of Florence*, 203. Lewis says that Machiavelli "tells the story in his history of Florence."

44 Quoted in Perlis, *Charles Ives Remembered*, 102.

45 LC, 1–7, 26.

46 Ibid., 77.

47 Ibid., 36, 171. Bettarini already lists many of these echoes between the letters and the poems in her excellent introductory essay for the collection (LC, vii–xxxix).

48 LC, 59.

49 Ibid., 49.

50 Ibid., 43, 60.

51 Ibid., 37.

52 Ibid., 47.

53 Ibid., 20.

54 Bettarini tracks down the popular song in her notes (LC, 294). The full lyric is available on the Internet.

55 LC, 29.

56 Ibid., 34, 35.

57 Ibid., 35.

58 Ibid., 39.

59 Ibid., 68–9.

60 Ibid., 77.

61 Bettarini's excellent note tracks down the Robeson reference (LC, 315), but it was Rachel Hertz who sensitized me to the relationship between the African-American lullaby and the fact that Montale was writing its lyric tenderly to his Jewish lover.

62 LC, 77–8.

63 Ibid., 85.

64 Ibid., 87.

65 Ibid., 157.

66 Ibid., 161.

67 IBJL, 72.

68 LC, 165.

69 IBJL, 80.

70 LC, 88. Trans. DMH.

71 Ibid., 82.

72 Ibid., 110, 116.

73 Drusilla's brother, Silvio Tanzi (1879–1909), was a composer who committed suicide. See LC, 337.

74 LC, 130–2.
75 This letter from Irma is in LC, 278.
76 LC, 133.
77 Ibid.
78 Ibid., 147.
79 Sarah Lawrence College Archives.
80 LC, 155.
81 Brandeis, "An Italian Letter."
82 I use Brandeis's titles for the translated poems here.
83 Levi, *Christ Stopped at Eboli.*
84 Sachs, *Music in Fascist Italy*, 213–14.
85 Mack Smith, *Mussolini*, 177.
86 Sachs, *Music in Fascist Italy*, 29.
87 Hibbard, *Florence*, 291.
88 Acton, *Memoirs of an Aesthete*, 8–9, and *More Memoirs of an Aesthete*, 47–71. Lord Acton's insider account of the privileged expatriate scene in Florence is indispensable.
89 Pini, *Incontri alle Giubbe Rosse*, 87–102. See the photos of Montale and Loria on pages 88 and 89.
90 LC, 176.
91 Ibid., 118.
92 Ibid., 168.
93 Testa, *Montale*, 30.
94 LC, 187.
95 Ibid., 186.
96 Ibid., 198.
97 Nascimbeni, *Montale*, 77.
98 IBJL, 94–5.
99 LC, 223.
100 IBJL, 98.
101 LC, 225–6.
102 Nascimbeni, *Montale*, 76–7.
103 The translation is mine. The most complete version of this important letter in the original Italian is published in Rebay, "Montale, Clizia e l'America," 173–4. Portions are also quoted in Testa, *Montale*, 33. A smaller excerpt is quoted in Tp, lxix.
104 Irma Brandeis returned to the United States in time to teach the fall semester at Sarah Lawrence. The semester began on 19 September 1938.
105 LC, 230–6.
106 Ibid., 238–9.
107 Ibid., 241–2, 249.

108 Ibid., 247.
109 Ibid., 252.
110 Tp, lxx.
111 LC, 256.
112 Nascimbeni, *Montale*, 77–80. Cannistraro, *Historical Dictionary of Fascist Italy*, s.v. "podestà."
113 Tp, lxx.
114 Montale, trans. Singh, *The Butterfly of Dinard*, 141.
115 LC, 260.
116 The apartment was at 38A Duca di Genova.
117 Montale clearly refers to Shakespeare's "only begetter" in his Dante lecture of 1965. See Montale, *Il secondo mestiere: Prose*, vol. 2, 2671.
118 LC, 271.

4. The Woman of *The Occasions*

1 The "I.B." dedication was not used in the first Einaudi editions of 1939 and 1940, but it appears in the first Mondadori edition of *The Occasions* (1949) and subsequently. See Eugenio Montale, *Le occasioni*, edited by Dante Isella (hereafter referred to as IO), xvii.
2 "I/Thou" is Cambon's term. Since Montale uses the informal *tu* in the Italian and not the formal form of address, I prefer "I/You."
3 While I.B. remains the dominant addressee of the book, Montale has pointed to other muses, such as Arletta and Paola Nicoli. See, for example, Greco, *Montale commenta Montale*, and Rebay, "Sull' 'autobiografismo' di Montale," 73–83. Greco's collection of Montale's comments on *The Occasions* is also available in Montale, *Il secondo mestiere: Arte, musica, società*, 1503–21. They are important enough to be included in Mondadori's edition of Montale's collected writings.
4 SLA, 303.
5 Most scholars discern traces in the poem of Arletta, Montale's early muse who appears towards the end of *Cuttlefish Bones*. Luciano Rebay spoke about the poem with Montale who told him that it was inspired by Arletta and that she was far too sickly to be Irma, and Dante Isella, author of the authoritative annotated edition, perceives traces of Arletta. See Rebay as quoted in JGCP, 485. Isella refers to the "crepuscular" Arletta in IO, 3. For further commentary on the light imagery here, see also Angelo Marchese, *Visiting Angel: Interpretazione semiologica della poesia di Montale*, 116.
6 Tp, 112.

7 Rebay, "Montale, Clizia e l'America," 186.
8 Nascimbeni, *Montale*, 90. However, Galassi points out that this is one of a number of possibilities for Liuba (JGCP, 491). For me it is the most plausible, judging from the text. See also IO, 49–50, for more detail.
9 Tp, 128.
10 QR, 254.
11 The translation of this remarkable passage can be found in JGCP, 492. It was republished in Grignani, *Prologhi ed epiloghi*, 60n19. It was taken from Montale's conversation with Giacomo Debenedetti, published in the *Corriere della Sera* on 21 December 1975.
12 Also, since Montale was estranged from his family, he may have thought that his memory of them was part of his personal ark of precious memories and that he was carrying those memories through his life like a "wandering Jew." See also the use of the ark image as "a private ark" of memories in "Sul Limite," Montale's short story published in translation in Singh, *The Butterfly of Dinard* (158).
13 JGCP, 490, 492–4. Galassi's excellent commentary examines Montale's remarks in Greco and in Montale's extensive letter to Bazlen dated 7 May 1939. See Greco, *Montale commenta Montale*, 34, and Montale, *Giorni di libeccio, lettere ad Angelo Barile*, 93–4.
14 JGCP, 493.
15 Tp, 285. See the earlier Arrowsmith translation of Montale's *Satura*, 7. *Euphuistic* refers to "artificial and excessive language," a criticism sometimes levelled at John Donne (a poet whom Montale and Brandeis read and translated together) and also at Italian "hermetic" poets.
16 See Bernard Knox's review essay on translations by Galassi and Arrowsmith in "The Heart That Howls," 27–31.
17 Cambon, *Eugenio Montale*, 34.
18 The use of the swan image is typical of the French Symbolist poets that Montale had read carefully. See Maurice English's version in QR, 257: "The cruel swan / preens and contorts itself / on the skin of the lagoon."
19 Rebay, "Montale, Clizia e l'America," 186. See also IO, 46–8.
20 Tp, 127. Trans. DMH.
21 *Lo Zingarelli,*, ed. Dogliotti and Rosiello, s.v. "barbaglio." For intriguing commentary on the range of light images in Montale's poems see Isella's list in IO, 4–5, n. 9; and also Almansi and Merry, *Eugenio Montale*, 72–3.
22 See O'Malley, "Literary Synesthesia," 391–411.
23 *Paradiso*, canto I, 40–93. In the heart of the passage Dante writes: "*Beatrice tutta nell'etterne rote / fissa con li occhi stava; ed io in lei / le luci fissi, di là su remote*" (I, 64–7). John Sinclair's translation is as follows: "Beatrice stood

with her eyes fixed only on the eternal wheels and on her I fixed mine, withdrawn from above." See Dante Alighieri, *Paradiso.* See also *Purgatorio,* canto XXXIII, 103–5. As the translator, Allen Mandelbaum, points out, Beatrice looks directly at the sun "as the journey of *Paradiso* starts, while Dante, who is facing her, will gaze at the reflection of the sun in her eyes. We are reminded that ever since it first rose over the shoulders of the mountain in *Inferno* I, the sun has often served as a symbol of God and of the illumination of Divine Wisdom. It is appropriate that it should appear at its brightest as the journey toward purification approaches its end" (Dante, *Purgatorio,* 408).

24 The occasional blending of sacred and vernacular is noted in most standard definitions of the *motet* that offer a sense of its great historical variety. See *Grove's Dictionary of Music and Musicians* and also *Harvard Dictionary of Music,* s.v. "Motet." See also Huot, *Allegorical Play in the Old French Motet.*

25 Hertz, *Angels of Reality,* 235–41.

26 Montale, *The Butterfly of Dinard,* 6.

27 See Galassi's excellent comments on Montale's "poetics of the snap-shot"; JGCP, 496.

28 DMH. The original Italian text is republished in Montale, *Il secondo mestiere: Arte, musica, società,* 1489–90. It is of interest that the Italian texts are inconsistent. Here "Querini" is spelled with an "e." In Tp, 256, it is spelled "Quirini."

29 Lawrence Kart, Jonathan Galassi, William Arrowsmith, Jeremy Reed, Dana Gioia, Maurice English, and Irma Brandeis are among those who have translated the Motets into English. I refer the reader to the bibliography. Also, the composer John Harbison has set the Motets to music and published his own translation along with his score.

30 She included Motets 1, 3, 6, 7, 8, 10, 11, 14, 16, and 20 (QR, 258–61). Montale also makes frequent mention of the Motets in LC.

31 DMH. Montale, *Il secondo mestiere: Arte, musica, società,* 1493.

32 Greco, *Montale commenta Montale,* 33.

33 LC, 115–16.

34 Galassi, citing recent scholarship, including experts such as Rebay and Forti, and Montale's own remarks, points out that the first three Motets are written to Paola Nicoli. See JGCP, 497. Cambon (*Eugenio Montale's Poetry,* 55) says that Montale "confirmed" that the first three Motets "were inspired by a lady other than Clizia."

35 QR, 258. Tp, 139.

36 Montale uses the term *ultima cena.* See LC, 122.

37 Farnsworth, *Provisional Conclusions,* 154, notes that San Giorgio is a symbol of Genoa. See also Isella on Sottoripa and the sound images in IO, 79.

38 DMH. Montale, *Il secondo mestiere: Arte, musica, società*, 1490.
39 See Jean Cook's unpublished preface to Irma Brandeis's letters and diaries. Also De Caro, *Journey to Irma*, 36.
40 DMH. Reprinted in the original Italian in the back of this book on page 311.
41 See Nascimbeni, *Montale*, 74–83, and Testa, *Montale*, 28–52.
42 DMH. Montale, *Il secondo mestiere: Arte, musica, società*, 1491.
43 QR, 259. Reprinted in the original Italian in the back of this book on page 312. Isella links the short story and the Motet closely. See IO, 88.
44 Galassi prefers simply "flash," and Arrowsmith "brightness."
45 LC, 363.
46 Tp, 145. QR, 259.
47 Tp, 146, QR, 259. Also, Isella refers to the "essential landscape of this poem." See IO, 93.
48 Cambon, *Eugenio Montale's Poetry*, 71.
49 See Greco, *Montale commenta Montale*, 34, for more of Montale's comments on these poems.
50 Maurice English translates the lightning image *tu fólgore* of the tenth Motet in QR as "a thunderbolt."
51 See especially Cambon, *Eugenio Montale's Poetry*, 74.
52 Dante, *Inferno.*
53 Tp, 147. Trans. DMH.
54 LC, 258.
55 Tp, 149. QR, 260.
56 The story is available in English in Montale, *The Butterfly of Dinard*, 88–92.
57 LC, 267. The notes probably come from a "popular antiwar song," as Rebay as proposed. See IO 102.
58 Tp, 150.
59 Greco, *Montale commenta Montale*, 34.
60 JGCP, 504. Noting the stilnovistic symbols, Isella points out the forehead can also signify the Volpe. See IO 103–4, n. 1.
61 IO, 106. See also Montale, *The Occasions*, translated by William Arrowsmith (hereafter referred to as WAO), 149.
62 QR, 260–1. Tp, 152.
63 Op, 913. JGCP, 505.
64 Hertz, *The Tuning of the Word*, 1–31, 100.
65 See Montale's complimentary remarks on Debussy in "Words and Music," the 1949 essay translated and reprinted in SLA, 230–3.
66 IO, 112.
67 QR, 261. Tp, 154.
68 JGCP, 505–6.

69 For pertinent early uses of *belletta* (mire, mud) Isella sends us to Dante, *Inferno* vii, 124, and D'Annunzio's *belletta* in the "Madrigali d'estate" of *Alcyone*. See IO, 119, and JGCP, 507. Cambon, who notes the connection between the scissors and the axe, points out the link with Dante's *Paradiso*, canto XVI, 9, where the Atropos figure has "murderous" scissors. See Cambon, *Eugenio Montale's Poetry*, 84–5.

70 Greco, *Montale commenta Montale*, 34.

71 Ibid.

72 This poem by itself is marked off as the separate *parte terza* of *The Occasions*, so Montale wanted a special presence for it in the book. The poem is generally assumed to have been written in 1939, but its date of creation is less exact than that of some others. See Montale, *L'opera in versi*, edited by Rosanna Bettarini and Gianfranco (hereafter referred to as Op), and Tp, 161–4.

73 Acton, *More Memoirs of an Aesthete*, 62, 65–6.

74 Montale, enigmatic as always, remarked that he did not go to Bellosguardo much. However, the lovely hill is a short walk from the Pensione Annalena, where he met Irma Brandeis. Greco, *Montale commenta Montale*, 35. See also Montale, *Il secondo mestiere: Arte, musica, società*, 1512–13.

75 Tp, 162.

76 Tp, 164. Trans. DMH. In his highly annotated edition of *Finisterre* Dante Isella points out that this is the first time the word *bufera* occurs in Montale's verse. See Eugenio Montale, *Finisterre (versi del 1940–42)*, edited by Isella, 3.

77 Trans. DMH. See Greco, *Montale commenta Montale*, 129–30. See also *Encyclopedia of Symbols*, s.v. "ivy," and see Galassi's comments (JGCP, 581). Isella comments on other Clizian images (IO, 136).

78 Cary, *Three Modern Italian Poets*, 296.

79 Hibbard, *Florence*, 300–1.

80 Vendler, *The Art of Shakespeare's Sonnets*, 66–9.

81 See, for example, Glauco Cambon's excellent commentary in Burnshaw, *The Poem Itself*, 322–3.

82 The second stanza is quoted in prose format in 1936. At that time Brandeis translated the title of the poem as "The Toll-Keeper's House." She changes a few words in her revision, which is presented in stanza forms that follow Montale's original in her *Quarterly Review* translation.

83 QR, 262. Here Brandeis's English title for "La casa del doganieri" is "The Toll-House," and in the first line of the translation she has "tollkeeper" with no hyphen. See the picture of the building in Contorbia, *Eugenio Montale*, 141.

84 Documents seen during my interviews with Jean Cook record the location of the apartment.
85 Montale, Op, 951. Galassi's commentary is particularly rich. See JGCP, 515–16.
86 IBJL, 84.
87 Tp, 173–4.
88 See Jonathan Galassi's excellent note, JGCP, 516.
89 Op, 921.
90 Tp, 173–4.
91 Op, 921. (See Montale's letter to Cambon, reprinted in chapter 6.) For Isella and Arrowsmith, the Idol is indeed Christ, but the failure of Christ here eventually enables Clizia to be reborn, Christ-like, as a feminine saviour in the later poetry, as Montale works her into a Dolce Stil Novo goddess and "Christ-bearer." See IO, 168, and WAO, 157.
92 LC, 172.
93 Tp, 173–4.
94 Rebay, "Sull' 'autobiografismo' di Montale," 75.
95 Barile makes an impressive case for "Eastbourne" as a Clizia poem in relation to the whole cycle. See Barile, *Adorate mia larve*, 30–42.
96 WAO, 113, 158. Contini, *Una lunga fedeltà: Scritti su Eugenio Montale*, 33–4. See also IO, 182–3.
97 WAO, 159. Isella also mentions a painting by Monet, *Barques sur la Seine à Auteuil*. See IO, 188.
98 IO, 192–93, 196. JGCP, 520–25. Both Galassi and Arrowsmith translate and reprint some of the extensive correspondence about this difficult poem that Montale had with Contini, Bazlen, and others. See also Rebay's groundbreaking "I diàspori di Montale," 33–53, which is cited in IO.
99 Tp, 199. Trans. DMH.
100 SLA, 303–4.
101 DMH. Reprinted in the original Italian in the back of this book on pages 312–13.
102 DMH. The Italian is in Op, 933.
103 DMH. Montale, *Il secondo mestiere: Arte, musica, società*, 1515–16. Also quoted in Greco, *Montale commenta Montale*, 109. Greco's whole commentary is excellent (109–13).
104 LC indicates that Irma Brandeis stayed in the Pensione Annalena during her last visit, but the poem describes a setting closer to the Costa San Giorgio apartment. See LC, 223.
105 The photographs are among the unusual and important archival materials preserved by Jean Cook. They were recently published in the Italian

edition of Brandeis's diary, edited by Jean Cook and Marco Sonzogni, *Irma Brandeis (1905–1990), una musa di Montale.* They are reprinted in this book as well, courtesy of Jean Cook.

106 The third stanza begins with language that is very similar to Mallarmé's in "L'après-midi d'un faune." Compare "Mon doute, amas de nuit ancienne, s'achève" and Montale's "Il mio dubbio d'un tempo era se forse." This is similar language used for very different purposes.

107 IO. 206–7. For a discussion of the outside/inside or external/internal opposition in *Le Occasioni*, see Angelo Marchese, *Visiting Angel*, 83–106, and his discussion of this poem in particular, 102–5. Alessandro Parronchi, clarifying certain points in his book of reflection and reminiscence on Montale, says that the "Martinella" was not actually the name of the bell in the Palazzo Vecchio. See Parronchi, *Quaderno per Montale*, 47.

108 See Cary, *Three Modern Italian Poets*, 300: "Clizia [is] keeper of the faith ... our Lady of the Chessboard." Cary sees this poem as the flowering of the themes of "suffering" and "sacrifice" developed from the last poems of *Cuttlefish Bones.* The poet, referring to himself in the third person, will stand by the self-sacrificing lady. Note the various scholarly views on *altri fuochi* (JGCP, 526).

109 Marchese sums up this opposition in semiological terms. See Marchese, *Visiting Angel*, 120–6.

110 IBJL, 56.

111 As quoted in JGCP, 527. See also IO, 208–9.

112 Op, 934, as quoted in JGCP, 427.

113 *Purgatorio*, III, 50.

114 For mention of Acheron in Dante, see *Purgatorio*, canto II, 104–5.

115 For a history and detailed analysis of the Palio see Dundes and Falassi, *La terra in piazza*, 1–2.

116 Ibid., 103–4.

117 Ibid., 133–5. Dundes and Falassi offer a rich account of how the subjectivity of perception is essential to the cultural practice of the race. Isella gives valuable context as well in IO, 214–16.

118 Jean Cook's archival materials document the dates. See also De Caro, *Journey to Irma*, 136, 174, as well as the helpful notes in JGCP, 529.

119 Cannistraro and Sullivan, *Il Duce's Other Woman*, 514.

120 From conversations with Jean Cook.

121 DMH. Reprinted in the original Italian in the back of this book on pages 313–15.

122 IBJL, 81–2.

123 Also note Carlo Bo's description of Montale's reaction to the coming war when it was announced in the Piazza della Repubblica. See Merisio, *Piazze d'Italia*, 150.
124 Fosco Doretto lists one more set of Palios in 1939. There were no races from 1940 to 1944. See Doretto, *Il mio Palio*, 269.
125 Stevens's "Credences of Summer" is an excellent example.
126 The great European masterpiece on crowds is Elias Canetti's *Crowds and Power*. Canetti won the Nobel Prize in 1981.
127 I thank my colleague Professor Giancarlo Maiorino for his insights on the connotations of these lines. He notes that the inference of prison is rather overt for the native speaker, which makes sense with respect to the notion of the prisoner in these lines.
128 Dundes and Falassi, *La terra in piazza*, 187. In their compelling last chapter the authors write, "The Palio represents the triumph of life over death."
129 Once again, see also the painters Filippo de Pisis and Giorgio Morandi.
130 Gombrich, "Moment and Movement in Art."
131 The photograph published in Contorbia's *Eugenio Montale* (177, photo no. 229) documents that Irma Brandeis was there with him.
132 Berenson, *Seeing and Knowing*, 17–19.
133 Op, 936; JGCP, 532. Isella thinks it may have been finished in early 1939 (IO, 222).
134 Greco, *Montale commenta Montale*, 38.
135 Keates, *Tuscany*, 146–9.
136 Montale to Silvio Guarnieri in 1964; Greco, *Montale commenta Montale*, 38. See Barzellotti, *Monte Amiata e il suo profeta David Lazzaretti*.
137 Barnstone, *The Other Bible*.
138 Eliot, *Notes towards the Definition of Culture*, 70.
139 According to the Italian scholar Umberto Carpi, Lazzaretti's views are analogous to the "Guglielmite heresy," which conceived of a redeemer who "suffered in feminine form for our sins and saved Jews and pagans": "a case of 'religious feminism,' of faith in Christ incarnate in female form." The interest in feminine religiosity is crucial because Montale wants to construct a "poetics centered on a saving female religiosity destined to end in the celebration of the Christian sacrifice of the absent one." See JGCP, 532. Isella's remarks are also important in IO, 230–1.
140 Lowell, *Imitations*, 122.
141 QR, 263–4. Reprinted in the original Italian in the back of this book on pages 315–16.
142 Greco, *Montale commenta Montale*, 108.

143 Merisio, *Piazze d'Italia.*
144 Arcidosso seems like a logical choice in its relation to the summit, but the small medieval streets of the medieval *borgo* of Abbadia San Salvatore seem very close to what Montale is describing. Also, Barzellotti includes pictures that emphasize the shadowy and narrow medieval streets of Abbadia San Salvatore. Montale would have seen these when reading Barzellotti's book.
145 *Rissa* also has the connotation of *zuffa*, a row or altercation. *Zingarelli*, s.v. "rissa." It is interesting to compare the very different versions of Arrowsmith and Galassi. Arrowsmith has: "This Christian wrangle which has nothing / but words of shadow and grief – / what of me does it bring you? Less / than the marsh, softly silting / behind its dam of cement, has stolen from you." Galassi has: "This Christian wrangle that knows only / words of shadow and lament – / what does it bring you of me? / Less than what the millrace softly silting / in its cement basin stole from you." There is great discrepancy in the answer to the question. See Silvio Ramat, *Montale* (138–9), for an Italian reading of the *rissa cristiana* and the elegiac motifs in the poem.
146 WAO, 133.
147 JGCP, 263. See also Isella's note on the *gora* in IO, 231.
148 *Zingarelli*, s.v. "veglia." See also the very similar "vigil" in *Webster's Dictionary* or the *Oxford English Dictionary*. The archaic meaning is "to keep watch on the night before a religious feast," but the modern definition is, more generally, "to keep watch when sleep is customary." See Isella's remarks on the *veglia*, IO, 231.
149 LC, 192–3. Bettarini also notes the relationship between the *porcospino* image and the "hedgehog" in the letter of 18 October 1934. See LC, 324.
150 Isella also feels that the *donna-angelo* (lady-angel) Clizia is not yet fully *investita* (empowered) to undertake her "mission" by the end of this book. IO, 231.
151 The library records at Sarah Lawrence indicate that Irma Brandeis signed out a copy of the second edition of *Le occasioni* on 31 January 1941.

5. Hitler and Mussolini at the Opera

1 Mack Smith, *Mussolini*, 188–212. Levi gives a penetrating account of the effects of the foreign war on the impoverished Italian south in *Christ Stopped at Eboli.*
2 Mack Smith, *Modern Italy*, 400.
3 Wiskemann, *The Rome-Berlin Axis*, 135.
4 "Herr Hitler in Rome," *London Times*, 4 May 1938.

5 The remarks by the two dictators are taken from "German-Italian Friendship: The Rome Speeches," *London Times*, 9 May 1938.
6 Lasansky, *The Renaissance Perfected*, 84. See Lasanky's general discussion of the visit to Florence, 83–96. Lasansky writes that Hitler was treated "as the ultimate tourist" (85).
7 "Fuehrer Leaves for Home: Day in Florence," *London Times*, 10 May 1938.
8 Lasansky, *The Renaissance Perfected*, 93–4.
9 Both the *New York Times* and *London Times* corroborate this.
10 As quoted in Hibbard, *Florence*, 292.
11 Acton, *Memoirs of an Aesthete*, 383.
12 Lasansky, *The Renaissance Perfected*, 88.
13 "Hitler Ends Visit: Spheres Held Set," *New York Times*, 10 May 1938.
14 Wiskemann, *The Rome-Berlin Axis*, 138.
15 Lasansky has found the guest list and cited some of the prominent figures there who also had been made members of Mussolini's Academy; *The Renaissance Perfected*, 95.
16 I examine the plot structure of the two operas performed for Hitler and Mussolini in "Hitler and Mussolini at the Opera," 169–86.
17 Carlo Alberto Salustri, trans. John Duval, *Tales of Trilussa*, 128–9.
18 Lyttle, *Il Duce*, 119. Mack Smith, *Mussolini*, 223.
19 Mack Smith, *Mussolini*, 221.
20 Ibid., 221–2.
21 As translated in Delzell, *Mediterranean Fascism*, 174–7.
22 Mack Smith, *Modern Italy*, 393, 396.
23 Rizi, *Benedetto Croce and Italian Fascism*, 223.
24 Mack Smith, *Modern Italy*, 361.
25 Delzell, *Mediterranean Fascism*, 177.
26 IBJL, 101.
27 LC, 257.
28 Lyttle, *Il Duce*, 132. See also Mack Smith, *Mussolini*, 225, 230–1.
29 Mack Smith, *Modern Italy*, 401.
30 Mack Smith, *Mussolini*, 242–50.
31 Acton, *More Memoirs of an Aesthete*, 42–3.
32 Mariano, *Forty Years with Berenson*, 244.
33 Merisio, *Piazze d'Italia*, 8.
34 Montale's translation reads: "*Quanto può giungere / quanto può andarsene, / in un mondo che non si muove!*" See Tp, 742.
35 Mariano, *Forty Years with Berenson*, 254–62.
36 Sachs, *Music in Fascist Italy*, 203–4.
37 Zuccotti, *Italians and the Holocaust*, 157–60.
38 IBJL, 107.

39 Telephone interview with Jean Cook, April 2005. Marangoni eventually stayed in the United States, marrying an American and raising a family.
40 The story is recounted in Zuccotti, *Italians and the Holocaust*, 198–9. See also Isaacson, *Einstein*, 506.
41 Herzer, Voigt, and Burgwyn, *The Italian Refuge*, 78–9.
42 Hibbard, *Florence*, 297.
43 The entire 1943 Lugano edition of *Finisterre* is reprinted in Tp, 923–98.

6. The Storm and the Sun Goddess

1 SLA, 303.
2 Cambon, *Eugenio Montale's Poetry*, 90; Cary, *Three Modern Italian Poets*, 304; SLA, 303n17.
3 SLA, 310–11.
4 Ibid., 312.
5 Trans. DMH. Reprinted in the original Italian in the back of this book on page 317.
6 Arrowsmith is one of the most perceptive commentators, in Italian or English, on the juxtaposition of the Fascist realization of Dante's hell and the light imagery of the beloved. He sees *bufera* as an especially Dantesque word. Eugenio Montale, *The Storm and Other Things*, translated by William Arrowsmith (hereafter referred to as WAS), 166.
7 Greco, *Montale commenta Montale*, 120. JGCP, 540.
8 Compare Montale's "e che ti lega / più che l'amore a me, strana sorella" in "La bufera" with Baudelaire's "Mon enfant ma soeur ..." in *Les Fleurs du mal*. Montale obviously knew this work intimately.
9 LC, 271–2.
10 DMH. The Italian is included in Greco, *Montale commenta Montale*, 118.
11 Montale brings out this problem eloquently in his Clizia story "Two Jackals on a Leash."
12 Pipa points out a lovely recycling of several images from Guinizzelli. See Pipa, *Montale and Dante*, 83n4.
13 Greco, *Montale commenta Montale*, 45.
14 Tp, 199.
15 SLA, 8.
16 LC, 10.
17 See, for example, Pipa's discussion in *Montale and Dante*, 85–8.
18 See ibid. for a reading of *Finisterre* as apocalypse.
19 The image of "blood beyond death" is one of the more carnal references to Clizia, in my view. Galassi points out that "blood" references are often

typical of Arletta, but he also mention the eighth Motet, which uses the blood image and is distinctly a Clizia poem. See JGCP, 541–2.

20 Greco, *Montale commenta Montale,* 45. The poem has the length of a pseudo-sonnet.

21 See also Bettarini's introductory essay, LC, vii–xxxix.

22 On 6 June 1942 Montale wrote the following to Contini: "*ti mando un altro pseudosonetto e ti ringrazio del Hoelderlin* numeroté." See Dante Isella, *Eusebio e Trabucco,* 74–5. See also JGCP, 546.

23 Tp, 731.

24 DMH. Reprinted in the original Italian in the back of this book on pages 317–18.

25 *Zingarelli,* s.v. "èlitra," or *Webster's 3rd New International,* s.v. "elytra." In the *Oxford English Dictionary,* it is "the outer hard wing case of the coleopterous insect." The zoological term is the same in Italian. Oxford English Dictionary Online, s.v. "elytra."

26 DMH. Reprinted in the original Italian in the back of this book on page 318. In addition to the Galassi and Arrowsmith versions, see also Cambon's translation in *Eugenio Montale's Poetry,* 123.

27 The speech can be found on the web at the Nobel Prize site. See http://www.nobelprize.org/nobel_prizes/literature/laureates/1975/montale-lecture.html. Arrowsmith also quotes this speech. See WAS, 171. Montale's liberal faith in the essential goodness of poetry here is also reminiscent of Shelley.

28 Montale's Shakespeare translations are in Tp, 731–40. The notion of sun and its eclipse, compared in various anthropomorphic ways in the Shakespeare sonnet, is brilliantly brought out by Helen Vendler in *The Art of Shakespeare's Sonnets,* 177. Also, compare Montale's *la sole luce* with *il mio sole* in his Shakespeare translation.

29 Greco, *Montale commenta Montale,* 46, 130. See also J.C. Cooper, *An Illustrated Encylopaedia of Traditional Symbols.*

30 Greco, *Montale commenta Montale,* 46.

31 Tp, 205.

32 Cooper, *An Illustrated Encylopaedia of Traditional Symbols,* s.v. "lily," "mistletoe." The entry for mistletoe is particularly intriguing: "Life-essence; divine substance; the all-healing; immortality. Mistletoe ... represents the sacred feminine principle with the oak as the male. It symbolizes new life and rebirth at the winter solstice."

33 Tp, 205.

34 See Cary, *Three Modern Italian Poets,* 312.

35 Tp, 206.

36 Greco notes this too but concentrates on the first "éventail" poem, not the second. See *Montale commenta Montale*, 46.
37 Hertz, *The Tuning of the Word*, 126–33.
38 Greco, *Montale commenta Montale*, 46. Also quoted in JGCP, 546.
39 *Zingarelli*, s.v. "ordegni."
40 JGCP, 547.
41 For a comprehensive list of images of "epiphanic ornithology" in Montale, see Angelo Jacomuzzi, *La poesie di Montale*, 104. There is also an *orda* image in "La primavera hitleriana," as Galassi reminds us. See JGCP, 547.
42 JGCP, 548. Translation of Greco, *Montale commenta Montale*, 46–7.
43 JGCP, 549.
44 *The Butterfly of Dinard*, 158. This amusing story was probably inspired by a taxi accident narrated in Montale's letter of 2 November 1934. A similar taxi accident turns up in "Nothing Serious," a story published in the *New Yorker* by Irma Brandeis in 1935. The difference between the two stories is fascinating. In Brandeis's version the incident is narrated rather simply; the taxi rider survives the accident without incident. In his version, the main character dies, and Montale invents a Kafkaesque vision of the afterlife. The rider goes to heaven, where he is entitled to take his "private ark" with him; this also includes his favourite pets and all lost loved ones. Both Rebay and De Caro have recently compared the Brandeis story and the Montale story. See Rebay, "Ripensando Montale," 64–8, and De Caro, *Journey to Irma*, 335–8. See Montale's recently published letter and his drawings of the accident in LC, 104–5.
45 DMH. Reprinted in the original Italian in the back of this book on pages 318–19.
46 The letter, a significant document in Montale studies, was originally published in *Aut-Aut* 67 (January 1962): 44–45, and again in *Sulla poesia*, ed. Giorgio Zampa (Milan: Mondadori, 1976), 91–2. It is now available in Montale, Il *secondo mestiere: Arte, musica, società*, 1497–99. I have made a fresh translation of this vitally important letter. A final paragraph, not translated in either the Galassi or the Arrowsmith version, shows how highly Montale thought of Cambon, and I have included it in my translation of this letter. Galassi's version (JGCP, 549–50) improves on Arrowsmith's (published in WAS, 174–5), which omits a crucial sentence.
47 Irma's hair is dark brown in the photographs. While Irma may have been a brunette for most of her life, Clizia's hair, part of a fictional composite, is another matter.
48 DMH. Reprinted in the original Italian in the back of this book on page 319.

49 Petrarch is quoted in the *Harvard Dictionary of Music*, s.v. "madrigal." See also the more extensive entry in the *New Grove Dictionary of Music and Musicians*, s.v. "madrigal."
50 See Rebay, "Montale, Clizia e l'America," 182.
51 For glimpses of Herma see LC, 98, 100, 102, 120, 131, 180–1.
52 One of the few places in which Arrowsmith is off the mark is in his commentary on the madrigal poems (WAS, 176–7). Mistaking the 1943 date for the beginning of the Allied occupation, he conjectures that Montale is critical of the post-Fascist scene. He will be, but that comes later. The very precise dates link the poems to the brief but violent German occupation of the northern provinces.
53 Op, 956–7.
54 See Arrowsmith on the "flashes" in WAS, 181–2.
55 JGCP, 561; Greco, *Montale commenta Montale*, 50.
56 Spaziani, "Un carteggio inedito di Montale," 321.
57 Tp, 233.
58 See *Fuori di Casa* in Montale, *Prose e racconti*, 292–7.
59 Greco, *Montale commenta Montale*, 51.
60 Ibid.; JGCP, 571–2. There is general agreement that Montale was aware of Hölderlin's Diotima.
61 WAS, 188.
62 Arrowsmith, who reads this as a Vixen poem, points out an intentional reference to Plato in the singing cicada in the poem and the singing cicadas described in Plato's *Phaedrus*. WAS, 188.
63 Tp, 243.
64 Cary, *Three Modern Italian Poets*, 319. Cary uses the *Oxford English Dictionary*. The Latin meaning of *silva* (wood, forest) is obvious to an educated Italian.
65 Angelo Jacomuzzi, *La poesie di Montale*, 34–57.
66 Savoca, *Tra Testo e fantasma*, 143. WAS, 107, 189–90.
67 LC, 223.
68 Op, 962. Trans. DMH. Galassi includes an earlier version in JGCP, 573. For further commentary on this passage and the woman/angel as "bearer of a message" see Giusi Baldissonne, *Il nome delle donne*, 115.
69 SLA, 303–4. The original Italian is quoted in Op, 963.
70 "Arsenio and the Nestorian are projections of myself" (SLA, 323).
71 While argument about the divine and human natures of Christ is at the heart of the Nestorian heresy, there were obvious rivalries and other political issues that contributed to Nestorius's downfall. See *Encyclopedia of Heresies and Heretics*, s.v. "Nestorian Christians, Nestorianism" and

"Monophysites, Monophysitism." *Encyclopedia of Religion*, s.v. "Nestorius." See also *The Catholic Encyclopedia*, s.v. "Nestorius" (available online at http://www.newadvent.org/cathen/).

72 *Oxford Companion to English Literature*, s.v. "Sphinx."

73 DMH. Reprinted in the original Italian in the back of this book on pages 319–21.

74 Jacomuzzi, *La poesie di Montale*, 41–2. WAS, 191.

75 Rebay, "I diàspori di Montale," 44–5. Clodagh Brook, *The Expression of the Inexpressible in Eugenio Montale's Poetry*, 108–11. JGCP, 574.

76 Dante, *Vita Nuova*, trans. Musa, 33.

77 Cooper, *Encyclopedia of Symbols*, s.v. "iris."

78 Cambon, *Eugenio Montale's Poetry*, 128.

79 Montale, *Il secondo mestiere: Arte, musica, società*, 1459. See also Galassi's excellent note, JGCP, 577.

80 LC, 237. Trans. DMH.

81 QR, 276–7. Both Galassi and Arrowsmith prefer to translate the title of the poem as "The Garden," not "The Orchard," opting for the most logical choice in English. However, Brandeis's translation has many excellent qualities, and her role in conveying Montale's message into the English-speaking world is of great interest. Moreover, the great care with which she undertook the translation is documented in the intricate details she discussed with Glauco Cambon in their correspondence. See the *Quarterly Review of Literature* Archives, Department of Rare Books and Special Collections, Princeton University Library.

82 QR, 276–7. Reprinted in the original Italian in the back of this book on pages 321–2.

83 *Quarterly Review* Archives, Department of Rare Books and Special Collections, Princeton University Library.

84 Brandeis translates *di dell'Ira* as "day of Wrath." Galassi prefers the Latin *Dies irae*, which also has distinct musical references. As the *Harvard Dictionary of Music* puts it, the *Dies irae* melody, which originates in the Roman liturgy, "has frequently been incorporated into program compositions having death or damnation as their subject." A famous example, certainly known to Montale, is "Dream of a Witches' Sabbath" from Berlioz's *Symphonie fantastique*.

85 I spend some time on parallelism in the deep structure of poetry and music in *The Tuning of the Word*.

86 See the typescript of the manuscript in Polimeri and Corti, *Catalogo delle lettere di Eugenio Montale a Maria Luisa Spaziani*, appendix V, folio 1–2. See also Jacomuzzi, *La poesie di Montale*, 39.

87 SLA, 323.
88 LC, 105.
89 WAS, 194.
90 The first line of the Mallarmé poem is "*Ses purs ongles très haut dédiant leur onyx*" (These pure nails held high dedicating their onyx).
91 QR, 278–9.
92 DMH. Reprinted in the original Italian in the back of this book on pages 322–3.
93 See Scarpati, *Invito alla lettura di Eugenio Montale*, 123–4.
94 Montale's original note is in Op, 963. Most editions include it. See JGCP, 582. See also Manacorda, *Montale*, 90. Note that *farfalle* can also means butterflies, a favourite image of Montale's.
95 Montale, *Il secondo mestiere: Arte, musica, società*, 1617. Trans. DMH. The original Italian, never translated into English until now, as far as I know, is of interest here:

"La primavera hitleriana" è una poesia molto difficile. A Firenze, il giorno in cui giunsero per l'incontro il Führer e il Duce, sull'Arno piovvero delle falene bianche, in quantità enorme: fu una vera nevicata, sotto ai piedi scricchiolavano. Naturalmente questo fu ricordato come un indizio funesto.

E qui c'è anche Clizia che parte (Clizia era una ebrea che partì per l'America).

Clizia non si chiamava Clizia, non è che il simbolo della donna mutata in girasole: qui nel "cieco sole" ch'essa porta in sé. In quel momento, mentre che l'orda s'abbatte sul mondo e anche su Firenze, c'è anche però una stella filante, una gemma che riga l'aria e distilla gli angeli di Tobia, la semina dell'avvenire. Tutto questo è sintetizzato in pochissime parole, naturalmente.

Proviamo ancora, per chiudere, a vedere se si può leggere questa "Primavera hitleriana" che porta una epigrafe, un verso di Dante, a Giovanni Quirini: "Né quella ch'a veder lo sol si gira …" (è sempre la donna "mutata al cieco sole").

96 An earlier version of this commentary on "La primavera hitleriana" was presented at the American Comparative Literature Association meeting held in Puerto Vallarta, March 1997.
97 It is generally assumed that Montale noticed the poem in the edition of Dante's *Rime* that was published by Gianfranco Contini. Since Montale often spent time with Contini, who was one of the great Italian critics of his generation, the two of them would have had ample opportunity to discuss Clizia and the Dante material. See Dante Alighieri, *Rime*.

98 Clytie's story is contained in the "The Sun-God and Leucothoe," book IV of the *Metamorphosis.* In the myth, Clytie arranges for the destruction of her rival Leucothoe, and that causes Apollo to spurn her completely. See Ovid, *Metamorphosis,* 87–90.

99 Ibid., 90.

100 These remarks are undated but were probably written around 1980. IBJL, 108.

101 While I admit that there is an element of sarcasm in the names of Eugenio Montale's muses (Fly, Vixen, Sunflower), I would also point out that the poet captures something especially perceptive about each of them. For pictures of Montale's muses see Baldissone, *Le Muse di Montale.*

102 SLA, 305. One of the clearest explanations of the intertextual elements in the poem, and one of the most compelling readings of it in general (written in the early 1960s), is to be found in Silvio Ramat, *Montale,* 194–8.

103 Compare how "Arsenio" begins with the lines "*I turbini sollevano la polvere / sui tetti,*" and "La primavera hitleriana" with "*Folta la nuvola bianca delle falene impazzite / turbina intorno agli scialbi fanali e sulle spallette.*"

104 Arrowsmith, a classicist, goes into some detail on the Platonic references in his note. See WAS, 196.

105 "Hitler Ends Visit: Spheres Held Set," *New York Times,* 10 May 1938. Birchall later won the Pulitzer Prize for his reporting.

106 Montale's 1948 article for *Corriere della Sera* indicates his awareness that the festival drew on a broad range of activities in Florentine cultural life. See "Celebrazioni fiorentine per la festa di San Giovanni," *Corriere della Sera,* 25 June 1948, republished in *Il secondo mestiere: Prose,* vol. 1, 738–9. This short piece was written around the time that Montale may have been revising his yet unpublished poem.

107 Several scholars have commented on Montale's probable interest in the reference to Tobias in Rilke's second Duino elegy. See, for example, Carpi, *Montale dopo il fascismo dalla "Bufera" a "Satura,"* 353.

108 Protestant Bibles from the seventeenth through the nineteenth centuries traditionally omitted the Apocrypha. Montale's use of Tobit is similar to Wallace Stevens's use of Susannah and the Elders, another Apocrypha story, in "Peter Quince at the Clavier." I treat that poem at some length in my *Angels of Reality,* 117–25.

109 Tobit and Tobias may have appealed to Montale for another reason. The first book that Irma Brandeis translated into English from Italian was Tobia Nicotra's *Arturo Toscanini.* In collaboration with Hannah Kahn, she published it through Dial Press in 1929. Since this was just a few years before she met Montale, she must have mentioned the book when she met him at the Gabinetto Vieusseux. Perhaps they both knew Tobia

Nicotra (this seems likely). At some point in the late 1930s Hannah Kahn may have been in Florence, looking for help from Montale, or possibly to visit him on Irma's behalf. Montale mentions her in "Senza salvacondotto," one of his late Clizia poems (see chapter 8). The Tobia in the poem, then, could be a double entendre, referring both to the good Tobias of the biblical story and to Tobia Nicotra, a messenger who brought knowledge of Arturo Toscanini, the great musician and anti-Fascist, to American readers via the angel-messengers Irma Brandeis and Hanna Kahn.

110 Galassi writes: "The controlling trope here is the opposition of her solarity, suggestive of her *senhal* name, with images of cold, activating the *stilnovistic* fire/ice contrast, evocative of the age-old erotic trope and embodied in the name Brandeis" (JGCP, 582). Rebay, in earlier scholarship, noted various forms of wordplay on the name "Irma Brandeis" in other poems. See Rebay, "Montale, Clizia e l'America," 182–85, 199 n. 45, 200 n. 52.

111 See Glenn O'Malley's remarks on synesthesia in the *Paradiso* in "Literary Synesthesia."

112 Op, 965. Glauco Cambon says that the poem was written in one fell swoop in 1938. See Cambon, *Eugenio Montale's Poetry*, 151. A more typical view, in keeping with the dating of Italian editors and critics, is to be found in Pipa, *Montale and Dante*, 96n17.

113 Galassi has pointed out the similarity between the long lines in the three poems and their indebtedness to the "versi Martelliani" developed by P.I. Martello and the sprung rhythm of Hopkins. For Hopkins and Montale, see Talbot, *Montale's "Mestiere Vile,"* 113–39.

114 In May 2002 I toured the family orto with Luca Tortorolo, grandson of the Montale cousin who built the house next to that of Montale's father. A large magnolia tree still grows there, and we both thought that it might be the very tree described in the Montale poetry. The home of Montale's family has been sold. Part of the old orchard area is now the grounds of the Hotel Cinque Terre.

115 JGCP, 588.

116 Trans. DMH. Reprinted in the original Italian in the back of this book on pages 323–4. Merrill's fascinating translation, though farther from the original, can be found in QR, 279–80.

117 WAS, 199–201.

118 Ibid., 199.

119 Galassi mentions a Dylan Thomas poem, which Montale translated, as a possible source for the poem. He also mentions Bergson. Michael

Hamburger refers to Boutroux and Bergson as Montalean influences; see his *Truth of Poetry*, 213.

120 Tp , 262.

121 JGCP, 594.

122 Tp, 262.

123 Italo Calvino has written that the poem is about "the horror of concentration camps past and future" (*The Uses of Literature*, 287).

124 Montale's rhetoric recalls the Vixen poem "Anniversario," in which the poetic "I" repeatedly claims that he is on his knees before his beloved. However, the moral reasoning of the poem is more typical of the Clizia Cycle, and the rainbows may be signs of Clizia. Montale does not give definitive clues in "The Prisoner's Dream" one way or the other.

125 WAS, 215; JGCP, 608.

126 Op, 962.

127 Tp, 275.

128 Calvino, *The Uses of Literature*, 284.

129 Valentini, *Lettura di Montale*, 282–3.

130 SLA, 319.

131 Tp, 275.

132 Ibid.

133 Eliot, *Complete Poems and Plays*, 48.

7. The Poet and the Modern Beatrice Spread Their Myth around the World

1 Nascimbeni, *Montale*, 105–6.

2 See the revealing sampling of Montale's art available in Scheiwiller, *Mantova per Montale*.

3 SLA, 19.

4 Nascimbeni, *Montale*, 108. Papa, *Storia di due manifesti*, 99.

5 Stephen Spender's review essay of three translations of Montale's writings – *Provisional Conclusions, Xenia,* and *The Butterfly of Dinard* – anticipated Montale's 1975 Nobel Prize by three years. See "The Poetry of Montale," *New York Review of Books*, 1 June 1972.

6 Testa, *Montale*, 53.

7 Ibid., 54.

8 De Robertis, *Giornata di studio*, 117–18. The translation is mine.

9 SLA, 22.

10 Montale, *Quaderno di traduzioni*. Testa emphasizes the importance of the *Notebook* in his account.

11 SLA, 198, 313. Talbot, *Montale's "Mestiere Vile,"* 113–34.

12 Nascimbeni, *Montale*, 122.
13 Jean Cook has provided the most complete bibliography. See also De Caro, *Journey to Irma*, 309–66. De Caro includes Brandeis's short stories in his very interesting appendixes.
14 Jean Cook has prepared the manuscript for possible publication.
15 Atlas, *Bellow*, 196.
16 The very interesting Glauco Natoli correspondence is in the Montale Archive at the Gabinetto Vieusseux, Florence, Italy.
17 SLA, "Self-Interview," 296.
18 Sonzogni, *Caro Maestro e Amico*, 129.
19 Michael Mewshaw discusses the role of Henry Furst in some detail in his review of Jonathan Galassi's *Collected Poems*. See "Montale as Couplet," *The Nation*, 29 March 1999. A full history of Furst's strange career is in Soldati, *Rami secchi*, 123–49.
20 SLA, 26.
21 As translated from Tp, lxxv.
22 *This Quarter*, April–May 1930. See the account of Beckett's life during this period and his work for Edward Titus in Anthony Cronin's *Samuel Beckett*.
23 Montale, *Il secondo mestiere: Prose*, vol. 1, 1494–9.
24 Ibid., 1754.
25 Ibid., 1649.
26 Pier Paolo Pasolini, "Poesia," *Nuovi Argomenti* (January–March 1971): 17–20.
27 SLA, 54. The entire speech is available in SLA, 49–58. For the Italian original, see Montale, *Il secondo mestiere: Prose*, vol. 2, 3030–40.
28 Ibid., 53.
29 John Ahern, "Between the Love of Clizia and Mosca," *New York Times*, 23 February 1986.
30 Irma Brandeis's correspondence with Theodore and Renée Weiss, *Quarterly Review* Archives, Department of Rare Books and Special Collections, Princeton University Library.
31 Irma Brandeis's major publications in Dante scholarship are *The Ladder of Vision* and *Discussions of the Divine Comedy*, edited with an introduction. There also is a list of small articles and reviews.
32 SLA, 318.
33 Montale, *Il secondo mestiere: Prose*, vol. 2, 2133–7.
34 Dalmati has a short piece on Montale and music in Iovino and Verdino, *Montale la musica e i musicisti*, 23–5.
35 The speech is available in translation in SLA, 118–33.
36 Telephone conversation with Theodore Weiss on 23 September 2002.

37 *Quarterly Review* Archives, Department of Rare Books and Special Collections, Princeton University Library.

38 Ibid.

39 Ibid.

40 Weiss lists something he transcribes as "Congedo provvisorio," which does not exist in Op or Tp. My guess is that he is referring to the "Conclusioni provvisorie," the last section of *La bufera.*

41 Archibald MacAllister, professor of Italian at Princeton University, hailed the book in the *Saturday Review* as "unusually readable, never pretentious, dogmatic, or precious ... she [Brandeis] writes clearly, with conviction, and with an easy authority born of sound scholarship." In *Italica,* Louis Rossi claimed that the book "will open up to many readers of the poem [the *Divine Comedy*] areas of understanding and feeling that up to now have remained closed to them." Colin Hardie cited what he considered to be missing bibliography and remarked that "Miss Brandeis' book is not a safe introduction of Dante ... But it is quite pleasant reading." See *Saturday Review* 44, no. 19 (July 22, 1961); *Italica* 40, no. 3 (September 1963): 281; and *Modern Language Review* 57, no. 1 (January 1962): 73.

42 Brandeis, *The Ladder of Vision,* 15–16.

43 Dante, *Paradiso,* Singleton commentary, 217.

44 Brandeis, *The Ladder of Vision,* 112.

45 Dante, *Purgatorio,* 280–1.

46 Brandeis, *Discussions of the Divine Comedy,* 79.

47 Brandeis, *The Ladder of Vision,* 118.

48 Ibid., 122–3.

49 Dante, *Paradiso,* 257.

50 Brandeis, *The Ladder of Vision,* 119.

51 Ibid., 120.

52 Ibid., 112.

53 While covering the pope's celebration of the Mass in the Holy Land that 4 January, Montale also provided a provocative account of Israel and the Arabs only three years before the Six Day War. See Montale, *Prose e racconti,* 503–8.

54 See the charming "The Paintings in the Cellar" in *The Butterfly of Dinard,* 167–70. In the story, which takes place in Trieste, Montale also mentions di Pisi and Morandi, two artists with whom he is closely associated.

55 Eliot's letter, in which he declined an invitation to speak, is reprinted in Scheiwiller, *Mantova per Montale,* 258.

56 "The Vistas in Retrospect," in *Società Dantesca Italiana e dell'Associazione Internazionale per gli Studi di Lingua e Letteratura Italiana, Atti del congresso internazionale di studi Danteschi,* vol. 1, 280–1.

57 The entire essay is available in SLA, 134–54.
58 Ibid., 136.
59 Ibid., 138–9.
60 Ibid., 140–1.
61 Ibid., 150.
62 Ibid., 151.
63 Brandeis, *The Ladder of Vision*, 186.
64 SLA, 150.
65 Brandeis, *The Ladder of Vision*, 15.
66 SLA, 154.
67 Irma Brandeis to Glauco Cambon, 14 August 1979. Glauco Cambon Correspondence, Archives and Special Collections, University of Connecticut, Storrs.
68 Carne-Ross, "A Master."
69 Letter to the Editors, *New York Review of Books*, 15 December 1966.
70 Ibid., 8 January 1967.

8. Clizia Becomes a Woman Again

1 Time and the relativity of its perception in relation to memory are important themes in late Montale. *Satura* and *Xenia* are late collections that are also full of important reflections on time.
2 *Lo Zingarelli*, s.v. "satura."
3 Ibid., s.v. "xenia." The Italian is as follows: "*Particolare caso di ibridazione fra due razze che provoca in una pianta alcuni frutti con i caratteri di un genitore e altri con quelli dell'altro*." Trans. DMH.
4 Paolo de Caro sees even more indications of Clizia in these poems than I do. See his chart of the full cycle in De Caro, *Journey to Irma*, 13–16.
5 Tp, 380; trans. DMH. Since the late Clizia poems have been translated less frequently than have the poems of *The Occasions* and *The Storm and Other Things*, I offer my own translated versions throughout this chapter. I encourage the reader to also consult Jonathan Galassi's renditions of most of these poems in his *Otherwise: Last and First Poems*. Arrowsmith has also translated the few Clizia poems to be found in *Satura* and other late works by the poet. See his *Collected Poems of Eugenio Montale*.
6 Arrowsmith's note indicates that the "you" is Clizia once again. There is no mention of Clizia in the notes for Op or Tp. See Montale, *Satura*, 218.
7 Scholars are just now starting to contextualize these poems, from *Satura* onwards to the end of Montale's life, in the context of the letters to Irma Brandeis. See Jacob Blakesley, "Irma Brandeis, Clizia, e l'ultimo Montale," published in 2011. For an earlier analysis of how Montale remembers the

women in his life in his old age see Éanna Ó Ceallacháin, *Eugenio Montale,* 149–174.

8 LC, 164.

9 Tp, 401.

10 Ibid.

11 Ibid.

12 Tp, 405.

13 I have been able to ascertain Hannah Kahn's married name thanks to Barnard College archivist Donald Glassman.

14 Gaetano Mosca was at first read by the early Fascists, but Mosca himself later turned against them. See Paxton, *The Anatomy of Fascism,* 35–9.

15 IBJL, 14. Jean Cook transcribes the letter in a note. In our interviews she also recalled the mid-1930s as the likely period for Hannah Kahn Barsky's visit to Montale.

16 LC, 174.

17 "Le revenant" is a title of a poem in Baudelaire's *Les fleurs du mal,* as Montale knew well.

18 The poet-scholar Rina Sara Virgillito makes a case for this poem as part of the Clizia cycle. See Virgillito, *La Luce di Montale: Per una rilettura della poesia montaliana,* 104.

19 Virgillito also sees this as a Clizia poem. See Virgillito, *La luce di Montale,* 95.

20 DMH. Reprinted in the original Italian in the back of this book on page 324.

21 The *Diario postumo,* which appeared in its entirety in 1996, is another story again. There are a few intimations of Clizia to be found in these poems, but the poet had by and large moved on to other topics. See Montale, trans. Galassi, *Posthumous Diary.*

22 Op, 1152. The date marked is in the typescript.

23 Tp, 714.

24 Tp, 652.

25 Donne, *Selected Poetry,* 82.

26 Tp, 663.

27 Svevo, *The Confessions of Zeno,* 392.

28 DMH. Reprinted in the original Italian in the back of this book on page 325.

29 Today the Pensione Annalena is only one portion of a larger building. Visitors have to climb one or two stories to get to the entrance, which is on the same level as the veranda.

30 Op, 1152.

31 Singleton gave two presentations at the International Congress of Dante Studies. Montale gave one speech. Both Singleton and Montale were later published in *Atti del Congresso Internazionale di Studi danteschi,* 2 vols.
32 O'Neil, "Dante, Montale, and Miss Brandeis," 32. O'Neil places Singleton in Florence in 1934, and Jean Cook's chronology and other facts document Irma's presence there that summer.
33 Tp, 715.
34 Ibid.
35 DMH. Reprinted in the original Italian in the back of this book on page 325.
36 De Caro, *Journey to Irma,* 105–6.
37 The current management of the Pensione Annalena has a copy of this poem ready for visitors who inquire about Montale and Brandeis. I received one when I walked in to inquire in April 2002. The veranda described in the poems is still in use. The door to the garden is still extant, with the inscription "Horti Annalenae" carved in stone over the entrance. Today the garden has been replaced by a nursery. The veranda on which Irma sat in the chaise longue looks out over that nursery.
38 Tp, 719–20.
39 "La vita fugge, et non s'arresta una hora, / et la morte vien dietro a gran giornate, / et le cose presenti et le passate / mi dànno guerra, et le future anchora." Both the Italian and the translation are available in Petrarch, *Petrarch's Songbook,* 320–3. While I suspected echoes of Petrarch, it was my colleague Julia Bondanella who actually found the sonnet for me, for which I thank her. Rosanna Bettarini's essay "Clizia e la Vita Che Fugge" expands on the connection with Petrarch and the overall *petrarchizzante* of these last Clizia poems. Bettarini cites the same Petrarch poem. See Bettarini, *Scritti Montaliani,* 155–63.
40 Tp, 719–20.
41 Stevens, *Collected Poems,* 404–5.
42 DMH. Reprinted in the original Italian in the back of this book on page 326.
43 Tp, 717.
44 Contorbia, *Eugenio Montale,* 177, photo no. 29.
45 LC, 241–6.
46 This is indeed a distinguished group. Leone Vivante is the author of *Essays on Art and Ontology* and *English Poetry and Its Contribution to the Knowledge of a Creative Principle,* with a preface by T.S. Eliot. Sbarbaro was a seminal influence on Montale. See the discussion of Montale's poem about Sbarbaro in chapter 3. Montale himself comments on these friends in *Il secondo mestiere: Prose,* vol. 2, 2624–5.

47 DMH. Reprinted in the original Italian in the back of this book on page 326.
48 Mudge, *The Poet and the Dictator*, 145–62.
49 See Galassi's helpful note in *Otherwise*, 152.
50 IBJL, 100.
51 Unlike many of the other late poems, the typescripts for these poems do not have a clearly marked date. Bettarini and Contini, who consider all the textual variants, give the date of "*forse*" (perhaps) 1979 for "Ho tanta fede in te" in OP, 1151. "Luni e altro" is not dated. My guess is that 1979 is a good estimate for both of these poems.
52 Tp, 711.
53 Greco, *Montale commenta Montale*, 46, 47.
54 Galassi, *Otherwise*, 151, points out that Luni was a "prosperous ancient Etruscan city at the eastern end of Liguria, near ... present day Sarzana. The port was located on the Gulf of La Spezia. Petrarch mentions it as an example of transience of human things and Dante refers to in Par XVI, 73–78." Today Luni is near the border of Tuscany and Liguria.
55 LC, 35–6.
56 Tp, 712.
57 Ibid.
58 This footage can be viewed in *Montale racconta Montale*, the RAI Educational video sold together with Testa's short volume on Montale.
59 Nalbantian, Mathews, and McClelland. *The Memory Process*, 10–13, 218–20, 260, 271.
60 Montale's last letters to Rosanna Bettarini also show that Clizia had become a mere code-name for Irma again at the end of his life, bringing her closer to an autobiographical character in his poetry. These letters, now published, are in Bettarini, *Scritti Montaliani*, 104–27. See especially the letter dated 31 March 1980 (122).

Coda: Montale, Brandeis, the "I," and the "You"

1 LC, 280.
2 See Saunders, *Self Impression*, 1–28. While Saunders concerns himself mostly with early Modernist prose as it emerges out of what he calls "the aesthetic auto/biography" of Ruskin and Proust, some of his argument does have implications for modern poetry as well. One important chapter treats Pound, and another examines Joyce and Pessoa in the context of Montale's friend Italo Svevo.

3 Montale, *Diario postumo*, published in Italian in 1991. A second expanded edition appeared in 1996, with a critical apparatus by Rosanna Bettarini. This, like so much else of Montale, has been translated by Galassi.
4 Rebay, "Ripensando Montale," 67.
5 De Caro, *Ludere pro eludere*, 91–221. Galassi has given a succinct account of the furor in his introductory essay, ix–xvii.
6 Marco Forti wrote *Il nome di Clizia*, and Angelo Marchese wrote *Visiting Angel*.
7 Merrill, *A Different Person*, 179.
8 LC, 274. See LC, 367, for a note regarding the misspellings of *pray* and *goddess*. Montale had misspelled *goddess* in exactly the same way many years earlier, in a letter to Irma written in January 1934. Another version of this letter was published earlier in Rebay, "Ripensando Montale," 69.
9 This June date, of course, does not correspond with Merrill's recollection of Irma Brandeis's statement that she heard from Montale sometime that winter.
10 Merrill, *A Different Person*, 179–80.
11 IBJL, 108.
12 While Montale did not think that psychoanalysis was particularly good for writers, a number of his Jewish friends from Trieste, including Umberto Saba, underwent Freudian analysis with Edoardo Weiss (1889–1970). Svevo, who did not seek treatment, used Freud's ideas as a symbol in *The Confessions of Zeno*. See Cambon, "Summer Days with Eugenio Montale," 88–9.

Poems of the Clizia Cycle

1 Please see the index for the page numbers of the Italian text, the translations, and the principal discussions of the poems. The scholar may also wish to consult the list of poems provocatively entitled *Per un "ciclo di Clizia" e per una ricostruzione del "romanzo" di Irma* in Paolo De Caro, *Journey to Irma*, 13–16. Our lists of Clizia poems overlap in many cases and differ in others.
2 Most or all of the twenty Motets could be read as Clizia poems, but the principal ones discussed in my text are listed.

Bibliography

Eugenio Montale's Principal Works

Montale, Eugenio. *La bufera*. 1st ed. Venice: Neri Pozza, 1956.

_____. *Diario del '71 e del '72*. 1st ed. Milan: Mondadori, 1972.

_____. *Diario postumo: 66 poesie e altre*. Edited by Annalisa Cima. Preface by Angelo Marchese. Text and critical apparatus by Rosanna Bettarini. Milan: Mondadori, 1966.

_____. *Diario postumo: Prima parte; 30 poesie*. Edited by Annalisa Cima. Milan: Mondadori, 1991.

_____. *Finisterre (versi del 1940–42)*. Edited by Dante Isella. Turin: Einaudi, 2003.

_____. *Meriggiare pallido e assorto: Poesie e prose scelte*. Edited by Giulio Nascimbeni. Milan: Longanesi, 1997.

_____. *Le occasioni*. 1st ed. Turin: Einaudi, 1939.

_____. *Le occasioni*. Edited by Dante Isella. Turin: Einaudi, 1996.

_____. *L'Opera in versi*. Edited by Rosanna Bettarini and Gianfranco Contini. Milan: Einaudi, 1980.

_____. *Ossi di seppia*. 1st ed. Turin: Gobetti, 1925.

_____. *Prose e racconti*. Milan: Mondadori, 1995.

_____. *Quaderno di quattro anni*. Milan: Mondadori, 1977.

_____. *Quaderno di traduzioni*. Milan: Edizioni della Meridiana, 1948.

_____. *Satura*. 1st ed. Milan: Mondadori, 1971.

_____. *Il secondo mestiere: Arte, musica, società*. Edited by Giorgio Zampa. Milan: Mondadori, 1996.

_____. *Il secondo mestiere: Prose*. 2 vols. Edited by Giorgio Zampa. Milan: Mondadori, 1996.

_____. *Tutte le poesie*. Edited by Giorgio Zampa. Milan: Mondadori, 1996.

Montale's Selected Letters and Incidental Writings

Montale, Eugenio. *Giorni di libeccio, lettere ad Angelo Barile (1920–1957).* Edited by Domenico Astengo and Giampiero Costa. Milan: Archinto, 2002.

_____. *Lettere a Clizia.* Edited by Rosanna Bettarini, Gloria Manghetti, and Franco Zabagli, with an introductory essay by Rosanna Bettarini. Milan: Mondadori, 2006.

_____. *Pastelli & disegni.* Milan: All'Insegna del Pesce d'Oro, 1966.

_____. *Quaderno di traduzioni.* Milan: Edizioni della Meridiana, 1948.

_____. *Quaderno genovese.* Edited by Laura Barile; with an essay by Sergio Solmi. Milan: Mondadori, 1983.

Montale's Poetry in English Translations and Bilingual Editions, Listed by Translator

Arrowsmith, William. *The Collected Poems.* New York: Norton, 2012.

_____. *Cuttlefish Bones.* New York: Norton, 1992.

_____. *The Occasions.* New York: Norton, 1987.

_____. *Satura.* New York: Norton, 1998.

_____. *The Storm and Other Things.* New York: Norton, 1985.

Brandeis, Irma, ed. and trans. Montale Issue, *Quarterly Review of Literature* 11, no. 4 (1962). Includes translations by Glauco Cambon, James Merrill, Ben Belitt, Robert Lowell, Sonia Raiziss,Alfredo de Palchi, and Irma Brandeis.

Cambon, Glauco, ed. *Selected Poems.* New York: New Directions, 1965.

Farnsworth, Edith. *Provisional Conclusions.* Chicago: Henry Regnery, 1970.

Galassi, Jonathan. *Collected Poems, 1920–1954.* New York: Farrar, Straus, and Giroux, 1998.

_____. *Otherwise: Last and First Poems.* New York: Random House, 1984.

_____. *Posthumous Diary.* New York: Turtle Point Press, 2001.

_____. *The Second Life of Art: Selected Essays.* New York: Ecco Press, 1982.

Gioia, Dana. *The Motets.* Saint Paul, MN: Graywolf Press, 1990.

Kart, Lawrence. *Mottetti / The Motets of Eugenio Montale in Italian; With Facing English Translations.* Limited ed. San Francisco: Grabhorn Hoyem, 1973.

Kay, George. *Selected Poems.* Edinburgh: University of Edinburgh Press, 1964.

Lowell, Robert. *Imitations.* New York: Farrar, Strauss, and Giroux, 1958, 1963.

Morgan, Edwin. *Poems from Eugenio Montale.* Reading, UK: University of Reading School of Art, 1959.

Reed, Jeremy. *The Coastguard's House.* Glasgow: Bloodaxe Books, 1990.

Singh, Ghanshyam. *The Butterfly of Dinard.* London: London Magazine Editions, 1970.

_____. *New Poems*. New York: New Direction, 1976.
_____. *Selected Essays*. Manchester, UK: Carcanet, 1978.
Thomas, Harry, ed. *Montale in English*. New York: Handsel, 2002.
Wright, Charles. *The Storm*. Field Translation Series I. Oberlin, OH: Oberlin College, 1978.

Montale Criticism, Biography, and Miscellaneous Montaliana

Almansi, Guido, and Bruce Merry. *Eugenio Montale: The Private Language of Poetry*. Edinburgh: Edinburgh University Press, 1977.
Avalle, D'Arco Silvio. *"Gli orecchini" di Montale*. Milan: Il Saggiatore, 1965.
Baldissone, Giusi. *Il male di scrivere: L'inconscio e Montale*. Turin: Einaudi, 1973.
_____. *Le Muse di Montale: Galleria di occasioni femminili nella poesia montaliana; Con antologia*. Novara, Italy: Interlinea, ca 1996.
_____. *Il nome delle donne: Modelli letterari e metamorfosi storiche tra Lucrezia, Beatrice, e le muse di Montale*. Milan: FrancoAngeli, 2005.
Barbuto, Antonio. *Le parole di Montale: Glossario del lessico poetico*. Rome: Bulzoni, 1973.
Barile, Laura. *Adorate mie larve: Montale e la poesia anglosassone*. Bologna: Il Mulino, 1990.
_____. *Bibliografia montaliana*. Milan: Mondadori, 1977.
Beall, Chandler. "Eugenio Montale's 'Sarcophagi.'" In *Linguistics and Literary Studies in Honor of Helmut A. Hatzfeld*, ed. Alessandro S. Crisafulli, 65–78. Washington, DC: Catholic University of America, 1964.
Becker, Jared. *Eugenio Montale*. Boston: Twayne, 1986.
Bertoloni Meli, Vasili. "Eugenio Montale: *Ossi di seppia*." *Die Neuren Sprachen*, vol. 11 (November 1969): 539–48.
Bettarini, Rosanna. "Per Dora." In *Le tradizioni del testo: Studi di letteratura italiana offerti a Domenico de Robertis*, ed. Franco Gavazzeni and Guglielmo Gorni. Milan: Riccardo Ricciardi, 1993.
_____. "Piccola indagine sul lessico." In Fondazione Mario Novaro, *Il Secolo di Montale: Genova 1896–1996*. Bologna: Società editrice il Mulino, 1998.
_____. *Scritti Montaliani*. Florence: Casa Editrice Le Lettere, 2009.
Biasin, Gian Paolo. *Montale, Debussy, and Modernism*. Translated by Gian Paolo Biasin. Princeton: Princeton University Press, 1989. Originally published as *Il vento di Debussy: La poesia di Montale nella cultura del Novecento* (Bologna: Mulino, 1985).
Blakesley, Jacob S.D. "Irma Brandeis, Clizia, e l'ultimo Montale." *Italica*, vol. 88, no. 2 (2011): 219–31.
Bonora, Ettore. *Conversando con Montale*. Milan: Rizzoli, 1983.

Boroni, Carla. *Le donne dei poeti.* Montichiari (Brescia): Zanetti, 1998.

Brandeis, Irma. *Irma Brandeis (1905–1990), una musa di Montale: Passi diaristici ed epistolari scelti, trascritti e introdotti da Jean Cook.* Edited and with an essay by Marco Sonzogni. Balerna, Switzerland: Edizioni Ulivo, 2008.

_____. "An Italian Letter." *Saturday Review of Literature,* 18 July 1936, 16.

_____. "Journals and Letters." Edited by Jean Cook. Unpublished manuscript.

_____. "Montale, Eugenio." In *Columbia Dictionary of Modern European Literature,* 16. New York, 1947.

Brook, Clodagh. *The Expression of the Inexpressible in Eugenio Montale's Poetry: Metaphor, Negation, and Silence.* Oxford University Press, 2002.

Calvino, Italo. "Forse un mattino andando." In *Letture montaliane: In occasione dell'80 compleanno del poeta,* ed. Sylvia Luzzatto, 35–46. Genoa: Bozzi, 1977.

_____. *The Uses of Literature: Essays.* New York: Harcourt Brace Jovanovich, 1986.

Cambon, Glauco. *Eugenio Montale.* New York: Columbia University Press, 1972.

_____. *Eugenio Montale's Poetry: A Dream in Reason's Presence.* Princeton: Princeton University Press, 1982.

_____. "Summer Days with Eugenio Montale." *Canto: Review of the Arts,* Spring 1978, 71–97.

Carne-Ross, D.S. "A Master." Review of *Eugenio Montale: Selected Poems. New York Review of Books,* 20 October 1966, 5–6, 8.

Carpi, Umberto. *Montale dopo il fascismo dalla "Bufera" a "Satura."* Padua: Liviana, 1971.

Cary, Joseph. *Three Modern Italian Poets: Saba, Ungaretti, Montale.* 2nd. ed. Chicago: University of Chicago Press, 1993.

Ciccarelli, Andrea. "Journey as Stasis: A Reading of Montale's Early Poetics." In *MLN,* vol. 124, no. 1 (January 2009, Italian Issue): 213–35.

Cillo, Giovanni. *Contributi per Montale / [scritti di] Giorgio Luti ... [et al.].* Lecce, Italy: Milella, 1976.

Cima, Annalisa. *Incontro Montale, 1973.* Milan: All'Insegna del Pesce d'Oro, 1996.

Contini, Gianfranco. *Una lunga fedeltà: Scritti su Eugenio Montale.* 2nd ed. Turin: Einaudi, 1974.

Contorbia, Franco. *Eugenio Montale, immagini di una vita.* Introduction by Gianfranco Contini. Milan: Librex, 1985.

_____. *Montale, Genova, il modernismo e altri saggi montaliani.* Bologna: Pendragon, 1999.

Corti, Maria. *I vuoti del tempo.* Milan: Bompiani, 2003.

Croce, Franco. *Storia della poesia di Eugenio Montale.* Genoa: Costa and Nolan, 2005.

De Caro, Paolo. *Irma politica.* Private ed. Foggia, Italy: Renzulli, 2001.

_____. *Journey to Irma: Una approssimazione all' ispiratrice americana di Eugenio Montale.* Parte prima: *Irma, un "romanzo."* Foggia, Italy: Matteo de Meo, 1999.

_____. *Ludere pro eludere: Alcune agnizioni e qualche ipotesi a rischio per il cosiddetto Diario postumo di Eugenio Montale.* Lugano: Annuario della Fondazione Schlesinger, 1994.

Forti, Marco. *Il nome di Clizia: Eugenio Montale, vita, opere, ispiratrici.* Milan: Scheiwiller, 1985.

Greco, Lorenzo. *Montale commenta Montale.* Parma: Pratiche, 1980.

Grignani, Maria Antonietta. *Dislocazioni: Epifanie e metamorfosi in Montale.* Lecce, Italy: Piero Manini, 1998.

_____. *Prologhi ed epiloghi: Sulla poesia di Eugenio Montale; Con una prosa inedita.* Ravenna, Italy: Longo, 1987.

Guerrini, Adriano. "Montale e Sbarbaro." In *Letture montaliane in occasione dell'80 compleanno del poeta,* ed. Sylvia Luzzatto, 443–52. Genoa: Bozzi, 1977.

Hertz, David Michael. "Two Meanings of Mutability in Montale's *La primavera hitleriana." Yearbook of Comparative and General Literature* 50 (2004): 105–20.

Huffman, Claire. *Eugenio Montale and the Occasions of Poetry.* Princeton: Princeton University Press, 1983.

Iovino, Roberto, and Stefano Verdino. *Montale la musica e i musicisti: Primo centenario della nascita di Eugenio Montale, Genova 1896–1996.* Genoa: Sagep, 1996.

Isella, Dante, ed. *Eusebio e Trabucco: Carteggio di Eugenio Montale e Gianfranco Contini.* Milan: Adelphi, 1997.

Jacomuzzi, Angelo. *La poesia di Montale.* Turin: Einaudi, 1978.

Knox, Bernard. "The Heart That Howls." Review of *Eugenio Montale: Collected Poems, 1920– 1954. The New Republic,* 23 November 1998, 27–31.

Luperini, Romano. *Storia di Montale.* 2nd ed. Rome: Laterza, 1999.

Manacorda, Giuliano. *Lettere a Solaria.* Rome: Editori Riuniti, 1979.

_____. *Montale.* 1969. Reprint, Firenze: La Nuova Italia, 1972.

Marchese, Angelo. *Amico dell'invisibile: La personalità e la poesia di Eugenio Montale.* Turin: SEI, 1996.

_____. *Visiting Angel: Interpretazione semiologica della poesia di Montale.* Turin: SEI, 1977.

Martelli, Mario. *Eugenio Montale: Introduzione e guida allo studio dell'opera montaliana; Storia e antologia della critica.* Florence: Le Monnier, 1982.

Melosi, Laura. *Profilo di donne dai fondi dell'archivio contemporaneo gabinetto g. p. vieusseux.* Rome: Università degli Studi di Firenze.

Mengaldo, Pier Vincenzo. *La tradizione del novecento da D'Annunzio a Montale.* Milan: Feltrinelli, 1975.

Nascimbeni, Giulio. *Montale: Biografia di un poeta.* Milan: Longanesi, 1986.

Ó Ceallacháin, Éanna. *Eugenio Montale: The Poetry of the Later Years.* Oxford: Legenda, 2001.

O'Neil, Tom. "Dante, Montale, and Miss Brandeis: A (Partial) Revisitation of Montale's Dantism." In *Montale: Words in Time*, ed. George Talbot and Doug Thompson, 27–42. Market Harborough, UK: Troubadour, 1998.

Parronchi, Alessandro. *Quaderno per Montale.* Novara, Italy: Interlinea, 2003.

Pell, Gregory Michael. *Memorial Space, Poetic Time: The Triumph of Memory in Eugenio Montale.* Leicester, UK: Troubadour, 2005.

Penna, Sandro, and Eugenio Montale. *Lettere e minute: 1932–1938.* Introduction by Elio Pecora; text, critical apparatus, and post-face by Roberto Deidier. Milan: Archinto, ca 1995.

Pipa, Arshi. *Montale and Dante.* Minneapolis: University of Minnesota Press, 1968.

Polimeri, Giuseppe, and Maria Corti, eds. *Catalogo delle lettere di Eugenio Montale a Maria Luisa Spaziani (1949–1964).* Pavia, Italy: Università degli Studi di Pavia, 1999.

Ramat, Silvio. *Montale.* Florence: Vallecchi, 1968.

_____, ed. *Omaggio a Montale.* Milan: Mondadori, 1966.

Rebay, Luciano. "Un cestello di Montale: Le gambe di Dora Markus e una lettera di Roberto Bazlen." *Italica* 61, no. 2 (1984): 160–9.

_____. "I diàspori di Montale." *Italica* 46, no. 1 (1969): 33–53.

_____. "Montale, Clizia e l'America." *Forum Italicum* 16, no. 3 (Winter 1982): 171–202.

_____. "Ripensando Montale: Del dire e del non dire." In Fondazione Mario Novaro, *Il Secolo di Montale: Genova 1896–1996.* Bologna: Società editrice il Mulino, 1998.

_____. "Sull' 'autobiografismo' di Montale." In *Innovazioni tematiche espressive e linguistiche della letteratura italiana del novecento,* 73–83. Atti dell'VIII Congresso dell'Associazione Internazionale per gli Studi di Lingua e Letteratura Italiana, New York, 25–28 April 1973. Florence: Leo S. Olschki, 1976.

Robertis, Giuseppe de. *Giornata di studio e mostra documentaria promossa dal Gabinetto scientifico letterario G.P. Vieusseux.* Edited by Lanfranco Caretti. Florence: Olschki, 1985.

Rovegno, Enrico. *Per entrar nel buio: Lettura di Finisterre di Eugenio Montale.* Genoa: ECIG, 1994.

Savoca, Giuseppe. *Parole di Ungaretti e di Montale.* Roma: Bonacci, 1993.

_____. *Tra Testo e fantasma: Analisi di poesie da Gozzano a Montale.* Rome: Bonacci, 1985.

Scarpati, Claudio. *Invito alla lettura di Eugenio Montale.* Milan: Mursia, 1973.

Scheiwiller, Vanni, ed. *Eugenio Montale: Immagini e documenti.* Catalogued and edited by Chiara Negri in collaboration with Gian Maria Erbesato. Milan: Scheiwiller, 1985.

_____. *Mantova per Montale.* Milan: Scheiwiller, 1983.

Singh, G. *Eugenio Montale: A Critical Study of His Poetry, Prose, and Criticism.* New Haven, CT: Yale University Press, 1973.

Sonzogni, Marco. *Caro Maestro e Amico: Carteggio di Eugenio Montale con Valery Larbaud (1926–1937).* Milan: Archinto, 2003.

Spaziani, Maria Luisa. "Un carteggio inedito di Montale." In *La poesia di Eugenio Montale: Atti del convegno internazionale tenuto a Genova 25–28 novembre 1982,* ed. Sergio Campanilla and Cesare Federico Goffis, 321–4. Florence: Felice Le Monnier, 1984.

_____. *Montale e la Volpe: Ricordi di una lunga amicizia.* Milan: Mondadori, 2011.

Surdich, Luigi. "Clizia dal 34 al 40." In Fondazione Mario Novaro, *Il Secolo di Montale: Genova 1896–1996,* 415–70. Bologna: Società editrice il Mulino, 1998.

_____. *La idee e la poesia: Montale e Caproni.* Genoa: Il melangolo, 1998.

Talbot, George. *Montale's "Mestiere Vile": The Elective Translations from English of the 1930s and 1940s.* Dublin: Irish Academic Press, 1995.

Testa, Enrico. *Montale.* Turin: Einaudi Tascabili, 2000.

Valentini, Alvaro. *Lettura di Montale: La bufera e altro.* Rome: Bulzoni, 1977.

Virgillito, Rina Sara. *La luce di Montale: Per una rilettura della poesia montaliana.* Milan: Cinisello Balsamo, 1990.

West, Rebecca. *Eugenio Montale: Poet on the Edge.* Cambridge, MA: Harvard University Press, 1981.

Mussolini, Fascism, and Italian History

Acton, Harold. *Memoirs of an Aesthete.* London: Methuen, 1948.

_____. *More Memoirs of an Aesthete.* London: Methuen, 1970.

Adamson, Walter L. *Avant-garde Florence: From Modernism to Fascism.* Cambridge, MA: Harvard University Press, 1993.

Becker, Jared. *Nationalism and Culture: Gabriele D'Annunzio and Italy after the Risorgimento.* New York: P. Lang, 1994.

Ben-Ghiat, Ruth. *Fascist Modernities: Italy, 1922–1945.* Berkeley: University of California Press, 2001.

Berenson, Bernard. *Rumor and Reflection.* New York: Simon and Schuster, 1952.

Bosworth, R.J.B. *Mussolini.* London: Arnold, 2002.

Calvi, Giulia. *Rinascimento e fascismo a Firenze.* Offprint from *Storica.* Rome: Donzelli, 2001.

Cannistraro, Phillip V. *Historical Dictionary of Fascist Italy.* Westport, CT: Greenwood, 1982.

Cannistraro, Phillip V., and Brian R. Sullivan. *Il Duce's Other Woman.* New York: Morrow, 1993.

Casucci, Costanzo. *Il fascismo: Antologia di scritti critici*. Bologna: Il Mulino, 1982.

De Felice, Renzo. *Mussolini*. Turin: Einaudi, 1993–6.

Delzell, Charles. *Mussolini's Enemies: The Italian Anti-Fascist Resistance*. Princeton: Princeton University Press, 1961.

_____, ed. *Mediterranean Fascism, 1919–1945*. New York: Harper and Row, 1970.

Di Scala, Spencer M. *Italy: From Revolution to Republic, 1700 to the Present*. Boulder, CO: Westview, 1998.

Falasca-Zamponi, Simonetta. *Fascist Spectacle: The Aesthetics of Power in Mussolini's Italy*. Berkeley: University of California Press, 1997.

Ferrero, Leo. *Diario di un privilegiato sotto il fascismo*. Milan: Claudio Lombardi, 1993.

Gatta, Bruno. *Intellighentia fiorentina: Le riviste eretiche del fascismo, 1924–44*. Rome: Settimo Segillo, 1997.

Griffen, Roger. *Fascism*. New York: Oxford University Press, 1995.

Hertz, David Michael. "Hitler and Mussolini at the Opera." In *The Finer Grain: Essays in Honor of Mihály Szegedy-Maszák*, ed. Richard Aczel and Péter Nemes, 169–86. Bloomington: Indiana University Institute for East Asian Studies, 2003.

Hoffmann, Henrich. *Hitler in Italien*. Munich: Verlag H. Hoffmann, 1938.

Lasansky, D. Medina. *The Renaissance Perfected: Architecture, Spectacle, and Tourism in Fascist Italy*. College Park: Pennsylvania State University Press, 2004.

Ledeen, Michael A. *The First Duce: D'Annunzio at Fiume*. Baltimore, MD: Johns Hopkins University Press, 1977.

Levi, Carlo. *Christ Stopped at Eboli*. Translated by Francis Frenaye. New York: Farrar, Straus, and Giroux, 1947.

Lyttle, Richard B. *Il Duce: The Rise and Fall of Benito Mussolini*. New York: Atheneum 1987.

Lyttelton, Adrian. *Italian Fascisms from Pareto to Gentile*. New York: Harper and Row, 1975.

_____. *Liberal and Fascist Italy, 1900–1945*. New York: Oxford University Press, 2002.

_____. *The Seizure of Power: Fascism in Italy, 1919–1929*. Princeton: Princeton University Press, 1987.

Mack Smith, Denis. *Modern Italy: A Political History*. Rev. ed. Ann Arbor: University of Michigan Press, 1997.

_____. *Mussolini*. New York: Knopf, 1982.

Manacorda, Giuliano. *Letteratura e cultura del periodo fascista*. Milan: Principato, 1974.

Mariano, Nicky. *Forty Years with Berenson.* Introduction by Sir Kenneth Clark. London: Hamish Hamilton, 1966.

Mosca, Gaetano. *The Ruling Class.* Translated by Hannah D. Kahn, with an introduction by Arthur Livingston. New York: McGraw Hill, 1939.

Mudge, Jean McClure. *The Poet and the Dictator: Lauro de Bosis Resists Fascism in Italy and America.* Westport, CT: Praeger, 2002.

Origo, Iris. *A Need to Testify: Portraits of Lauro de Bosis, Ruth Draper, Gaetano Salvemini, Ignazio Silone, and an Essay on Biography.* San Diego, CA: Harcourt Brace Jovanovich, 1984.

Papa, Emilio R. *Storia di due manifesti.* Milan: Feltrinelli, 1958.

Paxton, Robert O. *The Anatomy of Fascism.* New York: Knopf, 2004.

Pini, Arnaldo. *Incontri alle Giubbe Rosse.* Florence: Polistampa, 2000.

Rizi, Fabio Fernando. *Benedetto Croce and Italian Fascism.* Toronto: University of Toronto Press, 2003.

Sachs, Harvey. *Music in Fascist Italy.* New York: Norton, 1987.

Salvemini, Gaetano. *Under the Axe of Fascism.* New York: Viking, 1936.

Schneider, Herbert W. *Making the Fascist State.* New York: Oxford University Press, 1928.

Soldati, Mario. *Rami secchi.* Milan: Rizzoli, 1989.

Tambling, Jeremy. *Opera and the Culture of Fascism.* Oxford: Oxford University Press, 1996.

Tannenbaum, Edward R. *The Fascist Experience.* New York: Basic Books, 1972.

Ward, David. *Antifascisms: Cultural Politics in Italy, 1943–46.* Teaneck, NJ: Farleigh Dickinson University Press, 1996.

_____. *Piero Gobetti's New World: Antifascism, Liberalism, Writing.* Toronto: University of Toronto Press, 2010.

Wiskemann, Elizabeth. *The Rome-Berlin Axis: A Study of the Relations between Hitler and Mussolini.* London: Collins, 1966.

Italians and Jews

Arieti, Silvano. *Parnas: A Scene from the Holocaust.* New York: Basic Books, 1979.

Herzer, Ivo, Klaus Voigt, and James Burgwyn, eds. *The Italian Refuge: Rescue of Jews during the Holocaust.* Washington, DC: Catholic University Press of America, 1989.

Michaelis, Meir. *Mussolini and the Jews.* Oxford: Oxford University Press, 1978.

Stille, Alexander. *Benevolence and Betrayal: Five Italian Jewish Families under Fascism.* New York: Penguin, 1993.

Zuccotti, Susan. *Italians and the Holocaust: Persecution, Rescue, and Survival.* New York: Basic Books, 1987.

Italian Literature and Culture

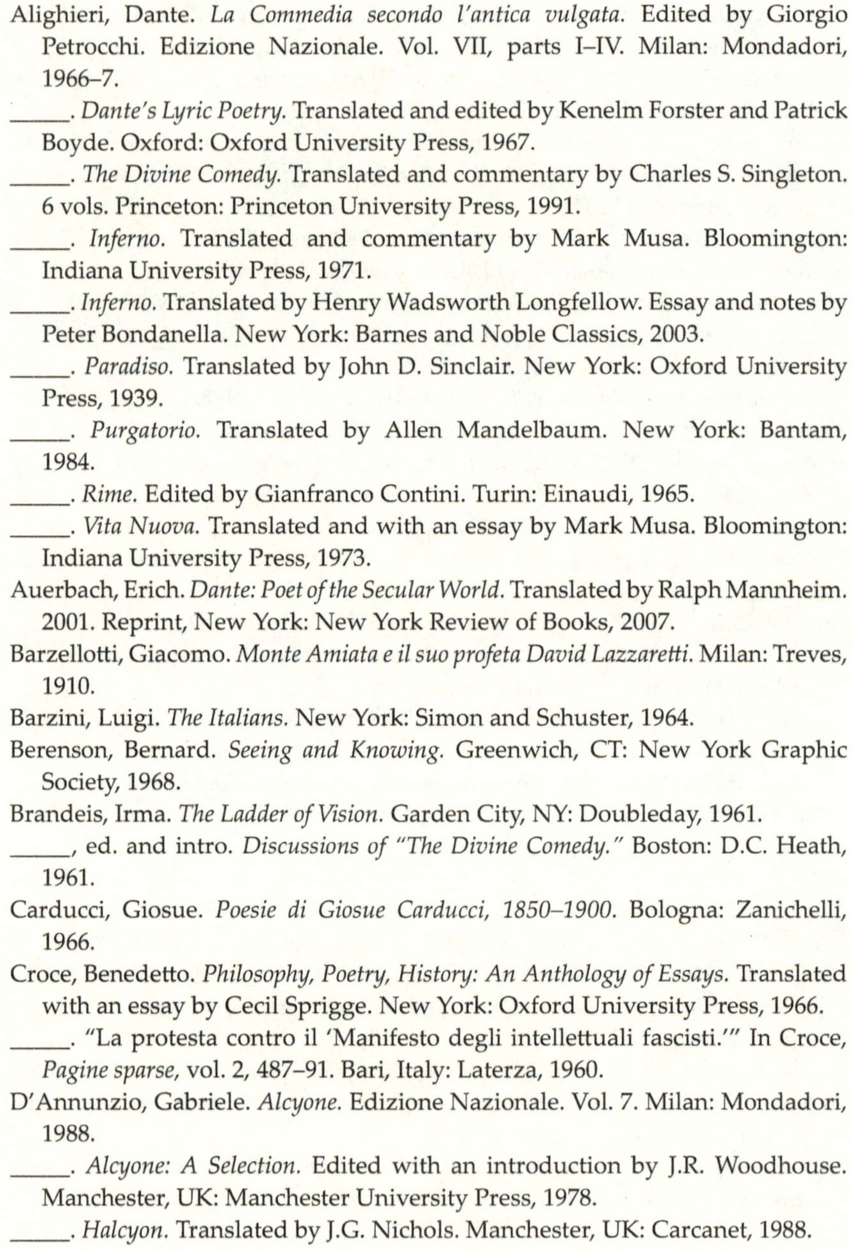

Alighieri, Dante. *La Commedia secondo l'antica vulgata.* Edited by Giorgio Petrocchi. Edizione Nazionale. Vol. VII, parts I–IV. Milan: Mondadori, 1966–7.

_____. *Dante's Lyric Poetry.* Translated and edited by Kenelm Forster and Patrick Boyde. Oxford: Oxford University Press, 1967.

_____. *The Divine Comedy.* Translated and commentary by Charles S. Singleton. 6 vols. Princeton: Princeton University Press, 1991.

_____. *Inferno.* Translated and commentary by Mark Musa. Bloomington: Indiana University Press, 1971.

_____. *Inferno.* Translated by Henry Wadsworth Longfellow. Essay and notes by Peter Bondanella. New York: Barnes and Noble Classics, 2003.

_____. *Paradiso.* Translated by John D. Sinclair. New York: Oxford University Press, 1939.

_____. *Purgatorio.* Translated by Allen Mandelbaum. New York: Bantam, 1984.

_____. *Rime.* Edited by Gianfranco Contini. Turin: Einaudi, 1965.

_____. *Vita Nuova.* Translated and with an essay by Mark Musa. Bloomington: Indiana University Press, 1973.

Auerbach, Erich. *Dante: Poet of the Secular World.* Translated by Ralph Mannheim. 2001. Reprint, New York: New York Review of Books, 2007.

Barzellotti, Giacomo. *Monte Amiata e il suo profeta David Lazzaretti.* Milan: Treves, 1910.

Barzini, Luigi. *The Italians.* New York: Simon and Schuster, 1964.

Berenson, Bernard. *Seeing and Knowing.* Greenwich, CT: New York Graphic Society, 1968.

Brandeis, Irma. *The Ladder of Vision.* Garden City, NY: Doubleday, 1961.

_____, ed. and intro. *Discussions of "The Divine Comedy."* Boston: D.C. Heath, 1961.

Carducci, Giosue. *Poesie di Giosue Carducci, 1850–1900.* Bologna: Zanichelli, 1966.

Croce, Benedetto. *Philosophy, Poetry, History: An Anthology of Essays.* Translated with an essay by Cecil Sprigge. New York: Oxford University Press, 1966.

_____. "La protesta contro il 'Manifesto degli intellettuali fascisti.'" In Croce, *Pagine sparse,* vol. 2, 487–91. Bari, Italy: Laterza, 1960.

D'Annunzio, Gabriele. *Alcyone.* Edizione Nazionale. Vol. 7. Milan: Mondadori, 1988.

_____. *Alcyone: A Selection.* Edited with an introduction by J.R. Woodhouse. Manchester, UK: Manchester University Press, 1978.

_____. *Halcyon.* Translated by J.G. Nichols. Manchester, UK: Carcanet, 1988.

Doretto, Fosco. *Il mio palio: Mossieri, cavalli, fantini, storia, curiosità, aneddoti delle carriere dal 1919 al 1992*. Siena: Il Leccio, 1994.

Dundes, Alan, and Alessandro Falassi. *La terra in piazza: An Interpretation of the Palio of Siena.* Berkeley: University of California Press, 1975.

Etlin, Richard. *Modernism in Italian Architecture, 1890–1940.* Boston: MIT Press, 1991.

Fantoni, Marcello, ed. *Gli anglo-americani a Firenze: Idea e costruzione del rinascimento.* Rome: Bulzoni, 2000.

Flora, Francesco. *La poesia ermetica.* 3rd ed. Bari, Italy: Gius, Laterza & Figli, 1947.

Guinizelli, Guido. *The Poetry of Guido Guinizelli*. Edited and translated by Robert Edwards. New York: Garland, 1987.

Hibbard, Christopher. *Florence: The Biography of a City.* New York: Norton, 1993.

Hollander, Robert. *Dante.* New Haven, CT: Yale University Press, 2001.

Keates, Jonathan. *Tuscany.* Topsfield, MA: Salem House, 1989.

Lewis, R.W.B. *The City of Florence.* New York: Henry Holt, 1995.

_____. *Dante.* New York: Viking, 2001.

Marti, Mario, ed. *Poeti del Dolce stil nuovo.* Florence: Le Monnier, 1969.

Merisio, Pepi. *Piazze d'Italia.* With text by Carlo Bo. [Milan]: Silvana Editoriale, 1985.

Moravia, Alberto, and Alain Elkann. *Life of Moravia.* Translated by William Weaver. South Royalton, VT: Steerforth Italia, 2000.

Orsini, Gian N.G. *Benedetto Croce.* Carbondale: Southern Illinois University Press, 1961.

Petrarch [Franceso Petrarca]. *Petrarch's Songbook: Rerum Vulgarium Fragmenta.* Translated by James Wyatt Cook. Italian text edited by Gianfranco Contini. Binghamton, NY: Center for Medieval and Early Renaissance Studies, SUNY, 1995.

Quasimodo, Salvatore. *To Have and to Give.* Translated by Edith Farnsworth. Chicago: Regnery, 1969.

Quinones, Ricardo. *Dante.* Updated ed. New York: Twayne, 1998.

Salustri, Carlo Alberto (Trilussa). *Tales of Trilussa.* Translated from Romanesco by John Duval. Fayetteville: University of Arkansas Press, 1990.

Società Dantesca Italiana e del'Associazione Internazionale per gli Studi di Lingua e Letteratura Italiana, ed. *Atti del congresso internazionale di studi Danteschi.* 2 vols. Florence: Sansoni, 1965.

Svevo, Italo. *The Confessions of Zeno.* Translated by Beryl de Zoete. New York: Knopf, 1958.

Woodhouse, John. *Gabriele D'Annunzio: Defiant Archangel.* Oxford: Oxford University Press, 1998.

Modern Poetry, Culture, and Miscellaneous

Atlas, James. *Bellow.* New York: Random House, 2000.

Avalle, D'Arco Silvio. *Sintassi e prosodia nella lirica italiana delle origini.* Turin: G. Giappichelli, 1973.

Balakian, Anna. *The Fiction of the Poet: From Mallarmé to the Post-Symbolist Mode.* Princeton: Princeton University Press, 1992.

Barnstone, Willis, ed. *European Poetry.* New York: Bantam, 1966.

_____. *The Other Bible.* San Francisco: Harper and Row, 1984.

Baudelaire, Charles. *Oeuvres complètes.* Paris: Editions du Seuil, 1968.

Bourdieu, Pierre. *The Field of Cultural Production: Essays on Art and Literature.* New York: Columbia University Press, 1993.

Braudy, Leo. *The Frenzy of Renown: Fame and Its History.* Oxford: Oxford University Press, 1986.

Brodsky, Joseph. *Less Than One: Selected Essays.* New York: Farrar, Straus, and Giroux, 1986.

Buch, Esteban. *Beethoven's Ninth: A Political History.* Chicago: University of Chicago Press, 2003.

Burnshaw, Stanley, ed. *The Poem Itself.* Reprint, Fayetteville: University of Arkansas Press, 1995. Originally published 1960 by Simon & Schuster, New York.

Canetti, Elias. *Crowds and Power.* New York: Farrar, Straus, and Giroux, 1995.

Celan, Paul. *Selected Poems and Prose of Paul Celan.* Translated by John Felstiner. New York: Norton, 2001.

Claghorn, Charles Eugene. *Biographical Dictionary of American Music.* West Nyack, NY: Parker, 1973.

Clément, Catherine. *Opera and the Undoing of Women.* Translated by Betsy Wing. Minneapolis: University of Minnesota Press, 1988.

Cook, Albert. "*Etendre, simplifier le monde:* The Philosophical Purchase of Mallarmé." In *Mallarmé in the Twentieth Century,* ed. Robert Greer Cohn, 31–52. Cranbury, NJ: Associated University Presses, 1998.

Cooper, Jean C. *An Illustrated Encylopaedia of Traditional Symbols.* London: Thames and Hudson, 1978.

Cremante, Renzo, and Mario Pazzaglia, eds. *La metrica.* Bologna: Il Mulino, 1972.

Cronin, Anthony. *Samuel Beckett: The Last Modernist.* New York: HarperCollins, 1996.

Dickinson, Emily. *Collected Poems.* New York: Crown, 1982.

Dogliotti, Miro, and Luigi Rosiello, eds. *Lo Zingarelli: Vocabolario della lingua italiana.* 12th ed. Bologna: Zanichelli, 1994.

Donne, John. *Selected Poetry of Donne.* Edited by Marius Bewley. New York: NAL, 1966.

Elias, Norbert. *The Civilizing Process.* Rev. ed. Cambridge, MA: Blackwell, 2000.

_____. *The History of Manners.* New York: Pantheon, 1982.

_____. *Norbert Elias on Civilization, Power, and Knowledge: Selected Writings.* Chicago: University of Chicago Press, 1998.

Eliot, T.S. *Complete Poems and Plays.* New York: Harcourt, Brace, and World, 1962.

_____. *Notes towards the Definition of Culture.* New York: Harcourt, Brace, 1949.

Ellmann, Richard. *Yeats: The Man and the Masks.* London: Macmillan, 1948.

Freud, Sigmund. *Civilization and Its Discontents.* Translated by James Strachey. New York: Norton, 1961.

Gasparov, M.L. *A History of European Versification.* Translated by G.S. Smith. New York: Oxford University Press, 1996.

Giamatti, A. Bartlett. "Italian." In *Versification: Major Language Types,* ed. W. Wimsatt, 148–64. New York: New York University Press, 1972.

Glauco Cambon Correspondence, Archives and Special Collections. University of Connecticut, Storrs.

Gombrich, E.H. "Moment and Movement in Art." *Journal of the Warburg and Courtauld Institute* 27 (1964): 293–306.

Gubar, Susan. *Poetry after the Holocaust.* Bloomington: Indiana University Press, 2002.

Hamburger, Michael. *The Truth of Poetry: Tensions in Modern Poetry from Baudelaire to the Nineteen-Sixties.* New York: Harcourt, Brace, and World, 1969.

Harewood, Earl of, ed. *Kobbé's Complete Opera Book.* London: Putnam, 1963.

Hartman, Geoffrey. *The Fateful Question of Culture.* New York: Columbia University Press, 1997.

Hertz, David Michael. *Angels of Reality: Emersonian Unfoldings in Frank Lloyd Wright, Wallace Stevens, and Charles Ives.* Carbondale: Southern Illinois University Press, 1993.

_____. *The Tuning of the Word: The Musico-Literary Poetics of the Symbolist Movement.* Carbondale: Southern Illinois University Press, 1987.

Hawkins, Peter, and Rachel Jacoff, eds. *The Poet's Dante.* New York: Farrar, Straus, and Giroux, 2001.

Huot, Sylvia. *Allegorical Play in the Old French Motet: The Sacred and the Profane in Thirteenth-Century Polyphony.* Palo Alto, CA: Sanford University Press, 1997.

Isaacson, Walter. *Einstein: His Life and Universe.* New York: Simon and Schuster, 2007.

John, Nicholas, ed. *The Stage Works of Béla Bartók.* English National Opera Series 44. New York: Riverrun Press, 1991.

Lockspeiser, Edward. *Debussy: His Life and Mind*. 2 vols. Cambridge: Cambridge University Press, 1978.

Mallarmé, Stéphane. *Oeuvres complètes*. Paris: Gallimard, 1945.

_____. *Selected Prose Poems, Essays, and Letters*. Translated by Bradford Cook. Baltimore, MD: Johns Hopkins University Press, 1956.

McCarthy, Mary. *The Groves of Academe*. New York: Harcourt, Brace, and World, 1951.

McLelland, J.S. *The Crowd and the Mob: From Plato to Canetti.*. London: Unwin Hyman, 1989.

Merrill, James Ingram. *A Different Person: A Memoir*. New York: Knopf, 1993.

Musgrove, Sydney. *T.S. Eliot and Walt Whitman*. New York: Haskell House, 1970.

Nalbantian, Suzanne, Paul Mathews, and James L. McClelland. *The Memory Process: Neuroscientific and Humanistic Perspectives*. Boston: MIT Press, 2010.

O'Malley, Glenn. "Literary Synesthesia." *Journal of Aesthetics and Art Criticism* 40 (June 1957): 391–411.

Ovid. *Metamorphosis*. Translated by Rolfe Humphries. Bloomington: Indiana University Press, 1955.

Paper, Lewis J. *Brandeis*. Englewood Cliffs, NJ: Prentice Hall, 1983.

Perlis, Vivian. *Charles Ives Remembered: An Oral History*. New York: Norton, 1974.

Preminger, Alex, and T.V.F. Brogan. *The New Princeton Encyclopedia of Poetry and Poetics*. Princeton: Princeton University Press, 1993.

Quarterly Review of Literature Archives, Department of Rare Books and Special Collections. Princeton University Library, NJ.

Richards, I.A. *Practical Criticism*. New York: Harcourt Brace, 1929.

_____. *Principles of Literary Criticism*. London: Kegan Paul, Trench, Trubner, 1924; New York: Harcourt Brace and Jovanovich, 1925.

Rilke, Rainer Maria. *Sonnets to Orpheus*. Translated by Willis Barnstone. Boston: Shambhala, 2004.

_____. *Werke*. 4 vols. Frankfurt: Insel, 1996.

Rosenbaum, Ron. *Explaining Hitler: The Search for the Origins of His Evil*. New York: Harper Perennial, 1999.

Rougemont, Denis de. *Love in the Western World*. Translated by Montgomery Belgion. Princeton: Princeton University Press, 1983.

Samuels, Ernest. *Bernard Berenson: The Making of a Legend*. Cambridge, MA: Harvard University Press, 1987.

Saunders, Max. *Self Impression: Life-Writing, Autobiografiction, and the Forms of Modern Literature*. Oxford: Oxford University Press, 2010.

Seferis, George. *Collected Poems*. Translated and edited by Edmund Keeley and Philip Sherrard. Princeton: Princeton University Press, 1995.

Slonimsky, Nicholas, ed. *Baker's Biographical Dictionary*. 7th ed. New York: Schirmer Books, 1984.

Spears Brooker, Jewel, ed. *T.S. Eliot: The Contemporary Reviews*. New York: Cambridge University Press, 2004.

Steiner, George. *In Bluebeard's Castle*. New Haven, CT: Yale University Press, 1971.

Stevens, Wallace. *Collected Poems*. New York: Random House, 1982.

_____. *The Necessary Angel*. New York: Random House, 1951.

Strum, Philippa. *Louis Brandeis: Justice for the People*. Cambridge, MA: Harvard University Press, 1984.

Vendler, Helen. *The Art of Shakespeare's Sonnets*. Cambridge, MA: Harvard University Press, 1998.

Vivante, Leone. *English Poetry and Its Contribution to the Knowledge of a Creative Principle*. Preface by T.S. Eliot. Norwood, PA: Norwood Editions, 1987.

_____. *Essays on Art and Ontology*. Translated by Arturo Vivante. London: Routledge and Paul, 1955.

Wellek, René. *Concepts of Criticism*. New Haven, CT: Yale University Press, 1963.

_____. *A History of Modern Criticism, 1750–1950*. 8 vols. New Haven, CT: Yale University Press, 1986.

Index of Titles and First Lines of Montale's Poems

General Index

www.ingramcontent.com/pod-product-compliance
Lightning Source LLC
LaVergne TN
LVHW040755070826
844660LV00025B/1153